Who Invented Heavy Metal?

Martin Popoff

WP
WYMER
PUBLISHING

Bedford, England

First published in Canada, 2015
Wymer Publishing
Bedford, England www.wymerpublishing.co.uk
Tel: 01234 326691
Wymer Publishing is a trading name of Wymer (UK) Ltd

Copyright © 2015 Martin Popoff/ Wymer Publishing.
This edition published 2019.

ISBN: 978-1-912782-12-3

The Author hereby asserts his rights to be identified as the author of this work in accordance with sections 77 to 78 of the Copyright, Designs & Patents Act 1988.

All rights reserved. No part of this publication may be reproduced or transmitted in any form or by any means, electronic or mechanical, including photocopying, or any information storage and retrieval system, without written permission from the publisher.

This publication is sold subject to the condition that it shall not, by way of trade or otherwise, be lent, re-sold, hired out or otherwise circulated without the publisher's prior consent in any form of binding or cover other than that in which it is published and without a similar condition including this condition
being imposed on the subsequent purchaser.

Every effort has been made to trace the copyright holders of the photographs in this book but some were unreachable. We would be grateful if the photographers concerned would contact us.

Printed and bound by
CMP, Dorset, England

A catalogue record for this book is available from the British Library.

Typesetting, layout and design by Eduardo Rodriguez.
Cover photograph © Monte Conner

Rock 'n' Roll Heaven

This book is dedicated to the passed-on folks I've had the pleasure of interviewing over the years who are also voices within these pages, arising from those fondly remembered chats:

Ron Asheton, Scott Asheton, Trevor Bolder, Jack Bruce, Michael Davis, Kim Fowley, Andy Johns, Clive Jones, Ronnie Montrose, Gary Moore and Dickie Peterson.

It's always poignant—and telling of how this all works—when we lose another old rocker. May their memories be extended through the words of wisdom you are about to read.

Table Of Contents

Introduction — 7

Chapter One – Trace Elements: 1250 BC - 1966 — 11

Chapter Two – Lead: 1967 - 1969 — 65

Chapter Three – Steel: 1970 — 161

Chapter Four – Titanium: 1971 — 213

Credits — 254

About The Author — 255

Martin Popoff – A Complete Bibliography — 255

Introduction

Yes indeed, who invented heavy metal? Of all the lively and lengthy debates me an' the metal buds have had over the kitchen table beers and acceleratingly heavy metal years, this question has always prompted the most significant, nuanced, hours-killing responses. And over those same years, either in my computer or in my head, the tally continued to grow, of the bands and songs and events that needed acknowledgement to flesh out the response toward the fullest, most complete answer to the question that's ever been mapped-out, fleshed-out, stuck between two covers, sent to the printer, put into your hands.

This is my modest attempt to foist upon ye that book. Through the years, as I plotted this thing, one of the key organizational debates has always been, do I construct this as some sort of timeline with quotes project, or do I render it with a narrative flow peppered by footnotes and the like? As you can see, I opted for the former. My favourite part of this whole argument is the massive stack of facts and figures and trivia associated with providing an adequate response to the question. And for that reason, I figured fashioning everything into one paragraph that flows to the next and creates some sort of entertaining "story"... no, this is an academic exercise. I wanted it all in there, no nonsense, lots of substance.

Having said that, I've really endeavoured to flesh out the entries, to explain why they are there, the significance of bringing up some song, or even some lick in a song from the early '60s that no one in their right mind would've brought up within the context of this argument. Still, at times, I've let the entry sit there enigmatically, silently prompting you to go to youtube to figure out why I stuck it there. As well, there are supporting quotes from all manner of music-maker and otherwise music industry person, most of it directly related to the advancement of the story, some of it simply about this important moment or song or album, in both cases, hopefully further casting illumination on this tiny bit of real estate before we move on to the next nugget of loud.

On the subject of pretty pictures, given that my relationship to the answer is on the strength of the recorded evidence, I decided to present virtually nothing but album and 45 sleeves, and more delectably, the period ads for them. These are most instructive when there's additional ad copy, in which I implore the reader (when you can see it—I've tried to make the key ads big enough for that) to look for words like heavy and hard rock and other descriptives that show that the writers had a clue as to what was most exciting about what they were trying to sell.

Now, another problem that I felt needed addressing is the manner in which to pull out the most crucial, salient bits of information, so the question doesn't become mired in a sea of a thousand ways to look at it. A large part of this concept of casting significance takes place right there at the entry, but what I've also done is come up with a summary—called Recap—at the end of the pre-'50s, the '50s, at the next five years up to and including all of 1964, and at the end of each subsequent year one by one, recapping the most important points through to the close of 1971, where the book ends. As well, the 1971 recap serves as a conclusion at the end of the entire book that provides an even more summarized and generalized answer to this hugely complicated question rife with grey areas, but hopefully given some shape by the assumptions and assertions that are very much the author's judgments.

Just to throw out a few of those assertions, one might be that heavy metal becomes invented when the blues is taken out of it. Another might be that heavy metal becomes invented when someone commits an album to the cause, pointing to a level of deliberation that is a level I personally think matters but you may not. Another might be that there is something heavy metal about aspects of a band other than the music, such as lyrics or album covers or general dark vibes, and thus there are entries that sit somewhat quietly and suggestive that we might think about these things.

Again, this is the author driving the process, making logical suggestions but some pretty wild ones too. It all becomes food for thought for the imagined dialogue I know this is becoming, in the ether, between me an' you.

A few points of format and process, just so you aren't confused. The sequencing of dates works like this. If all I was able to ascertain for a date was the year, then that entry goes at the beginning of the section for that year, i.e. everything dated simply "1970" is listed before January 1970. Same idea for having discovered month of an event but not the specific day of the month, i.e. "March 1970" is listed after all February 1970 listings but before March 1, 1970. What else? albums, films, TV shows etc. are italicized, while songs are in double quotes. Introductions of speaker quotes, I've tried to standardize by indicating their main association each and every time, rather than that ol' assuming you know who they are, let alone assuming you know who they are because they've been introduced earlier in the story. You'll see as well, I subtle change their descriptors from time to time, based on that person's relevance to the specific entry.

Now, the final point I want to address is that you will notice there are four parts, sections, chapters, to this book, allowing for a colourful compartmentalization to out titular conundrum.

Chapter one is subtitled Trace Elements, because it is about bits and pieces, slightness, hints, whiffs and traces of concepts we might consider as characteristics that contribute to heaviness.

Chapter two is subtitled Lead because it is about finding and hearing and experiencing true heavy metal elements. They are there, obvious and visceral, but usually not in alloy form, and usually not lasting for long enough, i.e. the duration of an album, which this book posits as the "gotta have" to git the crown.

Chapter three is designated Steel because it is about a dependable alloy, where not only do we get the dependability and assurance of album-length heaviness, but we also get (in what we deem the single-most accepted answer to the question), a marriage of heavy music with other very intentional visual, graphic and literary messaging toward this new kind of music being "invented."

Chapter four is designated as Titanium because for the final year of our survey, 1971, we are already post-invention, and into the future of metal. It is indeed a bit of an epilogue, a sift through the ashes of the momentous battlefield that was 1970. The question has been answered, and our mission now is to reinforce the verity of the answer proffered in chapter three, in part, through the "negative option billing" of demonstrating that no one has challenged our band that had been deemed the inventors of heavy metal in 1970, and through the positive reinforcement of that band's atom bomb dropped on our last year, incinerating any doubt once and for all. In effect, we will be going beyond the accepted and well-known answer to the question, by reserving judgment to see how the major contenders conduct themselves after the game is over. In other words, 1971 is a bit like the litmus test around sense of service applied to past Presidents—what do Democrats do after they leave office as opposed to Republicans? Exactly.

I suppose this isn't the place to give away further why these four sections exist, so perhaps all I want to say here is to have patience—the reason for each of these will become clear on three levels: 1) the entries themselves will reveal points about heavy metal through a thousand paper cuts; 2) the salient points will be driven home with BTO's proverbial sledgehammer in the conclusion to each chapter; and then 3) they will be put in greater context through ruthless summarization at the penultimate conclusion at the end of the book.

What else is this introduction for? I apologize to those who figured this is someplace where I was going to wax rhapsodic about anything to do with the nature of heavy metal music, but I am writing this before I do the whole damn book, and I know we are going to touch down on hundreds of concepts related to this music, so I'm really trying to just talk about methodology here. So, yeah, let's leave it at that and get to some power-chorded question answerin'.

Martin Popoff
martinp@inforamp.net; martinpopoff.com

Chapter One

Trace Elements: 1250 BC – 1966

In this chapter, ending at 1966, you will find no full albums to applaud, very little true heavy metal per se other than small clusters of songs, solitary songs, or even licks of sound within songs. Ergo there goes the title Trace Elements, where we begin way back in time, blasting through a couple thousand years punctuated with faint echoes of heavy metal messaging as it arrives through one of the five senses, but not always through hearing. I don't want to dwell on any of this material pre-, say, 1965, as it's obviously various grades of gravely tangential. So you won't see too many quotes or space-taking graphics supporting these points, because they are fragile and arguably spurious points through and through. So sit back, enjoy the ride, 'cos it's one that requires many leaps of faith.

1250 BC. Our story begins at the fabled Battle of Jericho. Joshua and his army make the Walls of Jericho fall with loud terrifying trumpet blasts, produced by an army marching around the walls blowing trumpets.

Jonathan Pieslak, author of *Sound Targets*:
Realistically the idea there is that unless you're a biblical literalist, the Walls of Jericho didn't really fall down because they blew the horn at them, but the point is that it was more to psychologically disorient and intimidate a combat adversary. You can look at Jericho as an example of that, but that has persisted through history up to the present day. Think about the famous scene from *Apocalypse Now*, when they play Wagner's "Ride of the Valkyries." The idea there is to psychologically disorient and intimidate a potential combat adversary.

250 BC – 250. Turks, Greeks and Romans put on the first wil rock 'n' roll shows.

Christopher Knowles, author of *The Secret History of Rock 'n' Roll*:
    The premise of my book is that rock 'n' roll is nothing new, and that it existed in a form almost identical to what we have today in the ancient worlds. When you talk about heavy metal, there were these rituals called the mystery cults, and the star attraction of these cults were certain groups. They went by several different names but they were, for all intents and purposes, heavy metal bands. These guys showed up dressed up in full hoplite armour, they had masses of drums, flutes, lyres, and then they would play their songs and use their shields and swords as musical accompaniment. They would scream at the top of their lungs until their throats were raw, and they would have lights shows using torches.
    This created a terrifying atmosphere to sort of kick off the show. These guys would come out and it's like Judas Priest. This starts very early on in Thrace, which is part of Turkey. It migrates to Greece, ended up in Rome. The interesting thing about this, is that this becomes a part of all the different cults—Dionysus, Cybele, Mithras, Samothrace—all these different cults around the ancient Mediterranean know these people and have experience with these people.
    Now, the interesting thing about that as well is that these groups—these heavy metal bands—were so well regarded and admired that a whole corpus of mythology grows up around them. They're said to be the music of the shields, and the swords and the screaming; it protects Dionysus, protects Zeus from Kronos—

you know, his father who wants to eat him—that the music has this protective power. But you have these rituals that make Woodstock look like a church picnic. There's really extreme music where they whip themselves into a frenzy. They had this dance where they twist their heads around so their long hair swings around, just like headbangers. We're talking sex, drugs, rock 'n' roll and craziness. I mean people would get so completely wound up. Women would get so crazed during the Dionysian rituals they were known to tear animals limb from limb and eat their flesh raw.

The whole point of these rituals was to take people out of their everyday existence, and that the state of terror that these musicians would instil would snap people out of their stupor and their routines and into this new mystery, into this new reality. It was very elaborate, with costumes and, again, torches, music, certain rituals and processions, like a Kiss concert would do. You're taken out of your everyday reality and you're put into a new reality. You're put into this new experience that transcends your everyday life, and so instilling this initial sense of terror was very much part of the process. You read a lot about this in the literature.

50 – 96 CE. A big chunk of The Bible is written, providing Trouble with a number of violent tales to go with their revivalist doom metal of the early '80s.

Trouble vocalist Eric Wagner:
I don't think it's any different now than it was 2000 years ago, the way people acted. We just have more things now. We have guns, we have jets, we have TV with thousands of channels. So all it is is that it's just being brought to our living rooms. But I think it's always been that way, just hating people because. Because of religion or the colour of their skin. They had the wars back then and they have them now. I mean Ireland, fighting between the Protestants and the Catholics. Who's right? I really don't think you're ever going to get the entire world together to believe in one thing. I was brought up Catholic. But you have to remember, back then in the early '80s, all the metal was kind of Satanic, and I didn't get into that vibe. And these people were talking about God and the Devil. As far as writing lyrics, I wasn't trying to save anybody, but just explore my life. Because you don't understand when you're 20 years old; you don't know what's going on. You're doing acid and stuff, so you're kind of like, what is the meaning of life? And I thought some of those subjects were cool too. And the Satanic stuff wasn't totally new either. You look at Lucifer's Friend's first album in '70, those lyrics could have been written by Slayer or Witchfinder General.

10th Century. Viking music and singing. With respect to Viking singing, an Arab merchant visiting Hereby, Denmark in the 10th century said, "Never before I have heard uglier songs than those of the Vikings in Slesvig (in Denmark). The growling sound coming from their throats reminds me of dogs howling, only more untamed." Another visitor compared their singing to the sound of a heavily loaded cart rolling down a hillside. The storyteller explains the sound was a result of lack of moderation in contact with alcohol. There are also various accounts of war cries, of a "harsh note and a confused roar" but this is a Roan account of pre-Viking Germania. With respect to the Viking horn, that's more of a drinking thing than a noisemaker. In fact, drums don't even seem to be a big part of the history of Viking music. It's a lot of aggressive singing, plus some woodwinds and stringed instruments. So there's a heaviness of voice, as well as the ties to pagan black metal, in that many Viking traditions are relived by the Scandinavian bands of the 1990s and beyond.

12th Century. Notre Dame organum, which was designed to fill gothic cathedrals with swirling sound, just like the immersive Leslie-driven technique of Jon Lord.

15th Century. Pipe instruments come from various cultures, but were invented as a Scottish instrument around 100 AD. They were popularized in the 15th century. The Great Pipes of the Highlands were a feared instrument to the English, as they led the Scots into multiple wars. The drone propelled bloodthirsty troops forward roiling with patriotism. The English eventually banned them as illegal upon fear of death.

> Jonathan Pieslak, author of *Sound Targets*:
> I would suggest that music has always been associated with war. There really isn't a single war that hasn't involved music. And I think it has been involved in a number of different ways. I think the first and primary way is a practical tactical usage on the battlefield. Because for centuries, wars have been fought without the baggage of radio communication. So drums, bagpipes, fifes, these types of instruments were actually used operationally to signal command on when to retreat, when to attack, those types of things. And so I think there is also a component of the beating of the war drum. You think of bagpipes and how they really inspired Scottish soldiers. We can even go back as far as Plato, who believed that certain musical scales or modes could incite aggressive behaviour. In the Republic, he talks about the Phrygian mode as being this sort of mode of, I wouldn't say war, but the mode that would incite aggressive behaviour, make you reach down to the depths of your soul and inspire warriors to create acts of heroism and self-sacrifice.

1547 – 1589. The development of the theorbo (or bass lute) for spectacles in the Medici court. The theorbo creates a form of power chords.

1553 – 1612. The acoustics of San Marco in Venice were exploited particularly in the multi-choral works of Giovanni Gabrieli and Monteverdi, pioneers in dynamics, volume, power and the manipulation of acoustic space.

1702. First documented usage of the term "diabolus in musica" or "the devil in music" to be applied to the tritone. Legend has it that centuries earlier, the tritone was banned by the church for its foreboding sound. The tritone is a musical interval, a "restless" one, a series of notes, but the main point within the story of heavy metal is its inherent dissonance, a "doomy" or "evil" quality. A clear and simple example is the main riff in Black Sabbath's "Black Sabbath" and later that band's "Symptom of the Universe." A modern term applied to this sound is The Devil's Interval. Although some believe the original term diabolus in musica had been used since the middle ages, the Andreas Wreckmeister 1702 reference is considered key, with other references emerging in 1725, 1733 and 1739, with variants that include "mi against fa," the devil in music and Satan in music.

> Musicologist Suzanne Cusick:
> I think it's a myth that it was banned by the church. And why is it devilish? Well because it's an extremely complicated ratio between frequencies and that's what produces the suggestive experience of dissonance. And in any case, whether it's a major seventh or a tritone, when we hear something dissonant, what we're responding to is our brain's effort to understand the ratio between the two frequencies. Or the multiple frequencies that are sounding together. And that's a particularly complicated ratio. It's also not an easy interval to sing into, and

so if you're sight-singing along and you don't want to produce this ugliness of either singing it correctly and producing dissonance or singing it incorrectly, you are troubled by it. And for the sight-singing in the middle ages and sort of pre-modern Europe, a great deal of the skill was based on trying to avoid singing difficult intervals, and that was the one that was most to be avoided because it was the trickiest.

So it becomes diabolical, not exactly because it's some symbol for a guy with a tail and a pitch fork in his hand or claw, but because it devils you. It's a hard problem to solve if you're sight-singing. I don't actually know if there's any evidence that it was banned by the church. It was to be avoided, which was a different thing. But you know, it was never listed as a sin. It was not banned as far as I know in the way that women singers were forbidden to perform on the public stage in Rome during the 17th Century; they did all the time, but officially it was banned. But as far as I know the singing of the tritone was not officially banned.

1703. Johann Sebastian Bach (1685 – 1750) enters the workforce, as the first virtuoso composer. Bach is the main classical influence cited by Ritchie Blackmore and Yngwie Malmsteen.

> Uriah Heep keyboardist Ken Hensley on classical in rock:
> Jon Lord, Keith Emerson, Rick Wakeman, Peter Robinson and guys like that, all the great Hammond players from the '60s and '70s were really great players and these guys were classically trained. Jon goes out and does these church organ concerts (laughs), which would not be possible for me. The difference for me was, it was good to have compatriots. It was good to see the Hammond organ being used in other rock 'n' roll contexts beside my own. Because in The Gods, I think we were about the only band on the road in the '60s that used it. But it was good to see it used later, and it was very amusing to be rated #2 or #3 keyboard player in all these big magazines, because you sit down, and Jon and Keith could quote any Beethoven, Bach, whatever you want, and I have no idea how to do that. I can't play anybody else's music, including the Beatles.

1720s. Turkish Janissary bands, which gave us our percussion instruments; we still use Turkish cymbals in our drums sets. These bands were used to frighten opposing armies into submission. Beethoven brings them into the last movement of his Ninth Symphony to recall that militant sound.

1776. George Washington apparently thought so much of martial music that he demanded that his own fife and drum corps practice regularly and get better with the threat of demotion and loss of pay if they failed.

1796. Beethoven (1770 – 1827) kicks it up a notch by embarking on a European tour similar to Mozart's. Beethoven is known for a majestic, blustery, heavy, dramatic sound.

1800. Date for Niccolo Paganini's early concerts. Lived 1782 – 1840. Rumoured to have sold his soul to the devil for talent, although very little evidence of anything along these lines exists. A cited influence of Yngwie Malmsteen, Paganini was an alcoholic by 16 and sober by 20. Paganini is cited as an early practitioner of the tapping technique, but tapping in various contexts has existed for centuries.

> Musicologist Suzanne Cusick:
> Paganini was a fantastic virtuoso and improviser, and a person who's reputed to have lived what we'd call a wild and crazy life that included access to 19th

Century mind-altering drugs. He left an image that's probably more colourful than the reality was. I believe that the people who do know a lot about Paganini are people who know a lot about Liszt, who is also a follower in the sort of creation of this public icon of the wild and crazy, almost diabolical virtuoso performer. Both of them were actually quite serious craftsmen behind the scenes, and a lot of the apparent diabolical-ness and inspiration onstage was indeed an act that they worked quite hard to acquire.

1812. American General Andrew Jackson's troops advanced to drum rolls written by Beethoven.

1820s. The best known Maori Haka is the "Ka Mate," composed by a chief named Te Rauparaha in the 1820s. It is a type of dance and vocal combination using shouting and stamping of feet. It's not necessarily a war dance, but sounds quite aggressive and scary. It is used in the modern day by the All Blacks rugby team from New Zealand to psych them up for matches.

1824. "Beethoven's "The Symphony No. 9 In D Minor, Op. 125," a recurring influence on heavy metal musicians of a classical bent; it was "covered" by Ritchie Blackmore as "Difficult to Cure" in 1981.

1836. When General Santa Anna wanted to frighten the defenders of the Alamo into either fleeing or surrendering, he played "El Degüello," a song that appealed to the enemy to surrender or die by the sword. It signified that no quarter would be given. According to various English-Spanish dictionaries, "el degüello" means no mercy or no quarter. The literal translation is "slit-throat." ZZ Top have an album called *Degüello*.

Sergeant Major and psychological operations expert Herbert A Friedman:
There are three forms of music used in military, right? The first one is very familiar, popular, very patriotic. I used to play "The Battle Of The Green Beret" when I was going in to train troops, you know, to stir me up. The guys attacking, in Iraq, a lot of them are playing a lot of heavy metal. When I go to battle with the Hummers going, they've all got iPods now and they're playing heavy metal all the way into the fight. In my articles I mention a whole bunch of the tunes. Basically, I asked people, "What are you listening to?" Because I was interested.

So that's one side, the pro side. Then you have the enemy side. You have music to scare the shit outta the enemy, and it's pretty much the same stuff. You go in and play Drowning Pool's "Let The Bodies Hit The Floor" (ed. official title: "Bodies"), a lot of heavy metal, when you're going into an Arab village. And then of course if you want to go back historical, for instance, to Texas Independence, the Mexicans played "Degüello," which basically said we're going to cut your head off and kill you. So you have the various threatening music.

The third use is for interrogation. Now once again, any music, any foreign music... It's crazy, when I was a kid there was a show called *Terry and the Pirates*, and they were hitting gongs and making strange sounds, and you're thinking geez, that's crazy music. Well, it's just the same today. So when you take an Arab, if you really want to torture him horribly, you play him Barney, "I Love You" or Mr. Rogers music. But what they found that they really can't stand (laughs), is heavy metal. They put them in, they leave 'em in a cell maybe, they put a bright light on them and they just play headbanging shit all night long. And it works. It just drives 'em outta their friggin' mind. You know, for some people, heavy metal is torture.

1837. The year of Berlioz' "Requiem" (multiple brass bands located around the hall to give surround sound) and the ride to hell from "Damnation of Faust."

> Blue Öyster Cult producer and musicologist Sandy Pearlman:
> I don't really know who was the first to create what we call modal music, but having said that, certainly the Celtic folk song literature, which is generally described under the academic title as Childs ballad literature, that Prof. Childs of Harvard collected, virtually the entirety of the Anglo Celtic American folk song literature in the late 19th century and the early 20th century. Of course this meant he was collecting a variety of music, which was preponderantly modal. The Celts, depending on who you believe, came west from Central Asia in some point in prehistory, were in Europe by the time they ran up against the Romans in all sorts of jurisdictions like Romania and Spain and of course England and Wales, and so forth and so on, England/Wales like Cornwall, France in Brittany, so they brought this music to Western Europe. This music became absolutely the foundation of what we think of as folk music today.
> There are so many crypto folk songs in Black Sabbath and of course in Led Zeppelin, that they are almost impossible to number because there are so many of them. I'm joking, but there are a lot of them. But this is a very potent combination. Modal music, as played on the guitar, is a virtual chord-finding Utopia. And you're a guitar player, you sit down, and you kind of play around with chords, and if you are operating out of a folk song platform, on a folk song platform, you'll find all sorts of really interesting chords. And it is interesting that the kind of progenitor of the gigantic European Romantic orchestra was Hector Berlioz, who kind of created the whole thing by 1837, which is "Requiem Mass," or as we say in Québec, "Mass de la Morte," and he composed on a guitar in bed. He's the only great, great, great classical composer who composed on guitar as opposed to on keyboard. His core repertoire is like staggeringly huge. And his influence on everybody else, everybody who followed him, starting with Richard Wagner, Anton Bruckner, Gustav Mahler, all of them are feeding off of the chord repertoire that earlier was pillaged. And that's a positive thing—to pillage mercilessly in the metal universe is the highest praise, right?

1843. The beginning of Giuseppe Verdi's productive years, or as he called them, his "galley years." Known for his "foreboding" sound.

September 5, 1857. The premiere of Liszt's "Faust Symphony."

March 6, 1869. Russian inventor and chemist Dmitri Mendeleev conducts a formal presentation on his extended version of the periodic table, which arranges the elements by atomic weight, leading to discussion of heavy and heavier metals. Not to be confused with Russian prime minister Dmitry Medvedev, who is a famed and documented Deep Purple fan.

1876. Richard Wagner (1813 – 1883) composes "Gotterdammerung (Twilight of the Gods)," a work for which metal has had kinship.

> Black Sabbath drummer Bill Ward:
> It's difficult for me to talk for the others, but for me, I thought that the first metal was actually classical music. There was some Tchaikovsky that I really liked, some Beethoven that I really liked. We didn't hear much of Richard Wagner in my early childhood; I think I first started listening to Wagner when I was ten or 11

years old. And the darkness of Wagner was very appealing; I liked the sadness and the almost monster-like chords that would evoke so much to the imagination. So yeah, classical music has always been there.

Musicologist Gavin Baddeley on why heavy metal is the ideal vehicle for dark themes: Bombast, I think, would be the obvious. Again, it's about theatre. The closest companion for heavy metal within the classical canon—if I can use classical in the classical sense—is opera. And so that kind of Wagnerian thing. And if you're looking for the shock rockers of the 1800s and the early 20th century, they are Stravinsky and Wagner.

July 1884. Anton Bruckner begins work on his imposing "Symphony No. 8 in C Minor."

Blue Öyster Cult producer and musicologist Sandy Pearlman:
    I think any long piece on heavy metal should actually pay serious attention to its roots in 19th century European Romantic music. And that's just a fact. That's an identifiable and supportable axis or origin point for heavy metal, and the transmission line is horror and science fiction written by the disciples of Anton Bruckner, who left Third Reich Austria, and came to the UK and America, and were recording for films.
    I do a class where we bring in Gary Lucas, and he plays his "Fantasia" for the crypto-orchestra, the heavy metal guitar, for him, one guitar player, one guitar, and 600 pedals, more pedals than you've ever seen in your life. And it's based along the last movement of Bruckner's eighth symphony, and it's a QED moment, and about 30 seconds into it it's like, "Oh my God! Has anybody ever doubted this premise?!" It's all over, within seconds. And it really does prove the point; you don't even need the whole band to do this—it's just the guitar. That's the point. And it's guitar which is inflated by the function of all these pedals which create impossible harmonies, and impossible stacks of octaves, you know, all the stuff that is actually all there in the Romantic orchestra, and it's actually all there from a heavy metal guitar player as well. But once you've got your army of pedals, your infinitude of pedals, you can do stuff in real time that is generally done only in overdubs, and Gary Lucas, I don't know if you're familiar with him, but he can do anything. He can do everything.

1895. Mahler's "Resurrection Symphony." The fifth movement, very dramatic, features prominently organ, which was by far the loudest, most power-invoking instrument available before electric guitar. Also see Virgil Fox playing Bach's "D Minor Toccata and Fugue."

October 10, 1902. Orville Gibson incorporates his company as Gibson Mandolin-Guitar Mfg. Co. Ltd..

1903. Bela Bartok (1881 – 1945), recognized here for his contribution to dissonance. In 1903 he wrote his first major orchestral work, "Kossuth."

1914 – 1916. Gustav Holst's *The Planets*, a seven movement orchestral suite. Heavy, grinding, including "Mars, Bringer Of War," an influence on Black Sabbath, and quoted by Led Zeppelin and Diamond Head—but first and most literally by pre-Atomic Rooster band Andromeda on "Return to Sanity" from their quite heavy 1969 self-titled album. Geezer Butler was a "medium-sized" fan of the *Planets* suite and had brought a melody from this to Tony who switched a few notes around and the song "Black Sabbath" was born.

1928. Frank Stokes, lesser known, unheralded bluesman who doesn't get the credit that Robert Johnson does, but is earlier with essentially the same kind of music.

> John Mayall on the earliest blues records:
> It would go back before Robert Johnson, who was in the '30s; I think 1935, 1936, somewhere around there. But the earliest recordings that I can think of would probably be Cow Cow Davenport, 1924. I mean, recordings of bluesmen... I'd say the blues evolved out of ragtime and jazz, early jazz. It's hard to pinpoint that. But from what I've read, it's a tradition that goes back... you never know from how long. Because when you read about people like Cow Cow Davenport, he was influenced by other players who weren't recorded, so eventually there's a whole list of names that crop up, names that, when you start doing research, were never recorded because it was before that was happening. So there's a long tradition of blues playing that no one knows where it came from. But ragtime is definitely one of the factors going on here.

September 17, 1931. RCA unveils the first 33 1/3 RPM LP record player, symbolizing the birth of album rock so heavy metal bands can make money too.

1932. Beauchamp, Barth and Rickenbacker, otherwise knows as the Ro-Pat-In Corporation, create the first electric guitars, the Frying Pan and the Electric Spanish. This is all happening in Los Angeles, to a soundtrack of Hawaiian music and lap steel.

1932. Hal Roach movie *Asleep at the Wheel* includes the phrase "rock and roll," while two years later, the Boswell Sisters have a #7 hit song called "Rock and Roll." If anything, it is the Sisters' hit from 1931 called "Shout, Sister, Shout" that includes an inkling of the rock 'n' roll genre to come, with its rapid fire vocals and talk of Satan.

1933. Pianist Peter DeRose writes the song "Deep Purple." Legend has it that it was Ritchie Blackmore's grandmother's favourite song, and that she often used to ask Ritchie to play it for her on guitar.

1934. Ro-Pat-In is renamed the Electro String Instrument Corporation, and one of their new models is called a Rickenbacker.

1934. Laurens Hammond invents the Hammond organ, the Hammond Organ Company selling its first model, the Model A, in June the following year. Keyboards were an integral part of early heavy metal, prominent in the work of Deep Purple (Jon Lord played a C3, as did Keith Emerson), Uriah Heep and Atomic Rooster. The Hammond sound was the heaviest keyboard sound available and allowed keyboards a place in the electric mud that is metal.

1935. The Model "B" Electric Spanish is the first solid body electric guitar, suggesting more reliance on electricity to get the job done over acoustic vibration and resonance.

1936 – 1937. These are essentially the recording years of Robert Johnson, who is said to have sold his soul to the devil at the Crossroads, but more importantly, influenced many future guitar players.

1938. LSD was first synthesized by Albert Hofmann from ergot, a grain fungus that typically grows on rye.

August 1939. Charlie Christian, at 23, gains national exposure in the Benny Goodman Sextet, arriving on that famed platform through the recognition and promotion of John Hammond. Christian is now cited by guitar historians as the first guitar hero, and the guitar that he is heroic with is electric. Part of this accolade is his work in bringing the guitar out from behind the brass, where it had been a struggling, quiet instrument, usually heard only through the hacking and banging of rhythmic chording. He would die three years later from tuberculosis.

1940. Les Paul, working after hours in the Epiphone factory, creates his prototype electric guitar called "The Log."

CEO of Gibson, Henry Juszkiewicz:
I would say that the guy who really invented distortion is Les Paul. He wasn't famous for it. I mean he was famous and he was famous for a lot of other things, but he had this effect box he called the Les Paulverizer. If you listen to his works in the songs he did with Mary Ford, you'll hear a lot of effects and one of them definitely is a distorted sound.

Let me step back for a second. Early on the guitar was acoustic. And I'll stick with the guitar because that's where my background is. And an acoustic guitar sounds great because of the way it's made, right? And once you buy an acoustic guitar, that's it, that's the sound. So you only have one good sound. People would buy the right acoustic, like a Stradivarius, to get the right good sound. Then in the late '20s and the early '30s, amplification came about. And it was absolutely essential for a guitar because the music of the day was ensemble, big bands, and you couldn't hear the guitar player. So very often the guitar player was in the background doing chording and percussive kind of rhythms, but with the amplifier the guitar player came to the front of the orchestra and became melodic. So that's sort of the second wave of instrument development. For centuries it was about the instrument and getting it physically to sound good.

Now you introduced this new dimension of electronics and volume, and you can get the guitar to sound louder and be heard in the mix, if you will. And then there were radio-style tone things introduced, knobs. So all of a sudden your guitar could sound like maybe a couple of different things. You could switch out pick-ups, you could switch out your tone selector, and you could get a variety of sounds. And also your amplifier had some tone and so forth.

So now all of a sudden you had a whole new dimension and your instrument was much more flexible. You could do many more things with it. From the '30s to Les Paul's time, that was where it was at and it was a new emerging kind of contribution to music. It was really Les and his early work with tape, which came from Germany, developed by the Germans during the war, that he started saying you know what? We can change the sound by using gear. And we can introduce all kinds of sounds. So he was using, through tape mechanisms, chorus and distortion and digital delays, sound... he was the first guy. He brought a third dimension to the instrument of effects, and it really made his sound. It wasn't heavy metal, it wasn't rock 'n' roll, and it wasn't too loud, but he was the guy who actually brought that into the music. Then it started becoming loud, all those things became a lot cooler, and musicians piled on with various effects boxes. That's kind of the history as I see it.

1942. At the siege of Stalingrad, it is reported that the besieged Soviets rolled giant loudspeakers to their front lines and played Argentinean tangos to their German attackers to keep them on edge through the long winter nights.

July 1942. Freddie Slack's instrumental "Riffette" includes an electric guitar solo by T-Bone Walker, a solo that is arguably the first rock 'n' roll guitar solo. Walker was a key influence on Goree Carter and Chuck Berry. Other contenders around this time include Sister Rosetta Sharp's "Strange Things Happen Every Day" from 1944, although the track is arguably a brisk blues, and Illinois Jacquet's "Blues, Part 2."

January 9, 1944. Jimmy Page is born, as WW II draws to a close and WW III begins over whether or not Jimmy Page invented heavy metal.

1944. 1979's *Apocalypse Now* includes a scene featuring the charge of the Air Cavalry while Lieutenant Colonel Kilgore's helicopter sound system plays "The Ride of the Valkyries" as they approached a Viet Cong controlled hamlet. Author on music in war Jonathan Pieslak couldn't find anybody to confirm if this actually happened, but says, "Strangely, there may be some truth to that scene since it has been reported that near the end of WWII, the Germans sometimes played that song to their soldiers to motivate them to continue the fight."

April 14, 1945. Richard Harold Blackmore is born in Weston-Super-Mare, on the Bristol Channel, England, the family transitioning to London when Ritchie was two, putting Ritchie at the heart of the metropolis that would be one of the centres of metal-making, if not steel production.

August 19, 1945. Ian Gillan is born (screaming?) in Hounslow, London.

1946. "Hey Ba-Ba-Re-Bop" by Wynonie Harris is yet another proto-rock number.

1946. Gibson introduces the P-90 single coil pickup which would soon make the first Les Paul come alive. The double coil humbucker would supplant it in 1957.

June 1947. "Good Rocking Tonight" (later "Good Rockin' Tonight") by Roy Brown, features the word "rockin'," and in the writing of it, the blues subtly flips over to boogie, something closer to rock 'n' roll. In 1973, the song was covered in a bold early metal zone by Montrose.

December 1, 1947. Aleister Crowley dies so heavy metal can be reborn.

February 4, 1948. Vincent "Alice Cooper" Furnier is born, in Allen Park, Michigan.

February 19, 1948. Frank Anthony "Tony" Iommi is born, in Aston, Birmingham.

March 17, 1948. The Hells Angels is born, in Fontana, California.

May 5, 1948. Bill Ward is born, in Aston, Birmingham.

September 1948. One of John Lee Hooker's early single, "Boogie Chillun'" is issued. The rhythmic choppy structure is similar to (though less electric than) Hooker's "Devil's Jump," which Pete Townsend had heard, citing the particular inspiration of seeing Hooker put a microphone inside his guitar, restring the guitar, and then play the song singing into the microphone that is inside the guitar.

December 3, 1948. John "Ozzy" Osbourne is born, in Aston, Birmingham.

1949. The first Fender Telecaster is issued, although it was known as the Broadcaster.

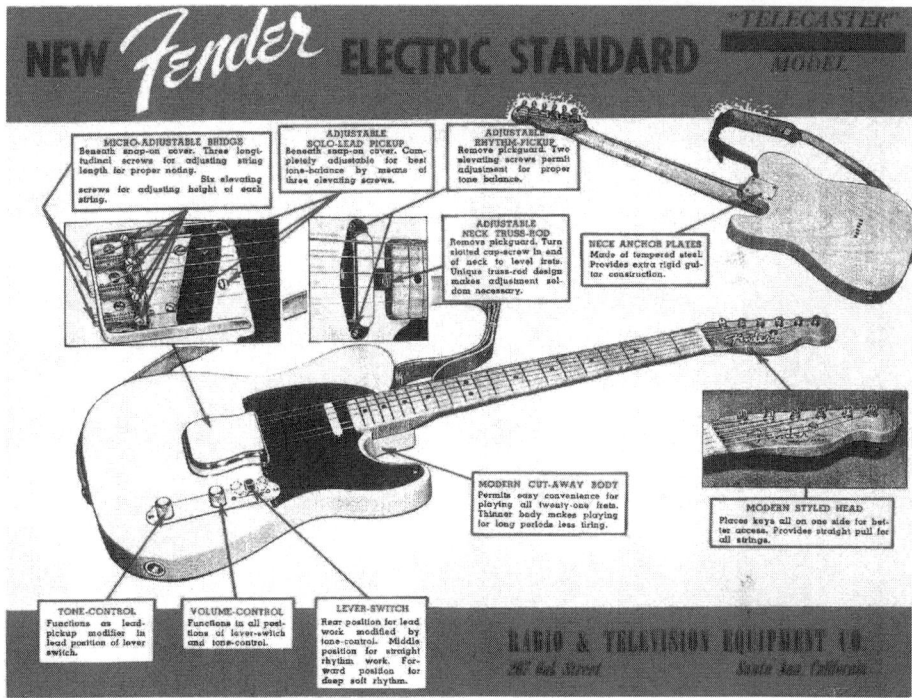

1949. "Rock the Joint," by Jimmy Preston and His Prestonians, is considered by some to be the first rock 'n' roll song. It's mainly piano and sax, but it's quite rock 'n' rollsy, with the circular boogie melody more pronounced over previous proto-rock numbers from the '40s.

April 1949. Music historian Robert Palmer considers Goree Carter's "Rock Awhile," recorded at this time, as candidate for first rock "n' roll song. Indeed there is an element of distortion on the guitar, but it sounds like distortion more due to rough recording values.

July 17, 1949. Terry "Geezer" Butler is born, like his Black Sabbath bandmates, in the Black Country.

Recap

The point of this section of our timeline as journey is more so to place in the mind certain characteristics of heavy metal that are not strictly related to the most important element of this music, which fundamentally might be boiled down to "music with predominance and prominence of guitar through a distortion pedal." Ergo, we've discusses war music, dramatic classical music, dark and evil sounding classical music, the birth of the blues (and maybe, just maybe, the birth of rock 'n' roll) as well as the birth of the electric guitar.

For fun, I've chucked in some important birthdays, Christopher Knowles' amusing look at the rock concerts of ancient times, and a couple of guys who pacted with Lucifer, and one who was the devil incarnate.

Suffice to say however, all of the above fall under the class of academic mind games. Indeed, a dimension of the argument that will quite legitimately come into play post-about 1966, namely the idea of the answer to the titular question depending on how old the answerer is… that's really not even an issue pre-1950. Essentially nothing that early approximates heavy metal without the stretchiest of stretches applied.

The '50s

1950 – 1953. During the Korean War, the Chinese "People's Volunteers" often attacked the UN forces en masse, blowing bugles or playing funeral dirges from their loudspeakers at night hoping to dishearten the American and South Korean troops. In one instance, the Chinese played a particularly eerie version of the Hank Williams song, "Your Cheatin' Heart" that fit well into the fog-shrouded night-time battlefield.

December 30, 1950. The Dominoes' "Sixty Minute Man" is recorded, later to become another contender for the title of first rock 'n' roll song. Little Richard says this is the first use of the term rock 'n' roll, with the lyric, "I rock 'em, roll 'em, all night long, I'm a sixty minute man." Amusingly, its co-writer Billy Ward would share a name with the man considered the first heavy metal drummer, or perhaps more accurately, drummer for the first heavy metal band.

1951. The Fender Precision Bass, or P-Bass, becomes the first mass-produced electric bass guitar, and the upright bass is methodically replaced in bands, with the bass player now allowed to roam the stage, or at least throw shapes, just like guitar players and singers.

March 3 or 5, 1951. "Rocket "88"" is first recorded, credited to Jackie Brenston and his Delta Cats. The band didn't exist however, and was put together by Ike Turner although Jackie Brenston did perform the vocal. It is the track most often credited as the first rock 'n' roll song, although it doesn't actually include any lyrics around rock 'n' roll, so the Billy Ward claim still stands. As well, the track is hailed as one of the earliest examples of distortion on the guitar, as played by Willie Kizart. The story goes that Willie's amp had been damaged in transit (either falling off the roof of the car, or receiving rain damage in the trunk), and that newspapers had to be stuffed into it to keep the speaker cone in place.

1951. "Lovin' Machine" by Wynonie Harris. Also considered important early rock 'n' roll, it is mostly piano-based. Not to be confused with Uriah Heep's much heavier "Love Machine" from only 20 years later.

October 6, 1951. Tiny Bradshaw records the first version of "The Train Kept A-Rollin'," which he co-writes with Lois Mann a.k.a. Syd Nathan. At this point it is a contender for first rock 'n' roll song. In 1956, intensified, it will become the first heavy metal song.

1952. The first Gibson Les Paul.

> CEO of Gibson, Henry Juszkiewicz on why the Les Paul became a quintessential heavy metal guitar:
> Well, it all goes back to Les. Les Paul was a really consummate guitar player, a famous player before he got involved in helping invent this guitar. But he was convinced that the guitars of the day really weren't right. And he experimented since he was a little boy trying to get guitars that were right, trying to get better and he experimented and experimented and spent days at the Epiphone factory in New York City trying different things. He was looking for a certain sound and a certain distain, and he tried everything. He literally put strings on a railroad tie and it turned out to sound really good. And so he said, wow, there are some principles here. A railroad tie, obviously, is not going to work as a guitar, but there's some principles here. Can we reduce that to a guitar? And over the years and in cooperation with some really hip designers at Gibson, they reduced his thinking and his drive to this Les Paul guitar named after him, obviously. And he got it exactly right about 15 years before it was needed.
> So Les was a studio cat. He was using effects and other things that were just way beyond the players of the day. And the guitar was only very modestly popular until one big thing happened and that is the one thing that was probably also the start of heavy metal, and that was big, loud, powerful amplifiers. When amplification volumes went up, the guitar just shone, you know? That guitar in conjunction with, say, a Marshall stack or one of the many powerful amplifiers of the day, it just rang and sang and it became an entirely different animal, because up until that time amplifiers were ten watts, five watts—very different.
>
> Kiss guitarist Ace Frehley:
> I still consider the Les Paul the best rock guitar made today. I had the pleasure of hanging out with Les Paul before he passed away; I did a jam with him at the Meridian in New York. Gibson just knows how to put together a guitar. And the Les Paul design is just classic. And it's still probably the #1 rock guitar in the world. A lot of people try to copy it and do variations of it, but you know, the interesting characteristic about the Les Paul is the fact that the neck is slightly arched against the body. If you take a normal guitar, you can lay it flat on a table, but you really can't do that with a Les Paul. The neck isn't attached, you know, directly; it's at a slight angle, about a 6% angle. And that creates a tension on the strings; when you tighten up the strings, that creates a sustain that a lot of other guitars don't have.

1952. Jimmie Webster publishes *Touch Method for Electric and Amplified Spanish Guitar*, in which he describes a two-handed tapping technique. It is said two-handed tapping was practiced by jazz guitarist Barney Kessel. Dave Bunker, who invented instruments, technology and wrote books for this, also cites Traktor

Topaz and Merl Travis, with Travis, according to Bunker, coming before Jimmie Webster, although Webster popularized the technique. Later, tapping will be practiced somewhat obtusely by Harvey Mandell, Steve Hackett and Billy Gibbons, but then become a heavy metal trademark at the hands of Eddie Van Halen.

1952. Jimmy Preston's "Rock the Joint" is covered by Bill Haley and the Saddlemen, and is pretty much just as rocky as "Rock Around the Clock," which clearly is based on "Rock the Joint." If not the first rock 'n' roll song in the original, "Rock the Joint" is considered by many, in this updated form, to be the first rockabilly song.

1953. Pat Hare is the guitarist on the early James Cotton solo recordings. He's variously credited as being the first guitarist to use distortion, at Sun Records in Memphis. Sam calls Pat, "the new guitarist with the angry, spine-tingling tone" and recruits Hare to play on Cotton's debut session for the Sun label, "My Baby"/"Straighten Out Baby" as well as "Cotton Crop Blues"/"Hold Me in Your Arms."

April 1953. Bill Haley's "Crazy, Man Crazy" is the first of the early rock 'n' roll numbers to reach the Billboard charts, reaching #12 on the Billboard Juke Box chart and #11 on Cashbox.

1954. The Hammond B3 first goes into production.

1954. Fender debuts the Stratocaster, which for years shared space with the Gibson Les Paul as one of the two quintessential heavy metal guitars.

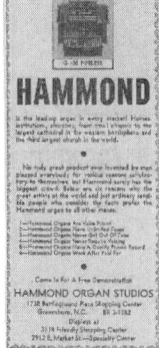

Deep Purple guitarist Ritchie Blackmore on his trademark Strat:
The Strat had more of a cut for rock 'n' roll. The Gibson is more of a jazzy guitar. It has a very mellow sound, full sound, great sound. But I wanted it when I heard Hendrix. I liked the way he cut through the notes, so I wanted to try and reach that more. I first got my Strat indirectly through Eric Clapton. He gave his roadie, who was my friend, a guitar, a Strat that he didn't want, and he gave it to me, and that's when I started playing with a Strat. It's all thanks to Eric Clapton.

April 12, 1954. Bill Haley and the Comets record "Rock Around the Clock" which is considerably rock 'n' roll, including a fairly wild guitar solo for the day, played by Danny Cedrone. Some argue that this should be called the first rock song because "Rocket "88"" never really charted, or never really charted as a rock song, and "Crazy, Man Crazy" is not heavy enough.

John Mayall:
Rock 'n' roll hadn't started when I first started collecting records. That came much later. First rock 'n' roll record is probably Bill Haley and the Comets, "Rock Around the Clock." That was one of the first ones that came up.

1955 – 1959. The key period for Hammer Horror films. Into the '60s, there's *The Mummy*, *Frankenstein* and *Dracula*–this is a much romanticized British franchise and institution. A lot of early rockers have been cited as having a fondness for these movies as kids. Crucially, the members of Black Sabbath had, over the formative years of their rockscrabble youths, internalized many of these films.

Musicologist Christopher Knowles:
I think Black Sabbath are really the prototype metal band. We had sort of the heavy blues, we had the acid rock. I mean really Blue Cheer are a group that don't get enough credit. I would say that in a lot of ways, Black Sabbath were directly working from the Blue Cheer template. But what they did is that they married this horror movie aesthetic to it, and they bring this intentional darkness, this intentional heaviness; this confrontational aspect that you don't see with a lot of the acid groups. It's really a melding of Hammer horror and heavy blues.

July 1955. Chuck Berry's "Maybelline." Berry intentionally over-drove his amp to get a fuzz sound. "Maybelline" is a good example of this.

September 14, 1955. Little Richard records "Tutti Frutti," which features a fairly extreme vocal, although the song is piano-centric. Little Richard's first album wouldn't arrive until 1957. Elvis includes his version of "Tutti Frutti" on his January 31, 1956 self-titled debut album.

Deep Purple guitarist Steve Morse on heavy metal in the '50s:
I don't think there was any. I think it was more... well, there's Little Richard, and the way that he used that really distorted raspy sound in his voice. Tons of control but tons of freedom, and playing a loose shuffle. When I heard Paul McCartney sing "I Saw Her Standing There," and then I heard Little Richard around the same period of time, I thought, well, of course, that's Paul doing Little Richard.

1956. Ritchie Blackmore gets his first guitar, a used Framus acoustic worth £7, and begins with classical training. Very soon, he starts learning rock 'n' roll from Big Jim Sullivan.

Gillan drummer Mick Underwood:
I played with Ritchie roundabout when I was 14, when we were kids. I had very few guitarists to compare him with, because nobody much could play in those days. When I saw him play I was blown away. He could actually do it. And we were playing in a little local band, little bits of gigs in Newcastle and things like that, and he played great. He was always a slightly complex character, shall we say. I got on great with him, super. He was a little bit nervous about standing up in front of a crowd, and he never wanted his mom and dad to see him play and things like that. That eventually changed, as you know.

1956. Screaming Jay Hawkins issues "I Put a Spell on You." Soon after, Alan Freed paid Hawkins $300 to emerge from a coffin on stage and thereafter the act incorporated horror or "shock rock" tropes like rubber snakes and his trademark smoking skull, prompting the tag "the black Vincent Price." Hawkins therefore is very much is an antecedent to Alice Cooper and even King Diamond and Marilyn Manson.

Musicologist Gavin Baddeley:
Screaming Jay Hawkins was someone who made very effective use of shock. People remember "I Put a Spell On You," but he sung songs about cannibalism and the Mau Mau and constipation, anything he knew you weren't supposed to talk or sing about. And he made a fairly good career out of that.

February 10, 1956. Little Richard records "Long Tall Sally," which houses an even more extreme vocal than the one heard in "Tutti Frutti." The vocal predicts the heavy metal wail, growl, and even falsetto of Ian Gillan.

April 16, 1956. Chuck Berry records "Roll Over Beethoven." The guitar licks are distinctive and repetitive enough that they suggest riff.

July 1956. Elvis Presley's version of "Hound Dog" is considered an early wailing, screaming vocal (although it's not that extreme). Elvis is also in effect the first rock star, dangerous, a threat to social order, with, perhaps, an intention to shock and awe. "Hound Dog" was first recorded by Big Mama Thornton on August 13, 1952 and was generally treated as a blues and country song. Presley's "Heartbreak Hotel" from six months earlier is also discussed as nascent rock 'n' roll.

Stooges guitarist James Williamson:
My very first records were singles, and they were actually Elvis Presley. My sister brought home "Hound Dog" and "Love Me Tender" and all those singles. I watched him on *Ed Sullivan* just like the next person at that time and was totally impressed. Probably if I had to name a single influence on why I bought my first guitar, he was it, even though I couldn't play it.

Black Sabbath drummer Bill Ward:
When I first heard Elvis Presley, I was bought and sold. I was completely grounded. I was just stumped. I got it immediately. I didn't have to be talked to about it or convinced about it. The first song I think I ever heard was "Jailhouse Rock." And then I heard "Heartbreak Hotel" and all the rest of it, and I was so gung ho on Elvis, I just thought it was brilliant. His singing to me was outrageous; he was singing stuff that was completely different. I had never heard such ferocity, like in "Jailhouse Rock," or the way he laid "Heartbreak Hotel" down, and then the lightness of him in 'Teddy Bear.' I still prefer Carl Perkins' "Blue Suede Shoes" but I love Elvis' version as well. So yeah, Elvis was just so different. There was just something about him, and I'm not talking about his gyrations or anything. It wasn't that, for me. There was a force and a different way of playing. The Jordanaires and his backing band, and the guitar solos, they were all different. And the drumming didn't seem to give a fuck about what was the normal type of drumming, how you have to play, blah blah blah, all that strict tightness or whatever. It was just loose and it just fitted and it brought freedom to me. That's all it was—freedom.

July 1956. Eddie Cochran records his first version of the brisk and energetic "Twenty Flight Rock," which is used in the movie *The Girl Can't Help It.*

July 2, 1956. Memphis, Tennessee's Johnny Burnette and the Rock 'n Roll Trio terrifically track, at Bradley Film & Recording Studio in Nashville, a version of Tiny Bradshaw's 1951 classic "The Train Kept A-Rollin'." Putting irrelevance upon the debate over first rock 'n' roll song, we will somewhat facetiously declare it the world's first heavy metal song, containing electric guitar licks, chugging, machine-gun propulsion, a driving 4/4 beat kept bluesy only by the walking bass line, distortion, menace, histrionic vocals to the point of tortured screams, reverb on the vocals, and a repeating three-note minor key signature not part of the original. It ends

with a prescient power chord. Not only would The Yardbirds and Aerosmith make the track famous again in two different later generations, but Led Zeppelin—as The Yardbirds and later as Led Zeppelin—would open their shows with the song in '68 and '69.

1957. Jazz legend Louie Bellson proves himself a double bass drum pioneer on "Skin Deep," although he had introduced double bass as far back as 1939.

> Motörhead drummer and double bass pioneer (on "Overkill") Phil Taylor: Keith Moon was probably the only one who played double bass drums during a song, but even then it was more or less like when he did a fill. His foot would go from the hi-hat to his left kick and he would just keep time just for the duration of the drum fill, and then he would go back. I think it was more of a nervous twitch than anything else. And the only other person I would really have to say that I listened to, but not intentionally to learn anything from him, was Louie Bellson. But I didn't even know he had two bass drums. It's just that my dad was into jazz and he had one record by this big band, where it featured a Louie Bellson drum solo and I thought it was great. But I didn't know it was two bass drums. But I've always admired, actually, Brian Downey from Thin Lizzy. Basically drummers only use two kick drums during solos, but I was always impressed with Brian Downey for double kick drums. But the master of them all, without two kick drums is, by far and beyond, Ian Paice—he's the man. He can play one kick drum like some people can't even play two.

1957. Memphis rockabilly singer Jimmy Wages records "Miss Pearl," "Mad Man" and other tracks for Sun Records, but Sam Phillips doesn't release the material, being talked out of it by producer Jack Clement, who doubted Wages could be successful. The vocal is fairly extreme and action-packed for the day, and the music is fairly brisk. Incidentally, another Sun track from 1957 with similarly aggressive vocals is Billy Lee Riley's "Flyin' Saucers Rock 'n' Roll."

1957. Blue Cheer's Dickie Peterson, ten years old, loses his mother, with his father dying two years later.

January 8, 1957. Rock 'n' roll arrives in Australia courtesy of a Bill Haley and his Comets tour. In essence, old time rock 'n' roll would prove tenacious down under, boogie figuring prominently in almost all of Australia's popular hard rock acts clear through the '80s, as evidenced by Buffalo, AC/DC, The Angels, Rose Tattoo and Heaven. Bill Haley was also the first American rock artist to tour the UK, selling over a million copies of "Rock Around the Clock" in that country.

1958. Ronnie and the Red Caps issue a rudimentary, tribal boogie instrumental single called "Conquest." The Ronnie is future metal great Ronnie James Dio. Co-writer of the track, he also plays trumpet on it—in the last 20 seconds, heavy metal trumpet.

1958. Duane Eddy issues his debut album, *Have 'Twangy' Guitar Will Travel*.

Ted Nugent:
Well, obviously, this was the opening volley of Les Paul's new creation. There was a bunch of, what I call, opening-day enthusiasts for the electric guitar. And you can't fail to mention Duane Eddy, "$1,000,000.00 Worth of Twang." He had that... I believe it was a Gretch Country Gentleman. Through various amplifiers, mostly Fenders, I believe. I mean, just listen to the richness of these tones. So here was a guy who took a brand-new invention, and figured it out immediately, and just took the adventure. I'd like to consider Lonnie Mack and Duane Eddy, and certainly Chuck Berry, Bo Diddley, those guys were the Lewis and Clark of guitar tone.

1958. A 13-year-old Ritchie Blackmore plays dog box and washboard with his first group, called The 2i's Coffee Bar Junior Skiffle Group. Skiffle music would figure prominently in the training of a young Jimmy Page as well. Later in the year, Ritchie's with his first band as guitarist, The Vampires. His Framus, now crafted into an electric, is supplanted by a Hofner Club 50. Also the same year, Roger Glover starts learning guitar and Jon Lord quits school, working in a solicitor's office and trying his hand at acting.

January 6, 1958. Gibson produces their first Flying Vs, the guitar that says heavy metal visually like no other. Early adopters were Lonnie Mack, Albert King and then by the mid-'60s, Dave Davies and Jimi Hendrix.

CEO of Gibson, Henry Juszkiewicz on the Flying V:
It's got all the heavy metal elements, including the high output, and it's got even more sustain. But it also has that look, you know? And in music, it's about the total experience. And so the Flying V has this really great look. It has an attitude that says heavy metal to a lot of people. So I think that's a large component of its popularity in that genre.

Early Flying V proponent Wishbone Ash guitarist and vocalist Andy Powell:
Until the Flying V came along, the coolest looking electric guitar was probably the Fender Stratocaster. There was the Les Paul, of course, which was considered more of a blues purist's guitar. This was until I saw a picture of Albert King with a V. Dave Davies and Keith Richards had also been photographed playing them, but it was so rare to even see a photograph, let alone the real thing. When I found mine, it was like it was meant to be. I just became one with it. I was very skinny at the time and simply made myself fit with the instrument, wearing it fairly low-slung, often resting it on one

knee on stage, so much so that I wore out several pairs of pants on the knee section. It didn't worry me that it was impossible to play sitting down—it was love at first sight!

March 31, 1958. Chuck Berry's "Johnny B. Goode" is released, giving clear definition to the idea of guitar riff as well as the magic of rock 'n' roll.

Ted Nugent:
I still live that garage band dreamer, trying to play Chuck Berry and Bo Diddley stuff with the spirit that those originators provided us. And I played bass for Bo Diddley and Chuck Berry for a couple of gigs, so I've been in the belly of the beast. I've ridden that angry stallion onto the mountaintop. A very happy angry stallion (laughs).

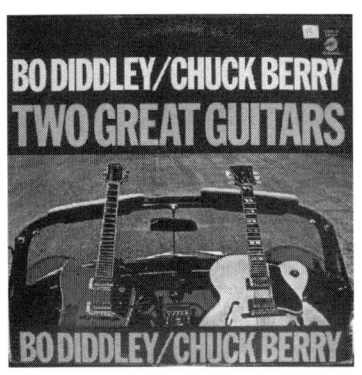

April 1958. Link Wray and his Ray Men issue "Rumble." Link (16 years old at the time) and this song are seen as influential for distortion, feedback and early use of the power chord, along with, as a bonus, a bit of a distorted guitar "lick." Apparently it was the first instrumental banned from radio. Then there is the story how Link poked holes in his speakers to make it sound more like the live version. Another legend has Wray getting this effect by dislodging a tube by accident, but then using it intentionally. One story has it that the inspiration was Johnny Burnette's Rock 'n' Roll Trio's "The Train Kept A-Rollin'" from '56. Link Wray charted again in '59 with "Raw-Hide."

Blue Öyster Cult producer and musicologist Sandy Pearlman:
I actually don't buy the theory that "Rumble" is the first heavy metal record. You know, it kind of proves the point with the chords, but that does not cover all of it. Because the truth is, "Rumble" is such a lame use of the electric guitar, the electric guitar pickup and the amp, that it's almost acoustic. That's my theory.

Deep Purple guitarist Steve Morse on the path to distortion:
I've heard that story about lots of people; I even heard that Hendrix did it. But I would have to say it's around the time of the Yardbirds, "Heart Full of Soul," when Jeff Beck achieved distortion. But he used an actual device to sound distorted. And then there's "Satisfaction," which had very obvious distortion. I also thought the Kinks stuff was really heavy, especially for the time. John Lennon... it's like he came straight from the Kinks with his rhythmic ideas, because when he played, it was always chunky and heavy and perfectly edited.

June 11, 1958. Eddie Cochran's "Summertime Blues" is released; light and acoustic at this point, it's nonetheless known for rocking versions by The Who and Blue Cheer only a handful of years later.

Blue Cheer bassist and vocalist Dickie Peterson:
"Summertime Blues" was just always a great rock 'n' roll song, and we used to use it more for filler. We didn't think anything was ever going to happen to that song. You know, most of my influences came out of the blues. And I know Paul was very influenced by the Yardbirds, and the whole concept of beefing up the blues. This is why we gelled so well together. And it was pretty much up to a guitar player to hang on.

October 1958. Eddie Cochran releases "C'mon Everybody," an eye-brow raising raucous song for the era, light because of acoustic guitar, but heavied a bit by fuzzy bass.

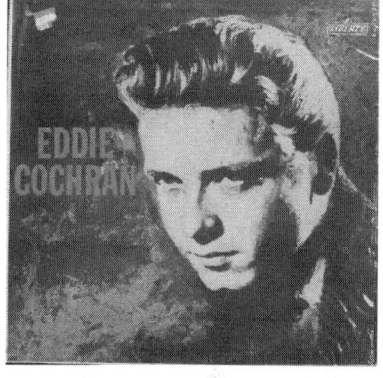

New York Dolls guitarist Sylvain Sylvain: The best record I ever had as a kid was Eddie Cochran, *Live in England*, and that taught me a lot of stuff, because, man, he's the one that could write them, he could play them, he could sing them, and he looked so damn fucking sexy doing it. But the first rock 'n' roll record I had was "The Peppermint Twist," Joey D and the Belmonts. And that was a rock 'n' roll record, believe it or not. Because it was a three chord progression. Anything that's a three chord progression, is really rock 'n' roll. Everyone brought something into the music, to what became the New Your Dolls, the soup. David was a big blues collector, and I like a lot of the girl groups, like The Ronnettes. Arthur liked the weird stuff, like 13 Floor Elevators, the strange things in music. He brought that in. That's how we came up with things like "Frankenstein." As far as heavy stuff: Jimi Hendrix. But heavy metal to us was T Rex. You know, because we hated it. We fought against all that. Heavy metal to us was big stadium rock, and we were a club band. We were right in your face and we wanted to touch you and we wanted you to touch us.

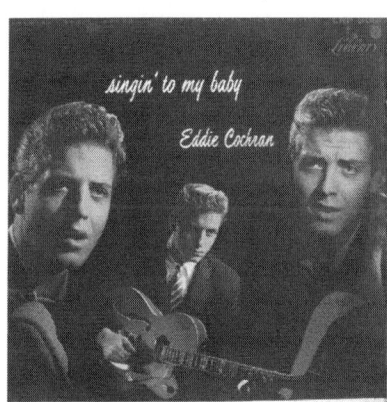

February 3, 1959. "The day the music died," namely the plane crash that claimed the lives of Buddy Holly, Ritchie Valens and JP Richardson (The Big Bopper). Did rock 'n' roll have to grow up quicker now that three of its stars were gone in one fell swoop? Did the wilder Beatles with their long hair fill that void?

July 1959. Eddie Cochrane releases "Somethin' Else," which drives pretty hard on top of a raucous rhythm section, topped further by a hoodlum vocal to get the boot in. This is one of Cochran's rockiest tune, the most electric, and also smashed by a violent rhythm section. But heavier than both "Somethin' Else" and "C'mon Everybody" are "Jeanie, Jeanie, Jeanie" and "My Way," which are also from 1958.

UFO drummer Andy Parker:
Pete Way loved Blue Cheer, loudest band in the world, but he also loved Eddie Cochran. That was kind of heavy stuff too. Phil loves Eddie Cochran too. You know, we covered a couple of his songs; on the first album we did "C'mon Everybody" and "Somethin' Else" made it on *Mechanix*.

1959. Howlin' Wolf's debut album is a collection of singles recorded from 1951 to 1959, entitled *Moanin' in the Moonlight*. Chester Arthur "Howlin' Wolf" Burnett's voice is considered quite extreme and growly even for 1959. He also had Pat Hare as a guitarist on some of his material.

Recap

I really feel that the most important candidates of all the songs discussed above as the first rock 'n' roll song, have to be the big anthems of the '50s, because of the inspiration they provided those who would advance hard rock in the '60s.

Ergo, I think more important, truly than first, would be the likes of "Johnny B. Goode" and "Tutti Frutti." Which brings up another point: important to mention in our recap is the birth of the wild man rocker, namely your Little Richard and Jerry Lee Lewis, and, yes, to some extent Chuck Berry.

Having said that, I am excited to push forward past games around the first rock 'n' roll song into the audacious idea of naming the first heavy metal song as one that came out of the '50s, namely Johnny Burnette and the Rock 'n Roll Trio's driving rendition of "The Train Kept A-Rollin'." See above for my arguably suspect justifications for going with something this gosh-darn early but there you go.

Finally, the '50s must be recognized for all the above listed early instances of distortion, however both accidental and weak they might have been.

In summary, we will look to the '50s more than anything for the birth of rock 'n' roll out of the blues—in short form, that pretty much means boogie—and then at the end of the ten-year span, harder and more extreme or wild manifestations of rock 'n' roll. And as celebrated above, rumbling down the tracks right in the middle of the decade, perhaps you'll allow me to declare our first heavy metal song, of which Joe Perry may concur.

The 1960s

1960

1960. Ritchie Blackmore leaves school at 15 and becomes an apprentice radio mechanic at Heathrow airport, early training that is quite similar to that of Nazareth's Manny Charlton. This becomes Ritchie's day job from '61 through '63. He eventually affords a red Gibson 335 hollow-body. Also this year, Ian Gillan—a vocalist with a stronger link to heavy metal histrionics than Ozzy Osbourne if not much wilder than Robert Plant—gets a taste of the rock 'n' roll life forming Jess Thunder and the Moonshiners.

February 20, 1960. Jimi Hendrix plays his first show, at a Seattle high school.

May 13, 1960. Johnny Kidd records, at Abbey Road, his original composition, "Shakin' All Over." Johnny Kidd & the Pirates (the single was issued under Johnny Kidd only) would be known for a fairly theatrical pirate-themed stage show, and the fact that they had a vocals, bass, drums and only one guitar lineup—Led Zeppelin had the same configuration and was known to play their songs in rehearsal. The Who was inspired by the band s well, crafting a famous, heavier cover version of "Shakin' All Over." It is said that The Who were inspired also by the configuration of the band, prompting Roger Daltrey to put aside guitar playing, a development in the persona of front man. Motörhead and Girlschool collaborated on a cover of Johnny's first single, "Please Don't Touch," which is actually a heavier, faster song than "Shakin' All Over," and could be said to contain a bit of the "machine gun" rhythm guitar riff that links "The Train Kept A-Rollin'" to "Communication Breakdown" and most impressively "Hard Lovin' Man." Finally, there's the obvious—Johnny Kidd & the Pirates invented pirate metal.

> UFO drummer Andy Parker:
> I don't know if you ever saw Johnny Kidd & the Pirates. Johnny, the bass player for The Pirates, was involved with managing us early in the day. Mick Green was the guitar player. Man, those guys were heavy as fuck! And you don't really think about it. Because it was kind of total pop, Johnny Kidd & The Pirates. But those guys were heavy.

August 25, 1960. The Shadows score the first of their five UK #1s with "Apache." Asked by the author on many occasions about his guitar heroes, Tony Iommi in one in-person chat elicited, with a chuckle, the one-word opening response, "Shadows." Tony, along with hard rock guitar legends Ritchie Blackmore and Randy Bachman, would participate in a Shadows tribute album called *Twang! A Tribute to Hank Marvin & The Shadows*, in 1996.

1961

1961. Nashville session musician Grady Martin gets credit in the development of distortion. A malfunctioning preamp circuit on a recording console is cited as the culprit contributing to the guitar sound on Marty Robbins' "Don't Worry," a soft piano track hit with some super-fuzzy six-string bass guitar come solo time. Same year is Ann-Margret's "I Just Don't Understand," which features almost synthesizer-like fuzz from guitar-wielder Billy Strange, using a hand-made pedal.

> Nazareth guitarist Manny Charlton:
> The first distortion pedal I ever got was a Gibson Maestro, I think. Distortion pedals came out way back, early '60s. The first distortion pedal I heard was Chet Atkins on a record by Ann-Margret; I heard a distortion pedal on that. So they really go quite far back, and they only became predominately used when Hendrix and Cream… it was to get that singing sustain they used, that long sustain on the notes. Distortion and sustain kind of went hand in hand. The distortion helped to make the note sustain longer. That's basically why guitarists used them. And it makes the note harmonically richer. Instead of it being quite pure like an electric acoustic guitar, where the note is very pure and very musical, they used the distortion pedal to make the note bigger in terms of its harmonic content. That's

what the distortion does. It creates all these extra harmonics that weren't there that derived from the electric guitar. So they liked it because there's more content in the actual note itself. The note becomes wider and thicker, and it has bass and an extended midrange and high end that you would not normally get if you did not use that pedal.

1961. The first use of the term heavy metal in popular culture is from William S. Burroughs' novel *The Soft Machine*, in which he introduces the character "Uranian Willy, the Heavy Metal Kid." The theme is developed in 1964's *Nova Express*, where the term is used with respect to drugs. It is of note as well, that in beatnik culture, heavy meant cool, and with music, it was something with some intensity to it.

1962

1962. Dick Dale rips his celebrated sinister-sounding guitar licks on "Misirlou Twist," from *Surfers' Choice*, the debut record from Dick Dale and his Del-Tones, on which we also hear distortion and aggressive vocals. Dale would pioneer many future heavy metal characteristics, including use of eastern scales ("Misirlou" is in fact of Greek origin, dating back to 1927), quick-picking *of* and *through* scales, reverb, plus increased intensification of distortion and amplification, working closely with Fender to come up with the first 100-watt amplifier.

> Blue Cheer guitarist Randy Holden:
> Dick Dale came on tour to Baltimore, and I had the only Fender Dual Showman on the east coast. Which was the biggest amp of the time. And when we played with Dick Dale at a gig one night, I didn't know who he was but I thought it was really interesting what he did. He had a Fender Dual Showman and he was doing this loud staccato guitar. I thought it was great. Dick Dale was awesome, a very potent force in heavy music. I mean, it just came to him naturally. And his melodies, I think, that was the really interesting part. He's of mid-eastern decent, Lebanese, so you can imagine the influence of the melodic structure that comes from. So that staccato picking would have come from way back when. So when it washed up on the shores of this country and Dick Dale found electric guitar, he was just translating what his genetics heard that he was doing with a lot of electric guitars. Then we kept running into each other way back then. It was really weird. He stole my amp the first time at that gig. They didn't know, they just put it in. They thought nobody else had any of that. They just loaded it up in their tour bus. And I saw my amp going, and I'm like where's my amp? I went out to the bus, said, "Oh, there it is. That's mine. Give it back."

1962. Alice Cooper's family moves from Detroit to Phoenix for health reasons. Alice, 14 years of age, attends Cortez High School. Alice would make his way back to Detroit through garage rock in Phoenix and freak rock in L.A..

April – May 1962. Ritchie Blackmore plays a couple dozen dates as part of The Condors.

May – October 12, 1962. Ritchie Blackmore gigs extensively as part of Screaming Lord Sutch & the Savages.

Producer Derek Lawrence:
In the early days when I first started hearing Ritchie, he would play on R&B and soul things, but the thing that made Ritchie absolutely brilliant was he used to play with a guy who was a big star in his country called Chas Hodges, who had a big act called Chas & Dave. And Chas, he's a great, great musician, and he always used to say to me, "Ritchie can't copy." And I think that's what made Ritchie absolutely brilliant, that he didn't have a mind that wanted to copy something. You would say, "Hey, that Smokey Robinson record, can you play the guitar thing for us?" And it would not come out like what you pointed him to. It would come out Ritchie. And that was what was great. Obviously, Big Jim Sullivan was a big influence on him in the early days but later I think Hendrix and Beck were the two that he really listened to. And I know Ritchie appreciated Jimmy Page. But then you've got to remember, I'd used Jimmy as a session guitar player playing ballads. We used to use Big Jim Sullivan on lead, and Jimmy on rhythm, and it was known as Big Jim and Little Jim.

Screaming Lord Sutch and Deep Purple bassist Nick Simper:
Ritchie was already a good mover. He was taught to be a good mover when he was with Screaming Lord Sutch, and the same thing went with me. I was with Screaming Lord Sutch too, and we used to do sort of similar antics and we kind of discussed this when we first started. Ritchie and I used to stand in a room with some mirrors up and we kind of used to work these things out in unison. It usually involved kind of gyrating the guitar around and trembling your knees. It seemed a bit old hat at the time, but ZZ Top are still doing it now (laughs). They're doing this stuff in "Waitin' for the Bus" and I thought, oh, that's what Ritchie and I were doing in Deep Purple, to try to impress the crowd. We always thought that moving was particularly important to the guitarists, and it goes back to the Screaming Lord Sutch days. And when we used to do it, sometimes it was to the detriment to the music, because we dropped so many bad notes because we were trying to be cool with the movements (laughs). So you had to compromise a little bit and make sure you played the right notes.

July 2, 1962. James Marshall Hendrix is honourably discharged from the air force after breaking his ankle in a parachute jump—his 26th and final.

August 17, 1962. "Telstar" (b/w "Jungle Fever") is the first British single to hit #1 on Billboard. It is written and produced by Joe Meek. A rumour at the time was that the sounds were obtained by sending signals up to the Telstar satellite for which the song is named, and then having them beamed back down.

Engineer on "Telstar," Derek Lawrence:
Joe was the first person, as far as I know, the first producer ever, to use distortion. And I mean, if you listen to some of his left-field stuff, the great story is, is that when we did "Telstar," and we sent it to Ed Lewis at Decca, the phone rang one day, and I answered the phone, and he said, "Derek, this record, I really like it, but it's got all this distortion at the front." And I went, "No, that's intentional." And I told Joe, and he threw a phone at me (laughs). So yeah, Joe had loads of distortion, and he would do various things. I mean, if he couldn't get the right

snare sound, he had the drummer play a telephone book. You know, it's very well-known that he would have the girl singers singing in the toilet. So yes, I mean, what I learned from Joe was that the bass and drums have to really stomp, and hit you in the chest.

To be honest, we didn't really know how he got most of his distortion, because what happened, the bands would do something during the day and we would all go home, and then we would come back the next day, and it would be all messed-up. I would think that most of it was about over-recording. You know, the first way to get distortion is, obviously, to play the loudness to a distorted level. Another way that we would do in the old days, is that, because we had heard the R&B drummers get like this great drum sound on their tom-toms, I had taken a snare drum and put feathers in it. And I remember Ritchie Blackmore, in the early days, would put sand in his speaker.

August 25, 1962. Bobby "Boris" Pickett & The Crypt-Kickers merges horror and (lite) rock with perennial Halloween favourite "Monster Mash." Two weeks later it is banned by the BBC as offensive.

October 1962 – April 1964. Ritchie Blackmore is now part of The Outlaws (as is Mick Underwood, on drums). Backup band on the band's October 26, '62 date is The Beatles. Multiple dates are logged supporting the likes of Jerry Lee Lewis and Gene Vincent, two of early rock's most mercurial personalities. On March 18, '64, not only are the Outlaws supporting the Rolling Stones, but it's also Ritchie Blackmore's wedding night.

December 1962. The Ventures hear distortion on the Marty Robbins track, and ask a friend of theirs, Red Rhodes, to help them achieve that sound. The first fuzz box is born, The Ventures using it on their classic "2000 Pound Bee."

Ted Nugent:
The Ventures certainly projected tone for this guitar freak. I mean, I was a guitar freak the minute I heard "Walk Don't Run," and "Perfidia."

1963

1963. Angus and Malcolm Young's parents move the family to Sydney from Glasgow.

1963. The Sandoz patent on LSD expires. The US Food and Drug Administration classified LSD as an "Investigational New Drug" which meant new restrictions on medical and scientific use.

March 1963. Liverpool's The Big Three issue a single called "Some Other Guy."

Quartz guitarist Mick Hopkins:
The Big Three were quite heavy-ish for the day. They did "Some Other Guy" and so did The Beatles, who we played with, as Gerry Levene & The Avengers. We played at a place called the Maney Hall, Sutton Coldfield, and we went on and then The Beatles. We were doing a double, because then we went to the Tamworth Assembly Rooms, and they came on after us again. While we were playing, our drummer, Graeme Edge, he started missing a few beats, and we thought, what the hell is going on? And Ringo was trying to pull him off his drums. There was a curtain behind Graeme, so Ringo, you couldn't see him there. You could just see this curtain moving while he was trying to pull him off his drum stool. And of course they were all falling about laughing, really. But The Big Three I would say were heavier than The Beatles. When you go and see something like that, when you're used to playing pop music, and all of a sudden there's really mad, really powerful playing, that's when you start saying, it's really going down. Liverpool's other fairly heavy band was The Undertakers, who used to go on all dressed in black and jump up and down on stage to this really pounding bass and drums.

The Big Three guitarist John Gustafson on whether they were rock's first traditional trio:
I can't recall another rock trio at that time in Liverpool, although I can't be sure. We got away with it at first by being loud and aggressive until we developed a trio playing style. Whether or not we influenced any other trios is open to debate. Anyway, I'm proud to be a Scouser and to have been lucky enough to take part in all that the city has achieved musically. I mean, we were signed by NEMS at the suggestion of John Lennon, as we were a favourite of his. To be there at the birth of rock 'n' roll was something that will never be repeated. I love the city and its people.

March 22, 1963. Beatles' first album, *Please Please Me* is issued. "Twist and Shout" is cited as an early example of a screaming or otherwise "extreme" vocal, the stock and trade, at the end of the decade, of one Ian Gillan. "Boys" is pretty rocked-up as well, and "I Saw Her Standing There" is famous for its own whoops and hollers.

Cream bassist and vocalist Jack Bruce:
The Beatles' work is very important to me because I was impressed by the fact that they did those great singles. And I thought they were really good because they compressed a lot of ideas into a very short period of time, two-and-a-half minutes, whatever. And that was a big influence on me in terms of writing songs like "I Feel Free," which were exercises in trying to write a pop song that would be interesting musically and would also sell a shitload of records.

> British producer Derek Lawrence:
> What I call rock 'n' roll, which would go back to Fats Domino and whatever, we copied it. There's no doubt about it. I once did a story and got so many phone calls from Americans about it, saying, well, the Beatles took black America and sold it back to white Americans. And that's what came from the '50s and the early '60s. And what I will say is, we took it on where America stayed where it was. I had a publishing partner who said that the Beatles took a cottage industry and made it multinational. But if you think about the Beatles, you know, that's rock 'n' roll! The Kinks, I would have to say that Ray Davies was different, because what he did was he took that Americans feel, but he put a London feel to it. The first couple of records, sure, they were just American rip-offs. But then he got into writing about his life.

June 1963. Portland, Oregon's The Kingsmen record Richard Berry's "Louie Louie," an early example of a riff rocker, or at least a song that centres on guitar signature of block chords that suggest the hummability of riff. The b-side of this single, issued this month in the US, is called "Haunted Castle."

July 26, 1963. Buddy Guy is captured live at Big Bill's Copa Cabana for the *Folk Festival of the Blues* album, making a huge impression on a young Jeff Beck, who saw the potential of the Fender Stratocaster open up to him. Buddy would go on to be cited as an early innovator in terms of feedback and distortion.

> Blue Öyster Cult producer and musicologist Sandy Pearlman:
> Buddy Guy was doing incredible counterintuitive stuff with the electric guitar, probably as early as... well, the first time I saw him was '65 or '66. So there was Buddy Guy, working feedback like no one had ever done before. Might've actually invented it, and in fact the historian at Universal Records, Andy MacKay, when I wrote that I thought that Buddy Guy had actually invented feedback, he called me to say that you're completely right. This is the first identified use of feedback, is in some Buddy Guy recording. And actually Buddy was interviewed by Terry Gross, *Fresh Air* on National Public Radio, and he said, "I think I invented feedback, and I think I know exactly what happened." So what that means is he invented the purposeful use of feedback rather than just a mistake.

Living Colour bassist Doug Wimbish comparing Buddy Guy with Jimi Hendrix:
Jimi was looking at other folks that were around him at the same time. You know, Buddy Guy was killing that shit too. Jimi was younger than him, but there were other exceptional, really flamboyant folks that were around encouraging him. Like Little Richard, saying, "Do your thing." But the blues stuff from Howlin' Wolf, Muddy Waters, the Chicago blues or whatever was going on, Jimi and Buddy were turning this stuff up and exploring with it.

November 17, 1963. The original Italian version of the movie, called *Black Sabbath* for English audiences, is released, entitled *I Tre Volti Della Paura*. Boris Karloff appears in the section called *The Wurdulak*, the other two mini-films being *The Telephone* and *The Drop Of Water*.

1964

1964. Tacoma, Washington's The Sonics release a single called "The Witch"/"Keep-A-Knockin'," on Etiquette. "The Witch" is a dark, driving song, with screaming vocals, that, in microcosm, tells the story of heavy metal by being part tritone and part blues structure; namely, it's arranged like a blues but its melody is doom. As with "Rumble," story has it that the inspiration for the band's fuzz sound was Johnny Burnette's Rock 'n' Roll Trio's "The Train Kept A-Rollin'" from 1956, but so much had happened in that eight year stretch, one wonders if it came from subsequent examples. Finally, lyrically, the song is about a witch, who, amusingly, even has a big black car.

Producer Jack Endino:
The Sonics, of course. They some pretty simple and direct riff rock, but it was crazy stuff, pretty pounding. And dark lyrically too, with "Psycho" and "Strychnine."

1964. Steven Tyler forms his first band, The Strangeurs, and later is part of Chain Reaction—he is a garage rocker soon to be bitten hard by The Yardbirds.

January 1, 1964. *Top of the Pops* opens for business. A big booster of rock acts of all stripes over the years, including many heavies, the inaugural show included one of the most hard-boiled acts of the day, the Rolling Stones.

Foghat drummer Roger Earl:
I used to go see the Stones at Eel Pie Island. Actually The Stones were great; in the early days when they first started playing I really enjoyed them. They were more like a rock 'n' roll kind of thing because they did a lot of Chuck Berry songs, and they tended to play stuff that is a lot faster. Not unlike how Foghat sorted of turned it up, the Stones didn't just copy the American blues artists and stuff they liked. They often changed things around.

Musicologist Gavin Baddeley on the most shocking acts from the days of proto-metal:
You get into the roots of heavy metal. Because a lot of people, yourself included, when trying to trace the roots of the genre, tend to look at things from a musical point of view, whereas I'm more inclined to look at things thematically. And so in the '60s, your shockers would be the Rolling Stones. I sometimes credit Rolling Stones as being the first heavy metal band. Because the themes are all there; the attitude is there. The Who, not so much, because, again, this is partially because I tend to see things from a thematic basis, and with The Who, I never thought of them as being a mod band, though obviously that's kind of their cultural context.

They obviously are a rock band, but the themes don't... there is some macabre stuff in there—"Boris the Spider" and so forth—but with the Rolling Stones, there was much more of a flirtation with Satanism and "Jumping Jack Flash" and the kind of sleaze and drugs and so forth. The Who certainly are in there on the periphery, but I think in some ways they're not theatrical enough.

February 9, 1964. The Beatles perform on CBS' *The Ed Sullivan Show*, playing five songs. The monumental rock 'n' roll event may not have directly invented heavy metal, but it sure inspired scores of future hard rock musicians—and musicians of many ilk, among the shows estimated 73 million viewers—to pick up a guitar and play.

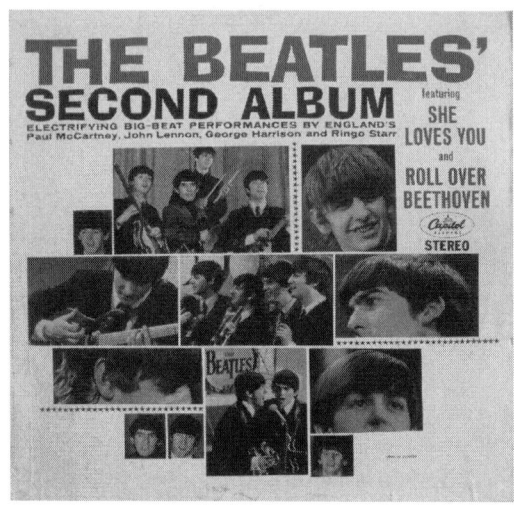

Trouble vocalist Eric Wagner: My older cousin was into it. Really when "Nowhere Man" came out, I was about six or seven, and that's the song. I mean it was Lennon's voice, his melodies. And to this day, he still freaks me out, when I see him. I had the shit on tape. It's just that his voice cuts through, and what he says, it's just hard to explain—whether it meant something or not, I don't know. I can't explain it. It's incomprehensible. He's incomprehensible to me, and now that he's dead it's more so. Like I can't even believe he was here. 30 years gone now and they're still selling big. They are my generation's Mozart. And 200 years from now, the Beatles will still be mentioned. They were the first ones to do it all. I still listen to Beatles records before it's time to make a record, just to get ideas. And they did all this on primitive equipment. A lot of bands today, you still hear Beatles influences. "Black Hole Sun," "All Apologies," those are Beatles songs. Even the first note of *In Utero*. To me that's the end of *Abbey Road*.

April 1964. The Outlaws (early band for Ritchie Blackmore) issue a cover of "Keep A Knockin'." Not much new or heavy to the rote structure and telling of the song, but Ritchie tears off four guitar solos that are indeed quite wild, heavy, electric, distorted and modern. The b-side of this last single for the band was called "Shake with Me," which English DJ legend John Peel once called the first heavy metal song. However, the author's assessment is much the same as for the a-side: nothing heavy about the song, but Ritchie indeed solos like the first guitar hero, if Charlie Christian hadn't already taken that crown 30 years earlier.

Producer Derek Lawrence:
If you go back to the Joe Meek stuff, and you go back to the Outlaws, "Keep A Knockin'"—that is Hendrix, before Hendrix. I just think, you know, Ritchie had these sounds in his body, and in his head, and nothing was going to stop him doing it.

April 16, 1964. The Rolling Stones issue their first album, a self-titled, all blues and rock 'n' roll covers save for one original, "Tell Me." The band is pictured on the cover in shadow, not smiling. The original UK cover featured no text on the cover other than the Decca logo, a ploy that Led Zeppelin would exploit a few years later to maximum promotional effect. An instant smash, the album stayed at #1 in the UK for 12 weeks.

Ted Nugent:
I would think because Les Paul had just electrified the guitar... a lot of those guys played nonelectric instruments in the beginning. Howlin' Wolf, just had a little acoustic guitar, you know, beating on it. And what the Stones brought to it was the same thing that I was bringing to it back home in Detroit, listening to the turntable, putting the needle on and learning those licks. But I heard Howlin' Wolf from the Stones, before I heard it from Howlin' Wolf. It was they that woke me up to the black American influence. Now be very careful. None of those guys would admit they were white. They all played the black stuff. They were addicted to Howlin' and Muddy and Lightning and Mose, and Robert Johnson, and Chuck and Bo, and Motown and James Brown. They were all obsessed with the black influence. And they did it in such a way... because, you've got to admit, those Stones albums, I mean, they did cover songs of all those heroes.

And Beck too, and certainly, whether it was Jimmy Page or Eric Clapton, they were all obsessed with playing those black guitar licks, and so they brought that to us via the British invasion. You've got to admit, Eric Clapton, kind of Caucasian-ized it, even though he never lost the soulfulness. But it was more in tune. Even old Keith Richards and Brian Jones, in their occasional semi-stupor, they at least, somebody, you know, Andrew Loog Oldman was demanding that they at least tune their damn instrument, because Howlin' and Muddy and Lightning did not (laughs).

Blue Cheer guitarist Randy Holden:
The Stones were very heavy. They just surprised me. I brought my band out to California and we were here when their first hit record came to Los Angeles. We were booked with them at the Long Beach Sports Arena, their first show in California, and I guess they were playing "All Over Now" on the radio—that was a hit song—but the sound of it on the radio was very tinny and light and a little hillbilly-ish. And my impression was they're very lightweight. I was kind of wondering why are these guys big? It wasn't making any sense. There was maybe a dozen bands on the bill at the Sports Arena. We were second bill to the Stones, so we tore the house down and then the Stones came on. But before they came on, they were setting up gear and Bill Wyman had two big Vox bass amps, and he hooked them in tandem. First time I'd ever seen anybody... well he was the first one that ever did it. God, the sound they had—real showmen, the other two guys, Brian and Keith—with that bass being doubled up like that. They had such power and were so heavy; it was like wow. Then you understood the record. I never understood the record until I heard them live. I heard them live—now I got it.

August 4, 1964. The Kinks release "You Really Got Me," a seminal, early song framed by overt use of power chords, albeit with an echo of blues patterning. Quickly, it is Dave Davies as well as Keith Richards who are popularizing fuzz applied to the guitar. For this song, Davies plugged the doctored amp into a Vox AC30 to record. Heavy metal's premier organist Jon Lord is cited as playing the piano on the track, recorded at IBC in London, although some say it is Arthur Greenslade providing the part. Consensus, straight from the recollections of Shel Talmy, is that Jimmy Page played neither guitar or tambourine on the track, but he played a bit of both on the full-length album.

Kinks guitarist Dave Davies:
When I was young I used to listen to records and just listen to the guitar work. I used to listen to James Burton, I used to listen to Scotty Moore, I loved John Lee Hooker, I liked Howlin' Wolf. Even before that, I was a big fan of The Ventures. And I used to like The Ventures' rhythm guitar playing. And if you listen to it, it's kind of like bar chords. They don't really play the whole chord, and I used to copy that. So it was a combination of different influences, coupled with my frustrations of not being able to get the sound out of an amplifier. Because the amplifiers in those days were very clean-cut-sounding and I wasn't very happy with that, so coupled with a variety of influences, and my own sort of aggression about how I wanted a guitar to sound, I got an amplifier and I just cut the speaker with a razor blade and I came out with this raunchy sound and that was the sound I liked, which was used on "You Really Got Me," which, oddly, has got one of my favourite solos because I didn't really know what the hell I was doing at the time.

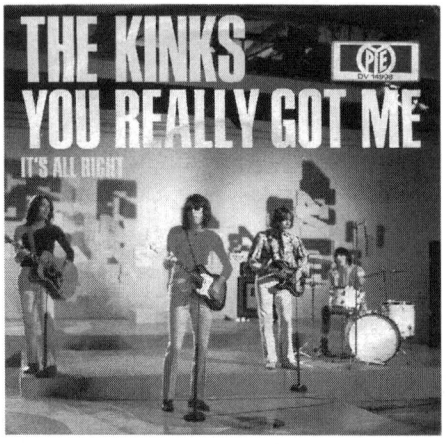

Black Sabbath drummer Bill Ward:
You had Cream, The Who, but also the Kinks, which Ozzy points out very, very well. When Dave Davies played "You Really Got Me" on that burnt-out amp... man, I tell you what, that sound, it was like, "Oh my God! What is that sound?!" That sound was great, and it just lands; it just puts itself to that really rough edge.

August 11, 1964. The Kinks issue "All Day and All of the Night" in the UK, on an EP. It's built on a riff, "incorporating B Flat after the chords F and G," but most importantly, it's a second popular song with blocks of power chords as prime propellant, power chords, that in fact, "lead" the song, with vocalist, bassist and drummer all following or responding. It's an example of this idea of heavy I talk about where heavy metal is invented where all the band members crouch around a fire, and that fire is a strong guitar line, built of either riff or power chords or a combination thereof.

August 14, 1964. Johnny Burnette, who gave us the world's first heavy metal song, is killed in a boating accident, at the age of 30.

October 2, 1964. The Kinks issue their self-titled debut album, in the UK. The American version has an altered track list and is called *You Really Got Me*. That song so crucial to heavy metal history is included on both versions. Little else rises above weak tea Beatles on the record other than brief Stooge-y instrumental "Revenge." Follow-up *Kinda Kinks* adds nothing to the tale.

October 20, 1964. Manager Chris Stamp and Kit Lambert create a promotional film of their new charges The High Numbers (previously The Detours and soon to be The Who) playing at the Railway Hotel. The performance is manic, dramatic, aggressive and noisy, mostly due to the band's firecracker of a drummer Keith Moon, but also to the surly punk rock disposition of guitarist Pete Townsend. The band's bass player is doing nothing much to invent heavy metal, but their lead singer, Roger Daltrey, is busy creating the persona of the cooler than cool blonde front man, heading up his band of strong personalities but also growling out some fairly carnal vocals for this nascent period in hard music's struggling birth.

Late 1964 - 1965. Tony Iommi is in his first band, the blues-based The Rockin' Chevrolets. Also around this time, Tony changes from left-handed to right-handed guitar, after an accident on his last day of work at a sheet metal factory in which he lost the tips of his ring finger and middle finger on his right hand. Django Reinhardt becomes an inspiration, given a similar disability—the suggestion that he listen to Django comes from his boss at the factory, who knew Tony moonlighted as a musician.

Recap

Perhaps the most important concert in rock history took place when the Beatles played on *Ed Sullivan* on February 9, 1964, given the wholesale intense inspiration the band ignited upon future generations of rock 'n' rollers. But there was a wider importance to the Beatles themselves, namely this idea of someone coming along—from Britain, significantly—that is kicking things up a few notches, mostly with their youth and their long hair, but also through some new sounds, though not many.

Wider still is that the Beatles were the first phalanx of a British invasion, which brought the bad boys along, the anti-Beatles, namely the Rolling Stones. Not much heavier, these guys however were a little rougher around the edges, and the blues they paid tribute to usually came with a hint of menace.

O'er to the side, we see Ritchie Blackmore twanging away with The Outlaws, pioneering distortion and the guitar solo with Joe Meek, building upon other minor advancements in distortion, some intended and some accidental. Surf music is also placing the guitar further forward in pop consciousness through the work of Dick Dale. Also, inspired by The Beatles and even more so the Stones, there are garage rock bands a' plenty, with some of them looking more closely at the blues, taught so by Mick and Keith, and yes, John and Paul.

The most significant advancements toward the invention of heavy metal come toward the end of this period with the arrival of The High Numbers and The Kinks. The High Numbers are not yet quite The Who, but live, as witnessed in The Railway Hotel footage, they are clearly presenting a new and harder rock with what they are calling "maximum R&B."

The Kinks, on the other hand, are making heavy metal (pre-) history proper with two widely celebrated milestones when this topic is discussed, namely the issue of the songs "You Really Got Me" and All Day and All of the Night" (along with equally heavy b-side "I Need You"). Both of these hit songs represent early and somewhat hard use of distortion, power chords and, more subtly, structures that are defined by the guitar part. In this sense, we are approaching the concept of riff, with one characteristic of riff being this idea of all other performances in the song falling in line or in a sense, following what the guitar and guitarist are doing.

Bottom line—and summarizing ruthlessly—"You Really Got Me" is regularly called by scholars of this stuff the first heavy metal song. And whether we track to that party line or not, fact is, up until the end of 1964, this is the kernel of heavy metal trivia that usually starts the discussion rolling—Dave Davies invented heavy metal with "You Really Got Me."

1965

1965. Ozzy Osbourne drops out of school at 15, does odd jobs and eventually winds up in Winston Green Prison for two months on burglary charges. It's a spot of heavy metal credibility that will come up in interviews often over the years, although it's talked about more as the poverty-stricken underdog getting nicked rather than Ozzy being a roustabout or "tear-away."

1965. The Rationals, from Ann Arbor, Michigan, issue their first of seven singles between 1965 and 1969. The band was a well-regarded early influence on Detroit's hard rockers of the late '60s and early '70s. MC5 manager John Sinclair's book, *Guitar Army*, is named for a Rationals song. The band's vocalist/guitarist Scott Morgan was a key figure on the scene.

1965. Garage rock band Sons of Adam, featuring Randy Holden of Blue Cheer fame, issue a single on Decca, "Mr. You're a Better Man than I" (a Yardbirds cover)/"Saturday's Son." The band is active from '62 until '66, beginning in Baltimore, Maryland and later moving to San Francisco. The original sound of the band was surf, eventually moving in a heavier direction. The band's other two singles are: 1) "Feathered Fish" (written by Arthur Lee of Love), backed with "Baby Show the World;" and 2) a second Decca single comprising "Take My Hand"/"Tomorrow's Gonna Be Another Day." The band's complete output is the above six tracks, although a Fenders IV single "Mar Gaya" ('64/65) includes a b-side called "You Better Tell Me Now" which is described as a Sons of Adam b-side. Fenders IV also had a '64 single for "Malibu Run"/"Everybody Up." This is significant because Fenders IV was more of a surf band, with Sons of Adam being the same band with a different drummer. But Fenders IV's "Mar Gaya" is some pretty intense surf music. As noted, Dick Dale and the whole idea of surf is a sub-story in the invention of heavy metal.

1965. Jim Marshall and his Marshall amplifier company, produce the Marshall Super Lead Model 1959. Soon after, Pete Townsend requests an 8 x 12" cabinet (later two 4 x 12"s) and the Marshall "stack" is born. Crucial to the story of heavy metal, advancements in amplification begins to serve as a catalyst for heavy music, with guitarists, bass players and singers first playing through PAs, and then drummers becoming fully mic'ed up as well. Also a nice twist on this story is that Pete essentially wanted an amplifier that he could use as a weapon, because he found it disrespectful that crowds would talk during his performances.

Who roadie in '65 and '66 Neville Chesters on early technical milestones in heaviness:

I guess the first one would be with The Who. We were the first band to get an 8 x 12" stack, not 4 x 12". Some of it Townsend designed were six foot high, but we were also the first band to get the 100-watt guitar heads. Those were overrun; as we know from Spinal Tap, we had it on 11 all the time. And then I think the advent of fuzz boxes, distortion boxes... off the top of my head I'm not really sure when we first got them. I just remembered everything with The Who was on overload the whole time. So we had distortion to start with before anything else was added. Before any fuzz boxes or wah wah pedals were added. I mean, Pete was overrunning his amp the whole time, so it was literally full on. That in itself was distortion. Yeah, The Who were heavy. They were doing "Summertime Blues." I mean, short of Blue Cheer, I don't recall anybody doing "Summertime Blues" quite that heavy.

Nazareth guitarist Manny Charlton:
To me, hard rock sort of came into being when they brought out Marshall stacks. Because then the guitars got really, really loud. And Clapton came out, the Yardbirds, the Who. All these bands were basically like power trios, and the power came from the Marshall stacks. Really, really loud amps. So everything else had to step up in volume. They started mic'ing up the drum kit, and putting it through the main PA where the vocal was. That's what they started doing. Usually the vocalist had the whole PA. At that time there was no putting the guitars through the PA system. It was basically just the vocals. Until the late '60s.

Status Quo guitarist and vocalist Francis Rossi:
The heavier metal thing came along people were tuning down. I remember Tony Iommi doing it—and we worked with Black Sabbath quite a lot. But also, you gotta remember that amplification in those days couldn't carry any bottom end. So once bottom end started getting in and decent PA systems started getting in there, then you could present a front house thing as high energy rock. Heavy metal has to have serious lows, otherwise it just has no bollocks, no bottom at all. And I think it couldn't have happened before those kind of systems came along.

CEO of Gibson, Henry Juszkiewicz:
One of the guys I really know pretty well is Jim Marshall, right? So when I first got in the guitar business in 1986 I flew to the UK and I had to meet Jim. He really was the guy that invented the big amplifier. So I said I want to find out what this guy's about. It's a wonderful idea and he's got to be a genius guy and I wanted to meet him.

So I went to meet him and he was kind enough to talk to me. So I went in his conference room at the Marshall factory, and the first thing I noticed was there was a big set of Ludwig drums in the conference room and no amplifiers. So I said, "Hey Jim, what's this with the drums?" And he said, "Actually I'm a drummer and a singer." So I said, "How did you come up with this amplifier deal?" And he said, 'Well I was also a retailer and I was a retailer in London and we had a lot of very famous customers, and they all needed amplifiers and they were not happy with the amplifiers of the day, and I saw that as a marvellous business opportunity. So I asked around and said what is the favourite amplifier that people are buying? They said it's a Fender amplifier. And Fender's circuit was patented."

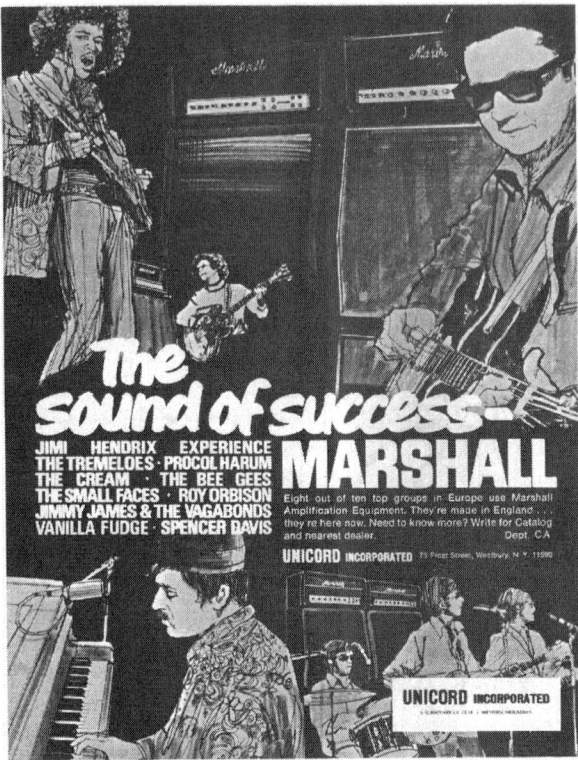

So he went to an engineering buddy and said, "What can we do to get close to this but not break any of the patents?" And this engineering fellow put in a diode into the Fender circuit, and what the diode does is it clips the waveform and causes distortion. So they weren't really going after distortion, they were going after trying to circumvent a patent. But it turns out that it sounded really great, especially when you cranked these big amplifiers up.

So I asked Jim, and Jim is really the guy who I think invented the genre. So I said, "Jim, how come these amplifiers are so big? What gave you that idea?" Because they don't have to necessarily be big to be loud. He said, "Well, I'm a big band drummer and a big band singer. The old days, when you were in a big band you had this podium in front of every musician, and on the podium, the band leader's name was in big letters." He said, "I wanted my name in big letters. So I said you gotta see it, so we gotta have a big cabinet with my name in big letters." And that's how it came to be. So if it's big, you can also stuff a lot of speakers in, of course, and had a lot of other wonderful aspects as to how it changed music, but that was really how it kind of got started.

Vanilla Fudge guitarist Vinny Martell on improving technology:
I used the wah-wah pedal myself; I used the Fuzz-Tone. We used the big amps. I went through every amplifier company imaginable and ended up with the biggest ones they had, which was the Marshalls. My ears are still ringing and I'm still coming down from those days. But I also used a semi-hollow Gibson ES-335 back then that I still have. It had a big sound, the semi-hollow body; I used a Gibson SG, which gave me a big sound, again with the humbucker pickups. Not that you can't get a big sound with the single coil Strat pickups—you can. You know it's a lot in the amplification in the guitar mix and it's a lot of with the group.

With the Fudge, a lot of the guitar parts I was doing were kind of supporting the sound rather than standing out to do a solo all the time. I was looking to get as much power and bigness out of the sound, so we would do chords together, myself and Mark, and get the most out of a build, and then break into a solo as opposed to just concentrating on doing solos all the time. So that's one of the things. It's on the *Renaissance* album, a lot of that; I did a lot of that with the chords and the heavy stuff.

But then as time went on we just kept moving out because we had more opportunity to do more stuff, so I could break into whatever I wanted to. But to support the group, what I did was I always had an eye to getting the most out of the mood. If we're doing a build, we're all doing the build. If we're doing vocals we're all supporting it tightly behind so the vocals stands out. Whatever is going to sound out, you want it to really give as much colour as possible. It's like preparation before you do anything. The preparation is 90% of the job.

January, 15, 1965. The Who issue "I Can't Explain" as their first UK single (released a month earlier in the US), which, although poppy, hangs its hat on block power chords with much breathing space in-between, a celebrated heavy metal trope. Both Roger Daltrey and Pete Townsend acknowledge the influence of The Kinks' "All Day and All of the Night" on the writing of the song. Jimmy Page is known to be a session guitarist at the recording of the song, but it is believed his contribution didn't make the final cut.

February – May 1965. Ritchie Blackmore logs a few dates with Screaming Lord Sutch & The Savages plus work with Jerry Lee Lewis, and into '66, The Three Musketeers, Riki Maiocchi & the Trips, and once again, Neil Christian & the Crusaders. Here we have arguably one of heavy metal's top four most historically important guitarists (along with Hendrix, Page and Iommi), cavorting with two early archetypes of the wild man front man, piano-burner Jerry Lee Lewis, and a dandy with "screaming" in his very name.

Early 1965. The Sonics release their debut album, *Here Are the Sonics* which includes "The Witch," "Psycho" and "Strychnine," all pretty rocking, extreme songs.

May 21, 1965. The Kinks issue their "Set Me Free" single in the UK (five days later in the US). The b-side, "I Need You," deserves mention along with "You Really Got Me" and "All Day and All of the Night" as the third but obviously lesser-celebrated pioneering proto-metal song disseminated by The Kinks. Six months later, "Till the End of the Day" would mine similar terrain.

June 6, 1965. The Rolling Stones issue "(I Can't Get No) Satisfaction," which is an early example of a song built around a guitar riff. This was one of the earliest uses—and certainly the biggest—of the new Maestro Fuzz-Tone Model FZ-1. The song's success soon caused shortages of the gizmo on the shelves of music stores.

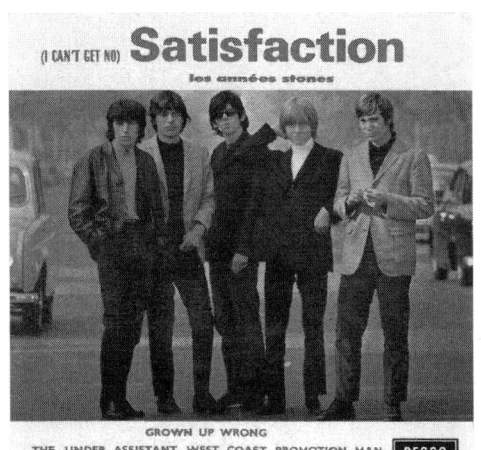

CEO of Gibson, Henry Juszkiewicz: Distortion is like a fine wine, okay? And you will never get two wine connoisseurs to agree what fine wine actually is. And so the technical description of distortion is basically harmonics from a clipped wave form, but it really breaks down to a lot more complicated kind of thing. And people will swear on a stack of Bibles on a certain pedal or a certain amplifier with certain settings, is the magic sound. And so there is not one magic sound, number one.

Number two, guitar players love to mess with their equipment. They loved to mess with it in the '50s, actually. They still mess with it today, and Les Paul is not alone. Everyone is trying to figure out a signature sound. Something that gives them something that's very unique. Sometimes you hack your equipment, sometimes it's your playing style, your guitar; everybody is searching for the Holy Grail of their signature sound. There are a lot of opinions on what that is. One of the essential elements of the signature sound is the distortion and how it sounds, so there are lots of ways of achieving it. There are lots of pedal companies, lots of amp companies, lots of hacks. You know you can get your Marshall amp hot-rodded or your Fender amp hot-rodded. You can get Russian tubes that are pre-selected for the amp. All kinds of mojo stuff to get that magic sound. So musicians achieve different kinds of sounds with all kinds of incredible things.

Stooges drummer Scott Asheton:
The first hard rock, you would have to say it was the Stones. Although I loved The Kinks very much. But as far as heavy and hard, the first band I would say was the Stones, although there were all kinds of littler bands that were heavy, like The Music Machine with "Talk, Talk" and Kingsmen, "Louie, Louie" and then The Nashville Teens, who did a pretty heavy version of "Tobacco Road."

Blue Cheer guitarist Randy Holden:
The original distortion pedal was the Fuzz-Tone, and that's what Keith used on "Satisfaction." And then so I got one just to play that song with, and it was a very cool sound. Wasn't much good for anything else though, because it was unique to that particular sound. I never managed anything else to do with it. But then George Harrison did something where he put the head of his guitar up against his amp and created a buzz saw kind of feedback. That was the first sustain of feedback. And then the Yardbirds came out, and Jeff Beck, he took it to a whole other level. I saw them play at... I think it was the Palladium. They were great. Jeff Beck was awesome then. He was not withdrawn and subdued. He was totally wild. He laid his guitar down in front of the amps, just feeding back and dancing around the stage like an Indian whooping. It was good fun. He took a small Vox, like a five or ten watt Vox, and then plugged into that and then plugged that into his big Vox, and out of that you got all kinds of power. I thought cool idea. I tried it with a Fender, and yeah, it was so powerful, it was overwhelming. But you couldn't control the hum.

June 13, 1965. Yardbirds first studio album, a US compilation called *For Your Love*.

Yardbirds rhythm guitarist Chris Dreja:
The band kind of grew out of two bands, that were both turned on by American black blues players, that sort of Chicago blues sound, also influenced

by people like Robert Johnson. So when Jim McCarty and I sort of started the band, we wanted to go electric. And in those days, in England, it was hard to get that sort of equipment. Like, we started electric, and amalgamated with Keith's band, which had Paul Samwell-Smith; they were known as The Metropolitan Blues Band.

But anyway, they liked what our influences were, so that band and us amalgamated, and we started electric. But in fact Paul Samwell-Smith made his own bass amplifiers. He was a bit of a technical wizard, a bit like Bill Wyman did with the Stones, all hand-made equipment, because you couldn't really get it. But basically it was a guitar band with Keith Relf playing harmonica. But of course, technically, we had very limited equipment. So it wasn't a big sound, but it was actually big compared to what was around, also because we played with a lot of energy. And then it kind of progressed as we started to record. We started to get access to Vox amplifiers, which, actually, we still play Vox amplifiers. And the sound started to round out.

And then of course Eric Clapton joined the band, and he was influenced by Buddy Guy and B.B. King, that sort of thing. So basically at the very beginning, it was a sort of British version of a blues band, which didn't last too long, because of course we were never going to be an electric Chicago blues band. So we started to experiment with other styles and things, introducing other instrumentation. We were just experimenting with this very early advent of distortion pedals, really embryo, really primitive, but they had a kind of funky sound. And we were pushing the equipment. There wasn't a number 11 on them, but we were abusing them well beyond the manufacturers' recommended thing. We were playing around with feedback and distortion and everything else, which often didn't come across too well in recording. We were recording in England, and the recording industry was pretty tame, and not used to a band that wanted to play with our sort of distortion levels etc. But of course, we pushed ahead, broke the rules, and I'm glad we did. We got some interesting sounds down.

July 25, 1965. Bob Dylan performs at the Newport Folk Festival, but electric and not acoustic, prompting boos from the folk faithful.

Summer 1965. The Spiders' (early version of the Alice Cooper group) first single, "Hitch Hike"/"Why Don't You Love Me." The band is an ambitious bunch of grounded, regular guys looking for a way to wake people up.

Late 1965. The Amboy Dukes, featuring Ted Nugent, start playing their first gigs. A guitar hero of the '70s is born through boasts made in the '60s.

October 25, 1965. The Who issue their anthem to youth, "My Generation" which is quite heavy, although no huge shakes over the two Kinks songs from the previous year or The Who's own "I Can't Explain." Until... the closing moments, where the song explodes in a fireball of noise. It is a significant heavy metal moment, if both brief and nihilistic. Conjecture, but The Who might not be in this discussion if not for Keith Moon.

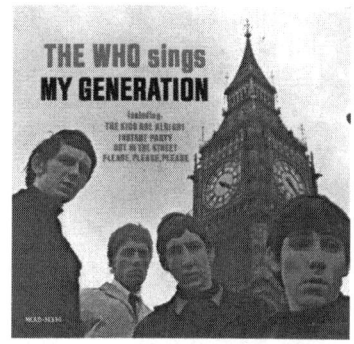

Blue Öyster Cult drummer Al Bouchard: The Who, who I saw many times, was a fantastic group. You just didn't know what was going to happen. It was like what the hell? They were just really high energy and sort of psycho. The Doors, too, were this psycho group that you just didn't know what was going to happen, but that was mostly Morrison. With The Who it was like all of them, except for the bass player. The rest of them, they were all a bunch of nutters. I saw Pete Townsend kick a cop in the balls. He came up onstage and started grabbing... apparently there was smoke from the restaurant next door to the theatre, and a cop came up, a plain-clothes policeman, so it just looked like some guy with short hair, got up onstage and grabbed the microphone from Roger Daltrey. And Roger Daltrey was like, "What?" So he pulled the mic back, and then Townsend ran all the way across the stage and kicked the guy right in the balls, and he went down hard. And then cops swarmed the stage and arrested Townsend. And it was like, "Cool!" (laughs).

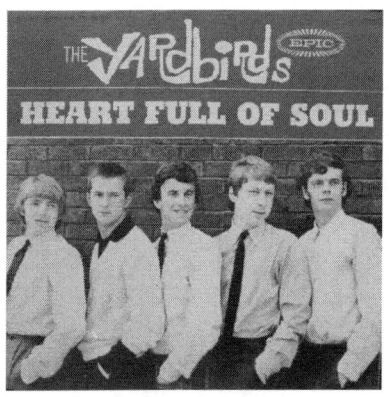

November 15, 1965. Yardbirds' second album is another US compilation, called *Having a Rave Up with the Yardbirds*. The album includes "I'm a Man," "Heart Full of Soul," "Still I'm Sad" and a legendary rendition of "The Train Kept A-Rollin'," which, in its second stage rendition by Johnny Burnette from 1956, has been pegged by the author as the first heavy metal song. The Yardbirds version, fully nine years later, surprisingly, does not add many heavy metal elements or advancements over the original, emboldening the claim of milestone importance we've bestowed upon Johnny Burnette's flag spiked to ground. Of note, the next famous version of the song would arrive nine years later, Aerosmith covering the song on 1974's *Get Your Wings* album, adding a slow and riffier vamp to it.

Aerosmith guitarist Brad Whitford on "The Train Kept A-Rollin':"
We may not have heard all the earlier or original versions of it. Our real driving force on that was definitely the Yardbirds. We were just huge into Jimmy Page and Jeff Beck and still are. We basically became just the two guitar band version of that. That song just had Aerosmith all over it. As soon as we started doing it, it just had such a powerful riff, and a touch of funk to it. As for the slow part on the front, I think we started messing around with that in pre-production, when we were working on the album. And also, being huge fans of James Brown and funk music, I think it just came up in rehearsal one day. It immediately clicked, and

we went, that's cool! So we decided to basically put two versions on it at the same time. I love the slow version. It's just so badass (laughs). We're all fans of many types of music, but certainly the basis of where we came from was just this deep appreciation of blues-based hard rock, really. We came into ourselves from being huge fans of a lot of what was coming out of England at the time. Like so many of our contemporaries, so many of us were blown away by people like the Stones and The Yardbirds—we so desperately wanted to do our own version of that.

Iron Butterfly guitarist Mike Pinera, drawing a connection between the Yardbirds and the Aerosmith versions:

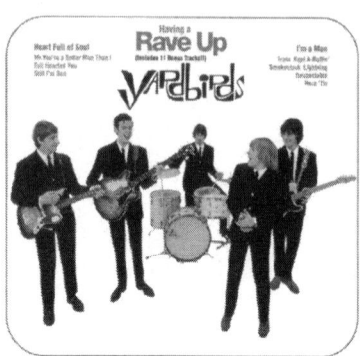

When the Yardbirds came over and John Mayall came over and then Cream came over, I had a chance to play with all those guys at a club that we had at Miami Beach called The Image, on Collins, right on the sand there, and we had everybody there. The Yardbirds with Jimmy Page... in fact I went to the airport to pick them up and that's when I first met Jimmy, and that was '68. And we became good friends then.

And I noticed there was this little kid tagging along with him, and I said, "Who's this guy here?" He says, "Oh, his name is Steven Tyler. He's going to be a musician one day." What happened was the Yardbirds had played in Boston and Tyler heard them playing and literally ran away. He just went on the road with them. Got on the airplane, paid his own way and just came. I had my car packed with some wild dudes. And then it wasn't but two years later that when I was in Butterfly and Jimmy started Led Zeppelin that we were, again, on the same stage together except as Zeppelin and Butterfly. And we were reminiscing about the old days when we first played together and jammed together. And I really thought he played some great licks and took the integrity of the blues and yet formed it into a sound all his own, and I love that. Stuff like "Dazed and Confused," where they would go outside the box with arrangement and then live, create jams that were just phenomenal.

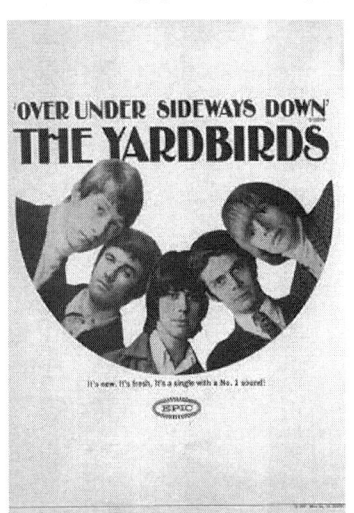

Stooges guitarist James Williamson:
"Train Kept A-Rollin'" and all those numbers were huge in my period of sort of growing up. Jeff Beck's lineup of the band was pretty smoking hot. I am very largely a rhythm guitar player although I guess I play a lot of everything. That's kind of why I play with one guitar in the band, because I don't leave a lot of air for people in my writing or in my playing. So, yeah, I always like a good beat and a good syncopated rhythm and so on, but Jeff Beck is much more than a rhythm guitar player (laughs).

December 1965. The Move form in Birmingham, England, becoming one of the first, biggest and most inspirational and influential of bands on the Birmingham scene in the '60s. Both punk rock and the heavy metal wind-up are born simultaneously, at least as far as the locals are concerned.

December 3, 1965. "Think for Yourself" on Beatles' *Rubber Soul* is arguably the first use of distortion on a bass guitar. In smart Beatles fashion, Paul applies both a regular bass line and the heavily distorted one, which sounds like a synthesizer part more than a bass part.

December 3, 1965. The Who's debut album, *My Generation* (or *Sings My Generation*) includes rockier tracks like "Out in the Street," "The Good's Gone," "My Generation" and "The Ox." "My Generation" is discussed as a mid-'60s hard rock anthem in parallel with the two big Kinks songs. As mentioned, distinguishing it is the manic performance of drummer Keith Moon who essentially thrashes out as the song explodes to a finish.

CEO of Gibson, Henry Juszkiewicz: Townsend definitely has heavy metal elements but would not go into heavy metal. Yet he definitely developed a lot of the style and stage presence and so forth of heavy metal. Clearly he was a pioneer in that area. Heavy metal is not just about the music, it's about the showmanship. It's the whole scene, the community. It's really an immersive kind of music that draws the audience and the artists together.

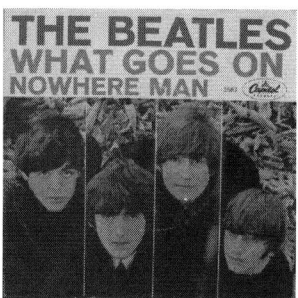

Recap

The pre-hippie generation year of 1965 nonetheless offers a few wild sonic moments, beginning with a Who single called "I Can't Explain," a Who album, and a wilder Who single in "My Generation."

Also in The Who's world, Pete Townsend and Jim Marshall butt heads and come up with the Marshall stack, an emboldening and enlarging of the Marshall amplifier system. Now vocalists and drummers have to compete with guitar and bass and the volume available on stage turns bands into four-headed monsters.

The other big story of 1965 is The Yardbirds, a band that is not as heavy as The Who, yet somehow manages to bring more focus to guitar and guitarist, indeed, inspiring a cult of the guitar that is central to heavy metal music. This happens due to the presence of not one but two new guitar gods, in Eric Clapton and Jeff Beck spread complicatedly across the two albums the band would issue in 1965, as the band hinted at the psychedelic era to come.

1966

1966. Blue Cheer is formed, an ill wind blown across San Francisco from Davis, CA, managed by an ex-Hells Angels named Gut.

1966. The Band of Joy form in West Bromwich, near Birmingham, England. Robert Plant is in the band at this point, but not John Bonham, who joins in 1967, replacing John Trickett.

1966. Tony Iommi's next legitimate band, The Rest, plies their trade about town.

1966. Ex-surf guitarist Randy Holden is now with The Other Half. Holden continues to pioneer volume live by using a half dozen 10-watt Fender Dual Showman amps hooked up in tandem on stage.

January 1966. Spencer Davis Group's Steve Winwood wields a heck of a fuzz sound on an otherwise tame minor hit from *The Second Album* called "Keep on Running."

Early 1966. Slade begins life as The N'Betweens. They are from the Black Country, West Midlands. Three of the members are natives of Wolverhampton, one from Walsall. Their substantial work in heavy metal will occur during the first half of the '70s, but their first original was called "Evil Witchman."

Producer Kim Fowley:
> I first encountered heavy metal as producer of Slade. They were the N'Betweens then. Same four guys with a different name. I recorded them in '66 and they were the loudest band in England. So when I came back and ran into fabulous Steppenwolf and Blue Cheer, I knew what was going on because I realized that England was the true birthplace of metal. And Bill Farley who engineered this stuff, was the engineer of "Iron Man" by Black Sabbath. You mean Kim Fowley did metal in the same studio with the same engineers as "Iron Man" and Black Sabbath before they ever existed? Exactly.

> This was Regent Sound, on Denmark Street. It was a tiny room like a cheeseburger box. And when the Stones recorded there they called it Impact Sound. Andrew Loog Oldham wouldn't put Regent Sound on the liner notes because he didn't want everybody to know where the studio was, so he made up a phony name and everybody was running around looking for Impact Sound, and in reality it was Regent. For £14 an hour. This was

downstairs on street level; just a crappy little studio. But Bill Farley was never given credit.

I also recorded Belfast Gypsies there, which is Them minus Van Morrison. So when Van Morrison left Them we recorded the remaining guys as Belfast Gypsies at the same time, that summer of '66, when we recorded the Slade, a.k.a. the N'Betweens. And then when I came jumping off the airplane back from England I noticed the records that were Top Five were "Talk Talk" by The Music Machine and Count Five, "Psychotic Reaction." But they were the forerunners of punk. So the seeds of punk were in California. The seeds of metal were in the UK at the same time.

February 1966. The Sonics issue their second album, *Boom*, for which they removed the soundproofing from the studio walls to get more of a live sound. The album contains considerably raw and rocking tunes, including "He's Waitin'" the band's carnal version of "Louie, Louie" and proto speed metal rocker "Cinderella," covered in 1978 by Boston punk-metallers DMZ.

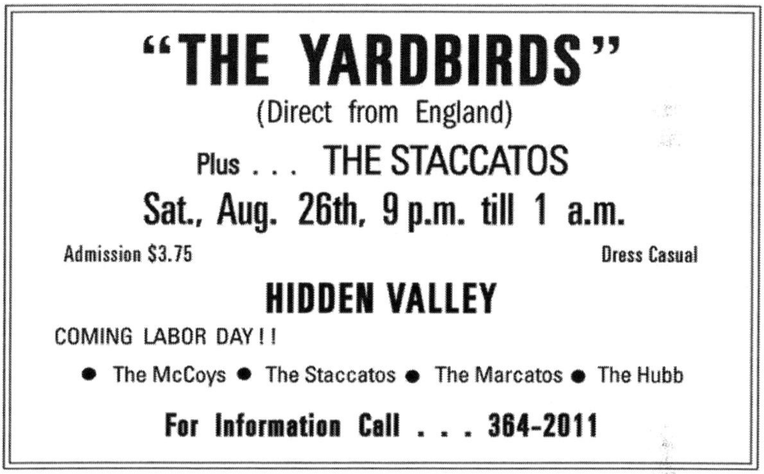

"THE YARDBIRDS"
(Direct from England)

Plus . . . THE STACCATOS

Sat., Aug. 26th, 9 p.m. till 1 a.m.

Admission $3.75   Dress Casual

HIDDEN VALLEY

COMING LABOR DAY!!

● The McCoys ● The Staccatos ● The Marcatos ● The Hubb

For Information Call . . . 364-2011

February 1966. Yardbirds issue "Shapes of Things" as a single, which is a fairly aggressive, heavy-structured composition, featuring Jeff Beck on guitar. The song comes up often in conversation with rock stars from the '70s in terms of tracks that influenced them.

Yardbirds drummer Jim McCarty:
We were making our songs quite original and we were trying to broaden our sound into something that was a bit unusual, especially when Jeff Beck was in the band. He had such a whole range of guitar sounds that it was quite natural for him to draw on those and we were all very happy to do that. So all of that quirkiness and strange originality became part of the sound. And it actually blended into the psychedelic scene quite well too. We would go to California, a bunch of young white guys from South London, and we'd be playing our stuff, and there would be all these hippie people jumping around going mad thinking we were all on acid trips.

Kinks guitarist Dave Davies:
A lot of the bands like the Beatles and the Hollies were more poppy-sounding, which was brilliant. The Yardbirds were quite heavy, a much heavier band, but that was rhythmically heavy. There's a great band called The Downliners Sect, which is a little bit obscure, but they were a big influence. It has a totally different connotation now, but we used to call it R&B, what we did, which is kind of like a mixture of Chuck Berry rock 'n' roll with blues, the Muddy Waters-type stuff. And the "Southern" music from London was much heavier than the music coming from Manchester and Liverpool.

Yardbirds rhythm guitarist Chris Dreja on the band's tendency to be much heavier live than on record:
Back to your interesting question about, was it the equipment that made heavy metal, I mean, before we did "For Your Love" as a hit single, the Yardbirds would've probably been one of the heaviest bands around, probably even more heavier than the Rolling Stones were, in terms of the onstage power, or the power on stage. And what happened was we tried to record that sound, with things like "I Wish You Would," and we were never successful in getting it onto vinyl, getting it onto tape. It always got so suppressed and compressed that it didn't happen, although, music-wise, it was a very frenetic and loud band. An audience would behave, if you like, like they were at a heavy metal concert. In other words, they would go fucking bonkers. Which was great.

But if you listen to some of the music we were playing on vinyl, you would go, well, that's okay, but it's a bit tame. But it wasn't like that live. When we came over to America and started recording in studios that were more geared-up to that more distorted in-your-face sound, it was more successful for us, like when we started doing things like "Shapes of Things." But I would agree with you, having played then and having played now, it is much easier to get your sound across now, because in those days you didn't have these huge rigs. Everything came off the stage. And of course guitar amplifiers could be loud, but you could never get a vocal out of it. So actually, it's very important. If you've got a lot of decibels and you're trying to reach a lot of people in a big hole, it was very difficult back in the '60s.

April 1966. The Seeds issue their self-titled debut. The dark, garage rock album includes "Pushin' Too Hard," which was issued as a single before the album, in November 1965.

April 22, 1966. England's The Troggs issue in the US their #1 smash rendition of Chip Taylor's "Wild Thing," a fairly gnarly, garagey and heavy song for the time, fitting nicely between "Louie Louie " and "I Can't Explain."

April 30, 1966. Anton LaVey founds The Church of Satan, in San Francisco.

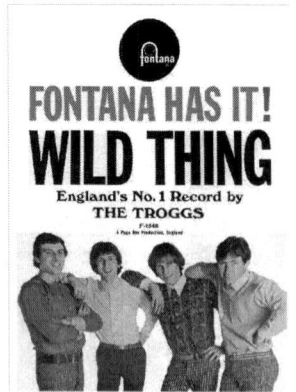

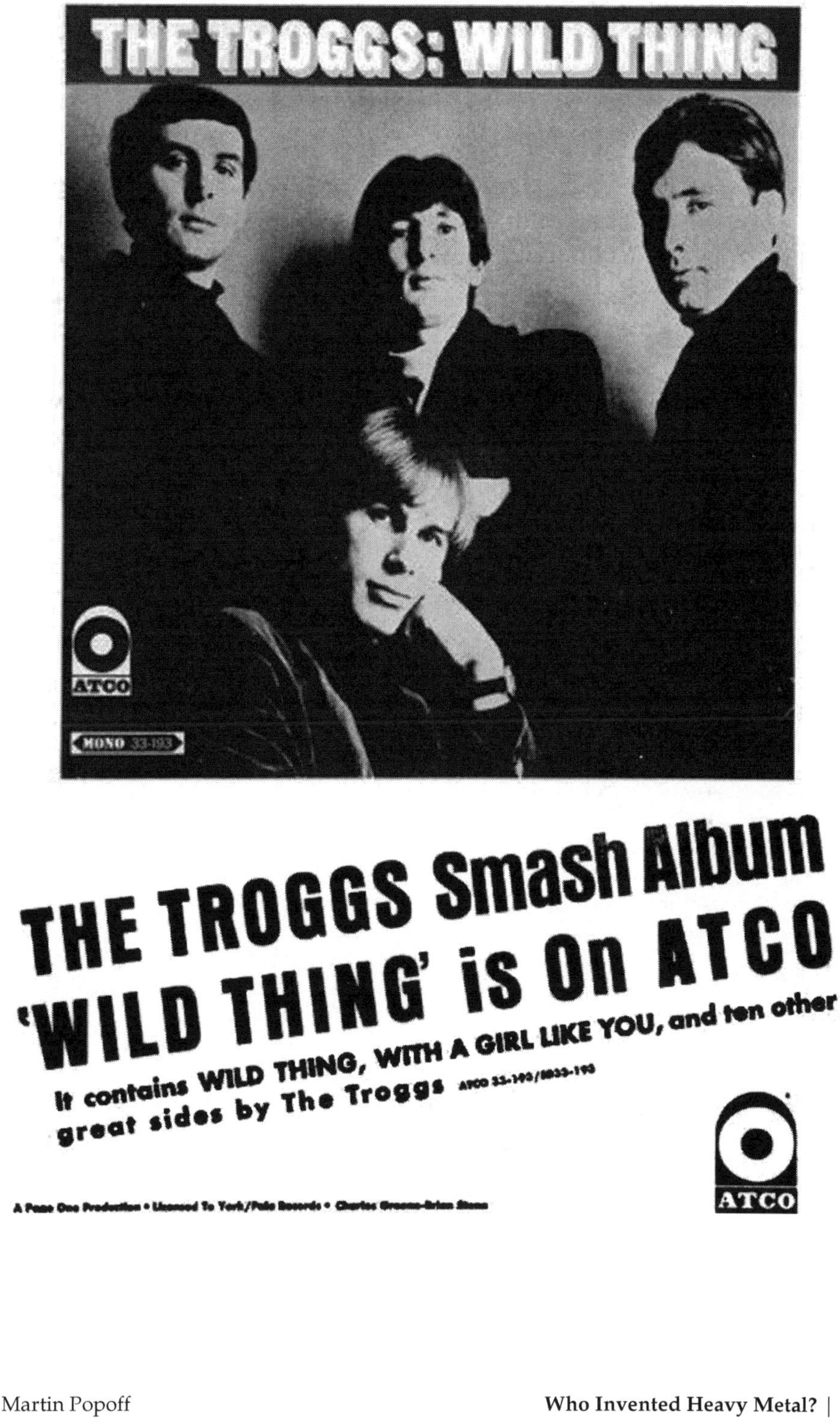
THE TROGGS: WILD THING
ATCO
MONO 33-193
THE TROGGS Smash Album
'WILD THING' is On ATCO
It contains WILD THING, WITH A GIRL LIKE YOU, and ten other great sides by The Troggs
ATCO

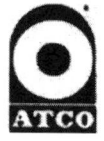

May 1966. Mitch Ryder & The Detroit Wheels' debut album, *Take a Ride*, is issued. Ryder is cited as the grandfather of Detroit rock 'n' roll and is noted for his gruff vocal style. In the same year, the band's second album, *Breakout!*, is issued.

Cactus drummer Carmine Appice on Detroit Wheels and Cactus guitarist Jim McCarty: He hasn't really gotten the credit due to him, but in 1966, when Jeff Beck was playing with the Yardbirds, his style of music, Jim McCarty was playing with Mitch Ryder & the Detroit Wheels, playing the same kind of guitar, bending with fuzz tone and doing all that stuff. Jim is one of the American originators of that kind of guitar playing.

Ted Nugent:
My band The Lourdes won the battle of the bands in Detroit, in 1963, against unbelievably killer rock 'n' roll bands, with the kind of musical authority that ended up creating, you know, Mitch Ryder & The Detroit Wheels, the MC5, Bob Seger and Kid Rock, and certainly the power and the soulful authority of what Motown had taught us. You see, the original creators of this incredible music, the black gods, were already the most influential in Detroit because of Mitch Ryder. He delivered it to us before they changed their name from Billy Lee & The Rivieras. So the competition to play tight, authoritative, powerful, soulful and really in the pocket, was already established in Detroit before the Rolling Stones were even aware of it. And Jimmy McCarty, what a genius!

June 11, 1966. The Rolling Stones issue "Paint it Black" as a single, which is a dark and somewhat proto-metal song both musically and lyrically. The track represents an early use of eastern melody, which will be used often in heavy metal, slowly entering the nervous system through the likes of Led Zeppelin and Rainbow in the mid-'70s.

June 20, 1966. The Beatles' *Yesterday and Today* is issued with the butchered babies cover. The artwork is quickly withdrawn, but one day there would be a fine metal band out of San Francisco called Yesterday and Today, plus another band called Cannibal Corpse that could relate all too well with the Beatles' woes around artwork.

June 21, 1966. Jimmy Page makes his live debut with The Yardbirds, playing London's Marquee Club.

July 22, 1966. Decca issues John Mayall's second album *Blues Breakers with Eric Clapton*. Kansas' Rich Williams says that although seeing the Beatles on *Ed Sullivan* lit the fire, this was the record that first featured guitar front and centre, and thus became the main inspiration for him to take up the instrument. The album is considered one of the most important of the British blues boom. Heavy metal was invented by kids raised on the British blues boom. My assertion is that heavy metal became invented when these kids eventually turned their backs on the boom.

John Mayall on the British blues boom:
It was very exciting. It was all happening in such a small country that everybody knew everybody, and we were all working the same circuits. It was probably much more personal, because it was so close-knit, like a musical society. The studio never accounted for very much time at all. The road is really where you did all your work. Heavy metal obviously evolved from the blues. I mean, all the major ones, Deep Purple and everyone else, they all started out with the blues thing. Jimmy Page was a blues guy; they all were. So it obviously was a very integral part in getting it all started. But I was never much into heavy metal. I still love the blues. It doesn't lack anything. It's the root music for all other rock music and several other genres. It's something that's very real, and something I've always been drawn to. I can't really give a better explanation other than it feels like the natural thing for me to do.

Iron Butterfly guitarist Mike Pinera on the British blues boom:
When I first heard that first wave of underground blues coming from England it reminded me of the '30s and '40s Delta blues, Mississippi area. And some of those songs were like flat-out copies. I mean, I know that some of the bands got in trouble for not giving credits to some of the original blues pioneers where they caught the riffs from. But other than that, there were nice people like Eric Burdon, who would say, "Hey, this is a Muddy Waters song" or, "This is a John Lee Hooker song." And all they would do is they'd crank their Marshall amps to ten. But I'd have chills go up my spine. And I got to play with John Lee Hooker back then too, and that was like playing with a hero, him being a blues pioneer. But I loved what the British did to it, especially the front-runners, who were the Yardbirds and John Mayall and the Blues Breakers with Eric Clapton.

Original Judas Priest vocalist Al Atkins on impatience with the British blues boom:
In my opinion, yes there was. I mean we all went through it. We needed something new, gotta go somewhere else. Cream and Jimi Hendrix, they set the standard, I think, becoming loud, more inventive, great musicians as well. Ginger Baker... best band I've seen in my life, Cream. Unbelievable. Still now, I've never seen another band that sent shivers down my back when I seen them play in the early days. Oh my god. And something comes on the radio now, Cream, I'll crank it up. But yeah, I just see that's the way we were going to do that. All of a sudden, music seemed to change, with Led Zeppelin, Deep Purple and Sabbath. Whoa, what's happening? We need to do this—we need to get on board.

Budgie drummer Ray Phillips:
Yeah, that's a good analogy because everything changes. Every musician that I've worked with over the years have all said, "I wish I was part of the '70s. That was the best music." So you're right, Led Zeppelin, Jeff Beck, Fleetwood Mac, all the people that had gone through the John Mayall club, they carried on their impression of the blues in their own way. Budgie used to do blues stuff as well. We took our little piece of the blues and took that to another place. But definitely without blues, I think it's fair to say that a lot of the Led Zeppelin or Budgie stuff wouldn't have felt the way it felt. It was an integral part of what we were about.

AC/DC guitarist Malcolm Young on the pervasiveness of the blues influence even in Australia:
The kids were just like that. The pub scene. Some of these pubs hold 1500, 2000 and they wanna rock out there. And the boogies, they could understand those straight enough. And we could boogie for half an hour, give 'em a boogie. It was like, "Give us a boogie! Give us a boogie!" So everyone played a boogie. But we would take it... you know, we used to like Canned Heat from way back, and we would just jam on stuff, around their ideas at the time, and we'd put a bit of boogie into our own material. But we were always into the blues and the rock 'n' roll stuff. We grew up on it. We had older brothers who were into Chuck Berry

and Little Richard and Jerry Lee Lewis, we grew up as kids hearing that. You know, it's in us. And we just tried to emulate that, these guys, with their feels, and get it really rockin' and then keep it going.

Thin Lizzy guitarist Gary Moore:
From the age of sort of 12, 13, I was just so into blues. I first heard the British blues stuff and then Eric Clapton, John Mayall, and then Peter Green, Albert King and Mick Taylor came along. It was just a great time to be growing up with all these great guitar players coming out of the woodwork one after another. And you had Jeff Beck obviously and then Jimi arrived on the scene and he still had huge blues influence. Obviously he wasn't making blues records per se—well, apart from tracks like "Red House"—but it was inherent in his playing. But I was totally swamped with blues.

You must remember, the guitar at that point was more in the background; it didn't have a really powerful voice until Clapton made the *Blues Breakers* album, from my standpoint anyway, for my generation. It didn't have a strong voice. That's when the guitar first really jumped out and spoke to people. Once I heard "All Your Love" on the *Blues Breakers* album, I'll never forget that moment. It's one of those things; when you're a kid, you'll never forget it. It was a pivotal moment for me; it was like, there was no going back. I saw how the guitar playing, in A minor, just playing simply but with a lot of passion, could be so devastating, so passionate, so amazing really.

And then I saw Peter Green play and that was another moment for me, when he walked into a club in Belfast. And I had never heard anyone play a Les Paul live before. And I remember the walls kind of resonating and the floors shaking. That's how I remember it. And he was just using a rented amplifier. It was an incredible moment for me. Same song actually, funnily enough: "All Your Love." He was playing Eric's lines. A hard act to follow, obviously. Only 20 years old; it was amazing, just walked onstage and fucking blew everyone away with his tone and everything. And when I heard all that, it was just so pure and so full of emotion and passionate, I really didn't want to play anything else. And it was some time before I started playing other music, actually, another three years after that.

August 5, 1966. The Beatles issue *Revolver*, which includes "Eleanor Rigby." Rather than give his heavy metal song to a garage band like The Beatles to wreck, Paul McCartney tricks a double string quartet into doing it. He patiently waits more than two years before handing his next heavy metal song to his own guys to work up.

September 24, 1966. Manager Chas Chandler and his new charge Jimi Hendrix arrive in London, Jimi with no more than the clothes on his back and a present for Great Britain in the form of heavy metal.

Late 1966. Punky garage rock heroes The Sonics issue their third and final album, *Introducing the Sonics*, which finds the band straying from their beloved core sound, or at least transforming their sound through sweeter production.

October 1966. Jeff Beck leaves The Yardbirds.

Motörhead guitarist Fast Eddie Clarke:
I always think of myself as a third generation blues player. Whereas people like Stones and the Yardbirds, I think are second generation, because they copied the old masters, as it were. I copied the Stones and the Yardbirds. Heavy metal came later, but I'd give Yardbirds some credit. The album *Five Live Yardbirds* was quite rocky with some quite heavy shit going, like build-ups and stuff like that and it had volume and they were thrashing out a bit. I was brought up on that, and that was kind of the start, I think, of heavy metal, really. But the music evolved; it got louder and the riffs got heavier and there was a natural progression. And then, you know, Hendrix was around '65 or '66, and he's the heaviest guitarist ever born. You had Cream, and then Deep Purple took it to another level, but they had keyboards. Ian Gillan was a bit of a screamer, which was not really the way I wanted to go. Robert Plant was probably my favourite vocalist at the time. Also early on was Humble Pie's *Rockin' the Fillmore*, which I think is a watershed and one of the greatest albums of all time.

Montrose guitarist Ronnie Montrose:
The only references I had were that I loved Jeff Beck, loved Eric Clapton, loved Hendrix, loved Deep Purple. Those were what I grew up on. Nothing else as a reference, because basically I was just so involved at that time in exploring my instrument with my limited experience. I was just trying to discover what it was I was doing. But I would say seeing the original Yardbirds with Jeff Beck and Jimmy Page at the old Fillmore was a pretty powerful influence on me. Seeing Cream at Winterland was very powerful for me. Hendrix obviously was without peer. But I much more liked the Yardbirds with Beck and Page than I did the live Zeppelin things. These guys, I idolized them and considered them icons. I always considered myself at best a second generation guitarists to the big boys, people like Jimmy Page, Ritchie Blackmore, Pete Townsend, Jeff Beck, and in America, Billy Gibbons of ZZ Top, that school, that one little wave before I started.

October 5, 1966. The Jimi Hendrix Experience is born when Jimi, Noel Redding and Mitch Mitchell pay together for the first time. This is five days after Jimi appears live for the first time in the UK, jumping on stage with Cream at the London Polytechnic.

October 7, 1966. Grand opening of the legendary Grande Ballroom in Detroit, featuring MC5 and The Wha?. MC5 would continue on through the coming months, becoming regulars.

MC5 drummer Dennis Thompson on the opening of the Grande:
Oh it raised the bar; it certainly did, but we also raised the bar for those bands. I mean The Who... the first place they performed *Tommy* was at the Grande. And the Detroit audience at the Grande was one of the toughest audiences that there were in the United States because they were exposed to all this great music—it was like kick out the jams or get off the stage. So it raised the bar for those bands; when they came, they knew they had to put on one of their better shows and it raised the bar for all the bands in Detroit because you know, let's face it—it's a competition thing going on. There was competition amongst those bands back in those days; there was a healthy competition. Going on like who's the best? You know, who's the fastest gun in the west?

Basically it's the nature of Detroit. It's a factory-based town; after World War II there was plenty of work for everybody here, and what we do here... what we did was we built cars. I don't know if you've ever been into a large factory, but it's loud, very loud and very blue collar, and that translated into drag strips and fast cars. The people of Detroit, the types of jobs that they had, the society—that's the kind of society that was built upon. Basically built upon a factory-type of town and you work hard in these factories. You work, you know, 50 hours a weeks and you work your butt off and so they work hard and they play hard. That's it. Hit us hard and hit us fast and give us our bit of happiness so we can go back and do it again.

Late 1966. The Music Machine issues their debut album, *(Turn On) the Music Machine*. The Music Machine is an L.A.-based garage rock band cited by some hard rock artists as a favourite from their formative years, especially through Top 20 hit "Talk Talk," which is one of 12 originals on the album and a hoary, fuzzy song of garage rock madness. A second album as The Boniwell Music Machine came out in 1967. The Boniwell Music Machine also issued as a single in '68 an a-side called "You'll Love Me Again," which is a spooky proto-fuzz psychedelic garage rocker about a stalker.

November 1966. The 13th Floor Elevators (includes Roky Erikson) issue *The Psychedelic Sounds of the 13th Floor Elevators*, which includes "You're Gonna Miss Me," later covered by DMZ.

December 1966 – April 1967. Ritchie Blackmore plays with Lord Caesar Sutch & The Roman Empire, including a date supporting Cream.

December 9, 1966. UK release date of Cream's debut *Fresh Cream*, which is more of a purist blues album than later, louder affairs. Instrumental "Toad" includes pioneering double bass drumming in a rock context from Ginger Baker as well as an early instance on a rock album of a drum solo, very much a heavy metal trope.

UFO drummer Andy Parker:
Ginger Baker is one of my all-time influences drum-wise. Paul Raymond remembers him with Graham Bond early on. He was one of the first guys I saw using two kicks, which opened a new door for me. I thought, man I gotta try this! 'Cause that was before they'd been to the double pedal for one bass drum—it's a lot easier than carrying another bass drum around, which I've always loved the look of anyway; I just loved the symmetry with the two kicks and I still use them today. But yeah, Ginger used them a lot, as did Jon Hiseman with Colosseum and Tempest; he was another guy with two bass drums. There were several guys, including Eric Delaney who was a well-known British drummer. But Ginger was heavy; I mean he was fat and heavy, especially on the solo on Blind Faith's album;

"Do What You Like"—that's got some great stuff in there with the two kicks. For me, it's cool for when you've got bass and drums to keep things going when somebody's soloing. I can be filling the bottom in a little more—the extra kick in there gives it a bit more oomph.

Cream roadie Neville Chesters on the British blues boom:
Was there a blues boom? It became popular but I'm not sure it was a boom. I mean, Cream was probably about as near as you get to it, and even they weren't considered that much. I don't think people really knew what the blues were until later on. It didn't sink in probably until the late '60s, and then not until a lot of musicians like Eric managed to get well-known enough to say, hey, there was the blues, you know? It came from America and people like Robert Johnson. And people were like, really? So even today, a lot of musicians don't know the real basis of the blues. John Mayall was obviously an early progressive of blues. I mean, there were blues bands, but it was just never a phenomenon like rock was. I don't think anybody knew who wrote "Crossroads," for instance. I think they probably all thought Eric wrote it, for years and years and years—nobody ever bothered to look stuff like that up.

December 16, 1966. Jimi Hendrix's version of "Hey Joe" is issued in the UK as The Jimi Hendrix Experience's first single, rising to #6 on the charts in January of 1967. Not a factor in the invention of heavy metal, the song nonetheless becomes one of Deep Purple's earliest jams, the band subsequently recording it for their debut album. More significant is the b-side to the single, "Stone Free" which features a fairly driving and heavy pre-chorus and chorus, plus a 4/4 beat clanged with cowbell. As well, Jimi's guitar solo is very heavy metal for 1966. Of note, Jimi's full name was James Marshall Hendrix. Jimi and Jim Marshall, probably the most important single figure from a gear point of view to the story of heavy metal, became friends early, sharing a laugh about the similarity in name.

December 26, 1966. Jimi Hendrix writes the lyrics to "Purple Haze" in the dressing room of The Uppercut Club in London, where the band had an afternoon show booked.

Recap

Garage rock continues to skulk in the shadows as rock's red-headed stepchild, led in heaviness by The Sonics, The Seeds and The 13th Floor Elevators. The Yardbirds step it up a notch with "Shapes of Things," again, not particularly guitar, but dark and well-written, strafed by wind-ups, licks and a howling mad solo section.

Also a highlight of the year is the continued nascent rock instruction of John Mayall through his second record *Blues Breakers with Eric Clapton*, with Eric soon to become part of a supergroup with similar aims, namely Cream, who issue *Fresh Cream* this year.

Do you sense a theme here? 1966 is the year of more Yardbirds, plus records from Blues Breakers and Cream. It's all happening in Britain and it's all deeply reverent of the blues, causing a boom to follow, which, like metal, was very much about the six-stringer as the draw, the sharp pencil in the drawer, the "hero" of the band.

Chapter Two

Lead: 1967 - 1969

Lots happens as we head into the combative and explosive late '60s. I'll leave the specifics to the end of year recaps, but suffice to say that in 1968 and 1969, the debate begins for real—that is, if you accept my premise that heavy metal gets invented not by a piece of technology, a song, live performance, a scream, a trace of mania or craziness, a shocking album cover or stage prop, but by sustained heavy metal over the course of most of a full-length album.

Forsooth, this is the framework we are hanging our Arthur Brown flame hat on: that we will drape the royal cloak upon the "who" that made the long-playing LP that is the first heavy metal album.

This is not the place to say that that happens for real in this chapter—"for real;" hah, there is no correct answer, just some near unanimous approximations of one—but indeed, within the timeframe of this chapter, full-length records are released that many scholars of this stuff thumbprint as the first heavy metal album. In other words, given our criterion, indeed lots and lots of smart people believe that heavy metal is invented by either a certain band in 1968, or one of to bands in 1969.

1967

1967. Stray is formed, in London, with the band later to achieve heavy metal credentials roughly on par with Atomic Rooster, but not quite as heavy as Budgie.

1967. Georgia's Bitter Creek issue their lone 7" single, which includes "Plastic Thunder," a roiling pile of noise rock that predates Blue Cheer but stomps that same terrain. Not much of a riff, but an impressive wall of sound for 1967.

1967. Dick Wagner and The Frost issue their first single, "Sunshine" which is fairly electric and driving psych, mentioned here because it arrives two years before the band's first album.

1967. Blue Cheer becomes not just a trio, but a power trio. The etymology of the band's name derives in part from the catchphrase, "Stay clean," and also a name for a type of acid.

Blue Cheer bassist and vocalist Dickie Peterson on additional connotations for the name Blue Cheer:
Another part of it is that we were all into the blues, but we weren't into being sad. And actually, in the blues medium, they have a name for this, and it's called jump blues. And the album title, *Vincebus Eruptum*… that came out of a friend of ours by the name of Richard Peddicord ("architect, artist, musician, freak, eccentric, acidhead," according to Paul), who showed up one day at the commune with a

big piece of butcher paper on it and put it on the kitchen wall. And we all looked at it, for quite awhile, didn't say anything, and finally said, "Richard, what is this?" And he said, "This is the name of your new album. This is what you should call it. *Vincebus Eruptum* means 'We control chaos.'" And we said yeah, that's cool, that's great.

1967. Blue Öyster Cult forms, on Long Island, NY, but under a different name and as a flower power psych band.

1967. Long Island garage rockers The Vagrants issue a cover of Otis Redding's "Respect," which quickly becomes overshadowed by Aretha Franklin's version. The Vagrants featured Leslie West and were considered a bit of a rough-looking, quite electric band. They were an influence to other New York-area rockers just starting to find their way, including people like Carmine Appice. In other words, they are proto- proto-hard rock, the way Mitch Ryder and the Detroit Wheels were in the Detroit area.

> Vanilla Fudge guitarist Vinny Martell:
> The Vagrants were like the #1 band in the New York area at the time. They were doing big arrangements and they were doing production numbers. The Vagrants were very instrumental to us because they had lights, which we didn't have anything. Originally we didn't even have a PA system. We didn't even have speakers. We had two horns. So that is a rough PA to sing through and that probably contributed to us perfecting the harmonies and the singing. It was tough to get a good sound out of that. You had no help. No reverb, no speakers, just horns. Anyway. So we played at the Choo-Choo Club and the Vagrants came in and they had lighting, and Peter, the front man, was a great front man. He looked like an Indian doing a dance up there with the tambourine twirl. He was great at twirling the tambourine, and moving. The thing that the Vagrants had that was tremendous was their moves. Peter moved wonderfully onstage to the music and so did Leslie West's brother, Larry, bass player; he looked like he was always in another world playing bass. Leslie—great guitar player with a big voice and a big presence up onstage. And in the back they had Roger on the drums who had hair down to his knees, and every time he would do a slam or something on the drums his head would go forward and all the hair would go flying. It was a show to watch these guys.

> Blue Öyster Cult drummer Al Bouchard:
> The Vagrants, oh my god. They were really heavy. You know, there were all these Long Island bands, like The Vagrants, Vanilla Fudge, The Illusion. The Vagrants would play like sort of slow and deliberate. Just like Vanilla Fudge, you know? And it was kind of fancy and loud, but there was a finesse there. I would say there was a finesse the Long Island bands had that Blue Cheer didn't really have.

1967. Tony Iommi is in a band called The Rest. Bill Ward is eventually in this band as well. Meanwhile, Ozzy posts an ad in a local music newspaper stating, "Ozzy Zig seeks a gig." Subsequently, Geezer forms his first band, Rare Breed, with Ozzy. The band breaks up after two shows. Across the ocean, Ronnie James Dio forms The Electric Elves, after a series of singles and bands reaching back to 1957, but none too heavy. Curiously, Ronnie James Dio is of no hefty significance to the evolution of heavy metal until his second album with Rainbow, *Rising*, way up into 1976—*Rising*'s importance is that it is arguably the first album in history with no non-metal songs.

January 4, 1967. The Doors issue their debut, a self-titled. Jim Morrison is the ultimate crazy, wasted front man in black leather pants as well as a really growling shouter. This album includes "Break on Through," "Light My Fire" and "The End," but other than The Lizard King himself, there is nothing heavy metal about the band, save for, perhaps, the influence of darkness, which all emanates from Morrison, the man.

January 11, 1967. Jimi Hendrix signs to The Who's Track Records, and records most of "Purple Haze," a significant moment where, on one level, heavy metal could be said to have been invented, at least at the song level. Invented here or not, "Purple Haze" is a first-level milestone in the story.

Black Sabbath drummer Bill Ward:
In Hendrix, Mitch Mitchell was playing jazz as well as hard rock. He played everything, but wherever Jimi went, Mitch went. And Noel Redding, he played that kind of free bass thing, which we hear so often in hardcore music. But of course, I know that Entwistle was, to me, the ultimate bass player, and the only exception for me would've been Jack Bruce—these were great bass players. And so when Geezer showed up, he started playing rhythm guitar (laughs), but then he changed to bass. And when he played bass, he was just like all over the place. He was just everywhere, and when we listen to Sabs, everybody is playing whatever they want to play, really (laughs). Everybody is playing a lead instrument.

Living Colour bassist Doug Wimbish:
I think what Jimi did, even before his hard rock, Jimi had to endure the reality of coming from Seattle, working his way through the R&B scenario. Which he didn't naturally, necessarily 100% embrace. Because he was kind of an odd guy, being in James Brown's band or in Little Richard's band. The blessing was that Jimi was able to work and meet up with Ronnie Isley. And it was the Isley Brothers that helped introduce him to the community, to R&B, to Harlem, and to his people. And he had some folks that believed in him. I think the Isley Brothers were one of the key components that helped translate Jimi's energy, before, during and after.

And I'll explain it to you like this. As Jimi started to become more popular in the white community, or in Europe, he was always trying to get back to his roots. So before he went to Europe, he was living at the Hotel Theresa in Harlem, pawning his guitar to try to survive. So he lived in Harlem, but he worked out of the village. So here you've got a person that is like, I've got to live playing R&B, but my heart and soul isn't necessarily all there. He was downtown in Greenwich Village, with Bob Dylan and other singer/songwriters and stuff, trying to hang on, trying to get a gig, trying to get a frequency going on, and he had to do that all in a very short period of time.

So what Jimi did was... Jimi was a badge of honour. Jimi was the one who was able to break out from the white community, and it wasn't until after his death, really, that the black community embraced him. Prior to that, I know, because I was one of those kids listening to Jimi Hendrix. They used to call me a white boy because I was listening to Jimi Hendrix. They didn't understand what was going on. I should've been listening to Sly, James Brown, Stax, Motown. I grew up in Connecticut which is kind of liberal. That's just the mentality of how the community was.

Now on the other side of the spectrum, Jimi was luckily able to go to England, UK, which is a country that has... let's just say it has its own thing when it comes to recording and doing certain things. There are less distractions. There are more recording studios and mixing studios in the UK than any place on earth. You only have three TVs channels. You don't have all these distractions. Pubs close at 11 o'clock. So people get together, socialize, write music, and he though, okay, let's get away from this.

So Jimi is your first—in sense and sensibility—your first international artist, that was able to completely break barriers down and do something. And let's recognize the reality of it: in a short period of time. I talked to Buddy Miles, and he says, you've got remember, in only three or four summers he did thing, '66 to '70. In that short period of time he did his music.

Alice Cooper producer Bob Ezrin, on the UK versus the US:
The reason why there were all these great British bands, and why they were always so tight and proficient, was because they were ten years behind the United States in diversions. In the development of diversions. They still only had three channels on television, there weren't that many cinemas around, and there was not that much disposable income. People had to work harder, and so it sort of forced people into pursuing some interest, and it didn't distract them. They weren't as distracted. America was full of distractions. By the '70s we were distracted beyond belief, and we were into a million things instead of just concentrating and doing one thing.

January 27, 1967. Jimi Hendrix plays the Bag O' Nails in London. Pete Townsend and Eric Clapton are in attendance, as is electronics specialist Roger Mayer, who meets Jimi for the first time and starts talking gear with him. Jimi decides to re-record the guitar solo using Mayer's new gizmo.

Who, Cream and Jimi Hendrix roadie Neville Chesters:
I do remember that when I started with Jimi Hendrix, this guy somehow came along called Roger Mayer, and he'd been with the BBC doing electronics, and he built this thing called an Octavia. That was a distortion box within itself, which Roger built, and he went on to build quite a few things for Jimi.

February 1967. Jefferson Airplane's second album, *Surrealistic Pillow* is issued, with Grace Slick (along with Janis Joplin), being a sometimes cited influence on hard rock singers, through songs such as "White Rabbit" and "Somebody to Love," both, additionally, dark hit songs melodically speaking.

February 3, 1967. "Purple Haze" is completed, with new guitar solo, prompted by Jimi's meeting with Roger Mayer.

March 1967. *Rosemary's Baby*, a book by Ira Levin, is published. It is inspired by the founding of the Church of Satan a year earlier. Both it and the movie are big hits. Satan lays the groundwork for his entry into the rock 'n' roll game.

March 12, 1967. The Velvet Underground issue their debut album, *The Velvet Underground & Nico*, which offers new levels of attitude and darkness.

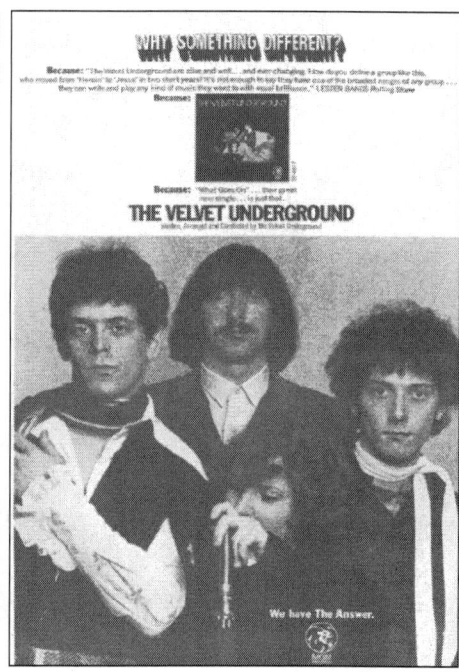

Mudhoney vocalist Mark Arm:
I'm more into stuff that is happening before it becomes a defined thing. The Stooges were out there on their own, MC5 were out there. It's funny how they get lumped in together. I guess it's because they knew each other and played together, but their approaches are very different. But they were both making up the rules as they went along, and the same goes for Black Sabbath and the same goes for Velvet Underground. In a sense you can say the Velvet Underground and Black Sabbath are basically the same idea. It's like the death of hippie. But it's sounding totally different in each case. But it's no longer this positive flower power kind of thing, where it was, "Let's kick ass and change the world." It was, "Let's kick ass and blow our minds," especially in the case of Velvet Underground.

March 17, 1967. The Jimi Hendrix Experience's "Purple Haze" is issued as a UK single; recorded January 11 and February 3, at De Lane Lea and Olympic Studios in London, UK. At a considerably raised threshold from earlier arguments plumping for "The Train Kept A-Rollin'" as the first heavy metal song (frankly, going that far back represents a stretch!), much argument can be made for this track deserving that trophy. A marked difference and advancement has occurred from the fuzzy garage rock that has come before, and indeed, many of the tropes of histrionic heavy metal guitar are on display right here.

So at a higher threshold, which we must necessarily rise to as we advance through the years, "Purple Haze" can be posited as one version of ground zero for the invention of heavy metal—at least within the language of single song. Ironically, one could say that the song competes with only one of two earlier Experience tracks. One is "Stone Free," issued three months earlier—lighter yet still quite rocky, but again, earlier. Additionally, b-side to "Purple Haze," "51st Anniversary," is in possession of a hard rock-written structure, but the lack of bite to the guitar and the meekness of the recording lessens its impact to the overall story.

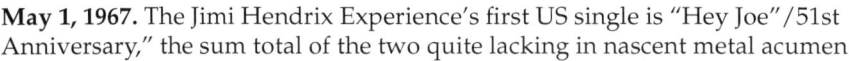

March 31, 1967. Jimi Hendrix sets fire to his guitar for the first time, at The Astoria in London.

Living Colour bassist Doug Wimbish on Jimi as entertainer:
Jimi had been around showmen. You had to be a performer. Jimi was around people who would do splits off the balcony, and so he learned the art of being a showman. And in the process of doing that, you find out you're in these bands, you had your R&B bands, you have a rhythm guitar player and a lead guitar player, you know what I mean? So I think the idea of his role as the lead guitarist started off when he was doing stuff with Billy Cox in the Army, and then when he moved on and came to New York.

May 1, 1967. The Jimi Hendrix Experience's first US single is "Hey Joe"/51st Anniversary," the sum total of the two quite lacking in nascent metal acumen.

May 5, 1967. Jimi Hendrix's "The Wind Cries Mary"/"Highway Chile" is issued as a UK single. "Highway Chile" is a bit of a roustabout boogie rock number, but it does include, come chorus time, a high-up-the-fretboard proto-metal lick.

May 12, 1967. Jimi Hendrix Experience's debut *Are You Experienced* is released in the UK. The UK version of the album contains heavy tracks "Foxy Lady," "Manic Depression," "Fire" and most notably pounding rocker "I Don't Live Today," which contains true metal riffery, feedback and manic drumming from Mitch Mitchell. Jimi is among the first to experiment with the new fuzz pedals, most notably on his heaviest track to date, "Purple Haze" which is left off the UK version of the debut.

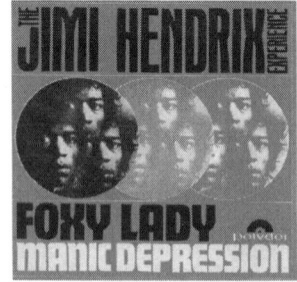

Jimi Hendrix roadie Neville Chesters:

It's really difficult to describe Jimi. I don't think many people really knew him, even though we were a five-piece unit on the road. Everything was so cheap that I used to bunk with Noel and Jerry used to bunk with Mitch, and Jimi always had his own room. But it's difficult. It was kind of magical, the way he touched the guitar and it made noises and you thought how the hell did that just happen? It was unique and it really is still today. I mean there are many, many people who compare to Jimi or try to be compared to Jimi, like Stevie Ray Vaughan.

Of course he was never called heavy metal. He was loud and he could be very loud, but there's a difference, really. I've seen some of the best musicians in the world comment on Jimi and you begin to see where he fits in. When he played with Little Richard, he would get pissed-off with Jimi very early on, like upstaging him, and that was just Jimi. And then so the early comments of Little Richard are, "Jimi, well he was too loud, he was too this, he wasn't playing what I wanted." And then he gets nicer and nicer until he's saying, "Well Jimi was unique; he really was." But Jimi would sit in his room... I think the term sleeping with the guitar is not just given to Jimi, it's quite a few musicians. But he did. He had a guitar with him the whole time and he would sit and do things, but they never really rehearsed and Jimi never did what you would call practice.

Ted Nugent:

Jimi, obviously, was an explosion of unprecedented creativity, was the next outrageous, defiance of the electric guitar via Les Paul. The bending of the strings and the noises and the feedback, the experiment with sound, distortion pedals... he was what I would call the front man for Lewis and Clark. He was days ahead of the expedition (laughs). He was the first guy to see an antelope. He's the first guy to see this black and white, prong-horned antelope, and was taking notes on the newly discovered species.

And in the world of Jimi Hendrix, the newly discovered species was dissonant overtone, sonic bombast and feedback. Even though I was doing it before Hendrix, Hendrix was doing it in a more outrageous way. Plus the song craftsmanship of "Foxy Lady," "Fire," "Purple Haze"... are you kidding me?! "The Wind Cries Mary"... are you kidding me?! His version of "Hey Joe"... are you kidding me?! So here's a black guy, who had a black upbringing, but was exposed to the white reinterpretation with minimal alterations. Here was an authentic black guy that had that genetic defiance. He did to the guitar what James Brown did to rhythm and blues, and what Little Richard did to, you know, to honky-tonk. I mean, come on. Thank God in heaven for those guys.

Stooges guitarist James Williamson:
Jimi was enormous and has to be noted. You know, I'm not even sure what heavy metal means but Jimi certainly raised the bar on what a guitar player could be and what it means. If you're gonna call somebody the best guitar player, I think it's him. All these guys like Eric Clapton and so forth... he was a fine guitar player, but they completely got smoked when Jimi Hendrix came around. Jimi was a really, really talented guy that had his own thing.

June 1, 1967. The Beatles' *Sgt. Pepper's Lonely Hearts Club Band* is released. Widely considered the first psych rock album, the front cover also features the first pop culture reference to Aleister Crowley—he's one of the head shots on the cover.

June 18, 1967. Jimi Hendrix sets fire to his guitar at the Monterey Pop Festival. The Monterey Pop Festival is considered the first widely promoted and attended rock festival and is also considered to mark the first major US performances by Hendrix, The Who and Janis Joplin. Arguably, many of the current generation of guitar gods, especially the icons of the British blues boom, quietly fold their tent upon the arrival of Hendrix, or at least become viewed as second rate and even obsolete (both Clapton and Townshend come to mind). Again arguably, it is Ritchie Blackmore that embraces the Hendrix phenomenon as a challenge, eventually becoming, perhaps paired with Jimmy Page, the first guitar god of the '70s, with Jimi Hendrix viewed as the second of the '60s, after Eric Clapton.

June 19, 1967. "Purple Haze"/"The Wind Cries Mary" is issued as a single in the US, and America gets a direct taste of what is arguably the first heavy metal song. The solo on "Purple Haze" benefits from, again, Jimi meeting Roger Mayer and utilizing his Octavia device, an early type of harmonizer that adds notes or harmonics an octave above on top of what's played. Amusingly, "The Wind Cries Mary" was suggested by Jimi's manager Chas Chandler, as a follow-up single because he thought another "Purple Haze" might freak people out too much. The softer track contains its own innovations though, with Jimi offering early use of wah wah.

Living Colour bassist Doug Wimbish on the origins of Jimi's heavy guitar style:
Well, all that came from Howlin' Wolf and all these blues artists that he was hearing out of Chicago. And out of the Delta. I mean, a lot of that stuff had been turned up loud already. It's just that it hadn't been recorded or even heard.

June 29, 1967. Actress Jayne Mansfield is killed in a car crash. Rumours that she was decapitated are untrue. Mansfield was an enthusiastic member of the Church of Satan and was escalated to High Priestess. She had apparently memorized most of the *Satanic Bible*. Her death was said to be the result of some sort of curse by Anton LaVey.

July 10, 1967. The Yardbirds issue *Little Games*, their last album, and Jimmy Page's last, before he jumps ship to Led Zeppelin. "Think About It" is a harder highlight, with a riff foreign to the blues, a key light bulb concept to the blueprinting of a harder rock worthy of a new name.

> Yardbirds drummer Jim McCarty on the band's contribution to the evolution of hard rock:
> I suppose definitely more the *Little Games* element, album-wise. But songs, yeah, "Think About It," "Tinker Tailor, Soldier, Sailor," "Dazed and Confused" obviously. It all came from heavy blues riffs. Like "I Wish You Would" for instance, quite a heavy blues riff. "Smokestack Lightning," which Jimmy actually sort of simplified. He used to do so many of these blues riffs very cleverly in his own way, simplifying some of them and making some of them more complex.
> But I think it was all about the riffs because we really grew up playing blues riffs. We were influenced by a lot of blues. Cyril Davis used to play with Alexis

Korner. Cyril Davis was the harmonica player. And he originally had this band that he'd been with, Screaming Lord Sutch, and they were a rock band and they were great. Every once in a while we would go see them and it was real rock 'n' roll, blues, you know? And I think that's a lot to do with where Paul Samwell-Smith got a lot of his bass ideas. They had a guy named Ricky Brown and there was a very good drummer called Carlo Little who had actually giving Keith Moon lessons. And Long John Baldry used to play around as well; he had really good bands.

Led Zeppelin expert Dave Lewis, on Yardbirds, Zeppelin and the birth of metal:

You've got to go back to the mid-'60s where the arrival of Hendrix, the early evolution of the Yardbirds, and that was where amplified rock began to take on a sound. Obviously the Who in there as well, and possibly the Kinks. So all that power chording material coming out, and with the Yardbirds when you had Clapton, and then Beck and Page, it was beginning to take it to a new level, and then the arrival of Hendrix in England in '67, you had Cream doing their stuff, and very much taking an extended format, which was way beyond the UK singles chart. If you went to see Cream there would be 25-minute tracks, which at the time was pretty unheard of.

So in England that was building, that explosion, which coupled with the blues boom going on with people like Fleetwood Mac and Ten Years After, that all began to flower, and then obviously when Jimmy came up with his concept of light and shade and loud and soft in a very encompassed way, that really was the beginning of it. And when you see the evolution of the Yardbirds into Zeppelin, I think they really begin to explore what could be done with power chords, with extended material, with improvisation, using the blues as maybe a backdrop, but then taking it much, much further—no one band took it much further than Led Zeppelin.

Deep Purple guitarist Steve Morse, making a connection between heavy metal and improvisation:
When we're talking about the heavy metal thing, Cream had a great contribution in rock 'n' roll in improvising and jamming, while they were playing concerts. And of course Hendrix did too, as did all the English bands—Deep Purple did a lot of improvisation on stage. I also saw Led Zeppelin live a number of times in the early '70s and late '60s, and they also did a bit of stretching out, definitely some long arrangements and things. And "Moby Dick," the one with the drum solo, that was one of the heaviest guitar riffs there ever was, around that time, I thought.

Also one of the cool things back then, I was at the Atlanta Pop Festival where there was Janis Joplin, this new group Led Zeppelin (laughs), Dave Brubeck Jazz Trio, Goose Creek Symphony and Ravi Shankar. It was okay to have variety. Nobody wanted to sound exactly like everybody else.

July 23, 1967. The roughly five-day-long Detroit race riots claim 43 lives along with the burning of 2000 buildings. The result was "white flight" from the city core and the inexorable decline of Detroit to where it is today.

Creem magazine journalist Jaan Uhelski:
The famous thing about Detroit is like the Wayne Kramer quote about how peace and love never made it to Detroit. So Detroit was always dark. Seriously, what flower power bands came out of there? I mean, it was The Stooges, it was the MC5; even the frivolous ones like SRC or The Frost really weren't light. So, I don't know if that would even pertain to us if we were going to keep that localized to Detroit. My personal theory is that we were used to that kind of clang, that industrial buzz and hum. It pretty much mimicked the car industry for us. I don't know if you've ever been there but it's not a really cheerful place. It isn't now and never was. It's kind of like you're pissed-off when you live in Detroit. Anything that will somehow blot out the lack of horizons and opportunities, you will take. I know for myself, I would put on that type of music and get in the car and drive faster. It's really escapist music in a way that it pushes every other thought, every other feeling, out of your psyche. I really think that that sums up who Detroit artists are. God, I mean we had Mitch Ryder but he seemed like an anomaly. He seemed like a male Arethra. Everything else just is this kind of soporific—not even soporific because that's too joyful—just this blot out the pain, knock your head against the windshield kind of music.

August 1967. The US and Canada issue *Are You Experienced* with different cover and different track listing. Significantly, the trio's heaviest track, the pioneering "Purple Haze" is added.

August 1967. New York's Vanilla Fudge issue their debut, on Atco in the US and Polydor in the UK. It's a virtual blueprint for what Deep Purple Mk. 1 would become. Over-rated—or at minimum over-stated—with respect to heavy rock influence, the Fudge were nonetheless influential with respect to grinding dramatization of rock standards as well as for power welling up from the keyboards. Ginger Baker and now Carmine Appice are the two drummers most associated with double bass drums, a staple of today's complex heavy metal music along many subgenre lines and really, not an instrumental dimension of too many other forms of music.

Vanilla Fudge guitarist Vinny Martell:
I come from kind of a classical background in so far as my sister took classical piano lessons. She's a little older than I am, so I grew up hearing classical music my whole life, and most of it had to have seeped in because my folks both play; they were both musicians also. My father played violin and guitar, and my

mother played guitar and mandolin, so I grew up around that. And the classical influences... you know, I'm Italian and all the relatives at Christmas time, everybody in the family played something, so this must have all influenced me. When I met up with the guys from The Pidgeons—because I had been playing music in Florida before that—Mark Stein looked like he was also into the classical aspect. So I don't know, we were able to get off on and develop into creative directions that made an impact.

Led Zeppelin expert Dave Lewis:
If you go back to the late '60s, the double drum kit was quite an accepted part of the setup, and Ginger Baker was a pioneer of that. So was Mitch Mitchell, Carmine Appice in Vanilla Fudge. John Bonham was in awe of Carmine, without a doubt. And I think when he got his first Ludwig sponsorship, which would have been February or March of '69, I think he wanted to have a double Ludwig. It was the maple kit he had at the time. There were days they played where there are pictures that exist in late '69 of him playing them.

But it was short-lived because it was so loud. Jimmy and Robert couldn't even hear themselves think. When he banged a regular kit it made a noise anyway. To bang two double basses, it was a bit too much. But in the end the good thing about it was he knew what he needed. Because if you look at the Bonham kit, it was one of the most simple kits you can have. He didn't need 16 tom-toms like Keith Moon did, half of which were probably for effect. John Bonham used the drums in an economic way that I don't think anyone else ever did. He really had what counted—the high hat, the ride cymbal, the tom-tom—it was all used to maximum. Nothing was spared. Again, with John Bonham, it's always worth saying that it wasn't so much what he played, it was what he didn't play. Because the spaces he left in between was the spaces Jimmy used to compose a lot of his greatest work.

Grand Funk drummer Don Brewer:
We played with Zeppelin, as The Pack, in this little club in Boston. Everybody was just raving about Led Zeppelin. I'd never heard of them before and the next thing you know, they're all over the radio and it was like, wow! They were a major influence on everybody for sure. The first time I saw John Bonham play this huge 26-inch bass drum, it was like, wow I gotta get a bigger bass drum than a 21; there were 20s too and it was like a cocktail kit. So I started playing the 24. Not only did it sound better but it looked cool.

Uriah Heep keyboardist Ken Hensley:
For me, there were two bands which I clearly recall as having influenced my attitude towards the presentation of the music, whether it was live or on record, and one was The Who and the other one was the Vanilla Fudge. Now, Vanilla Fudge I loved because they had such a great way of taking basically pop songs or R&B songs and turning them into balls-out rock 'n' roll songs. If you take "You Keep Me Hanging On," their version of that is absolutely magnificent! And so much so that we adapted it in The Gods as the opener for our live shows. Bear in mind with Timmy and Carmine, they had incredible vocal harmony, so here's this great rock sound with, albeit a little bit of a lame organ sound, but this great rock sound with incredible harmony and that moved me a lot. That deep vibrato harmony sound got its way into The Gods and subsequently Uriah Heep. And the funny anecdotal part of that is that we later went on to tour with Cactus, which had Timmy and Carmine in the band, and we used to laugh a lot, how basically their whole vocal style, their harmony style, how we stole it. But those

were the two bands that said to me, you know what? You don't have to wear a tie, you don't have to be nice, you can just play with balls.

August 5, 1967. Pink Floyd's debut album, *The Piper at the Gates of Dawn* is issued. A record of dark psychedelic rock, it includes a fairly heavy track in "Interstellar Overdrive." Billboard calls their music "virtually nerve-shattering in impact." If we are all agreed that heavy metal drew from the blues and garage rock, it's also quite plausible that psychedelic music deserves to be part of the story, at least the darker stuff. In essence, what will be shown is that a band as important to our titular question as Black Sabbath is, is in fact somewhat psychedelic in the beginning, even if acid rock is never mentioned as part of the band's sets of influences, and even if the second biggest band of 1970, Deep Purple, used to actually *be* a psych band through and through.

Fall 1967. Ozzy Osbourne and Geezer Butler are in their first band together, called Rare Breed.

October 13, 14, 15, 1967. Cream play the Grande Ballroom in Detroit, one of the most influential and galvanizing gigs on the Detroit bands that we will see have a huge hand in inventing metal, according to Grande owner Russ Gibb. The band gains a reputation for volume in the live environment, by-product of being early adopters of the most powerful new amplification equipment. Supporting on the gigs, variously, are The Rationals, The Apostles, The Thyme and the MC5.

> Cream bassist and vocalist Jack Bruce:
> We were loud by the standards of the day, but not loud by what followed, no. I mean now, people who use Wedges and so forth, they're using more power than we used. We used 100 watt amps but it seemed very loud at the time because people hadn't heard loud stuff before.
>
> CEO of Gibson, Henry Juszkiewicz:
> The amplifiers got big and they got loud. And the crowds got big. While there were always arena shows and so forth, really most of the sound came through public address speakers. Ten watts is not going to fill an arena, so these amps were mic'ed. When the mid-'60s hit, people brought this huge amount of equipment onstage and it started with big amplifiers and then it became walls of amplifiers, and now you still mic that, probably. But the sound went directly out to the audience, and directly out to the guitar player. Now you're engulfed in this sound and you can just feel it, and it's a more immersive way to play. It brought the audience and the guitar players together in a sense.
> At first it was just loud, and people were just trying to hear better, meaning they just couldn't hear it well because it wasn't loud enough. Then loud became part of the music. And it wasn't just about hearing what was being sung or what was being played, but loudness all of a sudden became part of the musical texture, right? So it penetrated you. You could feel the bass in your chest, so to speak, and it became part of the musical idiom. The early equipment wasn't that great, actually, so it took probably ten or 15 years for equipment to really become good. It was immediately loud, but there are all kinds of things that were added along the way to make it a much better experience.

October 14, 1967. The Who issue "I Can See for Miles" as the only single from *The Who Sell Out*. With journalists and Pete Townsend himself extolling the track's heaviness, Paul McCartney took up the challenge to respond with "Helter Skelter." The song indeed is chaotic and noisy, mostly thanks to Keith Moon. As well, the chord sequence is menacing and doomy.

October 31, 1967. The Stooges play their first gig, at their notorious band house.

Stooges drummer Scott Asheton on the band's original influences:
Actually we liked to listen to a lot of jazz—Earl Sanders, John Coltrane—and we played a much different style of heavy before that album. But we were asked to come up with some songs instead of just being a heavy, loud, jazz-influenced band. And so actually the whole band changed, just for the first album. That wasn't the band we were. Before then, it was jazzier, but to our way of playing jazz (laughs). We listened to so much jazz and a lot of African-style rock/jazz, it couldn't help but influence us. We couldn't help it getting into our music. But after, I would say we were heavy, but to be heavy metal, you gotta have that guitar sound; you gotta have that feeling of the heavy music. It is different from just rock 'n' roll, and I would say no, we weren't a heavy metal band. I would say we became a hard rock band, or a heavy rock band.

Grand Funk drummer Don Brewer:
We saw them at the Grande when we were probably still The Pack. Of course the audience is completely zoned-out on whatever. I mean, the place was just so full of pot and everyone was passing pills around and stuff, and we see this guy smearing hamburger all over himself and he dives off into the audience, and the audience is carrying him around on their hands all over the floor. It was almost like the music didn't matter, that it was just a part of the show, you know?

Grande Ballroom owner Russ Gibb:
Iggy brought show business. You gotta remember, that generation that made the Grande had been more or less weaned on television. My generation had been brought up on vaudeville and live shows and staging and plays and things like that. This generation did not know that. He brought that. If anything, Iggy—and I've told him this many times—he brought show business into rock 'n' roll.

And then of course we had Alice Cooper and a lot of the other famous people; they got involved there. And we would let anything go at the Grande. And Iggy was heavy because they were brought up and traveled in the same van with the MC5. They were all sort of buddies, and they all at one time or another shared apartments and shared lovers and whatever. It was a little community thing going on. Iggy, you know, musician-wise, you can argue whether Iggy's bands were that good, but I'll tell you, the energy level of Iggy. You know, the first time he fell off the stage, some people give him credit for inventing stage-diving. And the question becomes, did he or didn't he? All I know is the first time it was an accident, and then after that he started to dive in on a regular basis, into the audiences. And before long they were passing kids up to him on stage, because the stage was easily gotten to at the Grande.

November 1967. Cream's *Disraeli Gears* is released, which contains "Tales of Brave Ulysses" and "Sunshine of Your Love," the latter of which was tribal, doomy, wracked with power chords, feedback and bashing drums. Billboard compliments the band on selling so many albums without a single, calling their sound "wall-to-wall rock tinged with blues and 'flower' lyrics."

Jack Bruce, on "Sunshine of Your Love" Pete Brown, who is my lyricist, and myself, we always had to write the songs for the albums very quickly, because we never had much time. So we were trying to write some stuff, and we had been up all night and weren't really coming up with anything and we were in my flat in London and I just picked up my double bass and played the riff, the line of "Sunshine of Your Love" (sings it), and Pete looked out the window, and he wrote, "It's getting near dawn." Just like that. I think that's probably the best record that we did. It was the one that got us attention in the states. It was the first thing we recorded at Atlantic Studios with Tommy Dowd. There were a lot of good people around and we had a blast doing it.

Stooges drummer Scott Asheton: Depending on what you say a heavy sound is, if you're going towards heavy metal, I would say the big inspirational drummer for heavy metal had to be Ginger Baker, the drummer for The Cream. Because he started his drum solo thing with the double bass drums and everything... every drummer in the world wanted to do it.

Who, Cream and Jimi Hendrix roadie Neville Chesters on double bass drummers: Double bass drums came in '67, and it would be between Ginger and Keith; I think maybe Keith. But with Keith you had a guy that played lead drums. I mean, Entwistle played lead bass, if you like, would be the best way to describe it, and Moony was lead drums. I know that I did extensive work on Keith's drums to try and keep them in one piece, or as many pieces as they were supposed to be in. It's funny because I was instrumental in organizing the first deal that we had with Premier for Keith, and the only reason we did it, I think, was because we were going to get them for nothing. But I'm pretty sure you'd have to say Ginger. Keith made more noise with double bass drums, but Ginger was and always has been the more classic drummer. Ginger is one of my favourite drummers. Ginger was a drummer that was really into drums. I mean he'd been playing longer than Moony, of course. He played with Graham Bond. So he was capable of playing jazz. But he was a heavy drummer in terms of power and he was a fairly frightening character. He was tall, he could be aggressive in all shapes and sizes.

Skid Row and Thin Lizzy guitarist Gary Moore:
I wasn't a great Led Zeppelin fan. Anything that rubbed off was probably accidental. I think the other guys in Skid Row might have been more into Zeppelin. There weren't that many heavy bands around those days. Zeppelin were the first band who acknowledged the riffs, although Jeff Beck had been doing that sort of thing with Rod Stewart. A lot of the Zeppelin kind of thing, the concept, the riff ideas, came from the first Jeff Beck album with Rod Stewart. I think some of our jamming onstage was like Cream, but again, it was a lot more frantic. Cream was a lot smoother, more fluid. When you play with Jack and Ginger you can be very fluid and the guitar kind of floats over the top. And I can see why Eric was playing those long fluid lines because there was a lot going on, a bit of a volcano going on behind him (laughs). It was almost like Eric had to hold it together at times, but it became a really beautiful start of guitar playing, almost by necessity. But I enjoyed Eric's playing in Cream; it's just great.

Vanilla Fudge guitarist Vinny Martell:
Cream contributed a lot because they were a straight-out trio with a heavy drum and bass mood and with Clapton, who was a great player. What he did with the guitar, and what was beautiful about them to me, was the fact that since it was just a trio, he was able to really get into the guitar, the sound of the guitar. Every note was right out there; every chord, every nuance stuck out. It was a lot more of a bluesy feel than what we were into, but it did move me into a more bluesy feel, between the Cream and Hendrix. Big, strong sound, great tunes, great writing.

November 1967. The Amboy Dukes issue their self-titled debut album, on Mainstream Records. Not the heaviest band in Detroit, the Amboy Dukes nonetheless present a fairly "grungy" form of psych, with a guitarist in Ted Nugent who has learned how to fire off licks and elicit feedback from his odd hollow-bodied Gibson Byrdland, as experienced on "Colors."

November 1967. UK art rockers Hapsash and the Coloured Coat issue an album called *Featuring the Human Host and the Heavy Metal Kids*, drawing the William Burroughs reference into the world of rock music.

Late 1967. After making numerous trips to play gigs, the Alice Cooper group (still called The Nazz at this point, with the name change coming in '68) relocate from Phoenix to L.A..

Late 1967. Budgie forms, in Cardiff, Wales, as Hills Contemporary Grass, soon to be Six Ton Budgie, then Budgie.

Budgie bassist and vocalist Burke Shelley:
The name of the band, Budgie, it's ironic; it wasn't meant to be sort of like tough. Everybody was using occult names like Black Sabbath, or Led Zeppelin, which had connotations of heaviness; people went for those sorts of titles. We were originally called Six Ton Budgie, which you could say had that sort of inflection, but by the time we became Budgie, we lost that weight (laughs), and we were just called Budgie, which appealed to me much more.

Budgie drummer Ray Philips on why the band was so heavy:
From my point of view as a drummer I was always into classical music. I always loved classical music. I spent a lot of time pondering that music and the way music can move people. Take music out of films and all you've got is a picture. I would sit down, I'd play the drums to things like "Rhapsody in Blue," all sorts of classical music, and when I finally met up with Burke Shelley and Tony Bourge, I found that they were on the same sort of line. Only Tony was very blues-influenced. He was writing like John Mayall, while Burke then was more along the lines of The Beatles, alongside Led Zeppelin. I think a fusion of all those styles of music came together in Budgie. Black Sabbath wasn't so much of an influence. Black Sabbath are an excellent band and they live just a couple miles from here, or they used to. Excellent band, but we played a lot of Led Zeppelin stuff and Beatles stuff. So again we saw ourselves more classically-based and influenced.

December 1967. Meetings take place, in Hamburg, Paris and at points around England, between the management team of Coletta and Edwards and various musicians, and the first incarnation of Deep Purple, named Roundabout, would emerge by mid-February 1968. To get things going on a serious basis, management set the band up at (the haunted) Deeves Hall and buy them £6000 worth of equipment, including a Hammond C3 for Jon Lord. Vocalist Rod Evans is brought into the fold through an audition process, with Ian Paice joining on the strength of recommendation, replacing Bobby Woodman-Clarke. Both had arrived from The Maze.

Deep Purple drummer Ian Paice:
I met Ritchie on a boat on the way to Italy in 1967, and we bumped into each other again at the Star Club in Hamburg, where he was living at the time. He wanted me to join up with him then but I couldn't because I needed the money my band was earning. I made a real enemy of him because of that and used to cross the road if ever I saw him coming down the same street. Then in 1968, I went for an audition for Deep Purple and there he was again. Apparently he had been trying to find me but couldn't. They just hoped I'd see the ad in the paper and I did. I took along our vocalist, Rod Evans, and he got the job as Purple's

singer. At the time I joined I had a feeling that this band was going to make it. There was a will in the band to work hard and not sit around doing nothing."

December 1, 1967. Jimi Hendrix Experience issues their second album *Axis: Bold as Love*. More experimental than the debut, there are arguably three tracks in the proto-metal realm: "Spanish Castle Magic," "If 6 was 9" and "Little Miss Lover." "Spanish Castle Magic" would be the heaviest of the three and also, not coincidentally, the most distorted from a guitar point of view.

Living Colour bassist Doug Wimbish on Jimi Hendrix and his relationship with England:

I think a lot of the artists got pissed-off when Jimi came to London; everybody was saying he was stealing everybody's stuff. But I think it was the other way around. Everybody that Pete Townsend and all those guys were checking out, was nothing but the blues artists, period. That was it. But I think Pete and Jimi were both interested in the same thing. Pete might've been more on a high at that time, while Jimi was coming up. Jeff Beck had said to Pete, "Hey man, just went and saw Jimi at the 100 Club," and he went in and was blown away. But as he was leaving the club, Pete Townsend is coming in. Jeff's going, "Well, he's doing all you shit in there." And so that's an English thing, you know what I mean? I think Jimi was a person who came in and adapted what was going on, and said, I like the style of what's going on in England. I like the mannerisms of how you guys make record here, without the distractions.

So I think what Jimi was able to do was take advantage of the fact that this was a place where you could experiment. It was a perfect fit for him at that time, when he went there. It was the perfect, perfect, perfect time. But they didn't know how to deal with it. Because an English person's mannerisms are different from, let's say, a black American's mannerisms. We might be more friendly and blah blah blah and chatty. The English have—some, not all—more barriers. They'll sit down and give you a cup of Earl Grey tea, but they won't go, "Hey, I like what that guy's doing."

And Jimi was just such a blazing person that it was natural intimidation, and somebody had to find words to find a way to talk down the talent. Whereas Jimi's just like, "I just want to play my music." And he's like, "You know, I'm picking things up from you. Why not? I'm showing you something else." But the English press has a way of putting a spin on things. And you know, Beatles, Stones, Cream, Clapton, Eric, Jeff Beck, Pete Townsend, my man from Zeppelin... I think those four guys were like, "All right, we've got North, South, East and

West here. This is our shit here." And Jimi just came in and he was like, "Yeah, I hear it. You might think it's your shit. But I know where you're getting this shit from. You're getting it from... and you know why I know? Because I was there with the guys who made the shit. And I've been around and plus I know the way that things were translated. If you think it's yours, it's cool. But are you the owner of that? Are you the originator or are you another translator?"

Stooges drummer Scott Asheton:
I heard Pete Townshend say that when Hendrix first came on the scene, every other guitar player in the world wasn't any good. Because Hendrix made them all sound terrible. But Hendrix was very musical. He wouldn't just show up and turn up the amp, although he did play loud. I got the chance to see them live one time. Every guitar player in the world was influenced by Jimi Hendrix, at that time.

December 15, 16, 17, 1967. Vanilla Fudge play The Grande Ballroom, only the second really significant heavy act after Cream two months earlier.

December 28, 1967. A band called The Heavy Metal Kids play the Grande Ballroom, supporting The Woolies and Soap. Heavy Metal Kids included members of Billy C. & The Sunshine and the Four of Us, along with two members of the Mushrooms, one of which was future Eagles legend Glenn Frey, who assembled the act after the demise of the Mushrooms and having worked with Bob Seger. Maybe one of the Eagles invented heavy metal.

Recap

Given our necessary device of higher and higher thresholds for heaviness as we accelerate through the months of the late '60s, one phalanx of debaters o'er our titular question may wish to dispense with all previous claims and declare heavy metal invented in the year 1967, through the singles and two full-length albums of Jimi Hendrix, who dominates the year.

"Purple Haze" and a number of supporting flame-thrown salvos from the mercurial James Marshall Hendrix introduce a type of music that was hard to put into words at the time, exasperating critics as well as jealous (former) guitar gods. And when that happens, when you can't articulate something because all comparison points pack in accuracy, chances are you are creating something new.

Are You Experienced is perhaps the first heavy metal album, sure, although I would still hold off on that, waiting for the next higher threshold or bar. Still it's a bit unfair to deny Hendrix the badge to his regal vest, given that the sum total of the heaviest a-sides, b-sides and tracks from *Are You Experienced* and *Axis: Bold as Love* could fight at least to a draw against the likes of two records to come and feature prominently shortly, namely Blue Cheer's *Vincebus Eruptum* and Led Zeppelin's *Led Zeppelin*, the album so good they had to name it twice.

And speaking of Led Zeppelin, in 1967, one of those former guitar gods so summarily disposed of by Hendrix, Jimmy Page, would close shop on The Yardbirds through that band's thoughtful *Little Games* album. Arguably, what came next did more to blow to smithereens the British blues boom than it did to cause heavy metal to blow up big.

And sticking to the subject of dead gods, 1967 featured one more godly act fighting quite valiantly to hold one of the seats of power upon the stack. Eric Clapton's band Cream issues *Disraeli Gears*, their second and arguably most complete or completely succinct statement. Fact is, it isn't particularly heavy, those memories of Cream as mammoth really lying and relying on the band's crushing volume live, and their instrumental indulgence—forget guitar hero, Cream had a drum hero too, and only because there's no such thing as a bass hero (except to bassists), well, if there was, Jack Bruce would be one of those, plucking his thunderbroom with aplomb. No, what *Disraeli Gears* is, is an egregiously psychedelic album, albeit with a certain tribal brutishness (despite those sweet, sweet vocals from Jack), but also drugged to the teeth, with the album cover pretty much telling the story.

Still, as you might have been gathering from our future proto- and not so proto-metallers and the things they say about Cream, without the various arch-'60s charms of this band, these guys may not have turned out as loud and proud and proficient as they did.

Finally, bringing a little class to our hairy hippie world, classical music becomes an influence on rock and simultaneously hard rock, through the arrival on the scene of Vanilla Fudge and of Deep Purple. The latter would lean that way more than the former (and naturally so: there's a whole treatise that can be had on why classical is so much more imbedded in European consciousness than American consciousness), but a shared characteristic between the two would be the rise of organ and the Hammond sound, and what could and would be done with it. Sure, it would be a source for classical runs and melodies and even an inspirational starting point to quote or cover something actually from the classical canon. But what is also important is that soon sounds will be made by the keyboardist that contribute to heaviness, through use of distortion and bold chords, through wall of sound textural addition, and through the tradition of soloing.

1968

1968. Ritchie Blackmore said he and Jimi Hendrix saw Harvey Mandell use tapping technique at a nightclub. He also said in a separate chat that he saw Mandell use it at the Whisky A Go-Go. Both Mandell and Hendrix were influences on Ritchie.

1968. Up in the Black Country, Glenn Hughes joins Trapeze, the band signing to Threshold Records the following year.

1968. San Francisco heavy psych band The Other Half issue their lone album, a self-titled, on Acta Records. The band includes guitarist Randy Holden, known for his stint in Blue Cheer plus his solo album *Population II*. The band's "Mr. Pharmacist" is included on the *Nuggets* compilation of important garage rock songs, although it is a non-LP single. The Other Half's total output comprises the album plus assorted singles from '66 through '68. The sound is fairly urgent, brisk and rhythmic with wild vocals, and they were known to be quite loud live. A heavier highlight would be "Oz Lee Eaves Drop."

1968. Brian May advertises for a drummer. Roger Taylor answers and they form Smile, predecessor to Queen, a fine band with, much later, some of the most ferociously heavy songs of the '70s—sporadic in the catalogue as they may be—in "Modern Times Rock 'n' Roll" and "Stone Cold Crazy."

1968. Blue Öyster Cult (different name, different lineup), record an album's worth of wobbly psych rock material for Elektra Records. The album is shelved when lead singer Les Braunstein leaves the band.

1968. Sir Lord Baltimore forms, significant in that this would mean, ostensibly, that some considerably heavy sounds would likely have been worked up in rehearsal spaces by these gents in the late '60s, given the heft of their eventual recorded material.

> Sir Lord Baltimore drummer and vocalist John Gardner on guitarist Louis Dambra's influences:
> Louis used to listen to what I would listen to: the Yardbirds, Jeff Beck, Jimi Hendrix, of course. But you know, the funny thing about Lou, is that Lou is a totally untouched, musically, individual. He was never in a copy band. He never played lounge groups, never did that. So he's like a guitar-playing virgin, you might say. Untouched by the world. So when he plays, it's like whatever comes out of his heart—that's it. He's very special that way. There's no tainted stuff in Lou. Because he wasn't the kind of guy who sat down with a record and went, "Wow, I'm going to do that riff. I'm going to copy that to a T." He was never like that.

1968. A blues rock band forms in Australia called Head. It features Dave Tice, soon to be in Buffalo, and Peter Wells, later of Rose Tattoo. Buffalo would contribute much heaviness to the world, but more like two to six years after the scope of our survey.

1968. Grand Funk Railroad forms.

Grand Funk drummer Don Brewer:
When we put Grand Funk together, we were Terry Knight and the Pack, and that music in the mid '60s, it sounded very '60s. It was influenced by the English bands that were coming over but we also did some R&B covers. When we put Grand Funk together, this was right after Cream, Hendrix, Blue Cheer, and the whole thought of putting Grand Funk together was to go after that hard rock trio kind of a thing. We took with us all of our R&B influences and so whereas Hendrix and Cream and Blue Cheer were more blues-based, white guys playing the blues but cranked-up with all the feedback, we did the same thing but we did it with R&B. And I think that's really what defines Grand Funk is this unique combination between R&B and hard rock.

1968. Danny Fields signs The Stooges to Elektra.

Stooges guitarist Ron Asheton:
We were just sitting in our house here in Ann Arbor; we lived in a farmhouse, and we had played our shows and we were mostly just doing a bunch of riffs and just our shows were like free-form jams. So when Jac Holzman came to Ann Arbor to sign the MC5, Danny Fields said you've got to sign this band also, being the Stooges. So we played, and we did our regular show, like a solid half hour of free-form going off. And he said, "Well, do you have any songs?" "Yeah, we do." Oh-oh. So that was really... we didn't have much time. So it was just sitting in that house doing the same thing. Me coming up with riffs and pieces, and Iggy writing the lyrics and putting the stuff together. That 11th hour thing really worked great. We were good with pressure; we just kicked that stuff out.

1968. Somewhat murky lore, but 1968 is cited as the original birth date of what would become Accept, with lead singer Udo Dirkschneider and future metal producer Michael Wagener teaming up for Band X. Amusingly, Scorpions roots can be traced to 1965. Accept's first album wouldn't come until 1979 but admirably, *Accept* is uncommonly heavy even for 1979.

1968. Warpig form in London, Ontario, completing their debut album in 1970, although it wouldn't see release until 1973, through London, slightly altered, with new tracks produced by future Rush producer Terry Brown. In 1973, it's no more than an obscure footnote, but had it been released in 1970 when it was recorded, it would have been seen as somewhat heavy and modern for its day, a crude but spirited Deep Purple copy band caught somewhere between that band's Mk. 1 and Mk. 2. The album did indeed get released as an indie before 1973—red label on Fonthill— but two different members of the band interviewed by the author produce the timeline for that as, "Gee, I don't know, 1970" and "a little after 1970" with the material being written starting in 1968, and the independent record deal coming in the summer of 1970.

Warpig drummer Terry Hook:
We were pretty much influenced by the English scene at the time. We were big fans of Deep Purple. A few of the guys were really big fans of Sabbath. Personally

I was a big John Bonham fan. But I would have to say that Deep Purple in our eyes... that hard-driving rock we really enjoyed. We took a bit of their style, and a bit of Sabbath, and a bit of Zeppelin. There were even groups like Wishbone Ash, Uriah Heep, as much as they were very disappointing live (laughs). But we just liked that sound, and then of course we tried to put our own little twist to it. But that was the path we wanted to follow. As for the name, we just started dishing out names. Someone had War for part of it, and someone else mentioned Pig, and all of a sudden Warpig came up. I don't think it had anything to do with the Sabbath song. But I came on board when they were called Mass Destruction, and before that they were called The What. And then all of a sudden with the four of us together, like I say, with the influence from Purple, Sabbath, Zeppelin, all of a sudden we decided to do that English in-your-face rock, and then try put our own little twist to it. All the songs came within a very short period of time, a few months.

January 1968. Blue Cheer's debut, *Vincebus Eruptum* is released. A shockingly heavy album for its day, it is considered by many to be the first heavy metal album of all time. Here, we will assign it much weight, but deny it that title due to lack of skilfulness, lack of modern metallic flourishes, and assumed lack of visceral heavy metal intention.

Opener "Summertime Blues" is tribal and savage, wracked with low-humming fuzz and probably the best use of feedback on a record to date. "Rock Me Baby" is a go-nowhere, do-nothing blues, a second cover on an album that is half covers, a serious blow to credibility at the altar to our titular question. "Doctor Please" is our introduction to Dickie Peterson as writer of heavy metal, and it's a harrowing trip through thrashing garage rock turned up, more feedback and much firing off of guitar soloing, but not much for power chords—it's very much a jam track, at eight minutes without too many parts.

"Out of Focus" is another original, and it's not all that heavy, more like a laid-back Jimi Hendrix funk, albeit with all of Blue Cheer's noisy accoutrements. Admirably, the band do indeed turn "Parchment Farm" into a proto-metal scorcher, frantically blasting through it, yowling guitars pervasive. The album's last of six tracks is another original, "Second Time Around" being rudimentary but fairly metal like a Stooges track, tribal, repetitive, not much fuzz on the rhythm guitar, but noisy everywhere else.

Blue Cheer bassist and vocalist Dickie Peterson:
The Blue Cheer show is basically like it always has been, in that, we're not a pretentious band. We don't have any smoke, we don't have any mirrors. We come at you straight-ahead, face-to-face, rock 'n' roll. It's loud and it's powerful, and our attitude on stage... I believe firmly, that rock 'n' roll is 10% technique and 90% attitude. And we deliver when we walk onstage. We had the concept of making music something more than an audio sensation. We wanted to make it physical. And to a certain degree, we accomplished that. We knew we wanted to be loud,

and we knew we wanted to be physical. We just kept adding more and more amps. Plus I just have a unique style of playing. In a dressing room that I was in in Winterland, with Muddy Waters, at the Blues Bash, I finally got the courage to go and ask him for some advice. And he asked me, "What do you play?" And I said I played bass. He said, "Just play in the spaces more; just play in the spaces. Don't play more than you have to. You'll just get in other people's way." And that's what I've always done. And that's part of the reason why our music is so big and fat. I don't overplay.

Blue Cheer drummer Paul Whaley:
We were big fans of the Yardbirds and this blues-based approach, but with the feedback guitar and strong drums. More like The Who, you know? We were called either blues rock or hard rock. Heavy metal was not even a term. We were a blues band at first, and it was not until we saw Hendrix—me and Dickie and Leigh—at Monterey and then we went after this three-piece style. And you know, because of this we were considered copy cats and maybe not worthy of the attention. The audiences liked us but the in-crowd, the musicians, Airplane, the Dead, Quicksilver, Janis Joplin, not so much. Especially the Dead and the Airplane—they were a little bit snooty. But the audiences liked us and the record companies liked us. We picked up a good deal and they put a lot of backing behind us, and we wound up making a lot of albums.

Vanilla Fudge drummer Carmine Appice:
When we first saw Blue Cheer, we thought they were really loud and ugly (laughs). Because they were—they were very raw, ugly; they had lots of Marshall amps. We saw them, maybe in '68, on the East Coast, and they were really heavy sounding. They took what everybody else was doing and made it louder. And when you make it bigger and louder, it made it heavier. I know they had double bass drums as well. But a lot of these guys who played double bass drum back then, really didn't play that well. They were untrained drummers and they were just mediocre and didn't really know what to do with double bass drums—just go boom boom boom.

Detroit Wheels drummer Johnny "Bee" Badanjek:
Blue Cheer... they had ten Marshalls. They thought they were trying to outdo everybody else. We played with them a few times at the end of The Detroit Wheels there. They were very loud. Probably the loudest band I've ever heard. They might've been even louder than Hendrix. Some people thought they weren't that good of players and some liked what they were saying because it was so bombastic.

Blue Öyster Cult bassist Al Bouchard:
I didn't think *Vincebus Eruptum* was that heavy. To me, heavy was The Who. Blue Cheer just sounded like people playing loud, you know? I guess maybe it was just missed on me, but I didn't really like them that much.

Amboy Dukes vocalist John Drake:
We did gigs with Blue Cheer. That was the highest band I've ever seen on stage. I was with the bass player, and we were backstage and Blue Cheer was opening for us, okay? As I recalled they recorded on Pier 51 in California. They said no studio could capture—oh, in New York rather—no studio could capture their sound. So they had to record outside. Okay fine, they were loud, there was no question. They took a lot of pride in that. So I'm backstage and Dickie Peterson was plugged in. They had the equipment plugged in, and the curtains hadn't opened yet. I'd never seen anybody this high. He was dragging a bass or something by its cord plugged in and they hadn't gone on yet. Out in the audience you can hear boom-ba-boom-ba-boom; you know, it's making all this racket. I'm going what's with this guy? He kind of staggers out there and as I recall, that was like a power trio. He puts the bass on and they got loud. They got it together, but man, he was higher than a kite at that time. Crowd liked them. They liked them because they liked it loud, man. I mean we used to really play loud, and then I heard those guys and I go, "Man, what are we? Let's turn it up a little, boys."

Foghat drummer Roger Earl:
I played with Blue Cheer when I was in Savoy Brown back in the late '60s. Yeah, they were loud, but that was like a heavy metal band really, wasn't it? You know blues tunes but turned it up to 11. One more than ten, isn't it? One louder than Foghat. They definitely came from blues. They were a blues band but they just turned it up and just fucked with it a little bit. That's what happened.

Mountain drummer Corky Laing:
Blue Cheer was volume. Volume, plus the effect of the aggressiveness of the songs, and of course if you had any sort of rebellious attitude in the lyrics, you had to have volume. It was angst, volume, basically going over the top, just pushing as hard as you can.

Blue Öyster Cult producer Sandy Pearlman:
"I think the earliest heavy metal music that I remember seeing or hearing, was probably Blue Cheer, at the time of *Vincebus Eruptum*.

MC5 drummer Dennis Thompson:
I saw them and I wasn't impressed. They were loud; they were a very loud band. I really didn't mind their hit song "Summertime Blues" and there was another one; they had a couple of tunes. But they were probably like another little piece in the puzzle of playing loud and playing hard.

Creem magazine journalist Jaan Uhelski:
They were amazing! It was like that fuzzy wall of sound. It really was everything they'd say, that Blue Cheer was the loudest band in the world. They had all the great components of rock. They were good-looking, they were mysterious, they commanded the stage. In a way they ignored you but it was compelling. I think I still have at my parent's house, the little hand poster that they gave out at The Grande Ballroom. But I don't think everybody liked Blue Cheer, actually. I think it's like a fetish item if you like, kind of garagey. My tastes run really to The Stooges and the MC5; I mean that's just Detroit rock. I've got a wider palette given I've done this all my life, but that really does fit in my own personal aesthetic. They never got asked back, so that has to say something. Bands would usually play there two or three days, and if the attendance wasn't good, they wouldn't ask them back.

Frost guitarist Dick Wagner:
The crowds loved Blue Cheer. That was a band pretty much made for Detroit. Loud, aggressive... they got a good reaction.

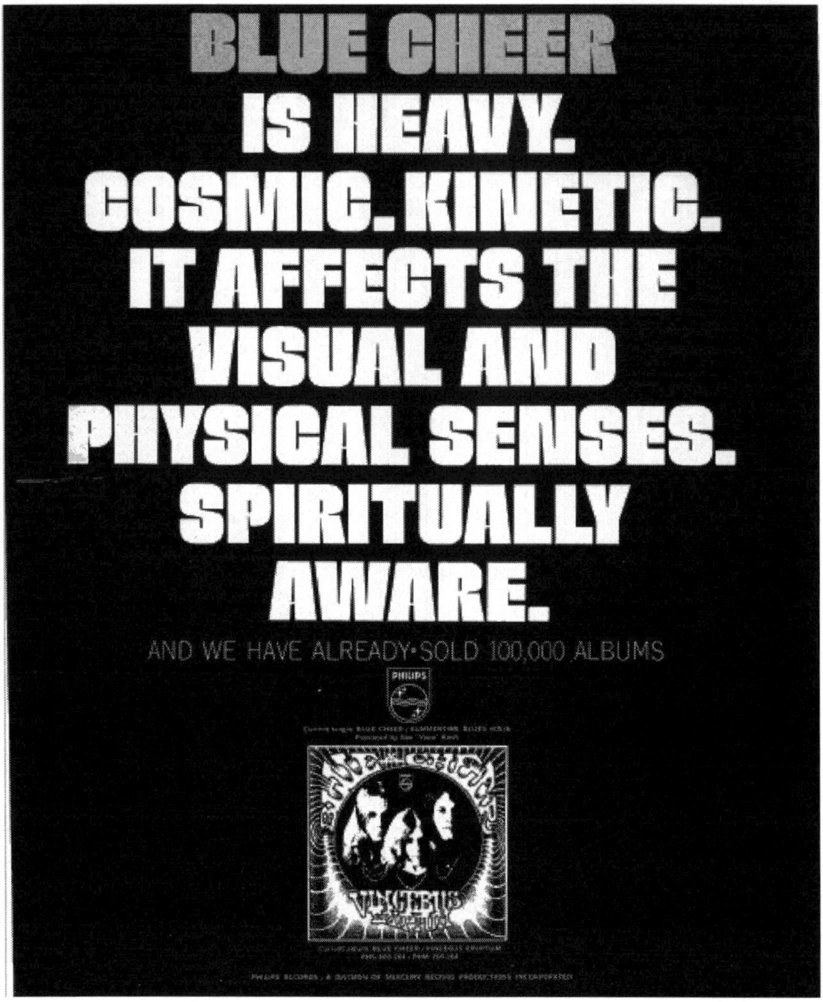
BLUE CHEER
IS HEAVY.
COSMIC. KINETIC.
IT AFFECTS THE
VISUAL AND
PHYSICAL SENSES.
SPIRITUALLY
AWARE.
AND WE HAVE ALREADY·SOLD 100,000 ALBUMS
PHILIPS

STEPPENWOLF
STEPPENWOLF
STEPPENWOLF
STEPPENWOLF
STEPPENWOLF
STEPPENWOLF
STEPPENWOLF
"EVERYBODY'S NEXT ONE"
"BORN TO BE WILD"
STEPPENWOLF
STEPPENWOLF

January 1968. Steppenwolf issue their self-titled debut album, which includes "Born to Be Wild," with the refrain, "heavy metal thunder" considered to be the first use of the term in a song. The song is popularized by its inclusion in the hit movie *Easy Rider* and is further remembered because it is indeed one of Steppenwolf's more heavy metal songs, featuring guitar over organ, and eschewing the band's usual dated psychedelic rock tendencies. The rest of the album is firmly not heavy metal, save for, at a neck-stretch, "The Ostrich," a brisk rocker with an amount of distorted guitar uncommon for this keyboardy and dated and over-rated psych band. Of note, the original mono version of the single is in possession of an extra kick of heaviness over and above the widely distributed stereo version—really, this is a very heavy song for early 1968, a fact that tends to get overshadowed by the etymological point.

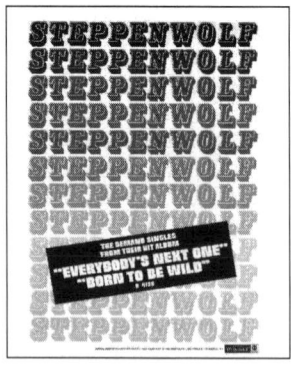

January 1968. The Sweet form as The Sweetshop; the band's considerable contributions to heavy metal will not manifest until 1973.

> Sweet bassist Steve Priest:
> We were all brought up by the same bands. I loved The Cream, or Cream and the Yardbirds. The Stones, in fact I saw them when I was 15 and I was knocked out with it. I mean, they're still going (laughs). But we all had the same Scousy, if you like, sort of upbringing, and we all had the same sort of heroes. Mick Tucker loved Ginger Baker and he loved his attitude. We all loved Cream. Andy Scott wasn't our first guitarist—Frank Torpey was. And we were around doing the circuit for three years before Andy was the guitarist. And we were doing pretty heavy stuff, but at the time in England, reggae was the choice of the month, so we didn't go over too well doing "I Feel Free" or "Eight Miles High" and "Sunshine of Your Love." They wanted this reggae stuff, and they were all wearing big bobber boots, they were called, and they didn't want to hear us namby pambies—they just wanted to hear reggae (laughs). That was a hard, tough beginning, I tell you, for all of us.

January 1968. Mythology forms, with Tony Iommi on guitar. Bill Ward joins the band in February of 1968. Some sources cite the band as forming in 1967, and others as early as 1966. Strongest alternative to our chosen date however is "the end of" 1967.

Black Sabbath guitarist Tony Iommi on his earliest heavy music:
Certainly not in The Rest. In Mythology there was, yes. It was more guitar-oriented blues. I'd be doing lots of solo guitar work in those days. So that was the start of it, really. I liked John Mayall's Blues Breakers. That was more the bands we sort of all liked. And when Clapton joined Cream, of course, I wasn't too keen on that. I did like them, but not as much as John Mayall's Blues Breakers—that was our early blues influence.

> Black Sabbath drummer Bill Ward on learning heaviness:
> We didn't have anybody who taught us that. The songs, when they came about... I don't know how that was. We just used to show up and we used to just play aggressively. I think it was just more the aggression that came out than anything else. I think we just pretty much turned up the volume. I mean, I didn't have a P.A. back then for my drums or anything, so there were no microphones. I had to play as loud as I possibly could anyway, and I think that sometimes the guys thought I was playing too loud (laughs), so they turned up. So we all just got louder, really. It wasn't anything that was planned or thought-out.

January 1, 1968. The era of album rock is born, with Billboard reporting that LPs, or long players, have outsold singles for the first time, essentially a blow to pop versus more substantive musical forms.

> Nazareth guitarist Manny Charlton:
> There were a lot of bands, for instance, like Spooky Tooth, Jeff Beck Group and Sabbath to a degree, that didn't really get played on mainstream radio, and that's all there was. There wasn't any alternative. So these bands became what they liked to call album bands. They did these albums and didn't really concentrate on singles. Even Zeppelin, at that point, weren't making singles. They didn't want any singles. So automatically they didn't go to *Top of the Pops* and they didn't get airplay during the day on mainstream radio. So that's where the kind of underground connotation came around, because basically they weren't as visible as, say, T. Rex and other bands that were on *Top of the Pops*.

January 20, 1968. The Stooges play their first show in public, as The Psychedelic Stooges, along with Apple Pie Motherhood, in support of Scot Richard Case, respected and somewhat heavy local act. The Psychedelic Stooges replaced The Amboy Dukes on the bill. Maybe Ted Nugent invented heavy metal not only through his pioneering of feedback and the concept of the guitar hero, but by making way for the introduction of the Stooges.

January 27, 1968. Iron Butterfly issue their debut album, *Heavy*, recorded in October '67. The title alone is a contribution to the term heavy metal in the conventional sense, although for the record, it must be said that the term "heavy," was more widely used to mean, simply, cool or impressive or far-out, with the added nuance of "with significance" or, logically, "with weight." The music on *Heavy* is, first off, most definitely convincing dark psychedelic rock, which is one stepping stone toward Black Sabbath, especially given scary opening track "Possession." Elsewhere, the album proves the perfect example of one that lacks in heavy metal intention despite heavy vibe. Although more than half of the record features heavy metal writing, the anaemic production, laconic vocals, lack of guitar, and the prominence of organ in addressing any sense of riffery, betrays a band that is quite spooky, but alas, not really inventing anything consciously or materially.

> Later Iron Butterfly vocalist and guitarist Mike Pinera:
> A couple of years before I joined the band, the band had that first album out called *Heavy* and a lot of people come up and say that's the first time they ever heard the word heavy alongside of rock, so they figure that's the pioneer of heavy rock, right there: Iron Butterfly. And indeed that album had a lot of things like "Iron Butterfly Theme," which was very dark, underground, psychedelic sounding, and then there was "Unconscious Power," which was really a cooker, a mover and a shaker, yet the lyrics were very, very deep.

January 30, 1968. The Tet Offensive, one of the bloodiest battles of the 19-year Vietnam War, an appalling conflict that darkened all of society through the '60s up until the end of the war in 1975.

> Blue Cheer guitarist Randy Holden:
> It was really bad over there. The influence on everybody's emotions from that whole thing was really crazy, and it was hard to deal with, just living in society. You're seeing so many people, young guys your age, dying and getting blown to bits, coming back with these incredible stories. I had one guy, Larry, he was over there and his brother Tony later played with Blue Cheer, but Larry came and he wanted to work with me as a road manager. And I said sure. And he was a really nice guy. But he was so wigged-out from 'Nam, it was unbelievable. The stories he told me, you just wouldn't believe. And he couldn't live with it. And he was with me only about two or three months, and he left. He had a hard time staying focused on anything. He was very hyper, and he committed suicide. 57,000 young US men died in Vietnam, but more than that committed suicide when they returned. That's how bad that was.
> So when you relate it to music, the music was nothing but a positive reaction against a great negative force that was going on. And then the music inevitably would have to turn dark, because there was a great dark force compelling the world. I think that's part of why my interests turned to discordance, and trying to look into the far future. I remember sitting once and trying to imagine what it would sound like for a nuclear bomb going off, and it

was so intense to me, it was so loud it was just silent. And I thought how can I create something like that in music?

Black Sabbath bassist Geezer Butler on *Paranoid*'s "Hand of Doom:"
In me former band, before Sabbath, and in the early days of Sabbath, we used to play a lot of American military bases around Europe, and in England. We used to talk to the soldiers who had just come back from Vietnam and stuff, and they used to always talk about the drug use over there. A lot of them were on heroin, and they used to have this stop-off point in England where they had to come off heroin before they could go back to America, because the government didn't want the American media to see the troops were on heroin and all that kind of stuff. And I used to talk to a lot of the soldiers about the drugs, and that's where "Hand of Doom" came from.

February 1968. Vanilla Fudge's second album *The Beat Goes On*.

Led Zeppelin expert Dave Lewis:
Vanilla Fudge were doing that heavy material based on what were more or less bubblegum records, "You Keep Me Hanging On" and things like that. But the Fudge were an influence on Jimmy. His influences have not always been vastly explored, but he definitely came into contact with them in both Zeppelin and the Yardbirds.

February 1968. Dick Wagner's early, heavy band, The Frost, play their first show at the Grande Ballroom.

February 1968. The Bakerloo Blues Line form. The significance to the story is that the band were managed by Jim Simpson, who, because he was having a hard time getting the band bookings, opened his own club in Birmingham called

Henry's Blues House, to provide a place for them to play. Early single-digit card-carrying members of the "club" were two Black Sabbath members. Soon Black Sabbath would be playing the venue and hook up with Simpson for management. Simpson was a jazz man, and surprisingly found an affinity for jazz within Sabbath, which he tried to encourage, amusingly, because calling yourself a blues band was beginning to kill a band's chance of success.

> Black Sabbath manager Jim Simpson:
> Black Sabbath were heavily influenced by jazz things in the very early days. Well, they were young, and especially early in their career, they were interested in anything, really. But Ozzy and Tony particularly, seemed to lean towards it. You can't tell with drummers and bass players, who express themselves fairly individually, but certainly if you look at the early Bill Ward stuff, you can hear some Kansas City Joe Jones high hat rides. And certainly Black Sabbath were the great riff band, and the great riff band in jazz was Basie, and that's where Joe Jones played. And Ozzy recorded a couple songs associated with the Basie band, Jimmy Rushing's "Evening," for one. And going slightly sideways, Tony recorded an instrumental called "Song for Jim," funnily enough, which was an absolute Charlie Christian take-off.

February 8, 1968. The Band of Joy play their first show in London, at The Marquee Club, venue for so many historic moments. At this point, both Robert Plant and John Bonham are in the band, which would break up within a couple of months.

> Quartz guitarist and early Bonham band mate Mick Hopkins on John Bonham:
> He was always loud. Years ago, I don't know if they had them in Canada, but they used have these special sound things, where if you played above a certain level, it would cut you off and cut the power off. And you could bet your life, if John was playing, he could knock it off on his own. He was so loud. There was nobody who could touch him. A booming drummer.

> UFO drummer Andy Parker:
> A lot of city councils had noise level things. There was this one gig we used to do in the west way of England. In the back of the hall there was this light bulb over the door, and as you play, the light bulb gets brighter and brighter. And if it stayed bright for too long, boom, the power would go out. And you'd kind of be watching the damn light bulb (laughs). Because cutting power doesn't do the equipment much good; it comes back on again and everything goes bang. So you'd take it down and it would be like just dimly flickering, and then you'd bring it up and you'd see that thing get brighter and brighter. Oh man, you gotta take it down again. All of a sudden there was this thing about, you're ruining people's hearing, and the younger generation is going deaf. With loud music. So there'd be some jobsworth in the back of the hall, with his sound meter or there was this frickin' lightbulb.
> But it was all new. You know, at first, the mic was for the singer (laughs). So to be heard, you had to play loud, which is a really good way of learning to play loud. I remember reading things about John Bonham back then, where he was chucked out of places for playing too loud. And he didn't have mics. You're in a little pub, and, you know, and you've got a great amount of Welly behind it, and I was like the same way. You know, get the front head off the bass drum, get as loud as you can. So it's actually hard for me to play quiet. In the last few years, I've been trying to hone my skills and gain some subtlety. But those early years are hard to repress.

Black Sabbath guitarist Tony Iommi:
We knew Zeppelin well, because they were friends of ours in the early days and we were from the same town, so we used to see them a lot, certainly Robert Plant and John Bonham. We were very familiar with what they were doing. When they started Zeppelin I remember Bonham saying, "We've got this band we're joining with Jimmy Page." He started telling us about it. And I remember the days from before he joined Zeppelin, he used to play in different bands around Birmingham. And he was always getting fired because he was too loud. So one week he would be with the band. We used to play these alternate weeks; this was before I was with Sabbath and before he was with Zeppelin. Bill and myself from Sabbath had another band and Bonham was with various bands. So we used to see him every other week playing at this place called The Midland Red Club in Birmingham, and he'd be there one week, and the week after that, he wouldn't be there. "What happened?" "Oh, he was too loud; we fired him."

March 1968. Birmingham's The Move issues their self-titled debut, more of a psych album with pop and some degree of heaviness.

March 3, 1968. Proving the power of hard rock, Columbia refuses to allow the MC5 (from arch-rivals Elektra) to open for the horn-boring Blood, Sweat & Tears at the Grande, opting for the Psychedelic Stooges to play their second Grande show ever, a move that backfired because heavy metal always wins.

MC5 manager John Sinclair on where the band got their heavy riffs:
Well, they made them up! (laughs). I know it's a radical concept to today's music, that you would make things up. In those days people would make things up. Jimi Hendrix came along with a whole new thing no one ever thought of—he made it up! You know? Beatles. There wasn't anything like the Beatles, and then there was the Beatles and then there was the Rolling Stones, The Who—they made all that shit up! They wanted to say something about the way they felt. Not the place you get rewards today, but there it was. It was an interesting period. I mean, the Beatles had to beg to get a record deal. They got turned down by Decca and shit. So it wasn't like they were looking for this. They had to storm the gates and pound and make them let you in. The hippies from San Francisco, the Big Brothers, Jefferson Airplane... they were jeered for not having any potential commercial impact. And then the Jefferson Airplane had the first hippie record that made the Top 10.

March 4, 1968. The Mothers of Invention issue their second album *We're Only in It for the Money*. The band come across as a bunch of heavy metal-looking freaks, and their album cover is a parody of *Sgt. Pepper*, Frank waging eye-winked war with pop.

March 16, 1968. The My Lai Massacre. Mass murder by US troops of 347 to 504 unarmed citizens in South Vietnam, all of whom were civilians, the majority women, children and the elderly.

April 1968. The Amboy Dukes issue their second album, *Journey to the Center of the Mind*. Still, really, not much of a heavy band, Billboard nonetheless says, "The Amboy Dukes power into the spotlight with a bruising brand of blues psychedelics and some of the hardest rock since Jimi Hendrix." The title track becomes the biggest hit of the band's career, and although it's a laughably purist psych number, Ted trundles through the riff, adding a choice bit of applied feedback squall.

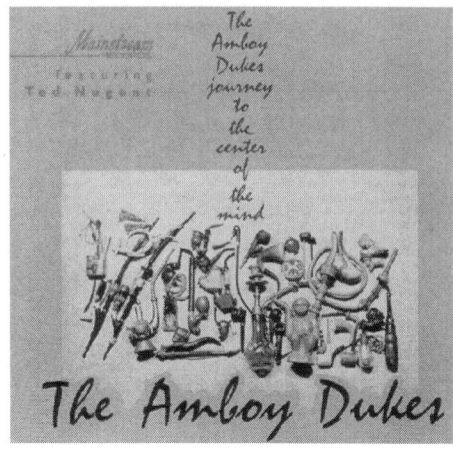

Amboy Dukes vocalist John Drake: We actually did consider ourselves hard rock, although some of our writing doesn't reflect that. I think when our first record came out, our first hit came out, "Baby Please Don't Go," I really wanted to stay along those lines. And then when "Journey to the Center of the Mind" came out, it was a hard rocker and I wanted to stay right there. But the music started to change; the next one that came out was "You Talk Sunshine, I Breathe Fire." That didn't do a lot for us. I just really wanted to stay along the lines of "Baby Please Don't Go." I thought we had been much, much better off with that. As far as Ted's influences go, he loved Beck. I don't think Ted really liked Hendrix all that much, although as a kid we copied him. In a lot of bands we'd do "Purple Haze" and "Foxy Lady" and all this stuff. He was an influence on our band, certainly Jimi Hendrix was, but Jimi Hendrix was another soul guy. He came out of Little Richard's band, and he had been in other bands, you know soul bands, and with the Isley Brothers too. Ted didn't like Jimi for the simple fact that he knew Jimi was a druggy. Ted, believe me, he loathed drugs. Believe me! This is Mr. Anti Drug himself.

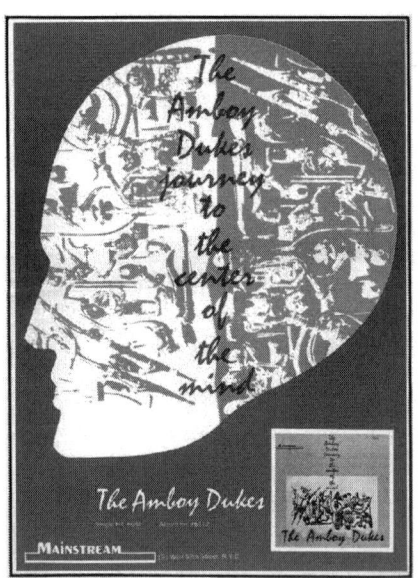

April 4, 1968. Martin Luther King assassinated. Riots take over 125 American cities (notably Detroit, Chicago, Washington DC and Baltimore); many people killed. Satan is alive.

April 19, 1968. Free's first show.

April 20, 1968. Deep Purple's first show, under the name Roundabout, in Tastrup, Denmark. A sample set list in October of that year was "Hush," "Kentucky Woman," "Mandrake Root," "Help," "Wring that Neck," "River Deep Mountain High" and "Hey Joe." Jon Lord indicates that if the trip over the channel was a failure, the band would change their name and start again. Woefully at this point Purple are still very much a covers act, but even in this dated psych rock guise, the band is beginning to feature precocious guitaring.

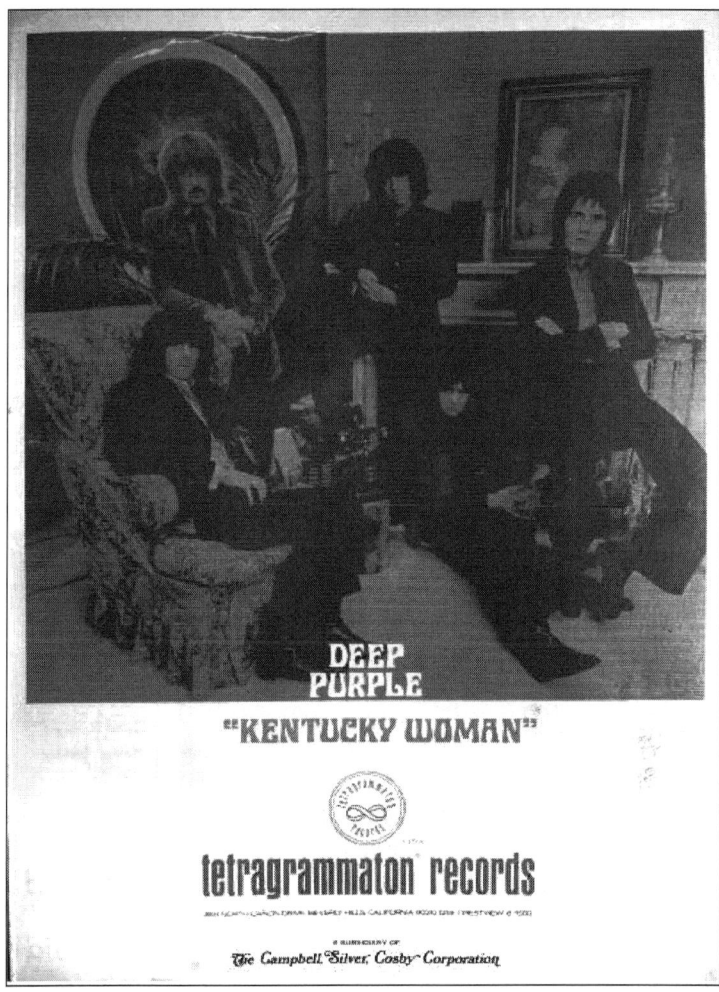

April 28, 1968. The Psychedelic Stooges play The Grande Ballroom for the first time.

Stooges guitarist Ron Asheton on why the band was so heavy:
Well, it was probably, at least for me, ignorance of my instrument. I had to play simple because I was just learning how to play. So I just picked up, you know, those three chords. When I go back now and talk to people like Thurston Moore and Mark Arm, they're going, "Well, we learned to play guitar from that record because it seemed like it was accessible to us. We could actually sit down and figure it out and get some joy out of it. Wow, I can play!" And they used that to start learning how to play. And that's pretty much just sheer bravado. That's

about being young upstarts, if you will, an extension of our personalities, our attitude, like anybody who plays, actually. We hung out together all the time, we were always together, doing everything together, so I guess that's what came out. When you put four minds together in a bad situation, they might turn into a killer. But you put four minds together in a nice musical situation, and something good is going to come out of it.

SRC guitarist Steve Lyman:
To me, initially the Stooges were kind of a joke, in the sense that for the most part the musicians that made up the Stooges were not that talented. And it was a real surprise to me when they finally got their act together, when they first started performing publicly. There was a show that was done on the University of Michigan campus that featured a lot of the Ann Arbor groups, including SRC, MC5, The Thyme, a lot of the groups that were managed by G Collinge, the producer that produced The Rationals; I know they were there too. But SRC played. We were somewhere midway through the show, and got a real good response from a really good crowd there.

And then when the Stooges eventually went on, I was amazed at how well the Stooges went over, even though musically they were, to me, sort of a joke. But I think it was due to the stage antics of Jimmy Osterberg, or Iggy Pop, that the audience just ate it up and went nuts over it. I know Scott Asheton was banging on oil drums and Ron Asheton was just sort of playing these power chords on his guitar without really doing any kind of lead stuff. It was mainly just Jimmy Osterberg out front with his shirt off being wild and crazy in front of the audience.

And I remember kind of shaking my head and walking away after observing their set, thinking man, that's what the public wants? But we were good friends with all those guys. That was the ironic thing, because one of the people, Ron Asheton in the Stooges, he was actually in a band called The Chosen Few, together with our lead singer Scott Richardson, before The Fugitives evolved into the Scot Richard Case, renamed SRC. So those guys, Iggy Pop, or as I call him, Jimmy Osterberg, the two Asheton brothers, they used to come over to our house all the time in the early days of our band and hang around with us. And we knew they were forming another band, but I never took it too seriously, because none of those guys were super proficient on their instruments.

May 1968. The Band of Joy break up; 1968 had found Plant and Bonham in the band at the same time, Plant still very much concealed in psych, folk and the blues, but Bonham, already known as loud beater about town.

May 3, 4, 1968. The Yardbirds play The Grande Ballroom, on their final tour before morphing into Led Zeppelin. It is said that Jimmy Page played most of the riffs that would show up on the first Led Zeppelin album and that he played through five Fender Dual Showman amplifiers. Supporting on the first date was Dick Wagner and The Frost, with perennials MC5 supporting the next night.

SRC guitarist Steve Lyman:
The first British group that I actually saw perform live was The Yardbirds, and that was not at the Grande Ballroom. It was at a club in Ann Arbor, Michigan called The Fifth Dimension. But the Yardbirds played at the Fifth Dimension right at the time when people started forming the Scot Richard Case, which became the SRC, and started practicing together. And I already had two albums by the Yardbirds at the time, so it was a real thrill for me to see a British group performing live. Jimmy Page was the guitar player at the time, because the Yardbirds went through various incarnations. Eric Clapton was their first guitar player, far as I know, Jeff Beck, and then Jimmy Page.

But the show was really good. The Fifth Dimension in Ann Arbor had some really good shows that we saw. We saw The Who there, Jimi Hendrix Experience there, right after they did the Monterey Pop Festival and they were supposed to be possibly the opening band for a Monkees tour. But yeah, I was mesmerized by that Yardbirds show. I was the lead guitar player in the autumn of '66 in the Fugitives, which became the SRC, so seeing Jimmy Page play became a real thrill for me, because I had been devouring these Yardbirds records on my record player and trying to figure out what they were playing (laughs).

Yardbirds drummer Jim McCarty:
We were a vehicle for what Jimmy wanted to do when he came in. He had a pretty free rein, as all the guitar players did and he pushed the Yardbirds sound into more of a heavy metal context. He really was the master of the riff.

Original Judas Priest vocalist Al Atkins, on witnessing The Yardbirds become Led Zeppelin:
I used to know Robert; we used to go for a beer together, and sometimes he'd borrow my microphone because he couldn't afford one, if I wasn't playing. We had one mic between the two of us (laughs). I had the best one. And a buddy of mine, "Are you playing tonight?" "No, oh go on." It was great times. Robert's roots have always been blues. He's a very intelligent guy when you're talking to him about the blues stuff. He knows everything about that. You can't argue with him about anything on that subject. But when I saw them, they went out on tour and what he said to me was... he was playing at Henry's Blues House again and Alexis Korner was playing on his own, a solo gig he got there, like a one-man band thing or something. And Robert got up and played harmonica and sang along with him.

And then with Jimmy Page, they formed the Yardbirds, went over to Europe, come back, and next thing they were called Led Zeppelin. I went to see them play at Mother's. They were backing Blodwyn Pig, and I think they got 75 quid or something. But when I saw him with Jimmy onstage that night I was totally blown away. And Bonham was absolutely out of his head. He was drunk, I think. And they did a set, and it was very mixed, including a lot of stuff that was going to be coming on the new album. They were loud, but they were brilliant. Robert's voice had just changed overnight. I couldn't believe the difference in his voice. Fantastic vocalist. And yeah, John Bonham, he couldn't come back onstage. They did an encore and the drummer from Blodwyn Pig came on and played this blues thing with them and they just jammed the encore. The good ol' days.

Led Zeppelin engineer Andy Johns:
Jimmy had made his mind up that they were going to blow everyone off the stage. That's what my brother told me. This is when Jimmy still had the Yardbirds thing going. Glyn said, "I was with Jimmy the other day, and Jimmy said, 'I've got this new lineup now, and we're going to blow everyone offstage.'" So that was an intentional thing, to be as dramatic and as riff-conscious as possible. And Jimmy was a fabulous writer, and had a lot of great ideas in the studio, and was just wonderful to work with.

May 6, 1968. Massive wildcat general strike in France, with riots, mass demonstrations by university students in Paris. The government is almost toppled. The hippie generation is going through some dark times globally, and soon there will be bands holding a mirror to the strife.

May 11, 1968. Although Lester Bangs is credited as being the first to use the term heavy metal in the early '70s, Barry Gilford, in the May 11, 1968 issue of Rolling Stone says, in a review of Electric Flag's *A Long Time Comin'*, "Nobody who's been listening to Mike Bloomfield—either talking or playing—in the last few years could have expected this. This is the new soul music, the synthesis of white blues and heavy metal rock." In reality, Electric Flag were not as heavy as their name.

May 11 – 13, 1968. Deep Purple record what will become *Shades of Deep Purple*, at Pye Studios in London. The album would be recorded in two days, a Saturday and a Sunday, and mixed by Derek Lawrence on the Monday, at a total cost of £1500. Quite aggressive for the day, with the power welling up from Ian Paice's at times Keith Moon-like drumming (this influence will abate over time), the album is nonetheless dated psych somewhere in the wheelhouse of Iron Butterfly, with decidedly non-heavy metal vocals from Rod Evans to boot. Ritchie Blackmore, however, is busy creating an electric din certainly as incisive as Hendrix on *Are You Experienced*. But alas, that was last year.

Deep Purple producer Derek Lawrence:
I worked with a guy called Joe Meek, and it kind of went from there, where I met Ritchie Blackmore and Chas Hodges and we just became friends. I went from there to a company called Film Music and did some things like English R&B bands, and from that I went to Radio Caroline and produced a band called The V.I.P.s, who eventually became Spooky Tooth. And Ritchie had called me and said, "I'm putting a band together; got these two managers who know nothing about music—would you get involved?" "Okay." So that's how the Deep Purple thing came about.

My feeling always was that most of the guys I worked with had started in skiffle, and so they were really good at rhythm and time. They'd learned to play in time, which, I find, a lot of the other bands speed up on the counting (laughs). And I always thought, and I still do, that most of the big heavy rock guitar riffs were actually R&B or pop bass lines, that were taken and made into guitar riffs. As far as the actual recording, we didn't really mess around that much. The idea was to record what they sounded like, and that was the hardest thing. You'll find that I usually did three albums with bands, and then didn't go into the fourth one. My opinion always was that the first album is to record them like they sounded like on stage, and what I liked, and the second one we got to more improvement, and the third was always as far as I could take them.

Deep Purple bassist Nick Simper on the original Deep Purple's inspirations:

The Graham Bond Organization, I mean, the music was just so far-out, and I think it would be termed sort of heavy rock, which it wasn't at the time. Graham was a bit into black magic and stuff. But the band itself, with Jack Bruce and Ginger Baker, it kind of changed the way everybody thought. It was just a different attack. And I was really getting into that stuff, and then along came Vanilla Fudge, which sort of compounded it really (laughs). Wow, these guys are playing so far-out and so different, the way they attack their instruments, the way they play, the volume and everything else about it. It was so different, and I think whoever came into contact with that realized that it was something very new. So when we got together with Purple, we knew we didn't want to do what had been done before, and we all kind of vaguely had liked Graham Bond and The Fudge as our, how would you say it... we didn't exactly want to copy that, but they kind of inspired us to try something entirely different. So when Purple first started, we got billed a few times in America as the English Vanilla Fudge, which we weren't really trying to be. We weren't trying to do the amazing vocal harmonies that they had because we couldn't sing that good. But they were an influence, without a doubt.

May 18, 1968. Uriah Heep forms, but under the name Spice. The band would perennially be compared to Deep Purple; indeed, the two bands rehearsed next door to each other (but never recorded in adjacent studios, as has been reported). Mick Box, famously jokes that the difference between the two bands is that Purple have one singer while Heep have five. Still, on the strength of what both bands would eventually produce in 1970, the focus will not be on the singing but a shocking nascent heaviness borne of a bold guitar/keyboard alloy.

May 28, 1968. The Rolling Stones issue in the UK "Jumpin' Jack Flash" as a single. The song is considered a repudiation of the band's fey attempts at being a psych band over the previous three albums, and its tough guitar line is another cited example within the Stones canon of a song built on riff rather than sloppy chording.

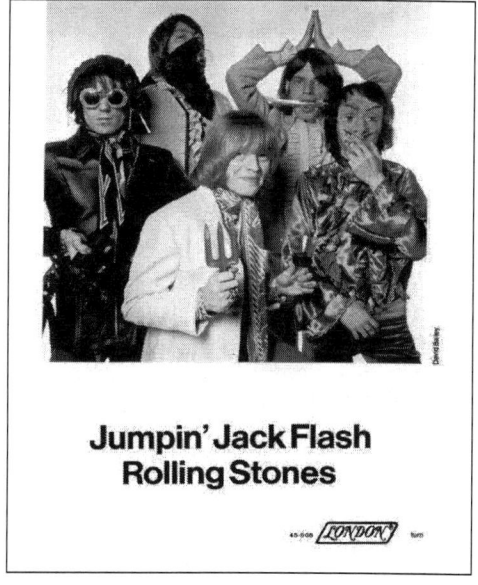

June 1968. Spooky Tooth issue a debut album called *It's All About*; the band sporadically approached and embraced heaviness but not for sustained periods.

June 1968. Vanilla Fudge issue their third album, *Renaissance*.

Vanilla Fudge drummer Carmine Appice:
When Deep Purple came out, they wanted to be Vanilla Fudge. I mean, if you listen two their first album, they were doing all the songs like we were, but heavier. And they loved us. Up until they made it really big on their own, they did have "Hush" as a single, but that wasn't where they really wanted to go. They wanted to do what Vanilla Fudge did. And you know, we have a song called

"Good Good Livin'," around '68, and I think it was a b-side to a single, and I think they took that concept and brought it home, with this heavy rock stuff that they came out with. Because if you listen to that song, it sounds like Deep Purple, before Deep Purple sounded like that. They didn't sound like that until 1970 or something. So they loved us, and Ian loved me as a drummer—he emulated me, got the big drums. You see, that was my trademark, the big drums. So he got a 26-inch bass drum and these big toms on the side, and he was a lovely guy also. So it was very easy for all of them to follow my footsteps. Once they got into that situation, they got endorsed by Ludwig, and they got a big drum set. That was the thing. Play this kind of music, you get the drums.

Led Zeppelin expert Dave Lewis on Carmine's influence on John Bonham:
I think he inspired him very much so in that first tour because John, again, had only seen the English drum setup, and he had a Sparkle kit in '68 into '69. And being on tour with Fudge he was obviously learning new things consistently, and I think Carmine had been working with Ludwig and they had the bigger bass drum, I think 26 inch or 28, and yeah, he was an influence without a doubt. I think John would be the first to say that and certainly did at the time. He was one of the most single influences, I think, on his playing, apart from the jazz drums like Gene Krupa and Buddy Rich.

June 5, 1968. Jim Hendrix goes all heavy metal and destroys a hotel room in Stockholm, Sweden, for which he's arrested on drinking charges.

June 6, 1968. Robert Kennedy is assassinated, and more hopes and dreams of the flower power generation become cloaked in doom.

June 12, 1968. *Rosemary's Baby*, the movie, is released to much success. The devil further ingratiates himself into the pop culture of the day.

> Black Widow saxophone and flutist Clive Jones:
> It was quite a big time for horror movies. Sort of the black-and-white things with Vincent Price and things like that. In fact, Vincent Price gave me... because he was on CBS, whenever he released an album, he gave me an album, which I still use to this day, of him talking about black magic and the war, and how black magic was used for good causes, as well as worshiping the devil-type stuff.

> Musicologist Gavin Baddeley on *Rosemary's Baby* and *The Exorcist*:
> Sure, those films had culture-wide impact. It would be strange if in heavy metal, you don't find heavy metal artists reacting to these films in some shape or form. And with *Rosemary's Baby*... well, *The Exorcist* is a very odd film in many respects, because

it's also an incredibly reactionary movie. The bloody novel itself is pretty much, "Get back into church, guys," for several hundred pages. And so it works for different people on different levels. But this is an area which bears a lot more attention than it's had up to now. I think it took a hell of a long time for horror movies and heavy metal to really kind of get into bed together to the extent they have today. Because any kind of mainstream horror picture will have not just the soundtrack album, but an album of songs inspired by, featuring all of the second division bands which labels are hoping to pump. But the connection goes way back. Of course, Black Sabbath took their name from a fairly obscure but very good Italian horror movie, which I understand, as far as I'm aware, they've never actually seen (laughs). Quite extraordinary.

June 14, 1968. Iron Butterfly issue *In-a-Gadda-da-Vida*, which includes the proto-metal classic title track, again a song written fully in the mode of doomy heavy metal, but arranged and produced without its sonic elements. The balance of the album is happy and dated San Francisco acid rock, save for the morose "Termination."

Later Iron Butterfly guitarist and vocalist Mike Pinera:
On *In-a-Gadda-da-Vida* the band told me that what they were trying to do was live up to their name—something heavy and something light mixed together. Doug Ingle had a lot of classical roots in his piano playing, and at the same time he could definitely write some dark songs. So that was the blend right there. So you'll hear really light, syrupy stuff like "Flowers and Beads" that was not so heavy. But on the other hand he would turn around and write "In the Time of Our Lives" from the next album, *Ball*. Very scary sounding, to tell you the truth. And so I liked that a lot. And you know it started to develop into a sound that was very much riff-based, where the guitar and bass would play the same riff, as in "In-a-Gadda-da-Vida" and some of the other songs.

Blue Cheer guitarist Randy Holden:
They had a big hit with "In-a-Gadda-da-Vida," and it was a long song. It's interesting because it had this compelling, hypnotic flow about it. That's one of the original things music was used to do, was create an entranced state so you could get into religious, spiritual mode. In the mid-east they still do that today and they actually use it as a control mechanism for society now, so I think that's what Iron Butterfly tapped into.

Now let me give you some interesting stuff to add to it. This is where musicians have always invented music from. The musical artist is someone who is hypersensitive, as a general rule, but the sensitivities are different. So throughout the ages, like in Europe, when the horses were galloping, the horses with the transportation, you heard all the Spanish dancing music and such—all those rhythms related directly to the horse. Today there's a couple guys who play nylon string guitar, and they play a combo of Spanish and mid-eastern influence; they're really outstanding. But you listen to their guitar melodies, and you hear this conversation between male and female going on. That's what's in their music. It's fantastic. And it's historic. And if you listen to mid-eastern music, like they play in the mosques over in the mid-east, that music came from the sound of the desert. These are the origins of music.

June 21, 22, 23, 1968. San Francisco's Blue Cheer play three nights at the Grande Ballroom. It might be argued that the third night out of the three constitutes the first heavy metal concert ever, with Blue Cheer (apologizing that they couldn't fit all their Marshalls into the venue), being supported by MC5 and The Psychedelic Stooges.

Blue Cheer bassist and vocalist Dickie Peterson:
That tour, I'd have to say, was probably the most gruelling. We left home and we didn't come back for a year. And we recorded the second album in the middle of that tour. The first album had come out already. We did one show with the MC5 in Detroit—Iggy & The Stooges, MC5 and us. And they were great; I loved what they did. I loved Iggy too. That night, at the Grande Ballroom was probably the first hardcore rock 'n' roll concert.

Grand Funk drummer Don Brewer:
Blue Cheer were just like this wall of sound, just loud for the sake of being loud, which was very in at that time. I mean, we did that too. We would get the biggest PA system we could get into these places and just turn it up. It wasn't about quality; it was how loud you could be. Because the louder you were, that made the audience think, "Wow! They're really big! Because they're so loud!"

SRC guitarist Steve Lyman:
I saw Blue Cheer at the Grande Ballroom, and the one thing I really remember about the show is that it was the loudest show I had ever heard. I mean, to the point, that even standing at the back of the Grande, I had to put my fingers in my ears, because it felt like someone was sticking knives in my ears. As far as what the public reaction, I almost think the strongest reaction from the public was, "Wow, they're awful damn loud." I mean, I'm used to having loud amplifiers behind me, but this was actually painful.

Blue Cheer drummer Paul Whaley:
I don't like to sound egotistical, but nobody could hit as hard as I could hit. It's just I had the lust to do it; I had the lust to be like Keith Moon, you know? This is the approach that I liked and I was able to do it. When I played a set, I didn't care if I got tired; I'd just keep playing. If I felt like I was going to faint I just pushed right on through. And this is why we could do 15 or 20 minute songs in one song, because if you didn't have the stamina you couldn't do it. So that's why we had this reputation of being a power group, because the drums could handle it. But it was a problem. Back home we didn't chum around with any bands. Big Brother was the only other band that would chum around with us. And a little bit of the Quicksilver. And the rest, they turned up their nose at us—too young, too heavy and too brutish.

July 1968. Deep Purple release *Shades of Deep Purple* in the US, which would be issued in September '68 in the UK. Oddly, the band's early success would be more so in America than on home soil, pretty much due to the priorities of the band's upstart US label.

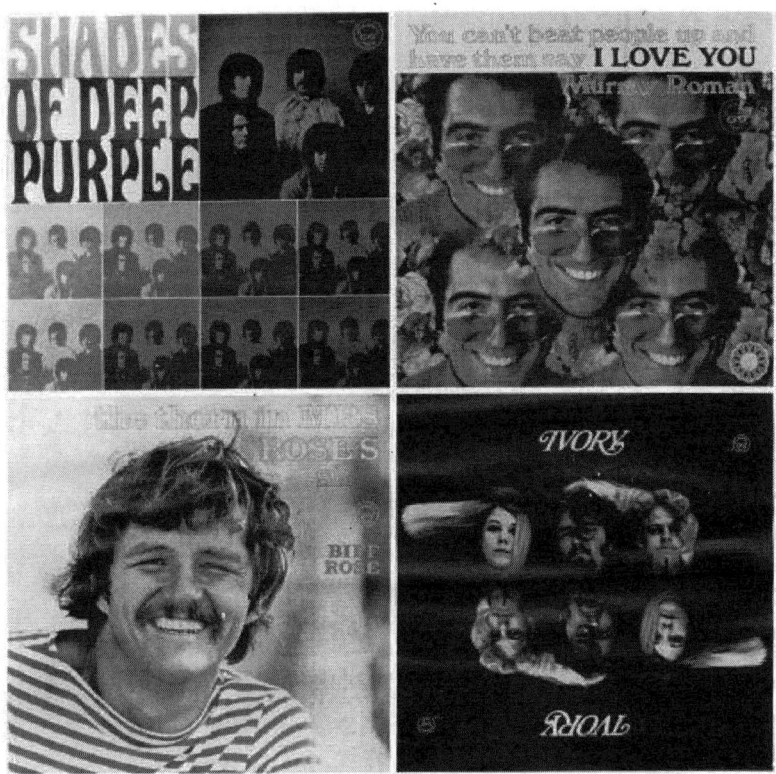

July 1968. Family's *Music in a Doll's House* is issued. It's Family's debut and is considered quite proggy and psychy for its day, but also hard-ish.

July 1968. The Yardbirds play their final concert, Jimmy Page essentially turning the page from the '60s to the '70s.

July 10, 1968. Eric Clapton says that once the current tour is done, that'll be the end of Cream.

July 13, 1968. Queen's Hotel, Silloth UK marks the last gig for Mythology, Tony Iommi's and Bill Ward's old band. The set list consisted of "Steppin' Out," "Top of the Hill," "All Your Love," "Help Me," "Dust My Broom," "All that Jazz," "Room with a View," "Morning Dew" and "Spoonful," basically proving the band a hard blues act. The band is said to have broken up because all four members of the band were arrested for possession of cannabis resin, fined £15 on May 27, 1968.

August 1968. Ozzy's and Geezer's band, Rare Breed, break up. Ozzy and Geezer from this band, join forces with Tony and Bill from Mythology, busted up a month earlier.

August 1968. Big Brother & The Holding Company's *Cheap Thrills* is issued. It's not that heavy, but includes quite extreme wailing vocals from Janis Joplin—Zeppelin-esque, even. This is the band's second and last album, as Janis goes solo in December of '68. It is the most successful album of '68, selling "nearly a million copies."

August 1968. Blue Cheer's second album, *Outsideinside*, is released, becoming a cogent candidate for first heavy metal album, given both the heaviness and riffiness of the songs "Just a Little Bit," "Gypsy Ball," Come and Get it," "Magnolia Caboose Finger" and "Babylon." Even "Feathers from Your Tree" and "Sun Cycle" contain loud, heavy parts, not to mention manic drumming and fairly aggressive vocals out of Dickie, both elements also a part of the band's speed metal version of the Stones' "(I Can't Get No) Satisfaction." All that is left is a cover of hard blues rocker "The Hunter," which, almost surprisingly at this point, stays in a garage rock zone, albeit, again, cantankerous, dangerous and loud, but alas, dated.

Blue Cheer drummer Paul Whaley on recording part of the album outside: That was a combination of everybody wanting to go another direction. I don't know how that really came up, but we just wanted to go outside and record and see how that would sound with the natural acoustics. Just some of the songs. And then the inside part of it, we got Eddie Kramer to record the inside part of it, and we did that at Electric Ladyland, and Hendrix was doing his *Electric Ladyland* album at the time. He was staying in one hotel and we were in another, and when he was not in there we would go in there and record. Jimi kept quiet about us. I never heard any comments from him at all about us. That was in New York City. And we did the outside part of it at a pier out there in New York City, pier 54 or pier 59, whatever it was.

Producer Jack Endino:
    Blue Cheer's *Vincebus Eruptum* is pretty much the first heavy metal album, as far as presenting a '70s aesthetic, almost a Zeppelin aesthetic, appearing in a '60s band. There it is—a whole blueprint is laid out. But their second album is almost like their *Physical Graffiti*, in a way. The production is way more advanced, but I don't think the concept is much different.

The thing with *Vincebus Eruptum* is that it's such a god-awful recording that it's really hard to enjoy it on any level unless you're already a Blue Cheer fan and you're already into it. It's a horrible recording, a four-track recording, and there isn't much to it. But if you pay attention to it and listen, I think it's still the same band that made *Outsideinside*. But I agree, *Outsideinside* is a much better record, and it is really like the Led Zeppelin blueprint ahead of time. I don't know if that band really got much respect at the time.

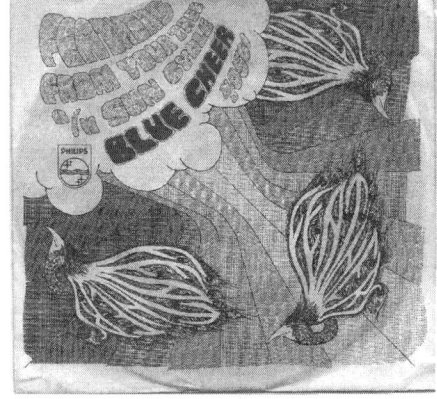

The first Black Sabbath record has something to be said for. You've got Cream, but I don't see it. You've got to give it up to the first Hendrix album too. You know, nobody called Hendrix metal. But of course they didn't really have the term heavy metal yet. It was blues, psych... what was it? Nobody calls it metal, and nobody calls Cream a metal band. We just always referred to it as hard rock. *In Rock* is a very relentless record—you can't deny that. But there you go, Blue Cheer is ahead of that time by a couple years. *Outsideinside* was '68, which is pretty early.

Stooges drummer Scott Asheton: Blue Cheer did come to Detroit, and they had a wall of amplifiers that everyone was just amazed at how loud they were, and they had the hair, and they were headbangers. I would say they were one band who evolved into a metal-type thing. The first band back then that you would call heavy metal now would definitely have been Blue Cheer.

Musicologist Christopher Knowles: Blue Cheer are really a heavy blues band; they're doing their version of Cream. They don't play as well as Cream so they make up for it with volume and intensity.

August 1968. Jeff Beck's debut *Truth* is released. The album is considered by some to be as important and pioneering in hard blues rock as Led Zeppelin's debut, although a studied playing reveals an album that is not as heavy or as imaginative as *Led Zeppelin*, or certainly *II* or the fourth. Too many covers, nonetheless there are connections. The band do Yardbirds proto-metal classic "Shapes of Things," plus "You Shook Me," which Zeppelin would record as well. Singer on the record is Rod Stewart who proves himself the closest antecedent to what Robert Plant would do with Zeppelin— over and above any actual blues singer, which, to be sure, is the way Robert would have liked to have been framed instead. Still, fact is, there's not a stitch of heavy metal on the album, just some heavy blues.

John Paul Jones on the incestuous nature of Truth, Little Games and Led Zeppelin:
Well, it was right around the same time. I was on the Jeff Beck album and Jimmy was with the Yardbirds, so my influence on the Beck album would probably be similar to my influence on the Led Zeppelin album, just like Jimmy. I don't know, I suppose. You can come to the same conclusion with any number of blues-based rock bands. But it soon took off from there. Most of the songs we had done on the first album had been done by Jimmy and the Yardbirds as well. It was only things like "Good Times Bad Times," which was a riff I brought in, that I wrote in the studio. That's got John's famous drum part, of course. John never used double bass. He did in fact bring in a double bass drum for rehearsal, and we played a couple of songs with it, but then we hid it when he went for lunch. When he came back it was gone.

Cactus guitarist Jim McCarty:
The first two Jeff Beck albums were hugely influential to me, the Truth album and the Beck-Ola album. I was with Buddy Miles at that time, which was a band with a horn section, an R&B thing. And the Jeff Beck thing was definitely what I wanted to get into. Those albums really hit me hard, and so when Tim Bogert and Carmine Appice called to form Cactus, it was kind of like perfect timing. Between Tim and Carmine, they had run their course with Vanilla Fudge, and Led Zeppelin had come over and opened for them, on their first trip to America, blowing people out the door. And Tim and Carmine looked at Zeppelin and said that's the direction we want to go in. So they wanted to do that kind of trio thing with a front man, and then I think Cream had just broken up too. So there was a huge hole there that a million different bands were trying to fill in, and Cactus was probably one of them. But nobody could replace Cream. But the Led Zeppelin thing, I think that was the motivating factor for Tim and Carmine.

August 9, 1968. Cream release *Wheels of Fire* in the UK, while America gets the record in July. Recorded from July '67 to April '68 and part live, part studio, the record would underscore the band's reputation as one of rock's new "album" acts, or "underground" bands.

Budgie bassist and vocalist Burke Shelley on "Politician" and the cooking up of heavy metal:
If you go back a few years, to Cream, you listen to something like "Politician" (sings it), you know, that's a heavy riff to me. What was appealing was guitar and bass playing in unison, which is what riffing is about, really. And making sure there's a few nasty semitones in there, slightly out of key, as a passing note into the key (sings "Politician" again). Those minor semitones. I don't know, certain classical music has that too; you can drag it out of certain classical music. But Tony Bourge's influences, he was very much into blues, as I said, and he would have some really obtuse ideas, where they came from, as you would say in America, left field or off-the-wall. He would mix his own ideas with big noise chords from Monaco or big brassy things he'd heard in musicals or something.

Blue Öyster Cult producer and musicologist Sandy Pearlman:
Vanilla Fudge had ended up doing a lot of touring with a lot of UK bands that became very heavy very soon, crushingly heavy. And Vanilla Fudge was the first band that I ever saw with way too many amps. I can't remember how many Fender Bandmasters they used, but if there were like eight or ten, tops, cabinets on stage, when they flourished in '67 and '68, if I say that, I don't think I'm exaggerating.

And I know for example the Cream, which was not heavy at all when they first came over, off of *Fresh Cream*, they went out with the Fudge, and soon enough they were OTT, completely over-the-top in terms of heaviness. We tend to forget this because *Wheels of Fire* is a magnificent record and extremely heavy, but Jon Landau trashed it so badly in Rolling Stone, that Clapton thought that he was doing unworthy and silly things, and discontinued the band, and started Blind Faith.

We can all evaluate whether that was a good idea or not, but Clapton's career, post-The Cream, from my viewpoint, is not equal to Clapton's career in the Yardbirds and of course Cream. And I think that by *Wheels of Fire* they had made some definitive statements about what textures a band should use, and the function of volume, distortion, overdrive, etc.—you know, the cult of Jim Marshall. It was completely brought to fruition by the time they made *Wheels of Fire*.

Uriah Heep bassist Trevor Bolder on Cream's Jack Bruce:
I started out from listening to a lot of the old blues players from the '30s and '40s, listening to a lot of Sonny Boy Williamson, a lot of early blues stuff, copying it. We didn't have a lot of blues albums in England when we were 14 and learnt to play, but we liked it so much that it was all we ever played. In Hull, we would go out on Saturday with what money we had from mid-day working or whatever, and we used to buy every blues album we could find.

Then along came a chap called Jack Bruce. I saw him play with Graham Bond and Ginger Baker, in Hull, before they formed Cream, and then I saw him play with Cream, and that was just unbelievable. I wanted to play like Jack Bruce, and I practiced to all his records continuously. He was unique; there wasn't anything like it before him. Before that, the bass players were just standing back playing along with the drums and leaving it for the guitar players and singers. But when he came along, he turned the bass up. For me, it was stunning to watch him play, and he was a great singer as well—it was brilliant, the way he sang, much more than Clapton. I mean, Eric Clapton was no one at the time, with John Mayall and The Yardbirds, and to me, the whole crux of the band was Jack Bruce.

Also there was John McVie from Fleetwood Mac, who was with John Mayall at the time; a lot of his stuff I liked and I copied a lot of his style. A little bit of McCartney and John Entwistle, but mainly Jack Bruce. He was the big influence for the feel; he had great feel—amazing!

August 10, 1968. Hard blues and psych act Ten Years After issue a live album called *Undead*, which features a rendition of the band's energetic "I'm Going Home." The heavy metal mania of the rote blues track is palpable, as is the nightmarish psych of the album's record cover, among others in this non-metal band's catalogue.

August 20, 21, 1968. Warsaw Pact invasion of Czechoslovakia. Czechoslovakia is invaded by the Soviet Union, East Germany, Hungary, Poland and Bulgaria to halt liberalization reforms. An estimated 500 Czechs are wounded and 108 killed in the invasion.

August 24, 1968. Polka Tulks Blues Band's first gig; they soon become Earth and then Black Sabbath, after some confusion with another local blues band called

Earth. It is said the band was inspired to call the band Earth from J. R. R. Tolkien's Middle Earth. Tolkien's fictional land Mordor was said to be inspired by the blast furnaces and steel mills of the Black Country, of which Tolkien was a local. Black Country boy Robert Plant name-checks Mordor in his own Tolkien-inspired song "Ramble On."

> Original Judas Priest vocalist Al Atkins:
> There was obviously Henry's Blues House, which was one of the main places right in the middle of Birmingham. It was above a pub called The Old Crown. Great gigs up there. You see, Black Sabbath was first spotted there. The guy who saw the band, they were called Earth at the time, and Jim Simpson, he was putting acts up there and he liked the look of Iommi and Ozzy, and he sent them up to Germany for a while, come back and changed their name because there was a band called Earth or something, and they wanted something to be heavier, a bit more blacker. You couldn't get much more than Black Sabbath, so they took off; fantastic time. There were a lot of bands coming out not just in Birmingham. Deep Purple were about the same time; I saw them in '68 and was just blown away by Deep Purple. I thought they were a brilliant band. But I think the actual metal started in Birmingham with Sabbath and then Priest coming a couple years later.

August 26 – 29, 1968. Democratic National Convention in Chicago. There are riots, plus MC5's penultimate moment, playing outside of it, the band putting on a true proto-metal concert of clang.

September 1968. Track Records issues *The Crazy World of Arthur Brown*. Arthur's histrionic vocal style—from his falsetto to his scream to his growl—becomes an influence on and inspiration to both Bruce Dickinson and Ian Gillan. The single, "Fire" (the album's heaviest and most demonic track) issued the previous month, hits #1 in the UK. An additional point about "Fire" is that its heaviness is partly derived from an ominous keyboard riff (courtesy of Vincent Crane), rather than electric guitar. The video for the track has Arthur pioneering the use of pyro, which shoots from a helmet on his head.

> Arthur Brown on the band being branded Satanic:
> Yeah, it varied from occult to... in those days everybody was looking for some spiritual, mystical answer. So we used to get people who would attach themselves to us, travel around with us, and regarded it as spiritual or occult. Oh yeah, we regularly had our equipment kicked down stairs. I remember coming to America on the first tour. It was 1967 and the leader of one of the witch's covens sent me a letter on black paper in black ink, that you had to hold at a certain angle so it would appear silver. Yeah, there was all those kind of people who read whatever they read into it. On the other hand, it was also regarded as avant garde and shock rock, with the makeup and the fire helmet, in those days. I think Alice Cooper has admitted a certain influence there. And the people in Deep Purple, Ian Gillan, from my vocal style, and then of course Marilyn Manson. And from what I've read in reviews and things, the Pink Floyd stage show was influenced by us as well. So yes, it's been there. There's been a reasonable amount of influence. And also, oh, yeah, yeah, yeah, George Clinton, Parliament Funkadelic, said he got all of his funk imagery from the *Crazy World*. Not the musical style, obviously.

Hawkwind guitarist and vocalist Dave Brock:
I saw Arthur many years ago in the late '60s, when he used to do his fire thing with his headdress on fire. Funny enough, Arthur ended up playing with us for two years as well, which is quite interesting. I went to see Arthur at a festival in Britain, and he made this great entrance, actually, which at the time, I thought he came down the steps of a helicopter, but it was a ladder (laughs). If you look, the Leslie, the organ, makes that sound, whooshing around and around, and it sounded like a helicopter to me at the time, and I was tripping at the time, and I thought wow, that's a fantastic entry, here he is coming down the steps from a helicopter. But it was a ladder, no helicopter, and he had his headdress on fire. Yeah, Arthur was good at doing that. Wonderful voice too.

September 1968. Deep Purple's debut album, *Shades of Deep Purple*, gets issued in the band's home country, three months after the record's US launch.

Deep Purple producer Derek Lawrence:
When we recorded the first album at Pye, Jon Lord, when I heard him on stage, the organ had bite. But when we went into the studio, it didn't have bite. And so the engineer on that was a guy called Barry Ainsworth, and I said to him, "Look, we've got to get something to reflect it to come back and bite, to make it really biting." So what we did was got four screens, put around the Leslie, and on the inside, we put silver paper, or tinfoil, treated it with tin foil. And that's how, if you listen to that first album, it really has a cutting organ sound. And we put like mics on each side of the Leslie.

September 1968. Cream's "White Room" is issued as a single. Not much of a heavy metal song, it nonetheless features busy lead drumming from Ginger Baker.

September 1, 1968. Polka Tulk/Polka Tulk Blues Band change their name to Earth, in and around their fourth gig. They play roughly 70 gigs in the next 12 months. By this time, the band have shed two members and become a four-piece.

September 7 - 17, 1968. Led Zeppelin mount their first tour, choosing Scandinavia. However, the band are billed as The Yardbirds. The first show is in Denmark. Significantly, the band have in their set proto-metal construct "Communication Breakdown."

Nazareth guitarist Manny Charlton:
We loved Zeppelin. They were just an extension to what was going on with the guitar bands like The Who, on from the Beatles. It went from the Beatles to The Who and then into that blues boom thing, with Jeff Beck Group. The Yardbirds and Cream, really, initially, were doing the electric blues thing. The Yardbirds moved from that blues thing to another area, where they kept the same sound but they started writing what you would call riffs, and in some cases, like pop songs. A pop song but played with that power trio lineup. Because initially when Cream started, they were doing "I Feel Free" and stuff like that, basically writing pop songs to get away from the blues, to get away from "You Shook Me." But the Jeff Beck Group took it to another level, and then Led Zeppelin obviously did as well. But their first album was basically electric blues songs.

September 27, 1968. Status Quo issue their debut, *Picturesque Matchstickable Messages from the Status Quo*. At this point the band are pure psych and not heavy, but the interesting thing about Quo is, despite their psych roots and later, major embrace of the blues, heavy metal would become so popular that the band would adopt many of the new genre's riffy characteristics, beginning with 1972's *Piledriver*.

Status Quo guitarist and vocalist Francis Rossi on discovering distortion:
We did about three singles or four singles before "Matchstick Men" was a hit, and there was this quite famous engineer. We used one called Alan Florence, and there was another one called Alan McKenzie. Now at the time, the Beatles had the whole thing of Father McKenzie, so he had the name Father McKenzie. But this was the point when there was some serious changeovers going on there because of the Beatles, really. They allowed the rest of us to start writing for ourselves, therefore dictating what we want.

And I was in the studio, and we were recording, I don't know if it was "Matchstick" or a track before. And in those days an engineer would come over and say, "Turn that down; it's distorting it, you see?" We'd already been over this with the producer at the time, saying, "Well that's how I like my guitar." A little bit of distortion, or that noise—we didn't know what it was called then. And the engineer came to me and he says, "You have to turn it down—that's distorted." And you can see it's me at 15 or 16 going, well the producer said I could leave it like that. So I was allowed to use a bit of distortion.

Then I saw everybody was starting to use fuzz box. Spencer Davis Group with "Keep On Running"—people like that had one. And Jimi Hendrix used one, and in fact I got a tax rebate, and the first thing I went out and bought was the wah-wah, which was used on "Matchstick." But the fuzz box in those days, there was a serious problem with the gain, because you would get the fuzz on the pedal, which would shrink down the size, and then you'd come back to the amp, which dynamically was twice as big. So the early fuzz boxes were a real problem but it's just great those things all came along slowly but surely.

October 1968. "Communication Breakdown" is recorded, to be issued on Led Zeppelin's debut in January of '69. It is possibly the best early example of a "machine gun" riff, or a "repetitive, down-picking guitar riff" or a heavy metal chug or, a term I've seen applied to Roger Glover of all people, "teenage eighth notes." The song would go on to be played on every tour, and it usually opened a show or was an encore. It's a rare track that Page sang a back-up vocal on. In the US it was the b-side to "Good Times Bad Times," another nascent heavy metal rocker on which all performances point to the overwhelming presence of riff. Incidentally, also in Zeppelin's early sets were various songs (some in medley form) that appear elsewhere in this story associated with different bands, such as "Hush," "The Hunter," "Somethin' Else" and "The Train Kept A-Rollin'."

October 1968. Gun, featuring the Gurvitz brothers, issues the lead-off track from their debut, self-titled album, "Race with the Devil," as a single. The song is a bit of a proto-metal classic, containing within it a driving Uriah Heep shuffle, maniacal laughing, a Satanic lyric, and a high-up-the-fretboard riff that is so much in the wheelhouse of Judas Priest, that they would one day cover the track. The cover art of the band's first album is also a first for the celebrated fantasy artist Roger Dean, and is quite a hellish and apocalyptic display. The band is called Gun. The album is very professional and ground-breaking, often proggy, shot through with horns, but also often very heavy, with some seriously distorted power chords and scorching leads. A level of intention is reinforced when Paul and Adrian Gurvitz, after a second and last Gun album, would form quite heavy band Three Man Army, and then the Baker Gurvitz Army with Ginger Baker.

October 1968. Steppenwolf issues their second album, called *The Second*. Again, the record is the work of a band rarely thinking of heavy sounds, but opener "Faster than the Speed of Light" is an interesting addition to our story, being a modern heavy metal but less so of the complex British variety, more proto- toward the simple party metal sound of Kiss and Ted Nugent. As well, "Magic Carpet Ride" from this record was a huge hit, and although it's pure toe-tapping pop rock, its opening squall of guitars is egregiously heavy—and it's a few seconds of glorious wattage that has been mainlined into pop culture continuously through radio since the day it came out. Also, there's a long, brisk jam that is quite proto-Purple, even if the rhythm guitars are weak. Point is, the music layman thinks Steppenwolf is heavy because of "Born to be Wild," the bits of this hit, plus, one supposes, John's voice and all these harrowing songs about drugs and the war and hippie life.

October 1, 1968. *Night of the Living Dead*, a key early horror movie, is released.

October 4, 1968. Led Zeppelin play their first gig under their new name. It is at the Mayfair Ballroom, Newcastle Upon Tyne.

October 16, 1968. Jimi Hendrix Experience issue their third and final album *Electric Ladyland*. Even more psychedelic and experimental than its predecessor (like *Axis*, undermining a love for heavy rock on Jimi's part), the album contains a few heavy tracks such as "Crosstown Traffic," "Come On (Let the Good Times Roll)," "Gypsy Eyes," "House Burning Down" and most impressive of all, "Voodoo Child (Slight Return)." Summary impression: even though there is much guitar lick and guitar soloing pyrotechnics all over the album, genre-wise and song structure-wise, *Electric Ladyland* is very much of its psychedelic time and not particularly modern or forward-thinking or pioneering (or intentionally heavy), certainly not to the extent that the debut was a year-and-a-half earlier.

Monster Magnet lead vocalist and guitarist Dave Wyndorf:
Hendrix is his own bird. Hendrix is totally his own thing. You can't pigeonhole Hendrix. It would be insulting him to say that he created anything besides Jimi Hendrix. I mean, Jimi Hendrix created imagination. He was just a beacon of like, guess what?! Look what I can do! And guess what you can do too, if you have half the brain of mine. As soon as you start to pigeonhole Hendrix, it doesn't fit very well. He's a fuckin' alien! Fantastic, unbelievable, untouchable. You hear his influences like blues, but they don't hang around long.

October 24, 1968. Possession of LSD is banned in the United States.

October 25, 1968. Jethro Tull issue their debut, *This Was*. The band's mix of blues, hard rock, prog and acoustic renaissance music over the next few albums impresses itself upon Ritchie Blackmore. Tony Iommi is even lured into the band... for two days.

Jethro Tull flutist and vocalist Ian Anderson:
Tony was someone we knew from the band that he played in before Black Sabbath was born. We ran into Tony at a gig when he and his band—who I think were the future members of Black Sabbath—were supporting Jethro Tull in some little gig somewhere in the latter part of 1968. He was a nice enough chap and had a nice clean straightforward guitar style, and he came to help us with a television show we were asked to do for the Rolling Stone, the *Rolling Stones Rock and Roll Circus*. We were very briefly at that and Tony came along to mime playing guitar, because actually I was the only one of us who was live on the show; the other guys were just miming. And Tony came along to do that because he was someone we played with briefly in a kind of jam session in a studio, and it's possible that if Tony's music and our music could be more complimentary at the time, then he might have become a member of Jethro Tull.

But Tony Iommi has some damage to his fingers from an industrial accident which meant that he was forced to evolve a particular style of playing guitar. For instance, it's quite difficult for Tony to play most chords across the whole six strings but he can play single notes and riffs and things, and the music that I was writing quite often was a little more adventurous from just being three chords on a monophonic guitar. So Tony would never really fit as a guitar player for Jethro Tull.

But his skills and the talents that were, I suppose, inherent in him allowed Tony to develop a physical dexterity to good effect with Black Sabbath who more or less invented an idea of riff-oriented heavy metal. But I think it was a logical step onwards from bands like Cream who were riff-meisters, and there were bands like Led Zeppelin and Deep Purple who employed these legendary guitar riffs in their songs. But Black Sabbath did it the most with riffs and the two or three note-opened chords that Tony can play with two damaged fingers on one hand. Django Reinhardt also developed his own style because he had, I guess, two working fingers on one hand.

You see sometimes this kind of adversity allows you to develop something that is your own unique style and you can excel in a way that other people might just give up. And Tony managed to turn his physical impairment around into something that makes him one of the guitar legends—if not for his dexterity of playing but at least for the fact that his contribution to rock music is a unique one.

October 30, 31, 1968. MC5 play the free admission shows, at the Grande Ballroom, that will be documented on their seminal *Kick Out the Jams* live album. Support comes from The Psychedelic Stooges.

Stooges drummer Scott Asheton on the MC5:
The MC5 were probably the heaviest, and I was a big fan. Well, so was the whole band. We loved the MC5. And I would have to say, if you wanted the #1 heavy band in Detroit, it would have to have been the MC5. The other bands were good, but they were not like heavy like the MC5 although Bob Seger had a song "Heavy Music." Then we started getting more bands from out of state that would come around that were pretty heavy.

MC5 bassist Michael Davis:
There wasn't any category of heavy metal. In fact, there was that writer who said that the MC5 sounded like a trash can rolling down a flight of stairs. It was heavy metal, but that term didn't come into usage until much later, and it didn't become a genre until much after that.

November 1968. Influential Detroit rockers, SRC (Scot Richard Case) issue their debut on Capitol Records. *Milestones* would follow in '69 and *Traveler's Tale* in '70. The band's sound is progressive psychedelic rock with very fuzzy guitar and Hammond organ.

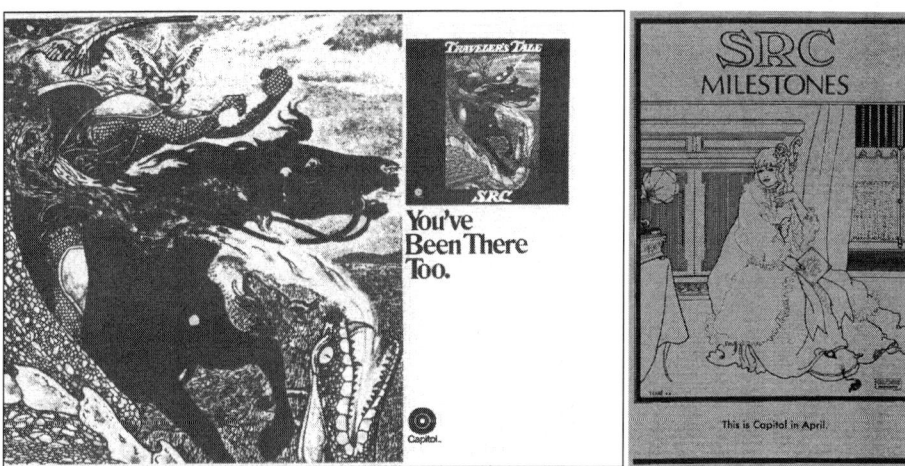

November 1968. Peter Grant negotiates a $200,000 advance for Led Zeppelin. Even the suits are crazy for that heavy music.

November 25, 1968. Beatles' *The Beatles*, or "white album" is released. Along with periodic bits of fuzz rock and quite electric guitar soloing, the album contains "Helter Skelter," a magnificently heavy, modern-sounding and riffy song, even for late 1968, proving that the Beatles (like Queen in the '70s) could be good at anything, when they tried. Paul McCartney's brief to himself was to write something as noisy as he could, and with screaming, partially as a challenge to Pete Townsend, who claimed that space for his own new single, "I Can See for Miles." Curiously, although I've had scores of hard rock stars extol the magical inspiration of the Beatles (primarily, the *Ed Sullivan* moment), rarely does "Helter Skelter" come up specifically as inspiration, although it usually comes up in their short lists of first heavy metal songs.

Beatles bassist and vocalist Paul McCartney:
I started off originally on guitar and then moved on to bass when The Beatles needed a bass player. So guitar was my first instrument that I learnt, so I love playing guitar. I didn't use to play much lead guitar because, obviously, in The Beatles we had George and then in Wings we would always have two lead guitarists, so my main thing was bass or a piano. But because I love it so much, I now like to play it. And if I'm underestimated that's okay; that means I'm better than you think.

November 26, 1968. Cream, as promised three months earlier, implode, arguably representing the death of the British blues boom, or certainly its decline. Amusingly, one of many reasons the band had thrown in the towel was because they were driving each other deaf on stage. Their last show was on this date, at the Royal Albert Hall, supported by Yes and Taste.

> Budgie bassist and vocalist Burke Shelley on the boring bits of the boom:
> Well, yeah, we were given license to do huge solos if we wanted to (laughs). Basically, you end up jamming for ten minutes in the middle of the song, don't you? And hopefully you don't bore the pants off them. But I mean, because it was new for the day, people accepted it immediately. We weren't the only who'd been doing that. The whole progressive blues thing allowed people to go off and try and be—without sounding too pompous, because it's a bit of a joke really, if you think about it—go off and try to create on the spot (laughs). But so much came out of that, you know. As you got into the '70s, it became boring. It had been done, dusted, and should have been put away, but people were still doing it and boring the pants off kids in the mid-'70s.

December 1968. Nazareth forms in Dunfermline, Scotland.

> Nazareth guitarist Manny Charlton on his guitar influences:
> Zeppelin, Jeff Beck Group, Spooky Tooth, Deep Purple—all these guys. We used to be a cover band before we turned pro and we used to do our versions of a lot of their songs. I wasn't that enamoured of a lot of the heavy bands that came out later on. Dan and Pete were very critical of vocalists. They had a very strong vocal identity and they tended to look on a lot of the bands from a vocal point of view. Dan and Pete are basically soul guys; they loved Otis Redding and Wilson Pickett—that's what they call singers. Mainly black guys. That's who their idols were as far as singing went. So a lot of the British bands, when they came out, unless it was Rod Stewart who they liked a lot, they'd scrape off the list. They didn't really care that much for the style of singing that went with these hard rock bands.

December 11, 1968. The Rolling Stones' mount the *Rock and Roll Circus*, which, as discussed, captures Tony Iommi miming a song with Jethro Tull. Tony was in the band for a brief spell (manager Jim Simpson says two days) but quickly realizes the match was bad and ran back to the lads. In essence, the event represents a moment of heavy metal intention on the part of Tony. Despite thinking this was something he'd better do for the advancement of his own career in music, at the risk of continued poverty, the guy would rather forge metal.

December 11, 1968. Deep Purple release, in the US, their second album, *The Book of Taliesyn*. It is the seventh release for the band's US label, Tetragrammaton, a venture founded only that year and going out of business by the end of '69. The album's UK issue wouldn't be until July the following year.

> Deep Purple bassist Nick Simper on Ritchie Blackmore the guitar-smashing showman:
> He was doing that right from the beginning. He had a guitar especially to break, but he couldn't break it. He bought this old Telecaster in Jim Marshall's shop; he used to drag it along the front of the stage and make noises with it and he set out to try and destroy it. Because it wasn't a very good one and he wasn't worried about it. And the funny thing was that he couldn't break it.

And I remember, I think it was about the second Deep Purple gig ever, after we came back from Denmark, and we were playing in this ballroom down on the coast. There was a big pipe that ran across the stage, tied to the ceiling, and he threw the guitar at it like a javelin, and it kind of wedged between this pipe and the ceiling, hovering there like an arrow. He couldn't break it, and in the end, the thing was so chipped and busted and smashed, he still couldn't break it.

But yeah, he was always doing that stuff. He always played a Gibson 335 which was his pride and joy for years, and once or twice he used to hold it up by the tremolo arm would kind of go to throw the guitar away but hang onto the arm, and the arm would bend. And a couple of times the screws came out and the guitar hit the deck and he was standing on the tremolo bar and the strings. So I think he realized pretty quickly that that guitar wasn't going to stand it. He turned to solids then and started bashing those about.

December 26, 1968. Promoter Barry Fey presents, in Denver, Colorado, Led Zeppelin live for the first time in the US, at the Auditorium Arena. Zeppelin supported, Spirit was the sandwich act, with Vanilla Fudge headlining.

Promoter Barry Fey on whether heavy metal was new in the early '70s:
No, look, new? Come on, I started touring Sabbath in '71, with Mountain. And I was the first one in North America to play Led Zeppelin, who a lot of people considered the first of the heavy metal bands. Although they were so much broader than that. And Deep Purple had been around, so it wasn't new. You have, actually starting in '64, the Beatles, who you just don't even put in... they're in comparable. And then you've got the holy trilogy of the Stones, the Who and Zeppelin, and you have individuals like Dylan, Janis, Hendrix, people like that. So metal might've come to the fore in the early '70s, but it certainly was in the music of the previous genre. But I think Purple was the first heavy metal. I mean, it was talked about with Zeppelin, but they were far more than heavy metal. But Purple was definitely metal.

Fellow western US promoter Don Branker:
The British bands in general had mystique and I have my own theory why. American bands for the most part were garage bands, basically with a limited amount of chords and very melodic. The English bands from that same era would go to tech school and art school. They would go to musician's school. So they were real musicians. When you look at it real quick, and you look at Keith Emerson, you look at a lot of guitar players, Jimmy Page, Eric Clapton, I mean they were real musicians. Not just players, they were musicians. So I think that had a lot to do with it, in the sense of the schooling. The English were generally more schooled musicians. We were more garage kind of bands. Look at a song like "96 Tears." That's my opinion. I've thought about it many, many, many times trying to figure out why and what happened. Why there was a difference between the mystique of one to the other.

Blue Cheer guitarist Randy Holden on Zeppelin live:
Led Zeppelin just came out, but they were doing something entirely different, and I went to see them at their gig at the Whisky, which was their first gig in California as far as I know. I liked their album; I thought they got a really heavy sound on the album, but then live they used these Rickenbackers and they're the most god-awful sounding amps I ever heard, which really surprised me. But the record really came off great.

Producer Kim Fowley on why heavy metal came from the UK:
   You had to have the English to invent it. Because you know what the Americans were doing? Joni Mitchell, Carole King and James Taylor. They were so guilty that people were fucking without rubbers in the '60s that they decided to stop being physical and be cerebral, hence you had the James Taylor, Joni Mitchell, Carole King singer/songwriter shit.

But at the same time that was going on, the English didn't embrace it as much. Instead they embraced Led Zeppelin, they embraced Black Sabbath, they were dealing with that German influence, where if you think of Judas Priest and those bands, even Wishbone Ash, people from that era, the initial gigs by those bands, Beatles-style, were in Hamburg. Germany had the air bases. The air bases had airplanes. What does an airplane sound like? A guitar in a heavy metal arena. So you had guys working on airplanes, and they want to hear the sounds of airplanes in a heavy metal state. Therefore the groups achieved that. And they also had air bases in England, and the air bases were the Liverpool Cavern Clubs for metal, and they would play in those big hangars out there in those places. You know how big an airplane hanger is, and that's where the heavy metal sonics began. And then it was recycled back through England. And when I met Kiss, they were stealing their tonal ideas from—or were certainly influenced by—Slade.

Recap

As a reminder, I'm trying to be ruthlessly reductionist with these recaps, and one of the conceptual slashing hacks that allows me to do that is to maintain the discipline that this book is, again, about looking for the band that made the album that invented heavy metal.

Ergo, our look at 1968 is mostly album-themed, although a couple of momentous stories of the live stage take place in this year as well. Beginning with the least important milestones (kilometrestones?), 1968 marks the arrival of Deep Purple, actually with two albums. Well, it's kind of a sweet and sour turn of affairs, as the band suggests to the world a confused mix of psych, classical, jamminess, covers, prog, blues and hard rock, looking not to metal with their album covers and wardrobes neither. Then there's Cream, who are stuck in the past too, but clanging away loudly at their drug rock to the point where it's impossible to ignore.

By far more important is the arrival of Blue Cheer, denigrated and stoned yokels from the country trying to make it in self-serious San Fran, also with two records in the one year. Now, their concerts, much talked about in 1968 as the next step in aural brutality—one observer said they turned the air into cottage cheese—were one thing, but this was actually a band that was able to capture and then press the mayhem onto vinyl. Which is perhaps the main factor why more people call *Vincebus Eruptum* the first heavy metal album over any other (by a slim margin), even if this book will wait until 1970 on that declaration. And the reason I disagree is because much of the record's bluster is in the sonics and not necessarily the writing or playing. So yes, although a large number of weight-watchers would declare this album the first, there is a sizeable army of us who wag our finger and say that you cannot stumble stoned into the invention of heavy metal.

But hold onto your fire hats, because Blue Cheer return before the year is out with the much more impressive *Outsideinside*, and the water are muddied. And it's frustrating, because not only do Blue Cheer return with an album that competes with their own first album, they do it before anybody gets one in in-between. Which makes the fair-minded inclined to say Blue Cheer invented heavy metal, because if the first album isn't the first heavy metal album, and even the second isn't good enough for y'all, surely the two combined—*before anyone else*—means Blue Cheer invented heavy metal.

And man, I love the way the loveable Jack Endino says *Outsideinside* is the band's *Physical Graffiti*. To me that's going way too far—no surprise on that, given that's my favourite album of all time—but he's onto something. It is a studio album, there's lots going on, and it's light years ahead of the debut. Plus it's really damn heavy for 1968. *1968*!

But here's where we lower the boom, the gate, swing the hatchet, so to speak, and I'll be blunt with it: there's still a weird and dated muddle to the band, a turgidness, even a haplessness, a confusion, a lack of intention, poor recording values, fuzz from pollution rather than high science, a psychedelic album cover, a drummer who drums like a '60s guy. I stack all this up, and yet I'm still tempted to give it to them. But in the end, I have to stick my thumb out and keep heading up the road. Still, *Outsideinside* and/or Blue Cheer have to be part of the one paragraph answer to our titular question, even if they aren't part of the one sentence answer.

Okay, enough. Closing off, the other big events of 1968 are a pair of live moments. One is the death of The Yardbirds giving rise to Led Zeppelin, who, very impressively, are playing live multiple times before the year is out, and playing some very heavy songs that will show up on their fairly important first album. Lastly, MC5 record their Halloween live appearance that will see unleashing as *Kick Out the Jams* into 1969. That's more of a 1969 story, but I just wanted to mention it because those sounds moved through the air in 1968, just like Zeppelin's, as we revisit this idea that maybe the metal is for all intents and purposes invented when the songs are written and performed in front of an audience, leaving aside that the very definition of invention might include the instance in which they are played by a band together anywhere, even in their jam space, where no one besides themselves are around to bear witness.

1969

1969. A late but disputed hypothesis about the origin of the genre or term heavy metal was brought forth by Bryan James "Chas" Chandler, co-manager of the Jimi Hendrix Experience in 1969, in an interview on the PBS TV program *Rock and Roll* in 1995. He states that, "It was a term originated in a New York Times article reviewing a Jimi Hendrix performance," claiming the author described the Jimi Hendrix Experience "…like listening to heavy metal falling from the sky." The precise source of this claim, however, has not been found and its accuracy is disputed.

1969. Guitarist Randy Holden, known for his brief stint within Blue Cheer, issues *Population II*, on Hobbit Records, although Holden himself is confused whether he would consider copies that emerged as legitimate or pirate copies only. The album is now considered a legendary and collectible album of loud, heavy psych rock. Holden by this point is sponsored by Sunn amps and is louder than ever.

> Randy Holden on *Population II*:
> Okay, now we're getting really different. Now it's way over the top. But that was the objective. There were a lot of objectives, and one of them was to be totally over the top. At the time, the music I was writing, I didn't really understand

where it was coming from within myself. I took an interest in discordant sounds. I always liked minor key scales, and I started fooling around with discordance. I'd never heard anything like that except maybe in orchestration or something.

And so that became really interesting because you had these gigantic chords through this massive wall of amplifiers, and it was so powerful. It was just unbelievable. And then you hit another chord, and there was discordance to it. And it was just like whoa, it'll scare you to death. There was a dark, ominous thing going on. It was almost like a phenomena, some kind of a magic element surrounding this *Population II* thing.

The number two kept popping up no matter where we were. There were two of us in the band and we were both born on the second of July, two years apart. And this good/evil, light/dark opposition kept appearing. The only reason my name was featured was because of the commercial interest, I suppose. And so one night in our house we were living in, Chris was walking around with a dictionary. It was right past sundown, there's some candles on, and he said, "Hey, how about this for a name?" And he pointed to Lucifer in the dictionary. I said, "Wow, that's interesting. Let me think about that." And then I forgot about it for a bit.

About two or three months later, it was like déjà vu, same exact time of day, same environment, both in the same room, and he did the same thing all over again, just opened it and pointed as he did the first time. "You remember you just did this?" He said no, he didn't remember it. I was like wow, this is weird. Okay, we have to do that. And then I took an interest in the concept because it was ominous. Most people thought of Lucifer as the devil. And I was curious why everybody thought that. Because I was trying to remember where I got the idea and I couldn't remember. And so I asked all kinds of people from all walks of life, and nobody knew. I thought isn't that strange? Everybody believes something but they have no clue where it comes from. Well is that a sign from God that you just stay away from that? Or is this just total ignorance and we're blind, deaf and dumb for some reason? Obviously, in the end we didn't go with it.

1969. Gun issue their second and last album, *Gunsight*, before the Gurvitz brothers transition to making fine, intelligent music with Three Man Army. "Dreams and Screams" is some serious wall of sound psychedelic metal mania, worthy of Hawkwind at their most fried, but the album is less persistently intense than the debut.

Gun bassist Paul Gurvitz on the softening of the band's sound for *Gunsight*: I liked the combination of strings and brass with the rock music and not many bands were using it at that time. I would say that we were one of the few bands doing that in those days. But *Gunsight* was just another side of what we liked to play. For example, "Drown Yourself in the River" was just a blues song I wrote, and the flamenco guitar was at the time something that Adrian was learning.

1969. Anton LaVey publishes *The Satanic Bible*.

1969. Michael Schenker and Klaus Meine join Scorpions, a significant personnel event. It must be said that 1969, 1970 and 1971 would feature a fair bit of hard "Krautrock," which is a genre describable as prog rock that is generally experimental, sometimes absurdist, sometimes with brass instrumentation, but also routinely dark and heavy. Scorpions would work this realm, arguably, through their first two albums, *Lonesome Crow* and *Fly to the Rainbow*.

January 1969. Brownsville Station forms in Ann Arbor, Michigan, home of the MC5, 45 minutes west of Detroit.

MC5 guitarist Wayne Kramer on the Detroit area's competitive spirit:
What most people don't know is that the culture in Detroit in the '60s was boomtown. After Korea, before Vietnam, after World War II, Detroit was a place that had four-and-a-half million people in it. Today Detroit has less than one million. But Detroit was a boomtown. It was the manufacturing center of the world. If you wanted it built, you could build it in Detroit and you *did* build it in Detroit. The factories were raging three shifts, 24/7, so there were good jobs. A guy could raise a family, buy a home, pay for his health care, his children's education, go on vacation, own a car, on one salary. Mom could stay home and take care of the kids and cook and clean. It was the deliverance of the promise after World War II, the American dream.

And with those swing shifts going around the clock, there was a great bar culture. I mean, Michigan Avenue was filled with clubs with live bands seven nights a week. And some of those places were where the MC5 learned how to play, along with bands like Billy Lee & the Rivieras and The Sunliners and Doug Brown & the Omens. They worked, week in, week out, playing Top 40 mostly. But the state-of-the-art was even more advanced because people got into comedy skits, clothes, pretty sophisticated stuff for a factory town. Because people in Detroit worked hard and they played hard and they wanted their bands to work hard. And it's a kind of sensibility that is embodied in the MC5, I think.

Mitch Ryder & the Detroit Wheels drummer Johnny "Bee" Badanjek:
It was basically a factory town; everybody had jobs working in a factory and then people wanted to party hard at night (laughs). That's the kind of town it is. So there was so much music here. Even going back to before Motown started, with the blues in '43 when John Lee Hooker and all the other blues acts that came up out of Chicago... they electrified the blues and added to what was there before. And in Detroit you've got these machines pounding and stamping out metal, and the people that do all that want to party. You know, they work hard in Detroit and they party hard and the music's gotta be hard.

January 2, 1969. Led Zeppelin begin a four-day stand at the Whisky in L.A.. Support is Alice Cooper, who perhaps slake a few ideas on a heavier future for their loopy psych rock act. It is said that the term headbanging is invented to describe kids at the front of the stages on Led Zeppelin's first US tour—a particular gig at the Boston Tea Party is often cited—banging their heads on the stage. But the accepted definition of the term, basically violently nodding one's head back and forth to the metal music, can be traced to the stage presence and persona of both Ozzy Osbourne and Geezer Butler all the way back to the beginning, both original metal-makers having been known to "bang their heads" to the music while performing.

January 4, 1969. Rob Tyner of the MC5 is on the cover of Rolling Stone.

Musicologist Christopher Knowles:
The Detroit bands, MC5 and The Stooges, they're really coming out of that whole soul, R&B tradition, which comes from the Pentecostal church tradition, which again through a very long and winding path, itself, is a result of the ancient mysteries. The tradition of the Detroit bands is definitely these R&B raves that get really intense. These guys are picking up on the energy, and what they're doing is they're bringing in this new technology of electric noise, the amps and

things like that. What Iggy and the MC5 were doing was much different than later groups like say Judas Priest or AC/DC, in that these groups are really about complete chaos.

January 12, 1969. Led Zeppelin's self-titled debut is released. The album contains seminal proto-"speed" metal track "Communication Breakdown," plus other heavy songs in "Good Times Bad Times" and doomy duo "How Many More Times" and "Dazed and Confused," both being a combination of dark, evil heavy metal and the blues. The band quickly become established as the first of the big, serious British hard rock bands, followed chronologically by Black Sabbath, Uriah Heep and Deep Purple Mk. 2.

Led Zeppelin bassist and keyboardist John Paul Jones on the band's early days: We didn't move into a style. I think we kind of created it. And if you would have asked me in 1969, as people did, what sort of band I was in, I would have said a progressive rock band. But then that became to mean something else. There you go banging up against categories again. That came to means something else entirely. And then it was just sort of like blues rock, because the band was quite blues-orientated. And it was just the style, the way the members of the band played together. But in terms of actual riffs, well, anything with notes (laughs), lots of notes, like "Black Dog," "Good Times Bad Times"... those were my riffs. And anything that was kind of lurchy and chordy were Page's riffs. That's how you tell them apart.

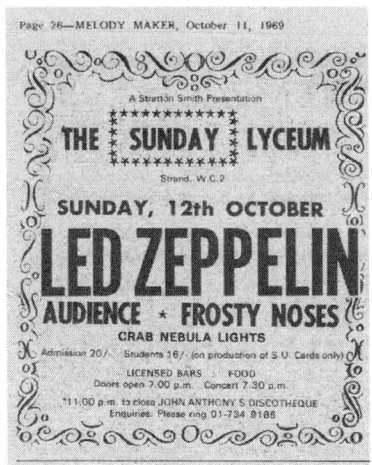

Deep Purple bassist Roger Glover, on the first Led Zeppelin record:
This album did influence me a lot because I was in a pop group called Episode Six and we were trying to get heavier and weren't making it because we were just playing the same music but louder. When the album first came out, you could tell it wasn't the loudness so much as a feeling, what you felt about the music rather than how they played it. Episode Six, as we were, weren't the right combination of people to be heavy, and I gradually gained the impression that heavy music wasn't for me because I didn't like what we were playing—loud pop music. And I decided for a time to go into folk music. I've never been so struck by an album as I was by Led Zeppelin I. It really left me open-mouthed. What they were playing was very simple stuff, loud and exciting, and it moved me. I suddenly wanted to be in a club playing that music—loud, straightforward, with simple guts. And by pure coincidence, just about that time I was offered a job with Deep Purple! But for Zeppelin, I might never have been in Deep Purple.

Yardbirds drummer Jim McCarty:
I remember Jimmy play me the first Led Zeppelin album. There was "Dazed and Confused" and there was a Howlin' Wolf-type thing, "How Many More Times" which is very similar to the stuff we'd been playing; it was similar to "Smokestack Lightning," I thought. And then there was another one which was similar. It was very well done, the first Zeppelin album; I thought it was very good. You can see the links, how easy it was to go from us to them.

Foreigner guitarist Mick Jones:
    At the time, I was cutting my teeth in France. Don't ask me how, but I'd become sort of the musical director and producer of Johnny Hallyday, who you've probably heard of. He's sort of the French Elvis, as it were. And so we would go over to England to record, and we ended up with an engineer named Glyn Johns, who at that time, he worked with Steve Miller and later The Eagles. I think he had been working with The Eagles even before their record came out. But he had worked a lot with John Paul and Jimmy when they were session musicians. And they happened to be session musicians on the stuff that I was doing for Johnny Hallyday. And so I was fully aware of who they were.

And every time I was playing with Jimmy Page, he blew me away every time we went into the studio. I had so much respect for him as a guitar player. So that's where our friendship developed. He would even come over to Paris with Glyn Johns and cut tracks over there. In fact, some of the music that we were doing with Johnny Hallyday provided the opportunity for Jimmy to work closely with Glyn Johns in preparing the first Zeppelin album. And I remember the day that Glyn took me into the studio, the back of Olympic Studios in London, and he said, "I'm going to play you a couple things on Jimmy's project." And he sat down and played me "Communication Breakdown" and it just blew me away. Just blew my mind. I couldn't believe it. I had never heard anything as mean and powerful in my life. It just left me staggered.

January 17, 1969. Iron Butterfly issue their third album, *Ball*, and by this point, the band have quite a few considerably doomy songs, that, had they all been on the same record, and had they been recorded with louder guitar, Iron Butterfly would have had a record as imposing as *Black Sabbath* (although *Ball* is the lightest Iron Butterfly yet, reversing trajectory). This is much the same argument that could be made concerning Led Zeppelin, that an amalgamation of the band's heavy material from *Led Zeppelin* and *II*—we are only having this discussion because both were issued before *Black Sabbath*—would have made one record nearly as heavy as Black Sabbath's debut, although not as doomy and not as forward-thinking or visionary—in a word, weaker.

January 17, 18, 19, 1969. Led Zeppelin play The Grande Ballroom in Detroit.

February 1969. The Amboy Dukes issue their third album, *Migration*.

February 1969. MC5 release *Kick Out the Jams*, recorded live October 30 and 31, 1968. Famous rock critic Lester Bangs' first piece ever is a negative review of this album. However, this is a very important moment for heavy metal, in that, arguably, *Kick Out the Jams* is the very first heavy metal album. To declare or believe this, we must discount *Vincebus Eruptum* as inept or unintended, *Outsideinside* as not quite power-packed or electrocuted or aggressive enough (in comparison, it arguably falls short in these departments), and *Led Zeppelin* as too dated, bluesy and at times, folky. One must also wish to plant the flag this early, putting aside the patience to wait to declare the fight for fully a year, with the arrival of Black Sabbath's *Black Sabbath*.

An analysis of the record yields solidly heavy metal tracks in "Kick Out the Jams," "Come Together," "Rocket Reducer No. 62" and "Borderline." Also, "I Want You Right Now" is heavy-ish and camp opener "Ramblin' Rose" is old time rock 'n' roll hugely heavied-up—almost made fun of. That leaves a mere two tracks. The one with the heaviest title, "Motor City is Burning" is ironically a boring, slow blues, and closer "Starship" is an acid-soaked art rock noise collage, essentially a non-track in the way an acoustic song wouldn't be, namely, it doesn't add or detract from heavy metal intention. In one respect, "Starship" is so nightmarish and squalled with distorted guitar noise that it is closer to a heavy metal experience than not.

Ergo, fact is, *Kick Out the Jams* is a very heavy album. Fact is also that it's live, which bestows upon the MC5 a particular type of unfair advantage. Adding to the discounting of the record, MC5 failed to prove intention with their next two records, *Back in the USA* from 1970 and *High Time* from 1971, and when you fail to confirm intention, your earlier set of statements feels somewhat coincidental, random, and/or accidental.

MC5 guitarist Wayne Kramer:
Kick Out the Jams was a great document if you're an MC5 fan and had witnessed one of those performances. I think it stands up pretty well as a phenomenally high-energy recording. But I always had some reservation about it, just in the nature of how events transpired around the sessions. Because the band was really rattled on that night. You know, there was so much pressure on us and Elektra Records had assured us, that if we didn't like the tapes, that we could record again. The MC5 was a very mercurial band, a very in-the-moment kind of band and was very good at rising to the occasion, to the challenge. It was not necessarily a consistent band in a lot of ways. And that was both a great gift and a great handicap. And sometimes we played not as well as other times; you know, in all candour, we missed the mark from time to time. It's what happens when you really stick your neck out. And I was felt that darn, you know, I have no regrets about it, but I know he went down and told us we could do it again and then after we did the show, they said, "No, no, that's fine; the record's done" (laughs). So that's what it is and listen, I'm proud of that record.

MC5 manager John Sinclair on issuing a live album as a debut:
I definitely wanted it. The guys say different things now, but I really thought it was a good idea. We thought it was a bold move. And we thought we could get it out faster (laughs). But I mean, the MC5 was a live band. They centered on performance. They developed the tunes to be performed by them. They would come onto them in a practice room and they would work it into a song, and they would figure out where in the set it would fit. So I mean, they spent a lot of time on the craft of presenting the show. Consequently, I thought they were the most exciting rock 'n' roll band I have ever seen. I saw them every night for two years. Every time they went on stage they were there to kill. And none of that material was old. They recorded it in October of '68, and they'd only really been writing songs for about a year. Those songs came out of performances and other jams in the rehearsal room, and they were developed through live performance. So it would start one way and then it would develop over the course of several shows. So it's really an exciting experience.

February 1969. Vanilla Fudge issue their fourth album, *Near the Beginning*.

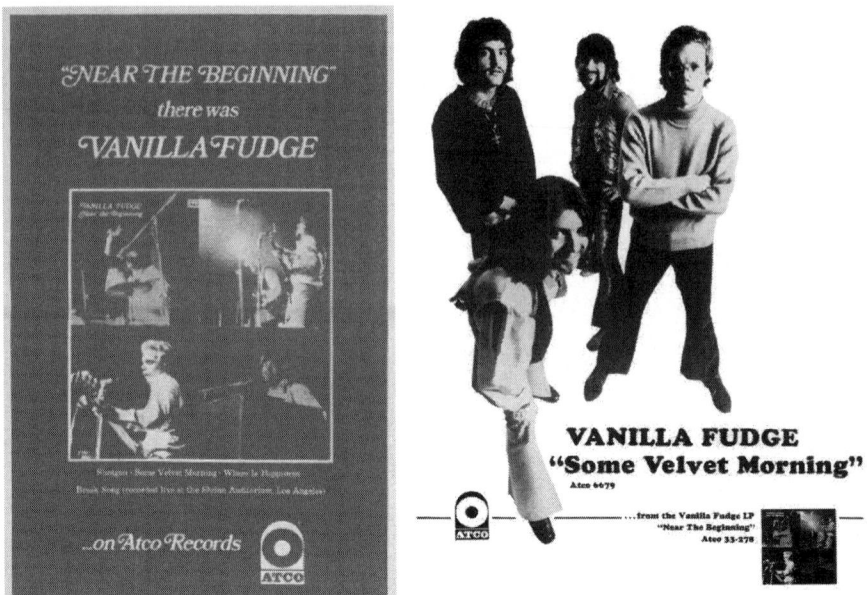

February 15, 1969. Last date of Led Zeppelin's first US tour.

February 24, 1969. Jimi Hendrix Experience play Royal Albert Hall, which turns out to be the band's last UK show ever, paving way for true blue British bands to take over the task of inventing heavy metal.

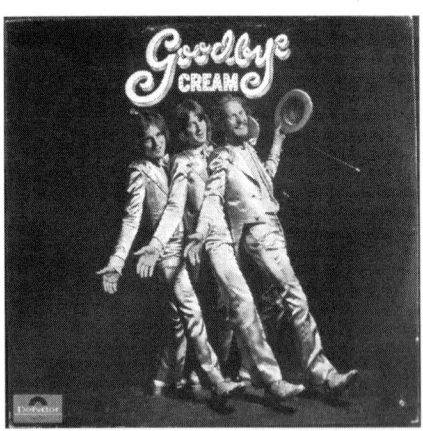

March 1969. Cream issue the gravely anti-climactic, post-break-up *Goodbye*. Recorded in October 1968, the album is an odds 'n' sods affair that fails to further the dialogue around hard rock and its advancement.

March 1969. Spooky Tooth issue a second album called *Two* or *Spooky Two*. Highly regarded, the album is a mix of bluesy, proggy and somewhat rocky material. "Better by You, Better than Me" will be covered on Judas Priest's 1978 album, *Stained Class*.

March 1969. Blue Cheer issue *New! Improved!*. It is neither. Recent arrival Randy Holden was in the process of being replaced by Bruce Stephens (not to be confused with original guitarist Leigh Stephens, who was, by 1969, onto heavy metal footnote Silver Metre), and subsequently Stephens plays on all the side one tracks, Holden on all the side two tracks.

Blue Cheer guitarist Randy Holden:
Dickie never thought of Blue Cheer as being heavy metal; he just thought of it as a rock 'n' roll band. And at the time I was interested in just being as heavy and loud as I could be, but do it artfully. And I was with Blue Cheer about a year. We just had different musical opinions. Dickie wanted to go kind of soft, quiet hippie music, as I would have called it then, and I didn't. I wanted to go bigger with more amps, and crazier and louder. And I did.

But back when I joined, I was always looking for somebody who liked to play at extreme volume like I did, and I could never find people who could get it. And when I saw Paul I went wow, those guys, they could play at loud volume. And then somebody came up to me after one of the Avalon shows. We were both on the same bill, and they said, "That's your band over there. Not these guys you're with." I said, "That's interesting."

We were actually louder when I was with them, but they just played with more distortion. Distortion gives the illusion of being loud. You could put on a pair of earphones and some of today's gear that is just latent with overdrive distortion and it would give the illusion of being loud. That's what it turned into, but that's not what it was. The illusion of loudness is totally different than the reality of actual volume. Actual volume, at great levels, can be absolutely beautiful. It'll take you away, where distortion can hurt your ears even at very low levels. Sound is a fascinating illusion.

March 1969. Alice Cooper issue their—yes, their—first album *Pretties for You*; the heaviest part of the band through the first two albums would be their long-haired, wild man band photos.

March 1969. Trapeze form in Birmingham, England; they are soon to be yet another heavy band from the Black Country and then funkier as time wears on.

British producer Derek Lawrence:
A lot of the really good heavy rock bands came from Birmingham. And my theory is, because when they were all kids, they worked at the car factories, and were surrounded always, all day by thump thump thump thump. I think most of the great American bands come from around the Motor City. We're also a bit more aggressive in our music because outside of New York, where they are so busy telling you they're busy, they don't do anything. Everything here is far more rapid. Everything is done at a higher speed.

March 1, 1969. Creem magazine begins publication, in Detroit. The magazine is started by Barry Kramer (dead at age 37 in 1981), and Tony Reay, with financing provided by The Grande Ballroom's Russ Gibb. The magazine's ample coverage of heavy metal would last through at least 1981, with much good-natured fun made of the genre's hairy personnel. Arch-rival Circus would also cover much metal, but with less of a hipster sense of irony.

March 14, 1969. Free issue their first album *Tons of Sobs*. Paul Rodgers is an example of an early hard rock front man with a powerful voice, even if the albums aren't that heavy in the aggregate. This record includes quite heavy blues rock tracks such as "Worry," "The Hunter," "Walk in My Shadow" and "The Mover." The band was slated at one point to be called Heavy Metal Kids.

> Free drummer Simon Kirke:
> I was pleased that someone picked up that awful name, and our refusal of it in the first place was justified when that group vanished without trace after a couple of years.

> Free vocalist Paul Rodgers:
> Looking at the beginning of Free, which was about 1968 or late 1967, there were a lot of things going on. There was a big blues boom going on in England, and that was very influential to us. And it influenced people like the Rolling Stones and Cream and Clapton of course. And actually Jimi Hendrix was going on too. But there was this music called... was it heavy metal? Heavy something? And there was psychedelia and there was Joe Cocker. But it was very much heart and soul music, non-synthetic. Synthesizers hadn't made any impact then. It almost looks manual, almost like a steam engine (laughs) compared to the way things are done today. But at the same time, it had the charm of a steam engine too.

April 1969. Influential Detroit rocker Bob Seger issues his first album, *Ramblin' Gamblin' Man*, the first of three records as The Bob Seger System. Seger first hit the scene in 1961, cycling through The Decibels, The Town Criers, Doug Brown & The Omens and The Last Heard, before becoming The Bob Seger System. Only relatively heavy to his times early on, he is nonetheless known for his growly voice and his salt-of-the-earth Detroit working class spirit.

> Stooges guitarist Ron Asheton on why Detroit bands worked hard:
> I know that of course New York will be a little snootier because they think they're a little more sophisticated (laughs). And California, the same. Sometimes they might really be into it but they won't be screaming and jumping around. But you go to places like Detroit, it's true, I mean, it's a little bit harder, I wouldn't say that much harder to please—they really want something for their money. You've got to really do something, and if you do, they'll let you know it. I've also always liked Cleveland. All the Midwest states seem to be pretty good party states and everyone's really got that attitude and it really does make the band play better. It drives you more and it's give and take. When they are throwing their energy at you, it's going to get you ramped up to throw that energy back.

Stooges drummer Scott Asheton on why Detroit bands rocked hard:
I think a lot of it had to do with the location, with all the factories. The people who lived there were all hard-type people, and it just reflected in the music. It's what people wanted to hear. Living in Detroit, you don't want to hear something wishy-washy and soft. You wanted it hard and drivin' and heavy. I've got a friend who says he hates the Detroit crowd. He says we've got the worst audience, worst crowd in the world, and they're all blue collar and rough and rowdy. But yeah, once they like you, they like you. They don't want you to change. They want you to keep doing what you're doing. And so in that sense I would say, yeah, they are demanding. It was hustle and bustle until the riots, and then everything changed, and everybody moved out of the city. But everyone would still go to the city, and it's still that way today.

April 1, 1969. Rory Gallagher and his band Taste issue their debut album, a self-titled. *Taste* contains a mix of very electric blues, acoustic rock, but also some pretty rocking moments, such as "Same Old Story" and "Blister on the Moon." Essentially the record is in a Cream and Hendrix zone, but with heavier production values. Follow-up *On the Boards* is much lighter, the band closing shop with a live album in 1971.

April 8, 1969. P.J. Proby issues *Three Week Hero*. It contains a medley that has as part of it, "Jim's Blues." It is significant in that it marks the earliest studio sessions ever of all four members of Led Zeppelin. Robert plays harmonica but doesn't sing.

May 1969. Screaming Lord Sutch and his famous buddies record some pretty rocking tunes, however they wouldn't be issued until early 1970.

Hawkwind guitarist and lead vocalist Dave Brock:
Yeah, Screaming Lord Sutch—poor old David—he used to play with us as well. Nice character. I saw him years and years ago in Soho, in the early '60s, because he used to jump out of a coffin. Do you remember Screamin' Jay Hawkins? He actually used to do a similar thing. He'd be in a coffin and throw the door open; Screaming Lord Sutch & The Savages, I think they were called. He was the only one who had really long hair at the time, as I remember (laughs). No, he was quite a good showman.

May 9, 1969. Slade issue their first album, *Beginnings*, under band name Ambrose Slade, on Fontana Records.

June 1969. Brownsville Station's first single, "Rock & Roll Holiday"/"Jailhouse Rock." The band would prove to be a footnote in heavy metal history, creating a hard-edged sound with a tough vocal, stylistically reminding music buyers of the boogie roots of rock.

June 1969. Killing Floor issue their visceral and professional self-titled debut. Much more than Jeff Beck's *Truth*, but significantly after it, *Killing Floor* matches up strongly to Led Zeppelin's debut, in that it too features old blues classics muscled-up in a hard rock context. In fact, the band covers Willie Dixon's "Woman You Need Love" before Zeppelin would take the root track and transform it into "Whole Lotta Love." Killing Floor also rework old black gospel song "Jesus is Going to Make up Your Dying Bed" as their own "My Mind Can Ride Easy" before Led Zeppelin would similarly do so for their own "In My Time of Dying" on 1975's *Physical Graffiti*.

> Killing Floor guitarist Mick Clarke on whether he'd heard "Whole Lotta Love" before they did "You Need Love:"
> Not at all! Had it even been recorded when we made that album? I don't remember hearing it until later. Anyway, we'd been playing "You Need Love" for some time; it was one of the first songs we rehearsed when the band was formed. It had always been a favourite of mine, and it was actually the first Muddy Waters song I ever had on record. In fact, Robert Plant was at one of our gigs in Birmingham when we performed the song. He wanted to jam at the end but we'd already started breaking down the gear so we told him no, sorry. So we like to think he got the idea from us! He'd probably tell you differently. Anyway we're not planning to sue for royalties.
> I don't know why I was drawn to the blues. Some people are, others not. Being the fashionable upcoming music of the day was certainly a help in getting the band out there, but I think I would've been a blueser regardless. We really made a conscious effort to be different. There were a lot of bands around who were really trying to emulate the original bluesmen note for note, and we didn't want to do that. So we drew influences from the rock world and pinched any idea that we liked from any source to incorporate into the music. Fleetwood Mac did indeed sound exactly like the originals in their early days, with Jeremy Spencer doing a perfect Elmore James impression and then Peter Green taking his turn to play a B.B. King song. But they were all so good, Fleetwood and McVie included, that it didn't really matter, and of course they later progressed to a more original approach. We were closer to the style of Savoy Brown, who were, like us, setting out to make their own statement about the blues.
> But they were turbulent times. We were all young and ambitious and things moved fast. If we didn't feel things were going right there would be arguments and people coming and going from the band all the time. But the reason that it finally finished really was that the blues boom in Britain was well and truly over and the European market hadn't developed yet. If we had managed to relocate to the USA as some of our contemporaries did, we might have found a new market and continued.

June 2 – July 8, 1969. High Tide work at Olympic Studios on tracks that will comprise their *Sea Shanties* album, important to mention vis-a-vis the finer points of the timing of heavy metal's birth, given the distortion and power of the finished album.

June 3, 1969. On live TV, proto-metaller Jimi Hendrix switches mid-stream in song and fires off a rendition of proto-metal anthem "Sunshine of Your Love," in tribute to the break-up of Cream.

June 4, 1969. Ritchie Blackmore and Jon Lord catch an Episode Six gig in London (Ritchie even jumps on stage for a bit of a jam) and ask Ian Gillan to join Deep Purple, their first studio jam taking place mid-month. Episode Six, having had some singles success, had begun work on their debut album which now stalls.

Roger Glover helps the in-flux Purple on some studio sessions and is also asked to join the band.

Deep Purple vocalist Ian Gillan:
I felt absolutely elated at joining Purple. When I first heard them, I had never been moved musically so much in my life. With Episode Six it was making commercial things all the time. At the time Deep Purple were the greatest band I could join. It made me realize I had to work much harder than I had ever worked before. It's very important to feel you are contributing a valid part to what is going on and I really try to contribute. I'm usually a bit of a dreamer and a hard person to work with.

Scorpions guitarist Uli Jon Roth:
Ian was fantastic from the beginning, even when he did *Jesus Christ Superstar*. You know, that was defining stuff. And I would say that if anybody in rock created the quote unquote rock sound that thousands of singers ended up copying, it was Ian. Before that we maybe have Robert Plant in Led Zeppelin, but Robert was a little bit more blues-based, coming from that kind of area. But Ian gave rock this kind of incredible bel canto edge, almost like an opera singer, in rock, without any of the opera kinds of sounds, but equally valid. That is so hard to do for most people, and I think he just single-handedly created that genre. Or least he's the first one who really had it down to a fine point with "Child in Time" and all that.

June 21, 1969. Deep Purple release their third album, a self-titled, in the US, with the UK issue following six months later. The album stalls at #162 in the US, the band's worst result yet, and fares even worse in the UK.

Deep Purple bassist Nick Simper:
When they said go in the studio and do the third album, we didn't have any

material. But we managed to cobble some stuff together, and because we had actually been together for over a year-and-a-half and we had done a hell of a lot of touring—toured America twice, been all over Europe—I think the direction was really starting to come together; we really started to change. There was a lot of pressure from Jon Lord to do this kind of semi-classical stuff, which Ritchie Blackmore always thought was a little... well, we didn't actually rebel against it until the third album. But we weren't as keen on it as Jon was, because he was dominating the band. And gradually it came around to the guitar being a bit more dominant.

Deep Purple producer Derek Lawrence:
The first three albums did great in the states. They did nothing in the UK. They were kind of seen as a singles band, because we put about five singles out. The musicians all knew that they were great musicians, but it wasn't looked at as anything different. I think they were a heavy pop band. The changes were when Nicky Simper and Rod Evans were let go—and that had probably as much as to do as my fault as anyone's. Because I was a song man. With Rod, we had to spend a lot of time tuning up his vocals. Nicky was a great bass player, but he was like a rock 'n' roll bass player. He had come up with Johnny Kidd and Screaming Lord Sutch. I mean, he put a band together, and I think at some stage I was supposed to produce it, but never did for some reason, called Warhorse. That, to me, just sounds like an insipid heavy rock band.

But my favourite on the third album is "Why Didn't Rosemary?" because they had all gone to the cinema to see *Rosemary's Baby*, and that was written about that. "Hush" as well, because it was a great pop song, and they did a new version of it; it was different and it was exciting. And I suppose I like "April" because that was starting to go where they were going.

Mid-1969. Andromeda release their self-titled, lone album. This is John Du Cann, pre-Atomic Rooster and the record is considerably heavy for 1969.

July 1969. Leslie West issues "solo" album *Mountain*, a considerably heavy record often left out of the discussion. Fully metal are "Blood of the Sun" and "Dreams of Milk & Honey." "Blind Man" is as heavy as one could take a slow blues. Elsewhere "Look to the Wind" and "Southbound Train" are mid-heavy, as is Leslie's carb-load take on Dylan/Danko's "This Wheel's on Fire." But added to that fairly weighty percentage of heavy songs is the muscular production job and the menacing, growling vocals of the big man himself.

July 1969. UK freaks Edgar Broughton Band issue their debut, *Wasa Wasa*, on Harvest. It is the first of a handful of albums, and the only fairly heavy one.

July 4, 1969. The Atlanta International Pop Festival, on which Grand Funk distinguishes themselves with a raucous set, leading to their deal with Capitol. Four albums later, Grand Funk would use a photo of themselves from this show as the gatefold for *Live Album*, even though none of the material on that album is recorded there.

> Grand Funk drummer Don Brewer on Grand Funk guitarist Mark Farner: Mark loved to reach into the outskirts of what a guitar should sound like. He didn't want to sound conventional. When we first hooked up with West Amplifiers, it was a little amp company that was out of Flint, Michigan, Mark went up to the guy and said I want it to sound like this; I don't want it to sound like a Fender. I don't want it to sound like a Sunn. I want it to be loud and big but I want it to have a certain... this real gravelly, edgy, overly clean and distorted at the same time sound. He was very much into creating his own sound. And he played a Messenger guitar, which nobody has ever heard of. It's all painted up, it almost looks like a Frankenstein, and the f-holes are taped over and it's just a ragged-ass looking guitar, but it had a very unique sound.

July 10, 1969. Ian Gillan's first show with Deep Purple, at The Speakeasy in London, ushers in the Mk. 2 era.

July 14, 1969. *Easy Rider* is released. it is a dark hippie movie with a shocking ending that graphically offers a literal depiction of the death of the hippie era. Furthermore, links are suggested between motorcycles, leather and rock music.

July 25, 1969. Deep Purple Mk. 2 issue their first release, the "Hallelujah" single, b/w "April Part 1," same b-side in both the UK and the US. The single is significant in that it informs us that despite the new lineup, Deep Purple is not yet crafting nascent heavy metal.

August 1969. Guitarist Mick Bolton introduces his band mates Pete Way and Andy Parker to a singer called Phil Mogg, and UFO is born, with the band changing their name to UFO from Hocus Pocus in October of '69.

UFO drummer Andy Parker:
When we first formed and did our first album, it was kind of a mishmash, but it had a bluesy background to it, because that's where we were coming from. The late '60s, blues was huge, with John Mayall & The Blues Breakers, Chicken Shack, Savoy Brown. That's where I was coming from when I met them, and then we went into our experimental space rock thing on the second album, and then naturally we start to progress, especially when we got Michael Schenker back in '73. It was a natural progression because he was in that genre of guitar playing. He was a harder rock guitar player than maybe we had before, because Bernie Marsden who was in the band, he was very much blues at the time. He went on to join Wild Turkey with Glen Cornick and that obviously led to Whitesnake. When Michael came along, we said this is what we want. Coming from Scorpions, they were a bit heavier, with that heavier, Teutonic influence.

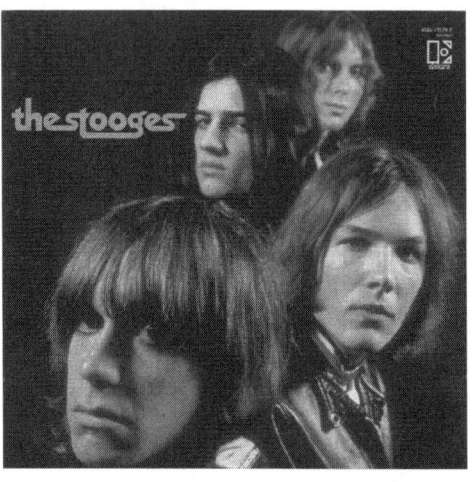

August 1969. The Stooges' self-titled debut is released. The album contains lots of proto-heavy metal songs such as "1969," "I Wanna Be Your Dog," "Not Right," and "Real Cool Time." Billboard says the band "feature a rough and raw Rolling Stones-type sound that glitters with the addition of strong lyric content and sophisticated pop execution."

The Stooges is another record in our growing list of full albums that can be called the very first heavy metal album. Once again, as we move through time, expectations of what constitute heaviness necessarily intensify and the bar is raised. If we can agree that we want to discount the first two Blue Cheer albums and *Led Zeppelin*, then we might put *The Stooges* up against *Kick Out the Jams*. And then *Kick Out the Jams* gains points for being heavier and earlier, whilst *The Stooges* gains credence by being a studio album.

Indeed, many watchers of this stuff will cite this album as one of the first, but let's not forget, there's a reason that just as many smart people call The Stooges the first punk band or frame *The Stooges* as a proto-punk album, perhaps the first within the punk genre but left out of the discussion altogether when it comes to heavy metal. And let's also not forget that the same sentiments get voiced about MC5. In other words, there's a validity there, a sense or a clue that the "metal" from these bands is from a whole different philosophical tradition, which can be tapped and examined to inform us why sonically and structurally, these Detroit bands are fundamentally different from Black Sabbath, Deep Purple and Uriah Heep.

Stooges guitarist Ron Asheton, on recording *The Stooges* with John Cale:

It was my first time ever recording, so that was a trip, a little bit nervous, and he was actually wearing a Dracula cape the first day. It was like wow, I knew who he was, but I'd never met him. I think we had seen him play in the Velvets, so I thought, well, this is cool. It was his first job as a staff producer at Elektra Records, so they thought that would be a good combination. It was our first time in the studio, but I knew he knew his way around the studio.

The one thing was, though, we only knew how to play loud. So we had Marshall stacks, Marshall bass stack, Marshall guitar stacks, and of course it's on ten. And he goes, "Wait a minute, this isn't how it's done in recording. You can't have this much volume and loudness." So we'd go, "Well, this is how we play. We kind of really need to have this to do what we want to do and get what we need to get." So we had a sit-down strike (laughs). We actually struck and said, well, we're not playing then. And just went in the other room and just sat there. And so he came in and, "Hey, we're working, all right?" I mean, we knew that too, but we were pretty stubborn. So I think our compromise was nine. Turn it down to nine.

It worked out well because it was just a little rectangular room, and it just had little baffles and barriers. So if there was any bleed, it was good. That's what we thought—well, it doesn't matter, it doesn't have to be that isolated. The simplicity of it really worked well.

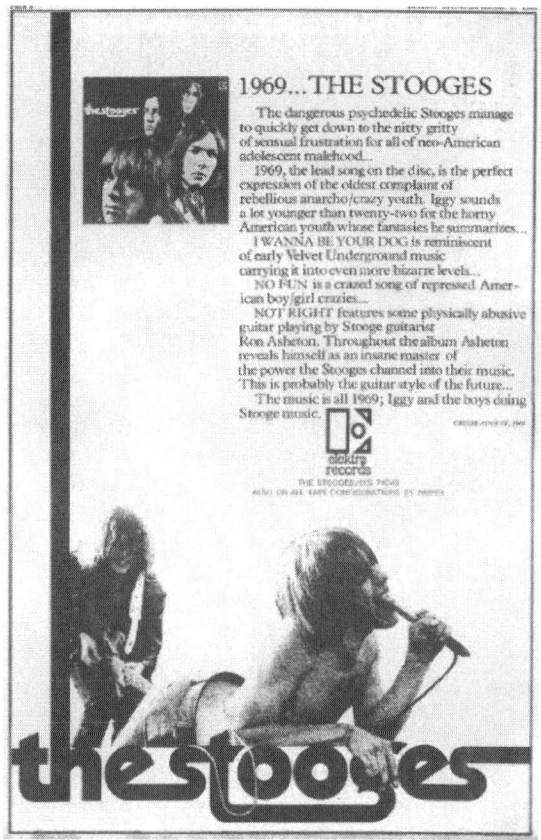

August 1969. Hard act around Flint, Ann Arbor and Detroit, Grand Funk Railroad issue their first album, *On Time*. It is the first of the band's three albums to be certified gold in 1970 alone.

August 1969. Blodwyn Pig issue their first of two (original band) albums, *Ahead Rings Out*. The band is an offshoot act for departing Jethro Tull guitarist Mick Abrahams, and their sound is folky, blues, proggy, with a bit of brass and heaviness—very much a Vertigo band but on Island instead. Producer on both albums is Andy Johns.

Blodwyn Pig brass player Jack Lancaster:
The only agenda I can remember was to play and have fun—and we did! Mick was very relieved to be able to play and record his own brand of stuff without hindrance. To my knowledge, he never regretted leaving Jethro Tull. Mick wanted to move in a different musical direction. If my memory serves correct, at the time he was thinking of going melodic/acoustic. However, he changed his mind and formed quite a loud band. After all, he is more than slightly mad.

August 1969. L.A. jazz guitarist Emmett Chapman discovers a new guitar tapping technique with both hands held perpendicular to the neck from opposite sides. Chapman would soon invent the Chapman Stick, made popular by bassist Tony Levin.

August 1969. Psych band The Glass Prism set the writings of Edgar Allan Poe to spooky acid rock on their *Poe Through the Glass Prism* album. Not heavy at all, even if "Alone" sets the blueprint for Cliff Burton's "(Anaesthesia)—Pulling Teeth" on the *Kill 'Em All* album. What is interesting is that the ad promises "hard rock guitar," yet there is very little of that on the album. Record ads hyping the heaviness of albums that turned out not to be heavy persisted through the '70s, which begs the question, if heavy metal sizzle sells, why not make the music, the steak, as heavy as the ad copy?

August 1969 – February 1970. Deep Purple work on tracks that would become their seminal *In Rock* album, variously at IBC, De Lane Lea and Abbey Road.

August 8, 9, 1969. The Charles Manson/"Helter Skelter" murders in L.A., which represent the death of the innocent '60s, although the event is one of a handful of cultural touchstones to do so. America finds out that hippies are not all peace and love, a revelation that would also come to Black Sabbath, who will represent a new pessimism, cynicism and fatalism amongst the ranks of the very hairy.

Black Widow saxophonist and flutist Clive Jones:
We were the first to do black magic in rock but it did bounce back against us. I mean, Black Widow had the most bad luck that any band could ever have. First of all, the BBC wouldn't play our records, because preaching the occult to the kids is not a good thing. And "Come to the Sabbat" would've gone to #1, but if you don't hear the song, that's the end of the story. And we were also going to tour the states, and then Charles Manson did the black magic murders over there, and they stopped us going to the states. And as you know, we were sort of rivals—or in the press anyway—rivals with Black Sabbath. And our management also took on Black Sabbath, which got very confusing. And when we couldn't go to the states, who did they send? Who didn't have anything to do with black magic?! (laughs). So they actually went on our tour, with our road crew, would you believe?! Which was a bit naughty, but fair enough. We always got on well enough with them.

August 9, 1969. Jethro Tull's second album, *Stand Up*, hits #1 in the UK.

Jethro Tull flutist and vocalist Ian Anderson on the band's hard rock influences:
That's kind of difficult, because then we're talking about real contemporaries. We're talking about Led Zeppelin, The Who, and people who we actually played alongside, and were contemporaries of, or rode quite closely on their coattails, just a little bit behind them. Led Zeppelin are a good example because they

weren't just about being hard rock. They too had a very folky and acoustic side to them and curiously, like I was, were also pals with Roy Harper. So there was some cross-fertilization. So Led Zeppelin were a good example of a band who were known for one thing but were not really trapped by it, where a lot of groups I think really were trapped by a certain kind of success. Whether they could, and just didn't want to do anything different, it must have been a bit of a limiting factor for the MC5 or the Ramones or even Status Quo. You did a certain thing and that was it. You really couldn't do anything else and get away with it. Even Black Sabbath, the same kind of feeling. You know, you would have to like that an awful lot to want to just do that and nothing else.

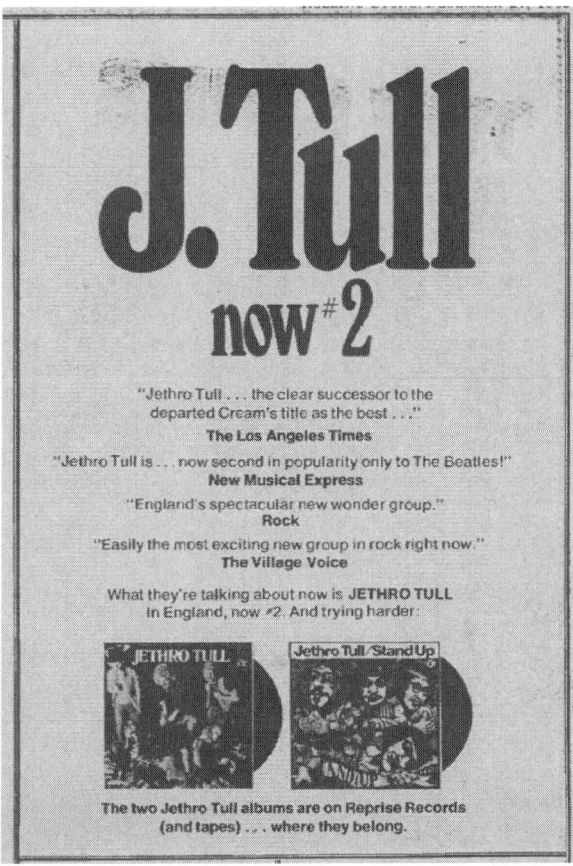

August 15 – 18, 1969. Woodstock takes place in a farmer's field. The monumental festival, rock's most famous, is considered the apex of the peace and love hippie generation, the good to Altamont's bad. The highlight was in fact a "heavy metal" moment—at the hands of Jimi Hendrix, who closed the entire three-day event at an ungodly 11:10 AM on Monday morning. Almost as brutal on the senses was The Who, turning in a raucous performance Saturday night at the wee hours of 5:00 AM into the Sunday morning. Conversely, the most heavy metal band on the bill, Mountain, hit the stage at a civilized 9:00 PM on the Saturday, sandwiched between two bands that I'm sure didn't approve of Leslie's noise, Canned Heat and Grateful Dead.

August 22, 1969. Earth/Black Sabbath record Norman Haines' "The Rebel" at Trident, with Rodger Bain producing.

August 30, 1969. Black Sabbath play their first show as Black Sabbath, according to Tony Iommi.

Black Sabbath manager Jim Simpson:
With Sabbath, a lot of people try and read into them more than they actually were. They were a blues band that had come to the end of the road with the blues. I mean, British blues was getting really bad press over here, because all the bands were playing the same thing, and they didn't really capture the feeling of... Not Zeppelin, but everybody else didn't really capture the feeling of the blues they were trying to copy. I mean, a few bands did make it on the blues thing, but there were ten million bands all looking the same, playing the same, wearing the same denim jackets and denim trousers, smelling the same—there were a million of them.

Promoters did not want to book blues bands. That's why I opened this club in Birmingham one night called Henry's Blues House—to give sanctuary to blues bands. There were some great blues bands being lumped in alongside the boring bands. And everyone tried to get out of it.

So the main thrust behind Sabbath was to create an identity, and not be seen as just another blues band. And that was the driving force—to be individuals. And that's why we looked at jazz, because nobody else was looking at jazz. There were some elements. They never, ever, wanted to become a jazz act. We thought together, because of my knowledge of jazz, there might be something from jazz that we could call upon and adopt, and we used it to make our sound different to everybody else's. In the end, when things like "Black Sabbath" were written, that was the turning point, that was the direction, and the word jazz was probably never mentioned again.

September 1969. Judas Priest is formed, with no classic lineup members, indeed with no one that would be in the band for their first record in 1974. The existence of Judas Priest is of huge importance because some would argue that Priest invented heavy metal, against the heavy rock or hard rock of their predecessors, through their very much "next level" albums of the late '70s, through their unified, codified and concise leather and studs visual presentation, and through their self-identification as a proud heavy metal band.

Original Judas Priest vocalist Al Atkins on Birmingham's ties to hard music:
It's maybe to do with the industrial area here, which we call the Black Country. You don't see many guys sitting on the foundries playing acoustic guitar here. It's a rough... well, it was rough; it's not so bad now. But in those days it was a lot of industry, steel mills and everything around the place. There's a lot of bands coming out of here. Led Zeppelin was coming out of the blues boom thing, weren't they? As were a lot of bands, who wanted to do a bit more Cream and Hendrix but spear-headed with a heavier blues feel.

I don't know, I just think Sabbath was the one. They came out about '68, they'd come out of the blues thing as well, called Earth. They were spotted up in Henry's Blues House in town, a lovely old crowd pub, which is a great place for everybody to meet. Plant, everybody. Judas Priest played there, I think it was '71 or '72, with Trapeze. I think that's what really happened. It was Black Sabbath trying to do something a bit heavier, a bit different, and they made the way for a lot of bands like Judas Priest.

Robert had teamed up with Jimmy Page, and I remember seeing them live in a place called Mother's in Birmingham, and they were still doing a bit of a blues thing there but gradually got out of that. I think everything went much louder, much heavier, and with some pre-shock tactics before punk come out. With the names, upside down crosses, Judas Priest, Black Sabbath; everybody's trying to shock the world into a heavier sort of music. Brilliant time.

September 1969. Vanilla Fudge issue their fifth and final album *Rock & Roll*. Even though none of the albums are too particularly important to the metal story, five albums of some heaviness is a significant accumulation.

September 1969. Status Quo issue their second album, *Spare Parts*—it is the last for the band in a psychedelic rock direction.

Status Quo guitarist and vocalist Rick Parfitt on the shift in Quo's sound:
In the early days, when you're young, one strives to find a direction to go in. I was playing guitar, and I didn't have a set direction. I could play this, I could play that style, I could pick a bit of country. And then Francis and I, in about 1969, we were in Germany, and we went to this club, the place called Bielefeld, in Germany, and we heard The Doors doing "Roadhouse Blues," which of course went "da-da, da-da, da-da." And we sat there and we looked at one another, and it was just one of those moments that you were never going to forget. This infectious boogie rhythm just got hold of us, and we thought well, we've got to have some of that. And consequently, Quo is known now for the 12 bar shuffle. And that changed our lives, just going into the club that night, and hearing The Doors play "Roadhouse Blues"—changed everything.

September 13, 1969. The Toronto Rock and Roll Revival, the site of the famous Alice Cooper chicken incident, in which a chicken thrown off the stage by Alice gets torn apart by the crowd.

September 24, 1969. Deep Purple perform Jon Lord's *Concerto for Group and Orchestra*, with the Royal Philharmonic Orchestra, conducted by Malcolm Arnold amidst exhaustive UK and mainland European Purple tour dates through to August 1, 1970.

Deep Purple guitarist Ritchie Blackmore on whether he was aware he was one of the first to incorporate classical into hard rock:
I suppose in a way. There was another band out at the time called The Nice, Keith Emerson's band, and they were doing similar stuff to what we were doing—they were doing classical music rocked-up. So I suppose the music I do with Blackmore's Night is not so different from the music I was doing then. It's just that I'm not doing it with such a loud guitar, but mostly acoustic. But the progressions are very similar and the arrangements are similar to what we would have done back in those days. But I've always been impressed with the classics. They have a sense of drama, a sense of depth that rock 'n' roll doesn't have for me so much.

September 26, 1969. The Beatles issue *Abbey Road*, which includes "I Want You" (She's So Heavy)," which is considered one of the first rock songs in drop D tuning, a future tool in the heavy metal box. The result is a hypnotic doominess.

September 26, 1969. This later date than those listed previously is another one for Earth changing their name to Black Sabbath, although to add yet another, other sources for this happenstance state August, 9, 1969. A small gig notice exists listing a Black Sabbath gig in early 1969, however this may have been for an obscure French band apparently called Black Sabbath. Further grey area surrounding the name of the band stems from an assertion that on August 23, the band is said to have played their last gig as Earth. We dwell on this because manager at the time Jim Simpson makes an interesting point upon the way that Sabbath had discovered heavy metal, intimating in interviews that it was somewhat inspired by Geezer coming up with the name Black Sabbath and the attendant lyrics and imagery, that the riffs were inspired by the willingness to talk horror in titles and lyrics.

Black Sabbath vocalist Ozzy Osbourne:
Why we got to be called Black Sabbath and why it was very dark, we used to rehearse early in the morning in a civic centre. And across the street was a movie theatre and it was Geezer or Tony that said, "Don't you find it strange that there's a horror film and people are paying money to get scared? Why don't we start writing scary music?" And we poor kids thought that was great. We didn't realize that there were people that practiced black magic and all that. But Black Sabbath was not all about Satan. We wrote about things that people were thinking, but not really talking about. Now they are talking about global warming. We were talking about wars and its effect on mankind. Geezer was a phenomenal lyricist— he still is.

Black Sabbath drummer Bill Ward:
    The name, Black Sabbath, Terry—that's Geezer—Terry got that from the movie by Boris Karloff. So when we had written "Black Sabbath," we were still the band Earth. And when we were showing up to play "Black Sabbath" as the band Earth, there was another band called Earth that was showing up as well, and they were playing popular songs and they were I guess putting on a very professional show (laughs), and they were nothing like these scruffy people from Aston. So we had to change our name from Earth, and Geezer had suggested using the name Black Sabbath for the band's name, and I think that happened when we were crossing from Dover to Dunkirk on the English Channel. He came up with that idea and we went, "Yeah, that's it, good, we've got it." We had made the song "Black Sabbath" first, and then Geezer suggested, "Let's just call it Black Sabbath." We had already named the song after the movie.
    All of us were interested. Just like a lot of people when they're growing up, they become interested in all that and Black Sabbath was no exception to that. So we were interested in scary movies, and it was observant. I mean Tony and Geezer in particular, they were very observant of and aware, that people liked scary stuff. So I don't know how much went into a contrived effort to make scary music. What was actually real in those first few songs that we did—in other words, the difference between organic and commercial—I always like to feel that those things came out of it naturally and exactly as they were supposed to be. But I know that those ideas of making something scary, that was something that was bantered around. But at the same time we were all looking into other aspects of the supernatural or God or religion or anything else for that matter. We were kicking the tires on everything, checking everything out.

Early booker of Black Sabbath Norman Hood:
They were originally doing sort of blues covers. I suppose it was their own interpretation of probably Chicago blues, but obviously with a bit more of the old pyrotechnics. It was probably only about 12 months or so from me knowing them until they evolved into Black Sabbath. We'd booked them at my club, The Pokey Hole, which was at the back room of a pub. They went to Hamburg for a little while, came back and it was Black Sabbath, in my pub. They announced the name change for the first time from the stage, then proceeded to take the roof off the place. Practically closed it down, in fact, because the people in the bar couldn't keep their glasses on the table, they were that loud. So the evolution was pretty quick. They went from doing quite a lot of derivative material to writing their own very, very quickly, and the black magic thing as far as it went was sort of... just icing on the cake, really. Part of the change in name and song. I was knocked out by it, totally. I'd heard one or two of their own numbers, obviously. They had been playing their own numbers. But I think the mere attitude they got, more than anything else... I mean Ozzy was always a bit of a nutter, but his attitude had totally changed when he came back. He was even more of a nutter and louder than ever.

CEO of Gibson, Henry Juszkiewicz:
Tony Iommi's an incredible musician. I remember talking to him and where his musical origin came from. Tony was an accordion player. I said wow, Tony, accordion to heavy metal. That's quite a stretch. And he still plays the accordion. But he's a great musician and he's innovative. It came from a deep part of him and once you get to know the individual you can kind of see where it came from and how sort of both those parts of his musicianship are able to co-exist.

Quartz drummer Malcolm Cope on the blues roots of Black Sabbath and the wider Birmingham scene:
There's a couple of their early songs, like "The Wizard," with the mouth harp, I'd call that's blues. And they were a blues band when they were Earth. Well, everybody was in that period. Everybody was copying John Mayall. Robert Plant, who grew up literally minutes from me, he was in a proper blues band as was John Bonham. John used to come around here and borrow my drums. Recently I teamed up with an old girlfriend who I was going out with at the time when I was 17, 18, and she said to me, don't you remember when Bonham and Plant used to knock on your door to borrow your drums, and you got fed up with it, that on one occasion, we hid behind the settee pretending not to be in the house? We also had The Move. What they were trying to achieve when they put it together was they wanted to be in the same framework as The Who. So basically it was aggression; they were trying to show a sense of power through aggression, that's where their link was with heaviness.

Black Sabbath manager Jim Simpson on fans' acceptance of the band:
    The kids always liked them from the beginning. From the very first date they played for me, for an intermission slot, the crowd responded. Not ecstatically to start with, but there was a response, which is more than you get from most intermission bands. The press were deafening in their silence, because they didn't fit any mould. You couldn't say they were like so-and-so or better or like so-and-so, but worse—there was no ticket to put on them.
    And we really battled with the media. The media was very cruel to us to start with, because they didn't understand what was happening. And I was constantly having to make excuses for them, the media, and explain why it was good. Maybe I wasn't aware of other bands around at the time as much as I maybe

should have been. But I mean, facts will prove me right or wrong, but my feeling was that Sabbath were in front of the bands, time-wise. The Purps, and who was the other one? Uriah Heep were later, weren't they? In fact, I lost a drummer from my other band, the Bakerloo Blues Band—he went to Uriah Heep. And the Purps, they were a bit pompous, weren't they? I mean it wasn't real people's music. It was stadium rock in its infancy.

With Sabbath, there's no pretension there at all. I mean, Ozzy's honesty showed through his vocals. That's what carried it. From the soul. Also, like some of the great jazz things like Jimmy Rushing, it comes from deep in the stomach in some way. It isn't conjured up from the back of the mouth. It comes from deep inside. And Ozzy did holler really well. That's a trademark of the blues. The blues were absolutely there. They were a blues band—you must remember that. They were a blues band.

October 1969. Free issue their second album, a self-titled, which is actually less heavy than the debut, *Tons of Sobs*.

Free vocalist Paul Rodgers on a shared blues influence with Led Zeppelin:

I do remember doing a show with Free and Alexis Korner actually, because he took us on tour with him. And he was a mentor for Zeppelin in the early days as well. See, that guy got around. And the Rolling Stones too. He was an amazing guy, now that I think about it, wow. We were playing at the Railway Tavern in Birmingham, I think it was, or the Railway Arches, it's a club underneath the arches of the railway, if you see what I mean. We were playing with Alexis and then he got up and played. And then he asked people up to jam.

Well, he asked this very tall guy with long blond hair and he was wailing away, playing blues, and it turned out to be Robert Plant, before Led Zeppelin. And we got talking. We stayed in things those days which were called bed and breakfast; so you got your bed and you got your breakfast and then you were out. So he came back for a cup of tea and we had a chat, and he said he had an offer from a guy in London to put a band together and the guy was called Jimmy Page—have I heard of him? And I said yeah, a lot of people are talking about him. He's a big session guys and there's a big buzz about him in London. And he said, he wants me to form a band and he's offered me like 30 quid a week or a percentage. What do you think? And I said, "Go check it out, but take a percentage" (laughs).

And it was so funny, because the next thing was Led Zeppelin. And of course, Peter Grant managed them, and then years later when Peter Grant was managing Bad Company, we got to talking, and I told him this story and he stopped and looked at me and said, "*You* told him percentage?! That was *you*, was it?!" And I said, "Peter, Peter, whoa, it was a long time ago. I hadn't met you guys yet!"

October 1969. High Tide issue the considerably heavy *Sea Shanties* album. The band's second and last, a self-titled, from '70, is quite a bit less heavy. *Sea Shanties* is nonetheless an important bridge record from the first two Blue Cheer albums to Black Sabbath in that the guitar tones are massive and distorted, and howling at the solo end. Musically, there's the brutishness of Blue Cheer, but also a frantic progginess, not to mention quite a bit of violin, given the presence of future Hawkwind violinist Simon House.

October 4, 1969. Deep Purple's set list at Montreux in Switzerland is "Speed King," "Hush," "Child in Time," "Wring that Neck," "Paint it Black," "Mandrake Root" and "Kentucky Woman." Also, along this tack of the band playing songs that would emerge on *In Rock*, it is likely "Speed King," known as "Kneel and Pray," with different lyrics, was played earlier. It is also known that "Into the Fire" was played in 1969. By mid '70, the band had "Black Night" as well. The important point about this is that Deep Purple had already written and performed some truly "next level" heavy metal songs in 1969, tightening the time span between Purple's contribution and Black Sabbath's with respect to what is essentially a newly invented style of music that officially arrives in 1970.

Earlier Deep Purple producer Derek Lawrence:
I just think that they wanted to be a real pumping band. You've got to remember, by the time *In Rock* had come, there had already been heavy rock bands out there. And so I'm sure they were influenced by that, or Ritchie kind of said, "Yes, that's where it can go. That's where I want to go. That's what I hear."

Deep Purple bassist Roger Glover, on the band's pathway to heavy metal:
   I think when Ian Gillan and I first joined the band, they had been to America, and "Hush" went very high in the charts. They'd done a couple of tours, and they were full of stories about America. We had never toured America as Episode Six. And they were full of stories, and certainly about the women, the music, the bands, the clothes, the experiences they had. And Vanilla Fudge and The Flock and It's a Beautiful Day, they got mentioned, but in the meantime, Jon had written this concerto which we did; I think it was our sixth gig with the band, Ian and I.
   And it was really right into the deep end, pardon the pun. And there was a feeling in the band that I think Ritchie wasn't that into it. He felt like we were a rock band, and this was kind of toying with artsy fartsy stuff a bit too much. But he gave Jon the okay, go ahead, we'll do it. And so we did it, and the reaction it got was that Jon Lord got hailed as the maestro of the band, the leader of the band, the main composer of the band, and that further kind of got right up the noses of Ritchie and Ian Gillan, in particular. And to a certain extent all of us.
   So there was a desire, really, to be a rock band, in the face of this diversity. And I think, looking back on it now, had we not done that concerto, Deep Purple *In Rock* wouldn't have been as hard as it turned out to be. There's a real determination to say who we were. I remember turning up doing several gigs, and promoters would be there, and they'd go, "Where's the orchestra?" You know, so the identity of the band was a bit mixed, going into *In Rock*. I read an interview of Jon's just a while ago, and he was saying that in the early days of the band, he was more of a musician and a writer. He had more the experience while Ritchie was the rocker. But he had more breadth to his composing talents. So I think yeah, it was more keyboard-oriented.
   But I love *In Rock*; it's where we found ourselves. So obviously, it's one of my top albums. And it's where the stage shows that we were doing... because we recorded it in-between gigs, and whatever studio at the time that was free. It was recorded in IBC, in Abbey Road, and finally in De Lane Lea Kingsway. And what was happening live was that the band was really exploding. And yet we were in the studio trying to make a sedate record. And I think on that album, the shows were coming into the studio. The live performance shows came into the studio. And I think that's what defines Purple. Because Purple is essentially a live band, and making records is a by-product. Because it really was vicious. And dutifully recorded by Martin Birch.

Deep Purple drummer Ian Paice on the band's influences:
Not so much the English bands. Fudge was very important to those first couple of albums, when we were into the big arranged stuff. But Mountain was on the scene then, and we thought they were great. So that sort of crept in. Hendrix was still really important to us, even though the heyday had gone and it started drifting down. Cream was very important. These bands that had the ability to play and then go somewhere else. Okay, that's the verse, let's do something else

for five minutes. Sooner or later we'll get back to the verse again—that's okay. So the bands that actually played were always in our consciousness.

October 7, 1969. Black Sabbath record a cover of Norman Haines' "When I Came Down" at Birmingham Arts Lab (Zella Studios). "The Wizard" is also recorded.

Black Sabbath drummer Bill Ward on "The Wizard:"
That was a real sod to figure out. There are a lot of movements, just like "Symptom of the Universe." So doing that live, way back when, because we don't do either of those songs now unfortunately. But being on stage in the middle of a tour, those songs are really quite, not difficult, but you had to be pretty physical to be able to play both those songs, especially "The Wizard" because it actually doesn't stop for the drummer from the beginning to the end. There's no actual time, so I'm actually just pushing it through with all the different rolls and things like that from top to bottom (laughs).

October 10, 1969. King Crimson issue their debut, *In the Court of the Crimson King*, which includes "21st Century Schizoid Man." If Deep Purple could be said to be a hard rock or heavy metal band with prog characteristics, King Crimson are the most obvious example of an original-era prog band with heavy metal characteristics.

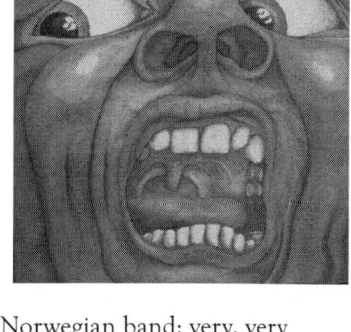

King Crimson bassist and vocalist Greg Lake on "21st Century Schizoid Man" influencing heavy metal players:
I think we did, in a way, yeah; I think we did. It is a very heavy track in that sense. Funnily enough, I heard a version of it the other day by a Norwegian band: very, very heavy, indeed! They played it at half-speed. So I see the connection with heavy metal in it. But again, it was used by Kanye West in his song "Power," so it has a lot of different ways of being interpreted, I think. But it still sounds contemporary to me, that song.

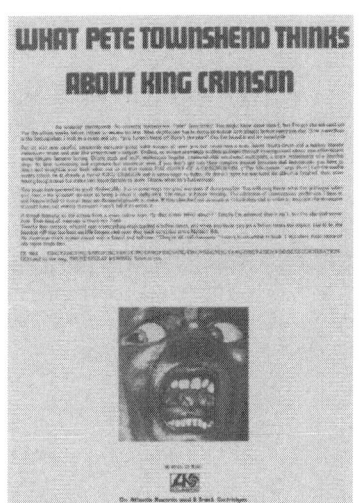

Author of *Mean Deviation*, a history of progressive metal, Jeff Wagner:
The book opens with King Crimson basically, and I put them in there for a number of reasons. Robert Fripp himself, the guitarist of King Crimson, said that he commented a couple times in the '70s how Crimson was metal. He said that when David Cross, their violinist left, "Violin has no place in heavy metal," and I'm paraphrasing a little bit. Then, he also described the song "Red" as "metal in 5/4 time." Also quoted in the book. I think that's interesting, and he's right: you can look at King Crimson as having a bit of a metallic element to it before there was even metal as we know it today.

October 16, 1969. According to Tony Iommi's autobiography, this is when Black Sabbath record's their debut album, *Black Sabbath*, at Regent Sound. He clearly states that it was recorded in one 12 hour session and then the band were off to play in Switzerland. There is some controversy however on these dates, as there is a demo tape that has the album being recorded on "17/11/69" and "18/11/69." This brings up the issue of whether the work took place over two days, and whether there was confusion over marking the tape with a 10 or an 11 for month, and whether Tony's date in the book was off by one day, lacking one extra day, and/or off by a whole month.

The demo tapes show "Beyond the Wall of Sleep,' "Black Sabbath," "The Wizard" and "N.I.B." being recorded on day one, with "Sleeping Village" and "Warning" being taken care of on day two. As well, other sources claim October 12 and October 13 of 1969.

The author is inclined to believe Tony's version, and indeed, through many interviews with all four members band, has been told on a few of those occasions that the album was recorded in one day, which plausibly then would indicate that it was recorded in one day and tinkered with and mixed the next.

In any event, is heavy metal invented at the point of recording, or is it when the *Black Sabbath* album—the one best answer to our titular question from an album standpoint—is disseminated to the public? In between those two solitudes—we've discussed this elsewhere but it's worth reiterating—is heavy metal invented when it's played live in front of people? And to put a finer point on it, is heavy metal invented when a certain number of songs of a certain heavy metal quality, are played in front of people?

October 22, 1969. Led Zeppelin's *II* is released. The album contains seminal metal track "Whole Lotta Love" (based on maybe the most famous old school metal riff outside of "Smoke on the Water"), plus "Heartbreaker," "Living Loving Maid," "Ramble On" and instrumental "Moby Dick," which represents an early example of drop D tuning in rock. "The Lemon Song" is a heavy blues and "What Is and What Should Never Be" balances a light verse with a heavy chorus.

Working against the album's positioning as smart new music is its pervasive blues structuring, but properly modern are "Whole Lotta Love" and "Living Loving Maid," the former for its chug, the latter for its briskness and its fiery response lick, a proper riff. Zeppelin, at this point, are now the undisputed kings of British hard rock, and pretty much the most obvious proto-heavy metal band, depending on one's opinion of the more "garage rock"-based acts from America, namely Blue Cheer, MC5 and the Stooges. As an additional trivia note, Eddie Van Halen has said that he was inspired to explore tapping from seeing Jimmy Page do it live on "Heartbreaker" in 1971.

> Led Zeppelin engineer Andy Johns:
> It was fairly obvious from the beginning that Led Zeppelin were of a different ilk. Pagey had taken it to a new place, and my brother did the first album, and there was a little bit of a falling-out about production, a bit of a war about that. The second record, they started touring in America and were breaking down some walls and doing very well. I did a couple of tracks on that, and then obviously Jimmy Page and John Paul Jones, I had known since I was about 14 or 15. I mean,

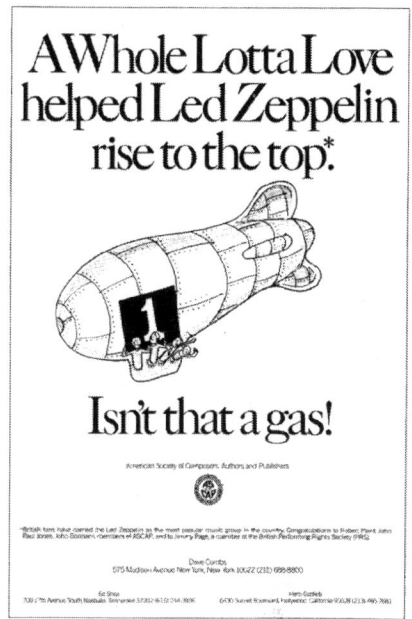

Pagey, in fact we were from the same town, Epsom, and John Paul, I had known from when he used to play a lot of sessions and he would do arrangements as well. And I had to deal with him where I was only 17, I would polish his bass and help him with his gear, and then I would go, "John, show me the lick from the Fontella Bass thing." "Oh, that's easy; well, it goes like this." And he would pass the bass over and he would go, "That's it; there you go." And then one time when he went on his lunch break, I picked up the bass and played it without asking! How he knew, I don't know, but he came back from lunch and looked at me and said, "You've been playing this, haven't you?" It wasn't all peace and love. It was, "Hey man, you can't do that." But then he started going on about, I'm going to make a million pounds in the next two years, and I went, "Yeah right, John." And of course he did.

UFO drummer Andy Parker:
There will always be the blues, but it was getting harder, edgier. If you think of Zeppelin's first album, there were so many blues songs and traditional arrangements. I wouldn't say they stole them, but you know what I mean? They were coming from the same thing as The Yardbirds. And then by the second album, "Whole Lotta Love," they'd taken it and hardened it up, and I think that's where we were all going then. There are always trends. Like I said, mid to late-'60s, we had the blues trend and you don't necessarily follow the trend, but you can't help but be influenced by it and swayed by it when you're surrounded by it everywhere you look and listen.

October 31, 1969. The Black Magic & Rock 'n' Roll Festival, otherwise know as The Black Arts Festival, Olympia Stadium, Detroit, which includes America's most prominent occult rock act Coven. A poster for the event reads: "Witches, Devils, 6 PM – 3 AM. Tickets 5:00." Acts listed are: Arthur Brown, Dr. Tim Leary, Frost, MC5 (whited out), Ralph Adams, Mystic Peter Murkos, Amboy Dukes, Bonzo Dog Band, Stooges, Coven, Pink Floyd, Savage Grace, Kim Fowley, Alice Cooper, Sky, Teegarden & Van Winkle, Satan (Ainsley), SRC, Frut, Bob Seger, All the Lonely People and Pleasure Seekers. A second poster reads: "Mike Quatro, Russ Gibb and Mike Keener present A Black Arts Festival" with the highlighted bands being MC5, Stooges, Frost, Bonzo Dog Band, Bob Seger System, Arthur Brown, SRC, Pink Floyd. One fan has documented that the show turned out to be a rip-off, with no performance by the likes of Pink Floyd, Bonzo Dog band, Alice Cooper, The Frost, MC5, Arthur Brown or The Amboy Dukes.

> Coven vocalist Jinx Dawson:
> That was in Detroit in 1969, Halloween. Iggy was there, Grand Funk was there. I would have to get out my old scrapbook to remember who was there. Anton LaVey was supposedly supposed to be there but he never showed. Timothy Leary was there. Timothy Leary, on the next night, we weren't allowed to do our full show at the festival, but we did the "Gran Dio," and Leary was there running up and down the aisles yelling, "Stop the show; this is evil" (laughs). So this was a great moment, and here I was thinking Timothy Leary was so great and he was saying, "Stop the show." The police pulled us off the stage in Detroit. They said if we spoke English to the audience that they would stop the show. So I, of course, after four songs, I saw it falling through, the whole thing, because we were supposed to do this big opera and stage show, and they came in, the government officials came in before the show and made us run through our show, a couple hours before they were going to open, and they censored everything we did, and no English. And I was really ticked off. We almost didn't go on the show, and after the fourth song all I said was, 'Happy Halloween, Detroit,' and they pulled us off the stage and took us back into the police holding area, and stopped the whole concert.

Fall 1969. The lineup for southern hard rock band Blackfoot solidifies, under the name Hammer.

November 1969. Dutch rockers Golden Earring issue their (depending on how you count) fifth album *Eight Miles High*. Often left out of the discussion of heavy metal invention, it's time to correct the record. *Eight Miles High* is a considerably heavy record for 1969, in general containing elements of Black Sabbath, Atomic Rooster and heavy Jethro Tull. The drums bash, the vocals soar and growl, the guitars are doomy, but there are keyboards and the guitars are often not bold in the mix. Also, one half of the record is a 19-minute jam of The Byrds' "Eight Miles High," which, in its original is often talked about as proto-hard rock. In the hands of Golden Earring, it sounds like the jammy bits of the *Black Sabbath* album.

November 1969. Black Cat Bones' only album, *Barbed Wire Sandwich*, is issued. The band is notable for having Paul Kossoff and Simon Kirke in the lineup at one point, who were gone by the time of this album. Foghat's Rod Price was also in the band, and on board for the album. It's an album that is heavy post-blues boom in nature, but it is more than occasionally brought up in kitchen table drunks about early heavy sounds.

November 4, 1969. The Allman Brothers Band issue their self-titled debut. It is mentioned here only because the Allmans are one of the originators/innovators of twin leads, courtesy of Dickie Betts and Duane Allman.

November 10, 1969. Black Sabbath record Crow song "Evil Woman," at Trident, with producer Rodger Bain. Recall that "Evil Woman" will emerge as both a single and as a track on the UK version of the album, but not the US version.

Early book of the band Norman Hood on where Sabbath got their heaviness:

I don't know if they actually had influences, as such. I mean, everything was happening so fast in those days. Bear in mind, I'd seen Cream on their debut performance a couple years before, and that was basically still blues rock. There was no psychedelic touch or heavy tinge to them, and they were the actual cutting edge then. Then all of a sudden it was like Zeppelin and Sabbath—I suppose maybe The Who were the newest link before Sabbath.

But the thing with Sabbath is they did it totally opposite to how bands had gotten noticed before. They didn't bring a record out, they didn't get any press other than some fairly bad press—they just worked. They played clubs, would go down really, really well, get booked back again; they were on the road all the while, and they built up a grass roots following that was just tremendous. It's not something that could be done a few years after that. All the smaller clubs had disappeared and the college circuit was probably preeminent then. But the mix of people as Sabbath got better known and as they played, they built up their own following, and this is before they recorded. We began to get people from the outlying areas and from Birmingham, travel across to us. People from out of town, which was unusual at that time. We had one or two other decent bands on, but Sabbath were the big pull, always.

But Tony, he developed his sort of 25-minute guitar solos, which were usually—bear in mind this was the back room of a pub—usually played with somebody hanging around his neck with a pint of beer (laughs). And of course the volume had gone up quite considerably. But once they sort of settled into it, then it was obvious that it was something that was going to be really, really special.

November 16, 1969. Black Sabbath play Rugman's Youth Cub. No significance to the show other that the fact that we know what songs they played: "Black Sabbath," "Let Me Love You Baby," "A Song for Jim," "The Warning" (an Aynsley Dunbar's Retaliation cover that will show up on the debut), "Wicked World," "Behind the Wall of Sleep," Early One Morning," N.I.B." and "Blue Blood Man." At this point, what is interesting is that there are still blues (boom) covers and that there are no songs that would show up on *Paranoid*. What is also interesting is that Sabbath are subjecting punters and liggers to a new kind of music, heavy metal, in 1969.

> Black Sabbath drummer Bill Ward:
> We were influenced by blues and some jazz, and some really standard-type blues things that everybody was playing. So we were still very much embedded in that, including versions of some John Mayall and Blues Breakers, like "Hideaway." I've forgotten the other ones. They were both instrumentals but Clapton played lead guitar. My turn towards Eric Clapton came with the Yardbirds, but when the Yardbirds were playing at the Marquee Club—that's when I first noticed Clapton. So we were still actually quite young, just coming onto 18 years old, 19 years old. But our first initial, really big influences were from the British blues scene, if you like, but also from what was coming from America. We had already learned all the basic rock 'n' roll stuff from America when we were kids. I mean, when I was 14, I learned "Johnny B. Goode"—we learned all the Chuck Berry stuff, like every band back then.

December 1969. Coven issue *Witchcraft Destroys Minds & Reaps Souls*. Jinx Dawson, vocalist, is an avowed occultist. Two more albums follow, in '72 and '74, and all have their heavy moments. The first song on the debut is called "Black Sabbath." While Black Sabbath wears regular crosses, Coven wears them upside down, right on their album cover. On the back, they also flash the devil horns made famous by Ronnie James Dio. Their bassist's name is Oz Osbourne!

> Coven vocalist Jinx Dawson:
> Well, we used to come out in coffins. Let's see, we did part of the mass on stage. It was very theatrical. I'd call it a rock opera, basically. And nobody was doing this. Nobody! Arthur Brown had some fire on his head, but that's about it. So we did actual real ceremonies and included the music in that and it was just something that wasn't done. I came from an opera background and I also came from a family that was left-hand path, and that is for real, you know what I'm saying? That is not a made-up thing. They had a big mansion on the farm, and

when I was a kid I grew up in all of that. And it was something they wanted to hide. I got in a lot of trouble with my family for even doing the first album, and letting out secrets that nobody had known before, like the sign of the horns. The inverted rosaries, nobody was doing that. I mean, find me one (laughs). Find me somebody who was doing it before Coven.

I don't know how we did manage to even get the first album made, because a lot of people were like, "What the hell is that?" I think it was a little more not known about, so I think at that point it was more like curiosity. But it really wasn't out there. Arthur Brown was more like a show person, more like shock rock, but we were a little more on the serious side. Nobody did the inverted rosaries. Nobody did a black mass. We were the first recorded ever black mass. Nobody did the sign of the horns. Again, it was just something that I felt I wanted to get out, because I had grown up that way. But I had a lot of problems getting it out.

Musicologist Gavin Baddeley:
Coven were a band who seemed to create quite a bit of shock. Again, rather localized. There is a common phenomenon within particularly occult rock, whereby you will record the one sort of demonic album that will attract all the negative press, and the fans looking for demonic material, and then someone in the band would pipe up and say, well we've been quite successful, wouldn't we be more successful if we got rid of all this hoodoo shit? And they would agree and record another album minus the hoodoo shit and disappear without trace. And Coven had had a hit single, courtesy of a drive-in movie, after their first album. And I've interviewed the lead singer Jinx Dawson, and she paints the picture of an incredibly lurid stage show, including a live crucifixion on stage, and at the climax of the gig, the ersatz Jesus leaps off his cross and walks off into the audience and then casts Bibles around.

December 1969. Black Sabbath signs to Philips Records. Their first single would emerge on Fontana, but newly poached record exec Olav Wyper has plans for Sabbath as one of the first acts on his hip new Vertigo imprint.

Vertigo founder Olav Wyper:
Yes, well, we were looking at the same time for where this was going to go, in terms of other acts, and I went to Birmingham for a meeting, and went on the wrong day, a day early, so I had to spend a day in Birmingham. I was staying in a hotel, and I went downstairs and said, "Is there any music in Birmingham?" And the chap, the concierge said, "Oh, I think there's a classical concert at the City Hall." And I said, "No, I wasn't looking for that. I was looking for some rock music." And there was a young lad who worked in the hotel who said, "Oh yeah, there's a pub that I pass on the way from the station to here called The Railway Arms, and they have music downstairs."

And I went in, and there was a band playing. And in those days they used to stamp the back of your hand with an ultraviolet stamp, so if you went out and came in again, you could prove that you had already paid. And the bloke stamped my hand and did a double take and did another double take, and I thought, "Oh shit, I've been recognized." Which indeed I had been.

But I went in, he didn't bother me, and the band wasn't particularly wonderful; they were coming to the end of their set, and then while they went off and the next band was getting itself ready, I suddenly noticed that the hall was filling up, the room was absolutely getting packed. Everybody who'd been at the back of the bar had all gotten fresh drinks and were all going down to the front. So they obviously knew who was coming and wanted to see it. And that was Black Sabbath.

So within a very short space of time I decided we had to have Black Sabbath. So I went, in the interval, out to the chap who stamped my hand and recognized me, and I said, "Are you something to do with the band or are you just promoting the gig?" And he goes, "No, I'm promoting it and I'm their manager as well, Jim Simpson."

My judgment, a lot of it, was based on what the audience's reaction was. If the audience loved them, then they had something. And on Vertigo, we didn't sign any band that wasn't a working band, and that couldn't deliver live. And the great thing about Sabbath was they had an instant communication. This was their very early days, their first album, and they had an instant communication with the audience. They had very good songs, very good rhythms, Tony Iommi, the guitar player, was absolutely stunning. His solos were just brilliant. Ozzy was obviously a good singer. The whole thing just worked brilliantly.

December 1969. The Frost, featuring Dick Wagner, issue *Rock and Roll Music*, the follow up to *Frost Music* from earlier in the year. *Rock and Roll Music* is recorded live at The Grande Ballroom, and both records are fairly hard-hitting psychedelic blues records.

December 1969. Deep Purple issue their experimental classical album—impossibly titled, but known as *Concerto for Group and Orchestra*—in the US. If anything (and it isn't much), the album underscores or represents the idea that heavy metal becomes invented when it sheds influence from the blues and adds influence from classical music.

DEEPER PURPLE

Deep Purple, once memorable for a gaggle of Top 40 hits, last summer embarked on a bold musical experiment with Malcolm Arnold's Royal Philharmonic Orchestra in London's Royal Albert Hall. For the occasion, Deep Purple organist Jon Lord composed a *Suite for Group and Orchestra*, which resulted in a couple of hours of intriguing music, uniting the more exciting ingredients of rock and the classics.

Fortunate are we to have a splendid stereo recording of this wildly-acclaimed event, now available at better record shops everywhere under the enticing title "Deep Purple and the Royal Philharmonic Orchestra." This live recording of a new and Deeper Purple, not to mention the Royal Phil, will amaze and delight the discerning.

Deep Purple deepens on Warner Bros. albums and tapes, where they belong.

December 1969. Thin Lizzy form in Dublin, Ireland, remaining quite acoustic and peaceful until 1973's *Vagabonds of the Western World*.

December 1969. Blue Cheer issue their fourth album, a self-titled. Dickie Peterson and Bruce Stephens have carried over from *New! Improved!* but the band has added a keyboardist, Ralph Burns Kellogg, while drummer Paul Whaley has been replaced by Norman Mayell. It is the band's first album as a four-piece. They were already out of the conversation on the last album and they remain out of the conversation with *Blue Cheer*.

December 6, 1969. The Altamont Speedway Free Festival in Northern California, headlined by the Rolling Stones, results in lots of violence, one murder, and three accidental deaths. The event-gone-wrong is considered the death of the '60s, or at least the death of '60s psychedelic rock, an idea foisted up the Manson murders as well. It is a rare large festival of the day with no heavy rock, just heavy security.

> Blue Öyster Cult bassist Joe Bouchard:
> Well, 1969 peaked with Woodstock, and then Altamont came along, and the first song that we did in Blue Öyster Cult, "Transmaniacon MC," referred to Altamont. So Altamont was the nail in the coffin for the hippie peace and love generation. The writing was on the wall, and that didn't bother us at all. That was okay.

> Black Sabbath drummer Bill Ward on dark music for dark times:
> I think the way that music was going, in this almost kind of, "Everything is going to be okay; all you need is to have love," and things like that, and again I have to say, categorically, that is not a slam on the Beatles. They're one of my favourite all-time bands. I love them; I love "All You Need is Love." But when

the songs were coming out, it wasn't like that for us in Birmingham. They were very good songs, but even the Beatles weren't living in Liverpool anymore. A lot of bands had moved to London, but poverty still existed, and crime still existed, and verbal abuse still existed. And not only in Liverpool, but in a lot of the cities, Newcastle, Manchester, tough cities, you know?

It was nice, the idea of peace, man, and wearing flowers in your hair, but the reality was, if you looked the wrong way on the streets where I came from, you'd get beaten to a pulp. That's the reality. So that's where all the emotional stuff comes in. That's where it's like the "Fuck you" comes in. And there was a lot of "Fuck you." And why there was a desire for us to play loud in Birmingham and why we just made these, almost like violent gestures in our music and in our live appearances—that was us. I think that was literally just reflecting where we were brought up. There may be more from a psychological point of view, but on the surface, I think that's what you're seeing; that's what we're getting at here.

December 29, 1969. Grand Funk's second album, a self-titled, is issued, after quite large and immediate success for the band, especially live. It is known as "the red album" due to its cover art but apparently also because the guitars were turned way up, with the band correcting for the loud bass on their debut record, *On Time*, i.e. "into the red." *Grand Funk* is essentially the band's heaviest album, and includes a track called "Paranoid."

Recap

If 1968 was the year of Blue Cheer, then certainly 1969 is the year of Led Zeppelin, who incredibly issue *Led Zeppelin* in January and then *II* in October. One of these bands had just a little more impact than the other.

We've sifted through the entrails of the first two Led Zeppelin albums and found them sadly lacking in different ways against the specific purpose of our study, namely the search for metal. Sure, we recognize that it's a fool's game, a bit like saying, nice Ferrari, but you can't bloody well move house in it, can you? But I stand by my sense of being underwhelmed beyond juvenile grounds like complaining that the nice acoustic songs aren't metal. No, fact is, even when Zeppelin tried to be heavy, they did it with a lack of imagination, smarts and creativity, conformed to their blues world, and for that, maybe they can be faulted.

But fact is, Led Zeppelin did attempt to rock hard fairly often, or specifically, about half the time, which over two albums is one album's worth of all the time. And they did this in 1969, so a smattering of applause, please.

Sticking with blues boom bloomers for a jiff, 1969 also gave us Free, Taste and Leslie West, with Leslie most deserving of notice as part of our reductionist recap. Why? Well, *Mountain* was at times very heavy, heavier than Zeppelin, just not often enough to lurch and perch above...

...the two heaviest albums of 1969, *Kick Out the Jams* and *The Stooges*. Now, again, we've talked about how punk claims these for its own as much as metal does and that is problematic. It's easy to dismiss both as descendants of the garage rock tradition, smartened by psych rock intricacy at times, and then only 10% or 20% visionary of this new thing called metal. Still, each of these are well over half heavy, with properly heavy metal distorted guitars embraced often and boldly and willingly.

If we diminish the importance of these records as rich heavy metal inventions, it is in part because we see what heavy metal becomes later, mot notably the canon of Black Sabbath and Deep Purple through the '70s, the New Wave of British Heavy Metal, thrash, hair metal, doom, progressive metal, power metal, black metal and the often very technical and fast stuff we get today, which we might call neo-thrash or, really, a vast and vague style of metal derived from the Swedish melodic death metal tradition, crossed with good ol' '80s thrash. That's a few mouthfuls, but the point is that a few records that happen in the next year of our analysis, 1970, will feel more like logical predecessors to all of that than do the MC5 or the Stooges. In other words, knowing metal now, it's easy to understand why punk, as well as grunge, stake claim to *The Stooges* and *Kick Out the Jams* more than do all these other more purist metal genres.

A couple other full album highlights of 1969 would have to be Golden Earring's *Eight Miles High* and High Tide's *Sea Shanties*. These of course fall under the umbrella of obscurities and therefore are subject to the debate over the importance of invention when so few are listening and by extension, being truly influenced or inspired. It shouldn't really matter, logically, but there's something to be said for giving some degree of credence to the idea of consensus o'er who invented heavy metal. No, it doesn't matter, does it? I'm thinking that one should not be bothered by the fact that few smart people recognize that these records are inventively heavy. Because they are not celebrated, doesn't mean that they couldn't be proof documents of invention for their makers and for us, the documenters. Of note, there are even greater levels of obscurity below this, and then finally to the point where we are getting into the era of unreleased recordings (from basement tapes or suspiciously unreleased albums) coming out on CD 20 and 30 years later.

So what we shall do is declare these obscurities as inventive as the four more acceptable choices discussed here—*Led Zeppelin*, *Kick Out the Jams*, *The Stooges*, *II*—each with different positives and shortcomings, and, frankly, neither holding a candle to *The Stooges* or *Kick Out the Jams* in relentless power chord churn.

A final note for our analysis of 1969 is that 1970 is set up beautifully with Black Sabbath coming onto their occult-ready new name (and sound), so much so that they record their debut album before the year is out—that's a big deal. On the other side of the English class system divide, Deep Purple finds its transformative Mk. 2 lineup, and is busy playing live and recording the songs that will fill, with headbanged wonder, its *In Rock* album of 1970.

Chapter Three

Steel: 1970

1970. New York City's (Mountain-related) Haystack Balboa issue their quite heavy self-titled debut, on Polydor.

1970. Bell Records issue a self-titled from Orang-utan, who apparently weren't aware the sessions were going to be sent to market. The band, composed of known London rockers about town, play a sort of slow, dated hard rock, impressively post-blues boom, very heavy for the day, quite loose and not well-recorded, which gives credence to the idea that the tracks were somewhat "absconded with," and may have been considered by the band to be demos.

1970. New England's Euclid issue their lone album, entitled *Heavy Equipment*, on Amsterdam, a subsidiary of Flying Dutchman. Members come from psych and garage acts such as The Ones, Cobras and Lazy Smoke. The sound is leaden and heavy post-psych, a little dated, but definitely bridging psych to metal in a distinctly American manner that leaves out the blues boom element.

1970. Ken Hensley is part of the legendary, quite-heavy-for-its-time oddball project album *Orgasm*, by quasi-band Head Machine.

1970. Aerosmith play their first gig, at a high school in Mendon, Mass.

January 1970. The Ghost issue *When You're Dead – One Second*, an obscure semi-independent album of frightening, dark, occult-ish psych rock with elements of Ritchie Blackmore to the soloing and some quality rapid-fire drumming. But the album's main link to the story of heavy metal is its superlative creepiness.

> The Ghost vocalist Shirley Kent:
> Sabbath, as were Led Zep, were all on "our block." We grew up in the same area, played on the same streets. Many of us went to the same schools. And the boys were friends with many of the group members. "Dark"... dark music, it's merely a colour, and that is the colour we used. We weren't Satanic, not at all. The "spin" then was new pagan. The media got mileage from that, and there were bands into marketing their dark side. Remember this was after flower power. The quasi-occult interested seekers. We were a God-fearing band of Christians.
> The songs and lyrics were about the time and the changes, young people growing in awareness. The lyrics may appear dark, but listen and you will hear hope on some tracks. A lot of bands pretended to be into dark arts mainly to get press. Remember, Alice Cooper was secretly playing golf, whilst looking like something from hell. We never associated ourselves with anything other than our music. As for the name, they were The Holy Ghost when I met them, but had

been Resurrection. As Holy Ghost was considered blasphemous, the band had to change the name to The Ghost.

January 1970. Frijid Pink release their pretty heavy, self-titled debut album, on Parrot Records. *Defrosted* will arrive later in the year, and is also loud, garagey psych rock. The band's final two albums would be much lighter.

January 1970. Lucian K. Truscott IV reviews Led Zeppelin *II* for The Village Voice, describing it as heavy, and comparing it to Blue Cheer and Vanilla Fudge.

January 1970. Man Myth & Magic, an encyclopaedia of the occult of sorts, is launched as a magazine, running for 112 issues and being anthologized in book form.

> Black Sabbath bassist Geezer Butler, representing the customer for a product like this:
> I was brought up an incredibly strict Catholic, and when I was about 12, all I wanted to be was a priest. And I used to collect crucifixes and statues of Mary and all that kind of thing, and in the end, I just got sick of going to Mass every Sunday, surrounded by a lot of drunks and idiots taking the piss out of me hair (laughs). And so, I just didn't want to go there anymore. It was terrible; I was one of the few people with long hair back then, and all these Irish guys used to take the piss out of me something rotten. And in the end, I just couldn't stand it and I didn't go to Mass anymore. And eventually, when The Beatles started getting into transcendentalism, there were a lot of magazines and assorted publications about the different religions, including Satanism, white magic and black magic and everything, and I just got interested in the whole spiritual thing. And I suppose it rubbed off in me lyric writing with Sabbath.

January 9, 1970. Black Sabbath release first single, "Evil Woman," a quite heavy metal cover of a Crow song, through Philips subsidiary Fontana. In essence, the track carried within it a hint of the doomy blues as explored by Led Zeppelin and UFO, as well as Deep Purple's soon to arrive "Black Night," which represents pretty much the end point of a heavy metal song that could be said to still contain vestiges of the blues.

January 15, 1970. MC5 release their second album, *Back in the USA*, which points to lack of intention to stick with the more kerranging end of the band's style as expressed on *Kick Out the Jams*, which, again, somewhat cheats at the game of power by being a live album. If there's one thing *Back in the USA* lacks, it's power, although "Call Me Animal" rocked the house.

> MC5 bassist Michael Davis: Our music is really based on fundamentals. Our records weren't full of production techniques and trickery or illusions of anything, synthesizer machines or whatever. We based our music on the fundamentals of blues and rock 'n' roll, and it's very basic stuff. And when you come right down to it, that's always good; it always works.

> MC5 drummer Dennis Thompson: The second album producer was Jon Landau who was primarily a great writer and enthusiast of R&B and whatnot, but he was not a producer. And a lot of people liked the second album better than the others, but the sound to me is bass-weak; it lacked a punch. The sound lacked the punch. The drum department, bass, all of it. It was too tinny. And the material, I mean you've got

"Tutti Frutti." You know, if you want to call it retro, yeah. But on that, when we did some of those tunes that was to show our roots. Without having your whole record be a tutorial, you'd like the audience to know from whence you came, where this music is coming from, to educate them. And you know, by doing "Tutti Frutti," we did that.

January 21, 1970. Rolling Stone run a cover story on Altamont, further framing, embedding and then ossifying the event into the fail column of rock history.

Early 1970. Asterix's self-titled, lone album is issued, on Decca. The band are pre-Lucifer's Friend and quite heavy for the time, again, one of many German acts that included metal as part of their tool box but with no clear intention to build everything with that iron implement. Oddly, Electric Food's self-titled on Europa is another heavy record that is part of this pre-Lucifer's Friend factory of heavy music, i.e. the entire band without their English singer, John Lawton. Electric Food would issue an equally guitar-charged album in 1971 called *Flash*.

February 1970. Trapeze issue their self-titled debut—quite folky, perhaps reflecting the tastes and style of the band's producer, John Lodge from The Moody Blues, who is also co-founder of the label Trapeze were signed to, Threshold.

February 1970. Screaming Lord Sutch, one of England's favourite underground wild men of rock 'n' roll through the '60s, finally issues his debut album, entitled *Lord Sutch and Friends*. The friends include the likes of Noel Redding, Jimmy Page and John Bonham, and the album is quite heavy, although more in the realm of the heavy blues boom and heavy psychedelic rock of the late '60s. Note the double connotation to the phrase "heavy friends." Overtop, Sutch sings with a fairly extreme hard rock growl. Nonetheless the album is a good place to hear the unmistakable sound and style of John Bonham outside the context of Zeppelin.

February 1970. The Move, from Birmingham, issue their second album *Shazam*, which is a considerably heavy album, the band making a fairly radical shift from their self-titled debut and their singles. *Shazam* features very powerful guitars, swooping Keith-Moon-styled drums and vocals that are more extreme than Ozzy's, but alas only on a few tracks, notably "Hello Susie" and the lumbering "Don't Make My Baby Blue," with the sum total sitting in Zeppelin's wheelhouse of heaviness mixed with folk and psych. Still, *Shazam* deserves note for its powerful, skilled, capable heavy metal production values, the band achieving a sound more action-packed than any other hard record from this year.

February 1970. Van der Graaf Generator issue their second album, *The Least We Can Do is Wave to Each Other*. The hard and heavy (and often melodically and lyrically dark) end of prog—much loved by hard rock fans then and even now—included the likes of Emerson, Lake & Palmer, King Crimson, The Nice, Jethro Tull and this band.

> Van der Graaf Generator vocalist Peter Hammill:
> We were an underground group in '69, and we were on that circuit with Deep Purple, what have you, Hawkwind, and on the other hand, contemporary with Soft Machine. But we came from somewhere a little bit different. I think we were always a bit more brutal than what rock people now think of as prog bands. There was an element of slight fey-ness and over-complication in the actuality of what prog bands did in that era, and in how they are perceived. And we were—and are—a lot more direct and brutal. I think there are heavy bands along the way who've picked up a few things from us. I think it's because, although, some of it is in funny time signatures, and some of the contexts are far away from heavy metal, there are quite a few heavy riffs. And in a way, particularly getting back to the old band, back to the early '70s, there was a point at which heavy metal was a very liquid form. There was a large part of our audience that was pretty heavy metal. Granted, we had organ and sax and no guitar, but apart from that, the absolute core of the thing, you know, here's a riff, let's belt it out—that was the norm.

February 1970. Atomic Rooster issue their debut album, a self-titled, but stylized as *Atomic Roooster*. The album is keyboard-oriented, proggy, but appreciably heavy, especially opener "Friday the 13th," All told however, it's closer to a cross between ELP, Van der Graaf Generator and Uriah Heep. The production is there and so is the guitar sound (when we get guitar), but the intention is more toward prog rock than heavy metal.

> Atomic Rooster and ELP drummer Carl Palmer:
> At that particular stage, when we came out, Atomic Rooster was an underground, cult figure-type of band, and that's exactly where I thought we should be. I actually put the band together originally, because Vincent Crane really wasn't in any shape to do it. But he seemed to be able to play well enough. So I carried on with him, and he carried on with the band even after I left, which I was quite amazed at—for quite a while actually; they had a hit here in England. I think I had been out of the group for about six months, and they had a #1 single here in England called "Tomorrow Night." And that was something that Vincent wrote, so there we go; that was his understanding of the commercial aspect of the music industry.
> Vincent Crane was an absolute superb arranger. On the very first album, he arranged all of the drum parts. He went to the Trinity College of Music, and he was an absolute fantastic musician, extremely talented. And a very good writer, and astute with the commercial side of the industry. He knew that one had to be original to really survive and to be able to hold your head up in the street and be somebody to be counted.

Unfortunately, he suffered with a lot of manic depression, so he got involved in drugs, because both of his parents were rather... they were sort of—how can I put it?—they were almost too intellectual. There was nothing but books and books and books in every room in Vincent's house. There wasn't even a radio or television. They just read all the time. And I think it was all just too powerful, too much for him. His depression, his manic depression, was really spurred on by, I would say, an excess of acid. If he would've stayed together, if Vincent's health would have stayed in good shape, possibly the group would have been something to reckon with, even today. Unfortunately, it never had a chance to develop. As I say, I was in the group for about 18 months, and I decided to make a move, mainly because somebody made me an offer I couldn't refuse.

Arthur Brown on Arthur Brown and Atomic Rooster keyboardist Vincent Crane: He was an extremely talented keyboard player. He was also a manic-depressive who eventually took his own life. He went on to form another band, Atomic Rooster, with Carl Palmer, later of Emerson, Lake & Palmer. And had a lot of success in Europe, I don't think they were very successful over here. He was a very, very funny man, extremely gifted player who could improvise. I mean, he could go on for six or seven hours without repeating much of what he had just done. It was quite astounding. And of course he was able to conduct orchestras and arrange strings, brass and stuff. So he was multitalented. He went to the Trinity College of Music, classical training, and played on the modern jazz circuit with people like Graham Bond, who of course gave rise to the Cream and all of that. He was a very funny, aware person in a lot of ways. But he had the manic depression, and he got spiked in America. I remember he had to go into a mental home. We had a lots of adventures with him.

February 5, 1970. Black Sabbath officially begin touring in support of their debut album. But *Paranoid* songs such as "Paranoid," "Iron Man," "Walpurgis" ("War Pigs"), "Hand of Doom," "Fairies Wear Boots" and "Rat Salad" are played at some point on this tour, strengthening the case for Sabbath against Deep Purple or Uriah Heep as "most first." In other words, Black Sabbath had *Black Sabbath* and a virtual *Paranoid* as part of their loud language, throughout the first half of 1970.

Black Sabbath drummer Bill Ward on "Fairies Wear Boots:"
That one, like "N.I.B." and some of the really early Sabbath stuff, was done at the Aston Community Center. I think the idea did come from the thing that was going on at the time between the Mods and the Rockers, which was a big thing back then. And I think it originally it might have been aimed towards the skinheads. But again it was Geezer and Ozzy who put the lyric together. And it's very much an early Sabbath feel, an early '68 feel in the sense of the jazz and again really no solid sense of time. We kind of just clumped my drums around Geezer and Tony really (laughs). Every time we do that song I can never play the same thing twice. Every time we go on stage it's always different. So we keep making these different versions of "Fairies Wear Boots." It's probably pretty close but every night I never know what I'm going to do. It's usually quite close to what I had played the night before but I'm never quite sure until I'm actually doing it because it's based on wherever I am physically and mentally at the moment; I don't base it on any level of criteria. I seem to be lacking in whatever it is you have to have to get it perfect or whatever every night.

Black Sabbath guitarist Tony Iommi on *Paranoid* tracks the band had early:
I think we used to sort of jam around with "War Pigs." Again, some of the songs were actually put together when we were in Europe, playing Hamburg. We used to play at these clubs playing seven 45-minute spots a day, and we would get bored, because there would only be a handful of people in them, and we would start making songs up. And "War Pigs" was one of them; we might have had "Fairies Wear Boots," as well.

Black Sabbath bassist Geezer Butler on heavy metal bass:
A lot of people think the bass player is supposed to be more melodic, like Paul McCartney, playing all these nice things to give everything more depth. But I couldn't do it that way so I just followed along with Tony's riffs. In addition, when we used to go into the studio, they'd say I couldn't have this much distortion on my bass, because bass players don't do that. But that's me; that's my sound. We used to have battles with producers and engineers about distortion and what bass is supposed to sound like. It was always an argument on every album.

February 7, 1970. Led Zeppelin's *II* hits #1 on the UK charts, which surely must have generated some optimism for Black Sabbath's backers, who had some heavy music of their own to sell.

Friday February 13, 1970. UK release date for Black Sabbath's debut, *Black Sabbath*. The album contains seminal metal track "Black Sabbath," plus "The Wizard," "Behind the Wall of Sleep," "Sleeping Village" and "N.I.B.," compositions of note due to their modern, innovative, visceral heavy metal construction, and to the pervasiveness of power chords recorded with fully powerful distortion effect, against the weak or simply buzzing distortion found on many previous hard rock contenders.

The UK issue of the album also includes quite heavy non-original "Evil Woman." Underscoring intention, when "Evil Woman" is swapped out for a different track for the US issue, it's yet another fully heavy original, entitled "Wicked World."

What is also heavy metal about *Black Sabbath*, adding synergy to the proposal or argument for this being the first heavy metal album, is its cover art, the depressive, horrific and sometimes occult lyrics, the name of the band, the name of the album and the name of the title track, "Black Sabbath" being the penultimate ground zero metal track for its massive power chords, it's tritone doom, its almost comically slow trudge, but then also its frantic heavy part.

What is not heavy metal about *Black Sabbath* is its bluesiness, although its blues is of such a twisted and dour nature, that it's barely recognizable as such. Really, the main expression of blues on the album is the Aynsley Dunbar's Retaliation cover, "Warning," which, unfortunately, is also quite long. What is also not metal about the album is its jazziness, although Black Sabbath's version of jazz is closer to the Krautrock-in-spirit prog that would become the beloved domain of so many badly-selling Vertigo albums through to the end of 1972.

Debatable also as metal is Ozzy's vocal performance. But again, it's complicated, because even if Ozzy isn't your standard screaming he-man with a rough 'n' tumble whisky voice—and we've been hearing these guys ever since garage rock and psych—there is no question the man is an excellent distressed narrator of Geezer's tales of mental, emotional and often demonic struggle. Bottom line, *Black Sabbath* is mostly shocked through with metal, and of the heaviest and weirdest ever constructed as of the record's release date in early 1970. And when it's not, its prog is prog metal, its blues is blues metal and its jazz is jazz metal.

What's more, the fact is, this is the first of our "first heavy metal records" that no smart students of this stuff find reservation over. There's no, "Yeah, but..." There's no weighing of the pros and cons. And thus we will declare *Black Sabbath* as the first heavy metal album. But, as you will see, we will not declare Black Sabbath as the inventors of heavy metal until the end of 1971. Those in the know see no surprise in the first demonic declaration—this has indeed been the consensus short form answer to our titular question for many years and across many students and academics of the sonic waveform we know and love as heavy metal.

But, as I say, there's something extra I wanted to do with this book, and it's the reason we are going to progress past February 13, 1970, through the rest of 1970, and toward the end of 1971. Even if most of us agree that *Black Sabbath* is ground zero for heavy metal, it's been messy getting here. What we will prove through the rest of the book, is that not only was *Black Sabbath* no accident, but that no other band will even come close to challenging its constructors by the time 1971 comes to a close (I worded that carefully, and you will soon see why). The effect will be a resounding affirmation for our picking of Black Sabbath as the inventors of heavy metal, and therefore a happy tidying up of the tale—a double checking, as it were, that confirms our choice. But before we move forward, let me repeat: *Who invented heavy metal? Black Sabbath.*

Black Sabbath manager Jim Simpson, essentially agreeing with the author that Black Sabbath invented heavy metal:
I believe it came from Sabbath. I believe that somehow, the members of the band dreamt it up themselves. There's no influence that I can see, before that, that goes in that direction. I think they made the leap. I saw it develop. I was very much involved in everything they did and had very close relationships, and we'd make use of regular meetings and thrash things out verbally, all the time. But the music, as far as I was concerned, seemed to have its own life. Once we'd imported my jazz thoughts and ideas, which may have gone into their psyche at one time, once the *Black Sabbath* direction emerged, that was all theirs. And they weren't listening to other

people. They weren't nicking things off of other bands. It was what they were doing. In Earth, they had songs like "Song for Jim," which was a jazz thing, which was produced under the Earth name. But I think "Black Sabbath," the song itself, that was the huge step—that song. After that, the rest sort of fell into place.

Black Sabbath bassist Geezer Butler:
Hell, we just thought we'd last two or three years and that would be it until we got real jobs. We weren't thinking like, you know, this is revolutionary music and it's going to be around for years. We just thought it was something to pass the time.

Black Sabbath drummer Bill Ward on the Sabbath vibe:
I love Led Zeppelin and I totally admire John Bonham as a percussionist. But Robert's lyrics were kind of like love lyrics. And that's not a put-down. But Ozzy was screeching his balls off singing, "What is this that stands before me?" And we were serious about it. It was a very serious band as well as a happy band. But those lyrics meant the world to us. They did then and they still do. So I could hear some really good rock units forming, but I always felt we were the odd band out. We'd come in under the gun all the time and I just loved it (laughs).

Black Sabbath guitarist Tony Iommi on building *Black Sabbath*:
Well, it was a new thing for Rodger Bain as well, because we were sort of his first project, I think. And because we were very green through the whole thing, we didn't know any different from who was going to come from the record company or what. We didn't know who was who. So they just sent Rodger Bain along to sort of work with us, to produce this album. So it was his test as well, really, for the record company. But he was very good, good for us in those days, because we knew absolutely nothing. I mean, by today's standards, he probably wouldn't know a lot, but he did at that point, certainly a lot more than we knew as far as the production side of it went. He seemed to work a lot with the engineer we had at that time. I think it was Tom Allom, who was very helpful as well. So it worked as a little team, to come up with ideas, like on "Black Sabbath" with the bell and the rain. But he didn't have much input musically, because all that was basically done. But the little effects and sounds was down to them.

Black Sabbath drummer Bill Ward on Black Sabbath inventing heavy metal:
Right, well, it's that place inside. It's called primal scream. And all of us wanted to go there. As a drummer, there's nothing better than playing drums in Black Sabbath, as far as I'm concerned. And in every song I could go to the primal scream inside me. I had to go to that place where you let go of everything, all your anger, all your frustration, everything of the day, and you place it on your cymbals, you place it on your snare, you put it in your bass drum. For me, it was the best way of staying well. You know, they called me the quiet guy in the band (laughs), but that's because I was kicking the crap out of a drum kit every night, and after that I was just real mellow. So that's how that one kind of works.

But yeah, with the way that we were playing, and the things we liked to go to, which again were all of the dark notes, you know, the flat fifths, all of the other discordant sounding notes, when Tony would go there, to me, that was like Valhalla. It was like, oh my God, that's great. And to Geezer and Ozzy as well; we all loved it. So that would be us kind of steering away a little bit from jazz? Because we wanted to go to that primal scream place, that place where we go, "Yeah, you bastards!" You wanted to go there, but you're just at that point of absolute laying in. That's the only way I could describe it. Pure anger.

Everybody had heavy bits of music. However, if you look at the whole picture with Sabbath lyrically as well, then it becomes completely different. And there were no other bands at the time that were sounding, or were putting the lyrical content into the songs that we were. And we were on our own. I mean, the big hit was friends of ours: Led Zeppelin. They hit enormously and are such a great band, a phenomenal sounding band. But—and this is no disrespect to Robert Plant; I've known Robert for years and years and years and I have no intention of saying something now that would upset him—but the bottom line was that Robert's lyrics were a little more about falling in love or boy/girl lyrics, type of thing. Which I think he did it his own way, in a very unique way, whereas the lyrics that Black Sabbath performed to, were "Figure in black," "What is this that stands before me?," "My name is Lucifer." So we had very poignant attitudes and were bringing in a very definitive statement about what we really liked and what we liked to play to.

Black Sabbath engineer Tom Allom:
   Well, I'd not heard anything like it. Bear in mind this was very early on in my recording career. It was about my second year as a recording engineer, and most of what I'd been recording before then was folk music (laughs), and sort of stuff for library music. Basically just learning my trade. So this band comes in, and I really wouldn't know what to do with them if it hadn't been for Rodger Bain, who was very clear about it, because he'd seen them live and he understood sort of what they were doing. And I just remember them being very, very tight, because in fact, not very long before that first album, they'd come in to do demos for it. And most of the songs that were on the first album had been demoed, I'd say, six months earlier or something, when they were called Earth.
   And I didn't have, really, honestly, an opinion whether it was completely something new. I certainly hadn't heard anything like it. About the only heavy stuff that I'd heard was that a friend of mine from California had introduced me to Blue Cheer, which was interesting stuff to listen to because it was such a racket. You could hardly hear what they were playing. It was just a din (laughs).
   Where we recorded that first Sabbath album, and the tracks for the second one, was in this little studio where I started out my recording career. It was a tiny place, with a low ceiling, dead as anything, acoustically completely dead. And of course if you listen to those records, they're very dry. Nobody had any idea that they were going to explode like they did. But they hit a nerve here and in America, of course, pretty well immediately.
   And by the time they made *Paranoid*, they were already quite a big band. *Paranoid*, we did that in the same studio, the basic tracks, and then we took them to Island to go eight-track, to finish off the overdubs, and there weren't that many overdubs. I was confronted with the original four-track tapes just about 15 months ago when I did a *Classic Albums*, and they found the original four-tracks with the backing tracks, and there's not much on the finished album that wasn't on those tapes, other than vocals, finished vocals. I think Rodger made a big contribution. I mean, he didn't have to do anything with the arrangements, particularly, not that I remember. He just wanted to get them recorded in a sort of raw way, and it was all done very live. God, the first album was finished in four days.

Black Sabbath guitarist Tony Iommi on the macabre graphics of *Black Sabbath*:
The upside down cross was certainly not our idea. When we saw the album cover, that was in there, but I suppose what it was, was that they were asked to do an album cover, and it went with the name of the band and they put this image together and did the album cover from that, whoever designed it. And they came up with that idea. From then on of course, we had all sorts of things happen over the years. Because playing under the name of Black Sabbath, you can imagine the sort of people we attracted. We had witches, Bible pushers, the church, of course, lots of different types of people. The churches, for a long time in different places, tried to ban us, because they thought we were extremely evil. And then we had

witches started coming to the shows and camping out in the hallway of the hotel. If anything, it created more interest. It made people more interested to see what was going on, especially the young kids. The parents of course, would stay away (laughs).

Future Black Sabbath manager Sandy Pearlman:
What Sabbath brought to the table is that the first Sabbath album is unrelentingly bone-crushing, right? There is nothing that does not participate in the exploitation of what we have come to regard as the definitive basic elements of metal. Modal, extremely distorted, overdriven, chordal, and in fact, they prove a point that I feel I also prove, and have proven in spades, that heavy metal is kind of a fusion of all of the hard rock trend lines of the mid-to-late '60s, plus something else, which is the influence of horror film and science fiction music, written for film, that started being made in the '30s, and then was made in the '40s, the '50s and '60s, through the '70s, when horror films changed radically and they were no longer doing the same horror and science fiction films. They started to do very different things, from the things they did before the '70s.

But my point is that every adolescent male who is not like completely lame, in the UK and in North America, grew up watching *Creature Feature* and Elvira and *Chiller*, whatever it is, and that includes the UK, on Friday and Saturday nights. They would just stay home and watch this stuff. And the music and the films that were being shown, in the horror film subculture, or rerun subculture on television, characteristically had scores written mainly by German and Austrian émigré composers who had come to the US and the UK before World War II, or during World War II.

Many of them were Jewish, and of course on the run from the Nazis. These composers had all studied in conservatories that were extremely, heavily influenced by the Austrian late 19th century composer Anton Bruckner, and of course this is why the dean of the music faculty at McGill and I teach this course called *Bruckner: From Chord Power to Power Chord*, how the gigantic late romantic symphony orchestra of Anton Bruckner is modeled by the single player, crypto-orchestra of the heavy metal guitarist, in the quest for sonic ecstasy.

And the point is that Bruckner's scores are extremely complex, with like whole vast stacks of overtone series and distortion. It's all built into the performance instruction and the composition; Bruckner was very aware of hall compression and the K space, things that heavy metal is completely reliant on for its impact. Even a band like Slayer, which kind of turns the idea of the K space on its head by playing so fast that they don't allow for much apparent K in the K space. But having said that, there is the K occurring, in the K space, and it complexifies and masses up the texture further, and it's a really neat trick.

And so when we teach this course at McGill, some people say, "You know, Slayer, they're just lame; they just play fast." And we say, "No, let's slow this down and take a listen to what Kerry King is really doing here before you ladle out the contempt for Slayer." And I'm able to convince them, in my finest moments, that this is as metallic as sludge metal is, and it's just that they are distorting these resources that metalists use, and turn it on its head.

But having said that, Slayer couldn't do what they do without the entire metal resource panoply, which was created in the late '60s. So Black Sabbath is the first place where this is a disciplined ideology, and everything they do is working off of this resource base. And not really going outside of the universe. Not until Dio gets there, that they stray much out of the universe, and having said that, *Heaven and Hell* is awesome anyway, even though it has acoustic guitars in it.

But *Black Sabbath* is where the ideology is laid out with absolute discipline, complete fidelity, and the resource base is exploited as well as it will ever be exploited by anybody, and again with extreme discipline, which most people aren't capable of. And they don't need to get out of the resource base to complete a completely perfect series of sonic events, songs, all which have tremendous impact, all which sound as good, maybe better, now, as they did in 1969 when the first Black Sabbath record was made.

Does that answer your question? And also, you've got to realize, that what I've just said about science fiction, horror, and heavy metal, is completely proved by Black Sabbath, the very name of Black Sabbath. And that's derived from, I think it's a horror film made by Mario Bava, an Italian horror film. And "Iron Man." I mean, I could go on, but I don't have to go on. Their obsession with the horror film and science fiction and literature are readily apparent in the song titles, and their obsession with Hammer films and the occult. It's basically like, these guys must've spent every Friday and Saturday in Birmingham, staying up as late as the BBC was on in those days, which was not that late, absorbing this stuff. And it was a youth well spent, in my opinion.

Early 1970. Fuse issue a self-titled debut, on Epic Records, after an introductory single earlier in the year, pairing "Hound Dog" with "Cruisin' for Burgers." The band is an early version of Cheap Trick (containing members Rick Nielsen and Tom Peterson) and impressively heavy for the time, mixing hard psych with doom, wild vocals, and regular psych.

March 1970. Steve Turner, in a shelved piece for Beatles Monthly, calls *Black Sabbath* "heavy, raw and doom-laden" and "like inner City Birmingham converted to musical notes."

March 1970. Silver Metre issue their lone self-titled album on National General/Buddah. Fairly heavy, the album features Blue Cheer's Leigh Stephens and Mick Waller from the Jeff Beck Group.

March 1970. The Amboy Dukes issue their fourth album, *Marriage on the Rocks/Rock Bottom*. At this point, Ted is off on absurd tangents, and will not be advancing metal again until *Ted Nugent*, his major label solo album in 1975.

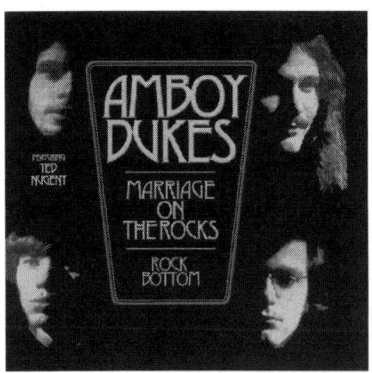

March 1970. Leicester's Black Widow issue their debut album, *Sacrifice*. Black Widow were known for being the most overtly Satanic band of the time although not that heavy. Still, the band's act, where they performed a Satanic mass, would capture the imagination of metal fans forever more, making the band a significant footnote in the pre-history of black metal, along with Black Sabbath (who Black Widow often were confused with).

Black Widow saxophone and flutist Clive Jones:
Black Widow actually started off as a soul band, and then the whole scene changed to psychedelic, so we went along that route. But we were just one of the bands, so we actually came up with the idea of doing black magic, but not just singing songs and every so often putting the word hell or devil in. We decided to take it a lot further than that, and met up with a guy named Alex Sanders, who was at the time the king of the witches, and his wife Maxine, and we learned as much as we could about it, and then had a little story, and then based the whole first album *Sacrifice* all around this black magic act. And of course the sacrifice that we used had to be naked, and in 1970 that was quite shocking, and we were sort of billed as, "Don't let your kids see this act!" And they flocked in like mad, and we had lots of publicity. I mean yes, it just happened to be a publicity thing, but we were doing it correctly, and the important thing for Black Widow was that we were the first.

Musicologist Gavin Baddeley:
You had a few of these occult bands—Black Widow for example. Though Black Sabbath sort of turned it around and said that Black Widow benefited from Black Sabbath's press where it was actually the other way around. You look at the papers at the time, a lot of people went to Black Sabbath gigs thinking they were going to see the Black Widow stage show, which had naked girls and whipping and who knows what going on.

March 1970. Bloodrock issue their self-titled debut album. It is a considerably heavy record, somewhat in the vein of Atomic Rooster. "Double Cross," "Wicked Truth" and "Melvin Laid an Egg" are downright Sabbatherian, while a few others are that way melodically, yet a little too lightly produced towards keyboards and jazzy arrangement. The cover of the album features the lurid band name, as well as blood, a rock, and shattered glass.

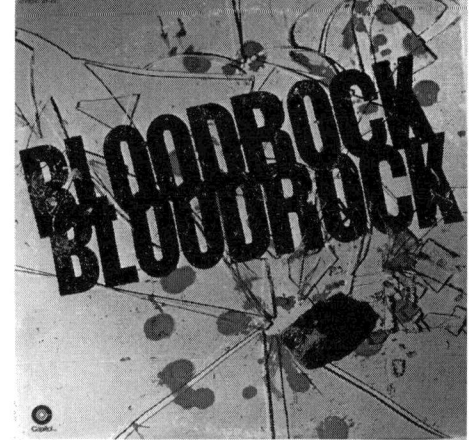

Bloodrock keyboardist Steve Hill:
I just remember that when we would get in the car, it would either be Jimi Hendrix or Cream. And Lee Pickens was a big blues fan, so Lee always had these blues recordings, like Freddie King and stuff like that, that he would listen to. I would say it was a combination of the psychedelic bands and the blues; Lee just really brought the blues thing into

it. Our original sound on that album... I think we were all going in the same direction on that one, as far as what we thought the band should sound like. We wanted the sound to be very aggressive, so I guess that was our mission. We wanted it aggressive, but we didn't want it to sound like anybody else, just kind of make our niche out there in the public.

Bloodrock vocalist Jim Rutledge:
The heavy metal thing, prior to changing the name to Bloodrock, first off, we all got off on Cream when they came out, and then when Hendrix came in, it was all over, and then Zeppelin killed us. And that's why we started writing that kind of material.

March 7, 1970. Mountain issue their official debut, *Climbing!*, which includes raucous, electric numbers like "Never in My Life," "Sittin' on a Rainbow" and "Mississippi Queen," a huge hit for the band. Despite its somewhat dated and simple construction, "Mississippi Queen" arguably offers the heaviest guitar sound ever captured on tape before the detonation of Black Sabbath's *Master of Reality* album in 1971.

Mountain guitarist and vocalist Leslie West on *Climbing!*:
I like the first side of Mountain *Climbing!*. The songs are all good; they used to play it as a perfect album side on the radio. That was the first real album of the group. The Leslie West *Mountain* album was my solo album. Felix was playing, but he didn't join the group until after that. Steve Knight was in the band because Felix didn't want us to look like Cream. I didn't really think we needed an organ player. A couple of songs, it paid off, but Steve was a bass player, really. And he played a little keyboards. But that was never my choice. I wanted to be like Cream, a three-piece. But it seemed to work at the time.

"Mississippi Queen," I wrote that tune in my apartment with Corky. The funny thing was that Corky had that song with another group. It was a disco song. I said that I had a great idea for a riff and some chords. We went into the studio and we needed a count off. Felix told him to count it off and to use the cowbell. That is how that started and ended! It was 2:16 of a freight train.

But actually "Never in My Life" was the first song we did, and Jimi Hendrix was the first one hearing it mixed, when we recorded at The Record Plant, in the next studio. Felix asked me to bring him in. I didn't know. I'm just a fat kid from Queens, "Go get Jimi and to come in and listen." And Jimi heard that, and he says to me, "That's a great lick, man." As soon as he said that, nobody could talk to me for like six months (laughs). And in our box set, there's a picture of me and Jimi playing at a club. He's playing bass and I'm playing guitar; it's on our web site too. The picture of me and Hendrix, I'll never forget that. It wasn't soon after that that he died.

Deep Purple guitarist Steve Morse on Mountain:
"Mississippi Queen" is written in such a traditional style, you would think it would be a cover. Mountain had the feel of, "Here is heavy guitar—let me tell you about it," you know? They really could nail it. They perfectly nailed it, even with *Nantucket Sleighride*. It was all about guitar: "Here we go."

March 20, 1970. The band formerly known as Spice play their first gig as Uriah Heep.

UFO drummer Andy Parker on the similarities between Purple and Heep:
Oh absolutely—it's that organ. That organ sound, that Hammond, which I still love. I mean Paul Raymond in our band digs that sound now and again. It's just something about it, man—it just grabs you by the nuts. It's the same with ELP with "The Knife." There's something about Hammond organ that just does that. Uriah Heep and Purple are very similar in a lot of respects, but I think that Purple's music was a little bit more intricate, a bit more virtuoso—is that the right word? I'm not trying to make enemies here. Uriah Heep was a little bit more down-to-earth, weren't they? I mean Purple, you listen to some of that stuff and it's just amazing—the musicianship on it is a little above.

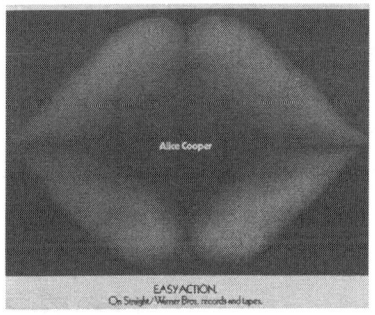

March 27, 1970. Alice Cooper's second album *Easy Action* is released, after which the band relocates to Alice's birth town, Detroit, and adopts a harder, more immediate, less psychedelic sound, in sync with the music scene of that rocking region.

Spring 1970. Hammer changes the name of their band to Blackfoot, and the south gets a load of riffs we wouldn't necessarily see with Skynyrd and certainly not the Allman Brothers.

April 1970. Cream issue *Live Cream*.

April 20, 1970. Jethro Tull issue their third album, *Benefit*. The band is still not (nor would they ever be) too particularly heavy, mixing blues, folk, flute, prog with just a hint of doom. Still, at the time, they were always— curiously, like Grand Funk—in the rock conversation, no doubt partly because they were so hairy.

May 1970. Free issue single "All Right Now," a quintessential party rocker built on power chords. Paul Rodgers' iconic status as a strutting front man is maintained.

Free vocalist Paul Rodgers on an early Free influence:
We had a mentor in a guy called Alexis Korner, who was a jazz musician. And it was great for us because he was from an older generation, but at the same time he was hip, you know? He could talk music with us and it was so great

because he had so much experience and he had seen bands come and go and he had seen trends and fads. I mean, he had seen a blues boom that came and went ten years prior to that, which was just awesome to us.

Of course, it was all new to us, the blues. But then we had to stop and think, of course this music is 40 years old; what are we talking about here? And he opened us up to the wisdom that says sometimes it's important what you *don't* play. And we would go away scratching our heads thinking what the heck does that mean? The gaps in between? And we finally figured it out and that helped us. You have to have some reserve and hold back so that the listener is urging you to play more. You're holding back and holding back and then you release.

The essence of Bad Company and what we do is a simplistic thing, just like Free. And I actually think that for me, that's harder to do. It's very easy to play a million notes a minute, which a lot of guys do. And very often, even the Buddhists say, "Life is lived between the notes." That's where the real atmosphere is. It's what you don't play. It's what you imply that is the real mastery of music. So I mean, I like the simplicity. The space that is left is where you can put yourself as a listener.

May 1970. Britain's interesting post-blues boom band Groundhogs issue their third album, *Thank Christ for the Bomb*. Tony McPhee and co. often come up in the discussion of early hard rock bands, although their sound is a smart mix of blues, dark blues, Cream-inflected prog and hard rock.

May 10 – 24, 1970. The Stooges record what will become the shabby and crabby *Fun House* album.

May 16, 1970. The Who issue *Live at Leeds*, on which the band retain their savage rockin' credentials in a live environment, albeit with songs not written to rock, Mose Allison's "Young Man Blues" getting the most radical up-ratchet from quiet to roar. And it must be said, typical of people not inventing anything, half the album is covers. Although the show that was recorded for the album takes place the day after Black Sabbath's album comes out, there isn't much significance here concerning the invention of metal, other than the fact that many rockers cite the album as one of the greatest live albums of all time, and by that, they surely are making tacit comment on its sonic violence.

Producer Jack Endino:
That's a pretty monster power trio record. And the thing is, nobody would call it metal, but what is it? It's a monster power trio with massive drums, crazy guitar and a great singer.

May 20, 1970. Four students killed by the Ohio National Guard at Kent State University in Ohio, where protests over the American invasion of Cambodia were taking place.

June 1970. Uriah Heep issue their heavy and modern *Very 'Eavy, Very 'Umble*, which was issued in the states as a self-titled. The UK edition's "Lucy Blues" was replaced by "Bird Of Prey," an incredibly flash, pioneering heavy metal classic. Other heavy tracks include "Walking in Your Shadow," "Real Turned On," "Dreammare," the Sabbatherian "I'll Keep on Trying" and a bulldozer of Hammond and power chord might called "Gypsy." That's a lot of hard rock, leaving essentially a couple non-heavy tracks.

Ergo, Uriah Heep's debut vaults into the foursome of the heaviest albums of 1970, the others being *Black Sabbath*, *In Rock* and *Paranoid*. However, given that Heep were neither the first (Sabbath were) or the most impressively heavy metal (Deep Purple were, but some would say Sabbath), as a band they clearly take third place in this critical trinity of acts. However, when it comes to being heavy metal with album covers, both the UK and the US covers of this album (completely different) are garishly scarier than anything we would see from all three of these bands until 1973's drop-dead shocking *Sabbath Bloody Sabbath* sleeve.

Uriah Heep guitarist Mick Box:
The thing is, if you listen to that album, there is heavy and light on there. That's why it's called *Very 'Eavy, Very 'Umble*. The heaviest is represented by songs like our anthem, really, "Gypsy," which is firing on all cylinders, and then you've got something very beautiful like a song played on acoustic like "Come Away Melinda." We realized early on that you could be just as powerful with an acoustic and a good melody and a good lyric, than offering all the power in the world. And we've married that all the way down in our career. We've always had those two things. We've never been a one dimensional band, if you like. We just played hard progressive rock.

The term "heavy metal" was invented way after us, Sabbath or Deep Purple were successful. Heavy metal was just a journalistic pigeonhole. I think we were the first band to use five-part harmony in a very effective way. Prior to us it was the Beach Boys which was very soft and sweet. We gave it an edge. We were once called "the Beach Boys of heavy metal." We always had comparisons to Deep Purple, but my stock answer was that they only had one singer and we have five. We are very proud of our legacy and what we are producing today but if you have your family and they are all healthy, this is all you could wish for.

Uriah Heep keyboardist Ken Hensley:

I don't have a classical background. I don't read or write music in a formal sense whatsoever. I never took the time to learn that. But I do take great inspiration from classical music. And the only thing I can say as a flat assertion, is that I never in my life ever wanted to do what anyone else has done or what I've already done. My goal was always to try to explore and do different things. Sometimes I had the freedom to do it and sometimes I had less freedom to do it. But the key to Uriah Heep was that I was pretty much the only one writing. So in a sense I was trying to stick to the rules and give the band what it needed and what the public would expect, but at the same time I still took advantage of the freedom I had as being the main songwriter for the band and took a little bit of liberty with that from time to time.

But the term heavy metal, I've never fully understood what it meant. I would never classify Uriah Heep as that in the contemporary sense of the word, the term, I would never classify Uriah Heep as a heavy metal band. Because I think Uriah Heep was more of a pop rock band than anything else. That's my feeling about it. I mean, a heavy metal band is probably something closer to Metallica.

Uriah Heep producer and Bronze Records founder Gerry Bron on the importance of Ken Hensley in Heep:

Oh yes, no question about that. You've got to remember that Ken was not only an outstanding personality, he's a great looking guy—long hair, right way down, very, very long hair—he looked fantastic. He sang as well as David Byron and higher, he wrote all the songs, he played guitar, he played all the keyboards, so he definitely was the strongest person in the band. No one came anyway near! Uriah Heep would've never been successful without Ken Hensley. They don't like I'm saying that, but it's absolutely so much true. If I was Mick Box and I was faced with a prospect of having my own band that was never going to be successful and being a part of a band that was successful all around the world, very, very successful all around the world, I'd take the second choice. But it wasn't Mick's band anyway: when I first saw them, it was Mick and David, so I never thought of it as Mick's band. When you talk about Mick and you talk about Ken, Mick never really expressed anything, he never said very much, whereas Ken was always talking. Ken had an opinion about everything.

June 1970. Michigan roots rock champions Brownsville Station issue their debut, a self-titled, also known as *No BS*.

June 1, 1970. The US release date for Black Sabbath's *Black Sabbath*, which contains squarely heavy metal track and band original "Wicked World" in place of UK cover track (and thus of lesser weight to the debate) "Evil Woman." Some sources say May '70. The album would reach #23 on Billboard, with the UK version peaking at #8 back home. Lester Bangs pan the album in Rolling Stone. See full analysis of the album at the entry for the UK releases date of February 13, 1979— it's important.

Black Sabbath guitarist Tony Iommi:
I think the first album was done in about eight hours and *Paranoid* was a couple or three days, because at the time, for us, it was just like doing a gig. We'd walk in, get the gear set up and play (laughs). We would just play through the songs

and Ozzy would sing in a little box and that was it. You would do one guitar overdub, and that was it, you're out, finished. I remember "Wicked World" was a "make it up as you go along," definitely the solo part. It was very much a jam; it would vary from time to time, night to night. That one I wanted to do again, but it was like, "Oh, no, no, there's no time," and that's the way it was in those days. You had a run at it, and then, "No, no, that's enough." (laughs).

Vertigo Records founder Olav Wyper:
Black Sabbath were very important to the label because we instantly got them off. It wasn't a huge, huge hit, but it was a big enough hit, and importantly, Europe absolutely loved them. The two biggest bands we had in terms of international success were certainly Black Sabbath and Uriah Heep. And Uriah Heep, which was another Gerry Bron act, Uriah Heep and Black Sabbath were very much the same sort of market. They were metal, sort of heavy metal stuff, and the Germans absolutely went berserk for them. There was always quite a bit of difference between them. In Uriah's stuff, there was an element of pop music being treated in a progressive rock way, whereas I don't think you could ever say that Sabbath had elements of pop in them. I think they both started out from a slightly different position.

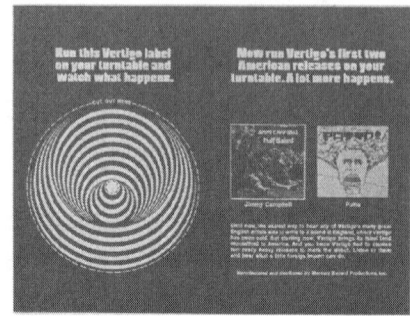

Monster Magnet vocalist and guitarist Dave Wyndorf:
None of these guys that made it called it heavy metal. They really did not. So you've got to watch that. That's a trap. It's like a critic's trap. But looking at it from a fan's standpoint, you're right. When all this stuff is stacked together on one album, that's when someone else can sit back and go, oh, this wasn't just some hard rock turned up for one song. These guys are going for this thing, whatever it is, volume and power as a form.

Black Sabbath drummer Bill Ward:
I know for myself, I knew we were doing something different because everybody hated us. We were thrown out of most places. I felt very alone, along with Tony, Ozzy and Geezer, which created tremendous unison by the way. That was one of our strengths. I felt like it was us against the world, and as a teenager of course, one can feel that way a lot. I knew deep down inside that we were into something that was not a part of anything else I'd been hearing. It was odd; I felt like an oddball. In hindsight I guess one could look back and go, oh my God, we did that and we did this and that got created and fashion came from this, and so much came from hard rock which then turned into metal. But it was different. It was raw. When Led Zeppelin's first album came out, one of the things I was particularly fascinated about was the smoothness of the album. And ours, when I compared it, was so raw and almost punk-ish, gritty—there's mistakes all over it and I just love it.

Mountain drummer Corky Laing on *Climbing!* tour support band Black Sabbath:
  Black Sabbath, nobody would touch them. In 1970, summer of 1970, no one would go near them. We were still touring Mountain *Climbing!*. *Climbing!* was actually recorded in the fall of '69, and came out in the first quarter of '70, and we toured it about a year. But Sabbath had a hard time, because they were trying to break them over in America. We were in Texas at the time, and especially in Texas, nobody wanted to know about Black Sabbath—just too freaking weird.

So Felix, myself and Leslie got together and decided it would be really cool idea to have a group like that open the show. And Ozzy was just so thankful after every show. He would run back and give us all kisses on the lips and stuff. He was just so boisterous. But even though the crowd booed him... the fans really didn't understand Sabbath, especially in Texas. The cops were looking at Ozzy like he was some kind of fucking alien.

But we always felt, get the best acts you can to open for you because it keeps you on your toes. And at the time, they were just a very different kind of band; they were the first Gothic band to come out. It was just very awkward. The police were there. Don't forget, they looked pretty strange. They weren't your pretty boys. And they were pretty strange. The only thing was, we had to keep an eye on Tony Iommi because he lost his finger. He has a fake finger. So one gig, we had to look for it; that was kind of weird. I just remember that because when we found it, we found it like a minute before the show. They didn't really know what they were going to do without his finger, because he only had one at that time.

June 3, 1970. Deep Purple release *In Rock,* which was recorded August '69 to May '70, intriguingly tightening the timeline with the *Black Sabbath* material. For indeed, if *In Rock* had been released concurrently with *Black Sabbath,* Deep Purple would have been deemed the inventors of heavy metal, given how much faster, riffier, and heavier more often, Purple's record is. In other words, although *Black Sabbath* and *Paranoid* (and records by The Stooges, MC5 and Blue Cheer) are earlier heavy metal albums chronologically, *In Rock* takes the prize for "impressiveness" without us having to take the liberty of reaching too far forward in the heavy metal time line. So, very soon after we meet Sabbath, here comes Deep Purple advancing metal further, being fast, innovatively keyboardy, and classical music-tinged.

An examination of the album yields six bona fide heavy metal songs out of seven tracks. "Speed King" and "Blood Sucker" are both complex of riff and even quite doomy, and "Into the Fire" mostly so, although the verse is a bit funky. "Living Wreck" also contains a bit of agedness in its verse riff, although the rest of the song is doomy of power chord. "Flight of the Rat" is a modern, flashy and fast bit of "happy" metal, but indeed, coloured with chord changes that routinely take it to a more menacing place.

Only "Child in Time" is not heavy on this record, and unfortunately it is also long. Then we get to the album's piece de resistance: "Hard Lovin' Man" is the best first example of a gleaming, modern heavy metal gallop, using the staccato machine gun style of "Communication Breakdown" but light years ahead in innovation, intellect and pyrotechnic advancement. What is an interesting quirk of history is the fact that as soon as Deep Purple finished with, arguably, inventing heavy metal, all of the rest of their albums for more than 40 years now would each have less hard rock on them than *In Rock*.

Deep Purple bassist Roger Glover:

I have one pet theory of why it's such a hard album. Although I think a lot of it has to do with the chemistry of the band. When I first met them they used to rehearse in this big old gymnasium called Hanwell Community Centre, big echoey, horrible sound, and I had never jammed before. I was in bands that you learn the songs and then you play those songs, so that was a revelation to me. They seemed to want to play their instruments; I was impressed with the way Jon and Paicey played their instruments to the full, loud, turned up... they didn't care what anybody else thought. That was a good impression.

But the main reason I think, is that when I first joined the band, the manager said to me that one of the first things you'll be doing is a concert at the Albert Hall with an orchestra. Jon Lord's written this thing which is a concerto, and meanwhile we started doing gigs. The first gig was at the Speakeasy in London, playing mostly Mk. 1 material, and meanwhile in one of our first rehearsals we had already written "Speed King," although it wasn't called "Speed King" at the time, and "Child in Time." "Speed King was actually called "Kneel and Pray," and there are several bootlegs of it with it called "Kneel and Pray." And I suppose we were evolving into quite a hard sound which even in the beginning wasn't exactly soft.

But I think the eighth gig we ever played was the "Concerto," and immediately it brought us to the attention of the media. We were in every newspaper—rock band and orchestra! But it was never meant to be that serious. And it had the effect of catapulting Jon Lord to the forefront of the band, to the point where he was being called the leader and the main composer, which got right up Ritchie's nose, and Ian Gillan's nose, specifically those two. And the rest of us really, because Jon wasn't the leader. We were pretty much a democratic band; even though we were new, everybody pretty much had their say.

This led to a great deal of resentment especially when we turned up to gigs, and the promoter would say, "Where's the orchestra?" And we realized that we were being misrepresented. People thought of Deep Purple as some sort of artsy, pseudo-classical thing. And we weren't—we were a rock 'n' roll band. And yes, you are correct when you say we were no longer based in psychedelia and not really based in blues, but there was this classical influence. And what would happen in the studio is that there was this resentment, which built up, so we had a determination to put, once and for all, our stamp on what we were, which was a rock band, and not a classical, pseudo-artsy progressive band. Very simple straightforward rock. And it became hard rock, because heavy metal wasn't even a term that was around at the time. I remember it that way, anyway. I remember we were rock, but we were harder than that, so hard rock became our epithet. And I think that's the reason that the album is the way it is. I remember Ritchie saying at one time, "If it's not dramatic or exciting, then it doesn't have a place on this album." And those were pretty good words to live by.

Deep Purple guitarist Ritchie Blackmore on whether he realized they were inventing heavy metal with the *In Rock* album:

Our biggest influences in the band were Vanilla Fudge meets Mountain, two American bands from Long Island. Paicey used to love the Vanilla Fudge drummer, and we loved the sound that Mountain got. So that was a big influence to us. And of course, Zeppelin had just done their heavy rock stuff in '69, so we were aware of that sound. But what I said to Jon Lord was, "Look, Jon, the trouble with what we're doing is that we're showcasing our musical abilities, but we don't have a direction here. One minute we're playing with orchestras, and then we're playing a rock song, and then we're playing a ballad." And I said, "I think we have to make a whole record of hard rock songs." Because I wanted to get that out of my system, at the time. And he said yeah, great. So we did that; we were very pleased with the way it came out.

And of course, it did very well, especially in England. In Europe, it was like #1 for like a year. Everything was so natural. You would go into the studio, play it, everything would work. You know, after three hours you were nearly finished, each song. Whereas sometimes, it's like pulling teeth, going into the studio. We would take two weeks over one track and have all sorts of problems and go through that period of thinking, it's just not a good idea. So everything just naturally worked. I love that. We just went into the studio and every song worked out the way it should have worked. And that's how Deep Purple *In Rock* worked. It was very easy to make.

Deep Purple drummer Ian Paice:
What happened then was the only thing that could happen. It couldn't have been anything else, because it wasn't a conscious decision to make that. With the personnel change, when you change two people in a five-piece band, that's a hell of a lot—that's a big percentage swing. And what you have is a totally different chemical balance, a totally different emotional balance. And so you have two totally different quantities in the band. Whatever they do will affect you, and whatever you do changes what the next guy feels. And just the way the music came together, the way the songs were written, Ian and Roger's take on what it was going to be lyrically, everything changed in an instant. It wasn't a conscious decision.

It was something we wanted to do before, but we couldn't. Because Rod, God bless him, didn't have the voice that could do that. He also didn't have the songwriting skills to create some of those things. But we didn't sit down and say, "Okay, we're going to make a record that's going to be like this." What happened was, as soon as we got together and started rehearsing, the music started coming out that way. Again, most things are not conscious creations, they just have to be that way. You have no choice in it. I think all the ideas that Ritchie wanted to use, but really couldn't with Rod and Nick, when Ian came into the band, all of a sudden he had a different vocal range to work with, and a different power and intensity vocally, to back it up, to use.

And Ian's voice, when he decides to make it shattering, is exactly that. So you can make it hard or you can make it high; you can do you want with it. So it opens up a vista in front of you. You're not stuck in this narrow lane of what is possible for a limited range voice. And Roger Glover's bass playing… Roger doesn't know how good he is; he never has done. But he is a superb player and he generally knows exactly what to do without thinking about it, so that was refreshing as well. Nick was a great bass player, but there was a lot of baggage from before, a lot of late '50s, early '60s stuff which he couldn't let go of. There's a lot of great stuff from that period—I love a lot of it—but you have to keep looking at how you improve. You have to keep taking more things on, while still holding true to your own beliefs about it. But you can't keep playing 1958 forever.

Ex-Deep Purple bassist Nick Simper:
As I have said before, the direction was not new, but the same direction that Ritchie and myself had pushed for from the start. This direction had been stifled by Jon Lord's classical influences, but finally emerged victorious, pushing aside the conflicting classical sound. As Jerry Bloom pointed out in one of the many Deep Purple documentaries, Warhorse was every bit as heavy, and rocked just as hard. The combination of personalities and original ideas was a huge antidote to the Deep Purple experience, and for me a far more rewarding time. Of course, success is only measured by record sales, but I will always think of Warhorse as the better band.

Deep Purple vocalist Ian Gillan on *In Rock* being the start of something new:
It is; you're right. With the benefit of hindsight, it looks to be a pretty significant record. And I think there are things like that, because I've listened to almost everything that came out of Seattle, and you can trace it almost directly to Tony Iommi, in my opinion. But we wanted to write our own songs. I think Jon, Ritchie and Ian... that's why they wanted to change the lineup of the band from the one that did "Hush" and "Kentucky Woman" etc. They wanted to be writing their own stuff, so that's why they brought Roger and I in—because we were already a kind of songwriting team. And so it just happened really, pure luck.

If you listen to Jethro Tull, you see that they're very obviously based in folk music; if you listen to Free, you see they're very obviously based in soul music; and if you listen to Zeppelin, it's blues as you've said. With Purple it's kind of weird, because Jon grew up in The Royal College of Music. So his background's in orchestral music and jazz. Ian Paice grew up in the Buddy Rich school of music, so big band, swing; stuff like that was the major influence in his life. Roger Glover was into Lonnie Donegan and every form of ethnic music you could imagine, folk music basically. And of course when Dylan came along, that was Roger's idol. And Ritchie and I were pretty much pop, rock, sort of country, and then delving into it blues and jazz. So we had a fairly diverse set of influences.

And so when the band came together, it was enthusiastic and loud (laughs). I don't know, I've always just been lucky I think, standing in the middle of these guys. They're just great musicians. We never had any ambitions to even have our photographs taken. There was never any ambition to be stars or anything like that. We just waned to play music.

Monster Magnet vocalist and guitarist Dave Wyndorf, disagreeing that the blues has been removed with Black Sabbath and Deep Purple:
It's all blues. It's just that it goes to minor chords. But the structure is all blues; they didn't remove any blues, except for the way they approached it. And that's the weird thing about it. I didn't understand that when I was a kid. I was like, this isn't the blues, this is fucking cool. I hated blues when I was a kid! I thought it was corny-ass bullshit. It's so weird! But yeah, I think when you take away that blues convention, there's a whole bunch of thing in it, such as minor chords. I think that has a lot to do with what we think of as heavy metal. And lyrical content. We could go on and on.

Deep Purple were looking for stuff to pad out there solos with. Some of those guys had classical music training when they were learning how to play their instruments. And the spirit of the age back then was to do something that somebody hadn't done before. So it's completely natural for a musician to go, well, you know, I've got a bit of Bach—put that in there. It's like they were looking for stuff to make the songs even longer.

When the Beatles, and before that Dylan, made the LP the preferred form of music, against the single, that was a literary thing meaning that all the songs together would outweigh individual meaning, that the sum of it would be something greater than the song. So that let them go, oh, well, we can do this here, do that there, do this there. I think they were just going for it, and I think it was the spirit of the age to do something that hadn't been done before. And then that fit in nicely with your idea of let's just not do blues. Let's remove this, and see what we've got. It was a fantastic time.

Led Zeppelin expert Dave Lewis:
In Rock was a very focused work, coming in 1970, and it marked the coming of Deep Purple, because they had the different lineups. You could say in the early day they were a bit of an English Vanilla Fudge. They did things like "Hush" and "Help!" with a bigger sound. But when they got Gillan and Glover, it was a much more focused band. I would say Deep Purple didn't always have the compositional strength that Jimmy Page had, but they certainly had the musicianship. Combined with all that, it was probably the right album at the right time, coming in 1970, which kick-started a lot of other bands to be very similar. Not always as good, I might add, but it was very focused at the time. Again, certainly the musical landscape in England was ready to take something like that on. So it was pretty accessible as well. It wasn't near anything you couldn't get your head around.

Nazareth guitarist Manny Charlton:
I think it was their seminal album, really. It really put them on the planet; put them right in everybody's face. They'd been messing around before that, and finally they settled their lineup and came up with *In Rock*. Great album, fantastic album. Just a classic. Hendrix and Zeppelin... it fit in with all that hard rock genre. It's the media that does all this splitting up, but it's all basically rock. But hard rock—we'll give it a distinction between Zeppelin and Eagles, for example. There's just that power trio thing, for example, with Marshall stacks and that sound.

June 5, 1970. Deep Purple issue the non-LP "Black Night" as a single (b/w "Speed King"), on Harvest in the UK, where it rises to #2. In the US, this constitutes the band's first Warner Bros. single, the label picking "Into the Fire" for its b-side. "Black Night" is a very heavy metal song for 1970, up to the standards of mid-level Black Sabbath, further, added to the evidence of the *In Rock* album, underscoring the intention of Deep Purple toward the invention of a certain new kind of music. In fact, given that Black Sabbath had under their belt the debut at this point but not *Paranoid*, "Black Night" was arguably as heavy as anything Sabbath had shown the world outside of the live environment.

Producer of Mk. 1 Deep Purple Derek Lawrence:
Ritchie would come around to my house and sit there all night and not say a word, and when he left, would say, "I really had a good night, man." And that was Ritchie. No, Ritchie was Purple, I mean, as far as I'm concerned. You know if you took what people regard as the great Purple things, they're all Ritchie guitar riffs. You know, I loved doing heavy rock, but I also wanted to do songs. I was a song man. But if you say to someone, "Black Night," they sing you the guitar riff. They don't sing you a song. "Smoke on the Water," they sing you the guitar riff; they don't sing you the song.

June 12, 1970. *The Band of Gypsies* is issued; it would be the last Jimi Hendrix album released while Jimi was still alive.

> Vanilla Fudge guitarist Vinny Martell:
> He blew everybody's mind. He was fantastic. We did a couple of great gigs with him. He was a quiet person, reserved. Not introverted off stage, but you know what it is with Jimi, he had a lot of business things going on in his life. He was being pulled and pushed in different directions, and as time went on the glamour and the glitter, the public is getting to notice you and how wonderful you are. You've already passed onstage and now you're into the business and being taken advantage of it. But he was generally a very quiet... not quiet, but very reserved, introspective. He had a lot of skills and was just the type of a guy that was just admired by everybody.

June 16, 1970. The recording sessions for Black Sabbath's *Paranoid* album commence. Over two days, June 16 and 17, the band record at Regent with Rodger Bain producing and Tom Allom engineering.

June 19, 1970. Black Sabbath complete the recordings for the *Paranoid* album, tracking vocals for "Rat Salad" and "Paranoid," and mixing, at Island Studios.

> Black Sabbath bassist Geezer Butler on *Paranoid*:
> We'd finished the album and had packed up all our gear and the management said they needed and extra three or four minutes to put on the album and we said we didn't have anything and they said, "Can you write something?" And Ozzy would literally be singing the lyrics as I wrote them. I was looking through the basement the other day and I found all the original lyrics from the *Paranoid* album, and verses from the song "Paranoid" that weren't used. It might be interesting for people to see the original versions some day. But it's just getting the time to do it. Lyrically, "War Pigs," "Iron Man," "Paranoid"... I used to try and give a message of hope or something at the end of each song and now I don't bother. Now I realize I can't change anything!

June 26, 1970. Free issue their third album, *Fire and Water*, which contains the hit single "All Right Now," the best example of Paul Rodgers and his concept of what you don't play being as important as what you play, a characteristic in a certain style of heavy metal song, the type built of big banks of power chords with much "space" between them. Other heavy-ish tracks include "Heavy Load" and "Fire and Water."

Mid-1970. Tear Gas issue their debut, *Piggy Go Getter*, on Famous in their UK home country and on Paramount in the US. The proggy hard rock act includes in its ranks, Zal Cleminson, who would go on to The Sensational Alex Harvey Band and Nazareth, plus Chris Glen of Michael Schenker Group fame.

July 1970. Toe Fat, featuring Ken Hensley and Lee Kerslake, later of Uriah Heep, issue their bluesy but loud and riffy self-titled debut, on Rare Earth Records; Toe Fat *Two* from March '71 would also be pretty heavy.

July 1970. The Stooges second album *Fun House* is released, containing heavy tracks like "Loose," "Down On the Street," "1970" and especially "TV Eye." However, given what has taken place in the advancement of heavy metal since the band's first album, *Fun House* adds little to the story, being, furthermore, arguably a regression from the debut in heaviness and certainly production values. Billboard says, "Hard rock and good improvisation are the settings of the album and the Stooges bring this off very well," adding that "the group has attained a grand musicianship."

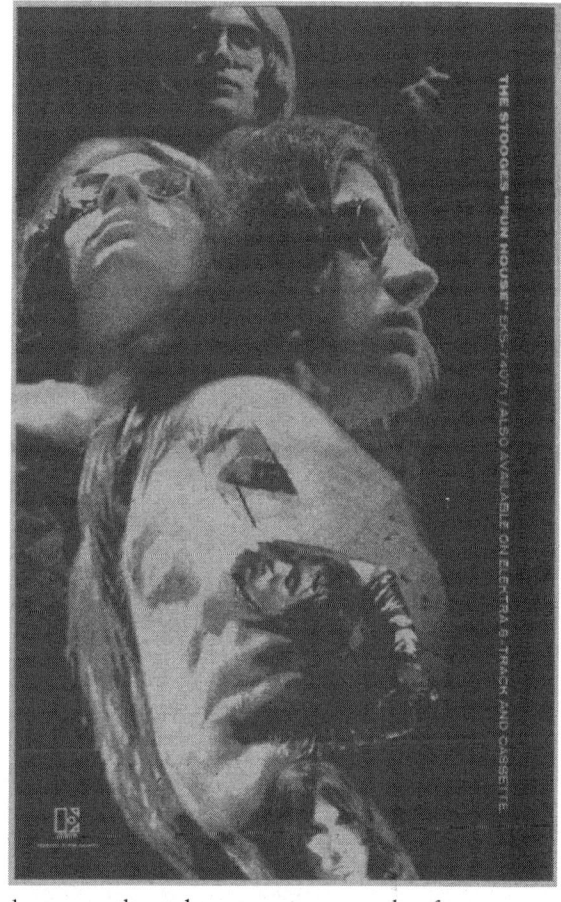

Stooges guitarist Ron Asheton: The first one is very minimal, but *Fun House* was totally different because we had started writing those songs in-between breaks between touring. We would be out for three weeks, a month, and try to write a couple of songs and then stick them into the act. So by the time it was time to record *Fun House*, unbeknownst to us, the producer, Don Gallucci had been following us around and he wanted to do our live set. So that's what it turned out to be. We played those songs live—which was so great for us—many times before we recorded them, which was the exact opposite of the first record. So when we went to record that record, everything, even the solos, was live—we performed it as we played it live. Iggy sang with the band, did all the tracks, but then I went back and added a couple of leads here and there and a couple of tiny rhythm parts, but pretty much it was live. So it was really different, but I still prefer the minimalism of the first one.

July 1970. Grand Funk issue their third album, *Closer to Home*. It is also the band's third album to go gold in 1970.

July 1970. Colorado's Frantic issue a self-titled debut, on Lizard Records, that bridges heavy psych to the stomping power chord rock of bands like Sir Lord Baltimore, Cactus and Grand Funk when they bothered.

July 1, 1970. Cactus' self-titled debut, on Atco is issued. Quite heavy, the band would share genre space with Mountain as loud hard rock with one foot in the blues boom from across the pond.

Cactus drummer Carmine Appice:

The Cactus sound is a very raunchy, raw, kind of basic sound. It's not really overproduced; there's a lot of energy and straight to the point. We do straight to the point rock music. We have some blues-based stuff on there, and a harmonica gives it more of a blues vibe as well. We were seeing the change from the Fudge stuff, where things were going more riff-oriented. And me and Tim... originally that band was supposed to have Jeff Beck in it. The idea was to change from Vanilla Fudge which was an organ-based band to a guitar riff band that originally was going to have Jeff Beck and Rod Stewart.

So that was going to be like the new... you know, Zeppelin had already been out a couple of years, and we were already planning to do this thing with Jeff Beck probably a few months after Zeppelin came out. But when Jeff got in a car wreck, that sort of upset everything so we couldn't pursue it on time. So we were probably about a year late from what we were trying to do.

The first album was a great, great album. I really love that album. I was a little unhappy with the production but as a whole, it sounded really great. It really kicked butt. It was an ass-kicking album. It was innovative because there was some different kind of playing on the album than there was on a lot of other albums at the time. It was very aggressive, very hard, very up-tempo. And that's what we were trying to do, try capture a lot of energy with some cool jamming and some cool bluesy-sounding songs.

Cactus guitarist Jim McCarty:
I guess the first thing that comes to mind about our sound would be a device that I used, the Ampeg Scrambler, that seems to have gotten a lot of notoriety in terms of the Cactus style. It's a rather unique overdrive device. It wasn't really a fuzztone, but more of a harmonic overdrive, and it produced a pretty unique sound, and I think I was pretty much the only person using it at the time.

July 17, 1970. Black Sabbath's "Paranoid" is released as a single. Its brevity and immediacy gain the band female fans, much to Geezer's amusement. The song represents a bulking up of the down-picked and muted chug concept pioneered on "Communication Breakdown" and then much more eloquently on "Hard Lovin' Man." The visceral beauty of this style of playing is what makes folks love Sabbath's own "Symptom of the Universe" from 1975 so much, with many musicology-inclined fans calling that particular track the quintessential heavy metal song from the first name in metal.

Vertigo Records founder Olav Wyper on whether Black Sabbath was inventing heavy metal:
I don't think that any of us really thought, hey, we're in at the birth of a new era of music here. What I was interested in doing— and if you look right across the broad spectrum of Vertigo when I was there—what I was after was a cross-section of really good music, whether it was rock, whether it was jazz, whether it was jazz rock, whether it was folk—we had some excellent folk stuff on the label as well. I just wanted a label of really good material, performed and written by young people, not by the establishment, but the young new artists, and almost everybody we had was a new band or new artist.

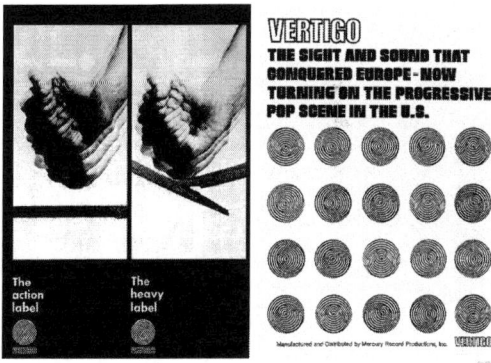

Not completely, because I also put out an album by Graham Bond, because Graham was a hero of mine, and when he became available I grabbed him. But most of the bands on Vertigo were new, untested, untried people, and they were all supremely creative and doing fantastic things. And I didn't care whether you could put them in a bag, as long as that that was a damn good bag. But to be honest, I don't think any of us thought that with Sabbath we were in the beginning of something brand-new. It was just one of several things that we were in that was brand-new. They were proggy, but I mean Tony Iommi's guitar playing drew a lot from jazz, I thought. I thought he was a terrific player, really terrific. And the band in the early days, certainly when I first saw them, the band were very much more musical and less formulaic than they probably became.

July 27, 1970. Attila issue their lone album, a self-titled. The band is essentially Billy Joel (ex-Hassles) on heavy keyboards and vocals plus a drummer, but *Attila* is composed of quite hard and heavy psychedelic songs, with titles such as "Brain Invasion" and "Amplifier Fire (Part 1: Godzilla, Part 2: March of the Huns)." Famous critical put-downs of the album can be interpreted as put-downs of hard rock, because on many levels, the record is solid and accomplished enough, stylistically landing between The Doors, Iron Butterfly and Bloodrock. *Attila* is arguably, at any rate, the most "exciting" or at least excitable and aggressive music Billy's ever done, and those terms can be viewed as complimentary inherently. Amusingly, in the same wheelhouse, Bruce Springsteen had his own pre-fame band with a heavy metal moniker, Steel Mill, and then before that, at 17... Earth!

Summer 1970. Thin Lizzy release their first single, "The Farmer"/"I Need You." Late in 1970, the band sign to Decca and relocate to London in March of '71. It would be years before the band would contribute to the story of heavy metal, most notably through twin leads.

Summer 1970. May Blitz are famously talked about as a somewhat heavy band, early on Vertigo, although on their self-titled debut, the songs are closer to prog, with a blues bent, punctuated occasionally by distorted guitar. A second and last, *2nd of May*, would follow in 1971.

August 1970. Gracious (no exclamation mark) are a very early progressive blues act on Vertigo, a label that was built on this sort of music at the beginning, with Black Sabbath representing by far the heaviest act, but still one that fit the adventurous prog rock mold of the label. *Gracious!* (or *!*) is issued this month, with *this is...Gracious!!* (sic) to follow in May '72.

> UFO drummer Andy Parker:
> I remember my impression when I first heard *Paranoid*. I think I still got my vinyl copy and I'm surprised it's not worn through. Who'd ever heard of guitar chords like that back then? It was just earth-shattering. Interesting enough I remember doing a festival outside of London and I was talking to somebody there from Sounds or NME or something, and she was talking about these new bands. One

was Sabbath and I remember there was a band called Gracious, and this girl was saying to me, "Oh man, I don't know about Sabbath but this band Gracious is going to be huge." I mean who's ever heard of Gracious?

August 1970. Status Quo's third album, *Ma Kelly's Greasy Spoon*, is issued; the band's ever-evolving sound is now inspired by boogie and the British blues explosion.

August 13, 1970. Iron Butterfly issue their fourth studio album, *Metamorphosis*. Not that heavy, the album nonetheless scored a considerable hit with its heaviest track, "Easy Rider," which features an early hard rock twin lead and punchy playing and production. "Butterfly Bleu" also contains convincing twin leads.

Iron Butterfly guitarist and vocalist Mike Pinera:

"'Easy Rider' was one of those demos I brought to the band with the guitar playing a riff sort of like the Kinks' "You Really Got Me" on slow speed, but it didn't translate that way in the studio. We loved playing everything from jazz to blues to fusion, but we knew the Butterfly fans were going to expect a certain kind of sound. So I started writing in that genre and the first songs I wrote for the *Metamorphosis* album was "Stone Believer" and that had big bass and guitar. I made a demo of it at my house on a four-track Teac and I brought it into the band. The only problem was the producer we had. Ritchie Podolor, great producer, but he was doing Three Dog Night and Steppenwolf, and he just didn't know how to get that big crunchy guitar sound. The guitar sounded bigger on my demo at home than it did on the final mastering. I think he put a little too much compression or something.

I did write some dark music there, such as "Butterfly Bleu," but we weren't as heavy metal as Black Sabbath, who we played with and who I liked a lot because musically speaking they sounded different than anything else I had heard. Whereas a lot of bands that were so-called quote unquote heavy were sounding a lot like other people. There were a whole genre of bands that came out that were supposedly heavy and they just kind of all mushed together. But Sabbath—and Hendrix and Zep on a good day— that was really new sounding music and I loved it. I liked what they were doing but I'm more musical where I would have loved it if they played some really bizarre, outside of the box chords, like minor ninths and diminished and stuff against those riffs. Then that would have just sent me through the loop completely. But I still liked very much what they did.

August 14, 1970. Space rockers Hawkwind issue their debut album, a self-titled that captures them not quite fully formed yet. Through the ensuing years, they would become heavy on and off musically, but tilted to the heavy side through album graphics and through the band's druggie stage show.

> Hawkwind guitarist and lead vocalist Dave Brock:
> Obviously, our music was somewhat shocking, and then we used to have strobe lights going a lot. We used to always get slagged off in the press, "Oh, three chords... all they know is three chords." Pounding three chord music with strobes going, and we used to have naked, statuesque dancers, gyrating around the place (laughs). And a good live show. So yeah, that's what was going on then. Nothing scary or black magic to it. I mean some people probably interpreted the danger of it all, because using strobes and heavy rhythms and things, using these frequencies that we used to use, it was dangerous. Some people would freak out over it. People would get pissed and fall over and they'd get sick (laughs). I mean, if you're going to get drunk and go somewhere where you've got strobes going, it's not the best thing to do.
> We did get banned actually, because we did a university up in Nottingham once, and of course most of the students used to drink a lot and we had our strobes going and we made a huge amount of people sick there and we got banned. That shows you how dangerous it is—it was a pretty damn big freak-out at the time. "Why didn't you say it was dangerous using strobes?" Well, if you're going to fucking drink a lot of beer and you've got strobes flashing in time with the music... because we used to have the strobes totally at whatever speed we were doing—we had the strobes flashing in time as it were. And consequently the worst thing you can do is drink and have that thundering away. Over you go backwards.

August 31, 1970. End of Black Sabbath's tour in support of *Black Sabbath*. The band would soon embark on what seems like an endless cycle of touring, with much of their time spent in the US, pointedly, away from the Black Country.

> Original Judas Priest vocalist Al Atkins on the desperation to escape Birmingham:
> Steel foundries and factories were just scattered everywhere. The main one was not in Birmingham but in a place called Netherton; that was a big one. There's one... Round Oaks Steel, it was called, a big one coming towards Wolverhampton way, that made the chains for the anchor for the Titanic. That was a big place. The one in Nethertown, they called it Hellhole. So these places already got names like that, because you didn't want to work in them. Let's start a band, let's get out of here, let's go to America. You didn't get many people sitting under palm trees playing acoustic guitar. It was a real bad area at one time.

> Led Zeppelin expert Dave Lewis on Birmingham:
> Well without doubt there was a lot of intensity of people wanting to be in bands, just as they did in Liverpool and London, and in the northeast with the Animals. But Birmingham being quite an industrial area, it was a very dour existence. If you go back to the mid '60s, it was very factory-based in terms of the industry, and to get away from that mundanity, people wanted to play loud rock music. Again, if you look at Black Sabbath in the middle of it, there was a first wave, really, of the Birmingham sound, which was the early '60s, which was people like Steve Winwood, Robert Plant and Band Of Joy, people like the Move. There was a whole early guitar sound, but then it graduated into Black Sabbath and Zeppelin with John and Robert. Birmingham bands, in the end, had to move to London to become famous. It's just never had the bright lights of London. Birmingham and the Midlands was a very industrial area and I know Tony Iommi

worked in a factory and that's how he injured his finger. It wasn't London and so Birmingham was screaming to be heard and it had a lot of creativity.

September 1970. Golden Earring's classic lineup solidifies as they issue their sixth album, a self-titled. Again, like its 1969 predecessor, *Golden Earring* proves to be quite heavy for the era, although, subsequent records will present the band as much more of a general and varied band, and indeed, even *Eight Miles High* is much heavier for 1969 than *Golden Earring* is for 1970.

September 1970. Atomic Rooster, admirably like Sabbath, issue a second record in the pivotal year of 1970. *Death Walks Behind You* is a considerably heavier affair than the band's debut, a rival for Uriah Heep's debut and certainly in that sphere of progressive, keyboard-laden hard rock, and powerfully produced to boot. John Du Cann's soloing style is very much like Tony Iommi's, which, arguably, is less heavy metal than Ritchie Blackmore's.

September 1970. Blue Cheer issue their fifth album, *The Original Human Being*. Dickie, Bruce and Ralph have carried over from the self-titled fourth album, while Paul Whaley is back in the bands on drums and they band has added a second guitarist, Gary Lee Yoder. The band is now far from their original cantankerous sound.

September 1970. Rock opera concept album *Jesus Christ Superstar* is issued, with one Ian Gillan singing the parts of the leading man. This provides close to nil in terms of heavy metal influence; it is conversely the 1973 movie, with its intense emotional musical scenes, some of them quite rocky and scary, that divinely touched many young future metalheads' heads as to the power of rock.

September 1970. Stray's debut album, a self-titled, is issued, on Transatlantic, with which the band signs in January '70. There's quite the Sir Lord Baltimore and Bang and Atomic Rooster doomy proggy joie de vivre about Del and his crew.

September 4, 1970. Jim Simpson is pushed aside as Black Sabbath's manager. Enter Patrick Meehan Sr. and Jr..

September 6, 1970. Jimi Hendrix performs what will be his final live show, at Isle of Fehmarn in Germany.

September 11, 1970. Official start of Black Sabbath's tour for the *Paranoid* album, the band taking heavy metal to the masses, materially proving to the world through the success of both albums so far and through brisk ticket sales, that there is an audience for this shocking music.

September 16, 1970. The Beatles are finally deposed after an eight-year run as best group in the Melody Maker readers' poll. This year's winner, Led Zeppelin, symbolizes a changing of the guard from pop to heavy rock.

September 18, 1970. UK release date for Black Sabbath's *Paranoid*, a record that is almost entirely of the already established Sabbath-born genre of heavy metal. "War Pigs" is a progressive metal classic. "Paranoid" is a short shocker with an arch-metal "machine gun" riff. "Iron Man," "Hand of Doom" and "Electric Funeral" underscore the doom element the band pioneered back on the *Black Sabbath* album. Only "Rat Salad," "Fairies Wear Boots" and "Planet Caravan" fail to take the genre forward past what was already established on the album that invented heavy metal a mere nine months earlier.

Finally, the only record keeping *Paranoid* from being the "most" heavy metal album of 1970 is, alas, Deep Purple's *In Rock*. *In Rock* may not carry the harrowing and foggy emotional weight of *Paranoid*, but it does do some other inventive nascent heavy metal things better. Billboard says that Sabbath "maintains their sound with a few slightly different twists."

Black Sabbath drummer Bill Ward on *Paranoid*:
I think *Paranoid* represents the late '60s, and where we were in the late '60s, because a good portion of the material on *Paranoid* was actually starting to be written, or was written, in '69 or '68. We started writing together in '68 and it might have even been earlier than that, '67. For that album cover, first of all somebody came up with the picture and we were like, "Hmm, okay, alright, not too bad." But I believe the working title for that album was *War Pigs*. And Warner Brothers didn't want it to be called *War Pigs*, which would make sense at the time. Record companies have to take care of how they look and everything. So I think that cover was based on *War Pigs*, and then they changed the name to *Paranoid* (laughs).

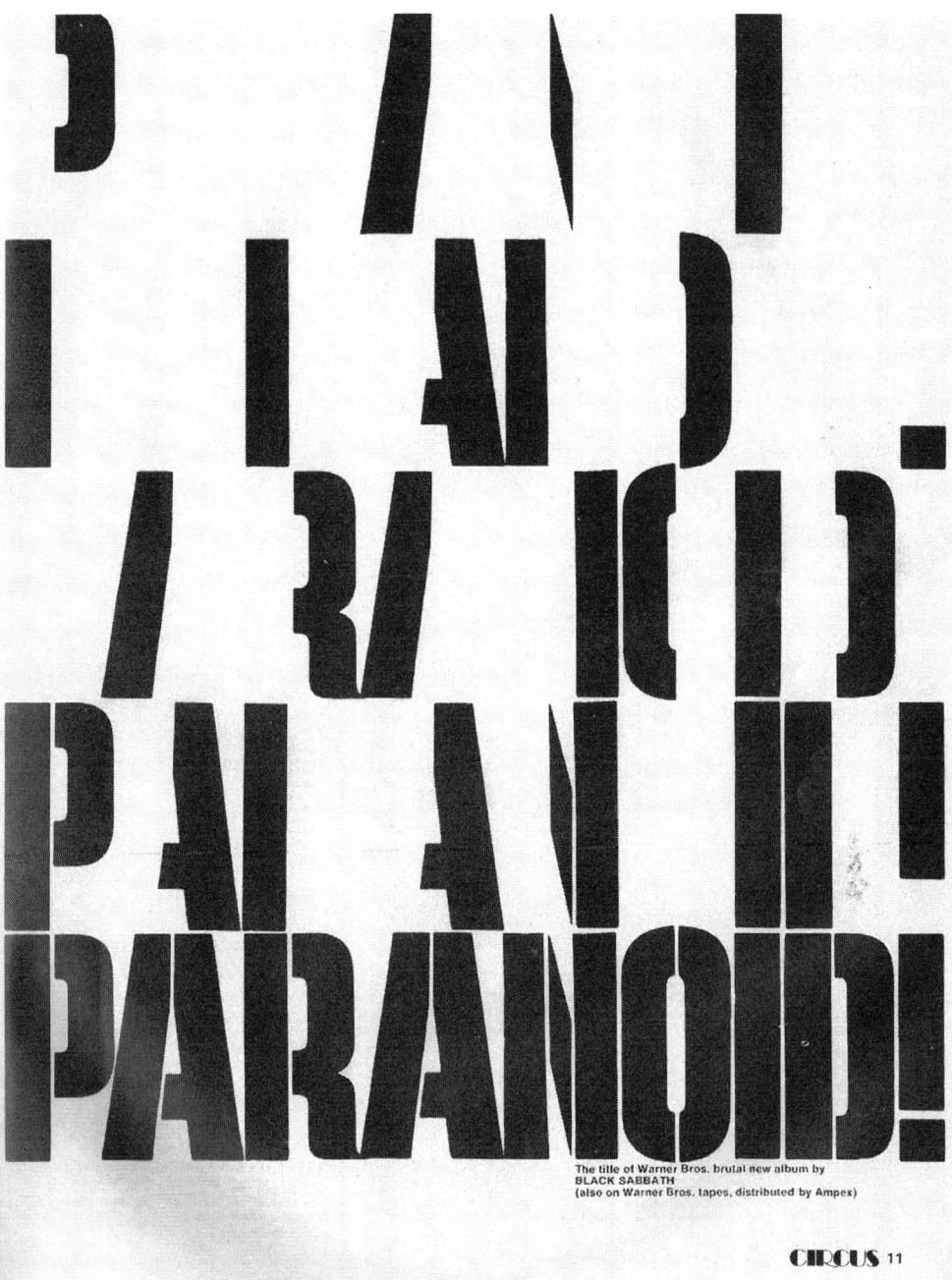

Black Sabbath bassist Geezer Butler on "Iron Man:"
I thought it was a really stupid concept (laughs), but it was from a comic book, *Iron Man*, and it was all about this being. It was an ecological theme. We were all very environmental at the time, and it was about this entity that turns into metal and is incapacitated at the end, just lying there. He can't talk at the end of it but he has all this knowledge that can save the earth from catastrophe. But yeah, I think science fiction played a big part in things like "Iron Man," science fiction and fantasy and the supernatural and a lot of politics as well in our lyrics.

The one thing we didn't want to do was normal love songs, because everybody in the world was doing them. And our whole band was against all that anyway, everybody talking about splitting up with their girlfriend and stuff. The reason we got together and made our music in the first place was because nobody else was doing it. So I just wrote about things that were interesting to me at the time. If I'd read a particularly good book, I'd condense that down to a song. It's just a reflection of society, real life. Everyone has their point of view. I used to write like that. "War Pigs," "Lord of this World," even "Paranoid." It's just an observation of society. I'm not preaching or trying to come up with any answers. But "War Pigs" is such a strong song. That's why we start concerts with that song. It has absolutely everything in it. It's a great song and it gets you up to play the whole concert. From there it's like, full steam ahead.

September 18, 1970. The death of Jimi Hendrix, arguably the person who invented heavy metal even more so than Tony Iommi, although he loses that mantle to Iommi by abdicating on intention, as demonstrated through evidence of the recorded works.

September 24, 1970. Black Sabbath perform "Paranoid" on *Top of the Pops*. Two days later, they film a performance of "Iron Man" and "Paranoid" for the German *Beat Club* TV show. On September 29, they perform "Paranoid" for Dutch TV.

Black Sabbath manager Jim Simpson on the band's dark image:
They never thought of themselves as being a scary band. It was always thought of as being a heavy band, a power band. The need to frighten people actually never actually came into the conversation. And although the name is taken from a horror movie, it's... I don't know, it was doom and gloom, sure, but that's not quite like horror, is it? To talk about "Paranoid," and Ozzy's vocal on the "Black Sabbath" track, those aren't scary, so much as doom-laden. It's a different thing. I always think of scary as being sudden shocks, and I don't think Sabbath were a sudden shock band. They were a batter-you-into-submission heavy band, weren't they?

We were more obsessed with being heavier and tougher than bands like Led Zeppelin. That was the target. We carried a strapline saying, "Black Sabbath makes Led Zeppelin sound like a Kindergarten house band." That was the prime objective. And neither them nor I were political as such. We all felt badly served by society; we all came from the wrong side of the track. But there was no conscription. Had we had conscription at the time, ongoing wars and things would have had more places in our consciousness. And in America, the Vietnam

War, there was conscription, wasn't there? So any young man growing up, 13, 14, would be start sort of counting down the years until he was going to be called upon. But that wasn't the case over here. The IRA thing always happened to someone else. All these tragedies, they're never your tragedies; they're somebody else's.

Black Sabbath guitarist Tony Iommi on generating the building blocks of heavy metal:
Anything can do it. You can be in a good mood one day and you can reel off a bunch of riffs. I don't have a problem that way. I enjoy it when we go in for a writing period. Once you get rolling, they just come out. There's no mystery behind it. I just go in there and play. In fact, when I'm at home in my studio, I'll put a tape on and run through a series of riffs that are just coming to my head and I'll take the tape off, throw it in a box, and it may never see the light of day again. I have so many of them, and I never go back to them really. By the time I go back to them, I could have written another riff. I write material far quicker than I ever have before. You could put me in this room here and say, "We want a riff in five minutes" and I'll come up with a riff. I'm not blowing my own trumpet; I'm just that way. That's one of a few things that I can do.

Mountain drummer Corky Laing on Black Sabbath drummer Bill Ward:
Bill Ward is a very solid drummer. He never considered himself a well-rounded drummer. He was just really great with the Sabbath. He had a way of playing, a plodding nature about the way he played. Everybody would bounce their heads really slow, you know, that sort of dolls or dogs at the back of the car, the way that doll goes up and down. He had a nature for playing like that. He wasn't a speed freak at all. He's a plodder. He started that whole plodding drum thing. Man, when they were in England, they invited us over. They played so loud—I'm serious—they played so loud, I was a block away driving to the studio. And in London, it's a very strange town. I just followed the sound. It was like three or four blocks away, and we're talking about these buildings. And it was so loud, you could open your window and all of London could hear it. This was when they recorded the second album. We were over their touring or something. I remember going to the studio over there, with their manager and their agent. We hung around quite a bit. For some reason there was an affinity there. Oddly enough, my father was born in Birmingham, and this is where they're from. They're all from Birmingham. It's a real blue-collar worker upbringing. I don't know if you've ever been to Birmingham, but it's a tough place. Manchester... these neighbourhoods were tough. These guys had to be hard-assed. I don't know, I got along with them very well and so did Leslie.

October 1970. Clear Blue Sky issue, on Vertigo, their lone album, a self-titled. The first song on the album is subtitled in parts, "Sweet Leaf," followed by "The Rocket Ride" and "I'm Comin' Home," which are both close to Kiss titles. The sound of the band is a form of psychedelic prog rock but most of the time buttressed by fuzzy guitars. Quite heavy for 1968 and 1969, but dated by late 1970.

October 1970. Irish band Skid Row, with future Thin Lizzy guitarist Gary Moore, issue a debut called *Skid*, on CBS. The sound is Cream on steroids, theoretically wild for the late '60s, but dated in late 1970.

Skid Row bassist and vocalist Brush Shiels:
Before us, there was only really, as far as I can remember, Van Morrison, and then Rory Gallagher and ourselves around the same time for Irish bands. But yeah, one of our missions was to be the fastest and the loudest band in the world (laughs). It was very fast and it was very loud; we came out of listening to The

Cream and Jimi Hendrix, and we thought, we're going to take it up a notch. That's basically what we were going to do. And we were also influenced by the jazz and Dave Brubeck, a little bit of Charlie Parker, the bebop. And for some reason, we were born showman. At the time you had The Who and Jimi Hendrix burning guitars and all that, and if you're going to go to America, you want to have a show. So we would've went on stage, at the Fillmore West, with Frank Zappa, and we never used monitors; we didn't want to blow him off. We were touring America with the Allman Brothers, and we played at the Whisky A Go-Go, and Led Zeppelin turned up to hear the band, and John Bonham and Robert Plant got up to play with the band.

October 1970. Bloodrock issue *Bloodrock 2*, which, like the debut, is fairly heavy, pointing to a degree of intention around hard music. As well, like Black Sabbath, they issued their debut early in 1970 and their second record in late 1970. *Bloodrock 2* actually found its way to gold, certified 20 years later, on the strength of doomy and depressive hit single "D.O.A.," which, as sinister as it sounds, is more Black Widow and Iron Butterfly than Black Sabbath and Iron Maiden.

> Bloodrock keyboardist Steve Hill:
> Immediately, for the second album, we were just getting a bit more focused. I think we only had one ballad on it, and if I remember right, it was only a three-minute song. So *Bloodrock 2* has a bunch of songs that are kind of the same mood. I've come to believe that when people put an album on, they're not really wanting to hear how many different kinds of songs you can play. They like albums that, whatever the mood of the album is, they want all the songs to kind of fit that mood when they play it.

October 1970. UFO release, in the UK, their first album, a self-titled, which shifts the blues boom fulcrum toward something faster and more distorted. As well, like Sabbath, the band find doom in the blues, on songs like "Boogie," "Evil" and "Shake it About" and even slower tracks like "Treacle People" and "Melinda." Elsewhere there's a Who influence, with the band unsuccessfully searching for hard rock mania. The album would see issue in the US on Rare Earth in April of 1971.

> UFO drummer Andy Parker:
> When we I first got together with these guys, we were doing old blue stuff like "Loving Cup," "Goin' Down," just more blues-influenced songs. You know, the first Zeppelin album, the songs they did on there, they weren't attributed to Willie Dixon (laughs), but same thing there. They were extremely blues-influenced, and into the '70s they got more into rock, as we did. It's your roots.

The first album, with songs like "Follow You Home," "Timothy" and "Boogie," that's kind of where the band was at when I joined them. A lot of the songs were written already. But you know, I just remember at that point in our lives, Phil was totally into the blues. He turned me onto, that *Electric Mud* album, the first Muddy Waters album; I'd never heard that. And Phil was a huge Jeff Beck fan from *Truth* and *Beck-Ola* and Howlin' Wolf—all those guys he really loved. And he had a lot of that stuff in his album collection that I'd never heard, the more obscure stuff.

Mick Bolton, maybe not as much; Mick was a bit more poppy. He had the poppy side of it. Pete, not sure, but he liked the Small Faces, and they had a huge blues influence in there. I think it's where we parted company with Mick along the line, because we wanted to go a little heavier, and he wasn't really that way inclined. It wasn't a personality thing. It was really just a music thing. He was still kind of like that airy fairy trippy acid-type player, and we wanted to go heavier, which is why we went to Larry Wallis and then to Bernie Marsden and then finally Michael. You were blazing a trail but you didn't know it. You know what I'm saying? It's just what we wanted to do. But you look back at it now, and you go, oh, you guys, you were heating it up. But you didn't think about it at the time. And the bigger the amplifier you got, the heavier your sound was.

UFO vocalist Phil Mogg on the band's origins:
There was a club in London called UFO. We were living in a place in London—me, guitarist and a bass player—when we had just formed the group, and we were going down to The Roundhouse when it was all acid rock and Pink Floyd. Jimi Hendrix had just come over and Free had just started, so we were between doing that kind of spacey stuff but more blues-based; we started to lean more towards R&B and blues. I was into old artists like Screamin' Jay Hawkins and Sonny Boy Willliamson, Muddy Waters and Howlin' Wolf. Of more modern, Stevie Marriott was one of my favourite singers, and Arthur Brown I used to really like. Then, Joe Cocker and Terry Reid; they're from the same period. We'd been playing for a very short time and we didn't actually have any direction. Literally, when we got the contract to do the album, we'd never been in the studio. We just played The Marquee—it was the first time, our biggest gig. There was our first shot at writing and recording, and then we started writing more, and had a big transition when Michael Schenker joined the band too. Before that, we were signed to a record company called Beacon, and that was the company that put out this space rock—whatever it was—album, and then we got a deal with Chrysalis.

October 5, 1970. Led Zeppelin's *III* is released. Three records into Zeppelin's career, one into the new Purple, and two into Atomic Rooster, Zeppelin offer up a record widely viewed—and denigrated, indicating new hard rocking times!—as the repudiation of their loud rock roots, even though "Celebration Day" and "Out on the Tiles" are weighty numbers, with "Immigrant Song" going further, by inventing Viking metal.

Led Zeppelin bassist and keyboardist John Paul Jones on "Immigrant Song" and its legendary bass licks:
Yes, well, the first part is fairly easy (sings it), but then I decided to do these runs which are quite fast. But in fact, it's nowhere near as fast... I heard some bootlegs once. I'm not sure, did we used to start the show with it? But it was enormously fast, almost twice as fast! How we played that, I don't know. And we still made them swing. I remember, one funny thing. In the old days, black music was always taken at a much slower tempo, and it had that groove. And white groups used to speed up too much. Except for rock 'n' roll. Black rock 'n' roll, like Little Richard,

was always really fast and I remember Little Richard quoted as saying that we used to speed them up so the white bands could never play them and swing at the same time (laughs). That was quite funny. But Zeppelin could play fast and swing at the same time.

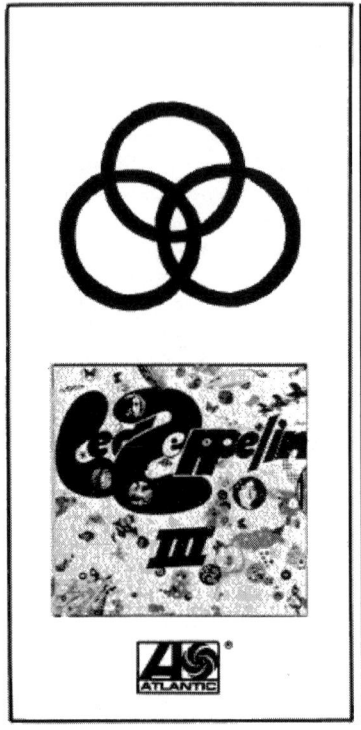

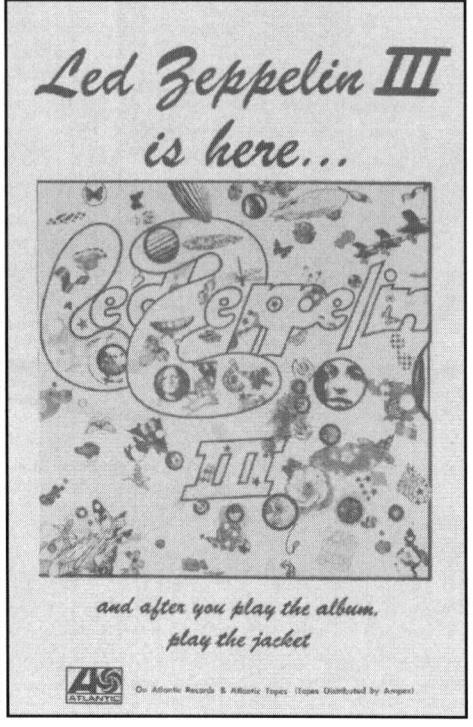

Aerosmith bassist Tom Hamilton on what drove Aerosmith in the beginning: I just think we were just trying to do something that sounded almost as good as Led Zeppelin. Our aim was to put something out that that made us feel as inspired as when you listen to The Who or Zeppelin or The Stones or the Beatles. We grew up on it, and we were all imprinted it with it really powerfully during that period. So when it was our turn to go in the studio, you know, we wanted to hear something that made us feel the same way. That's how we knew we were doing it right.

Black Sabbath bassist Geezer Butler:
    One of the biggest influences was Zeppelin because two of them were from the same part of England that we were from, from Birmingham, and we used to see them in clubs and stuff around town. So we sort of associated more with Robert Plant and John Bonham than anybody else, I suppose, 'cause we were doing the same kind of circuit before we made it. There wasn't competition, just friends. We'd see each other out and have a beer or whatever, and just socialize, really. Everybody seemed to be doing their own kind of thing. There was like lots of new kinds of music coming out around, and everybody sort of had their own originality.
    But bands lasted like two or three years and then you wouldn't hear from them again. When we did *Paranoid*, the Beatles had only been together for eight

years and broken up. So we thought, well, if the Beatles break up after eight years then we'll probably last about two or three years and that'll be it—and never to be heard of again. Which is a good thing, because if you could get a time machine, you probably would go back and change the music so it's perfect and everything, and it just wouldn't be the same.

Our families had sort of thrown us out 'cause we wouldn't get proper jobs, so they didn't believe in it. The friends I had thought I was nuts. They just didn't have the—I don't know what it was; ambition's the wrong word—I suppose the belief in the music and we just wanted to do the music more than anything else on earth and luckily it turned out well for us. We were just doing music that we liked writing together. We never thought about it as heavy metal or anything like that. We just thought it was rock, heavy rock kind of thing. We all loved Hendrix and Cream and John Mayall, that kind of heavy, Zeppelin. And so that was the natural sort of progression when we started writing our own stuff.

Led Zeppelin bassist and keyboardist John Paul Jones on why *III* was fairly acoustic:
I don't know, we were into Joni Mitchell a lot and listened to a lot of Fairport Convention as well. There was a lot of music around that was softer. Remember Ian Matthews' Southern Comfort? And there was an American group, Poco. We listened to a lot of that and thought, we had done a couple of heavy albums. It's funny though, a lot of heavy Zeppelin songs were written on the acoustic guitar. Plus there was a lot of acoustic stuff on the first album, which people forget. You know, after the second album, they always go, "Oh, the third album's acoustic. What are you doing?" And we were like, "What about 'Babe I'm Gonna Leave You?'" I mean, there are acoustic numbers, but they had heavier parts. And I had started playing mandolin by then as well, so like "Going to California" and "That's the Way;" those were all my mandolin parts. It just seemed a nice thing to do. And by then we realized that again, there were no rules. We didn't have to do it this way or that way. We just made our own judgment and said, well, this is nice, this is good, let's use it.

Led Zeppelin engineer Andy Johns:
By the time we were doing their third album, which I did all of... you know, the musicality of that band, because Jimmy and John were extremely well-trained, and Bonham was just a natural. And so was Robert—a natural. They would bang out two, three tracks a night, sometimes, and it'd go by quite quickly. Because of the standard of musicianship. As soon as I got a decent sound, off we went. And that record, I think turned out okay. There are some very nice things on it. "Gallows Pole" was wonderful, and "Since I've Been Loving You" is still a favourite of mine. One was distinctly aware that you were dealing with real class. They were a step above the others, and nobody could really imitate them. People have tried ever since, and they never really quite get it.

Montrose guitarist Ronnie Montrose on the his favourite guitarist for versatility:
There's only one. Led Zeppelin. In my book, Jimmy Page is, was, and will always be, the most prolific rock riff writer on the planet Earth. Prodigious output! Of rock riffs, acoustic, electric, recognizable rock riffs. Nobody has ever done that since.

October 28, 1970. Black Sabbath arrives in the US to begin their first ever set of dates there. October 30, 1970 marks the band's first US gig ever, at Glassboro State College, Glassboro, PA. Roughly 15 US dates are logged, rooted by Fillmore West and Whisky A Go-Go multi-day stops on the west coast which featured two shows per day.

Late 1970. Farrokh Bulsara, otherwise known as Freddie Mercury, joins Smile and soon suggests the new name Queen.

November 1970. Trapeze issue their second album, *Medusa*, which is quite hard rock versus the debut.

Trapeze bassist and vocalist Glenn Hughes on why the second album moved the band in a heavy rock direction:

Well, in '69 in the Midlands of England, from the era in the north of England, there was still a heavy contingent of American music, like Beach Boys and the Beatles and the whole harmony thing. Between '67 and '69, there really wasn't much intense hard rock. And then Zeppelin and Cream in '68, started to raise their heads and when we started putting Trapeze together in early '69, we were also on the Moody Blues label and the Moody Blues were extremely mellow. We were sort of in the same genre as they were with the big harmonies influence and Hammonds and the mellotrons.

And then, of course, we switched. That black and white record and that first band was only around for nine months before we switched into the trio. We realized that America was going to be our calling ground and we needed to go hard rock. The producer, John Lodge, unfortunately, I think John was great on the melodic stuff. On the first record, Trapeze, with a five-piece, it was all basically California-sounding, three or four part harmonies, Hammond organ, lots of Gretsch guitar, more Beatle-y influence, and it was more akin to what the Moodys were into.

Well, when I started to write as a trio for *Medusa*, it was a little different for John. He never really dealt in the hard rock stuff. But John is a great guy, and I also owe a lot of my career to him, and he was like a big brother to me, very, very influential in my coming to America in 1970, and he was a great producer, for the first record. I think for the second record, it was getting a little heavy for him. So by the time the third one came around, he opted to let someone else come in and produce.

Original Judas Priest vocalist Al Atkins:
Good bands coming out of Wolverhampton. Glenn Hughes was incredible. Trapeze was soon to come on the scene and they were a really good band. They started out being a five-piece and they ended up being a three-piece band. We played with them as well at Henry's Blues House. Why they got heavier, I'm not sure, but I know they started doing some stuff in America in Texas and maybe that's some influence on playing live, wanting to get a bit louder. I have got a story but I can't tell you. But I do know that Glenn was hanging around with John Bonham at the time, and I did hear that John was trying to get him signed to Atlantic, Led Zeppelin label. There were big bucks being thrown around to

sign Trapeze up. And something happened, which I can't say, but they didn't go there. But maybe John was trying to influence them to go a bit heavier, not sure.

Led Zeppelin expert Dave Lewis on John Bonham as the quintessential hard rock drummer:

Well you hear stories about when he was in the Wildlife and Dave Pegg was in that band, who went on to be in Fairport. There was always that thing where he wanted to bring the drums closer to the stage. He was never one for wanting to be in the background, and I think that was also something that was taken on into Band of Joy, where he always wanted to be billed as Robert Plant with John Bonham and the Band of Joy. He didn't always get his way by any means, but they knew he was good, John Bonham. He knew that he had talent and he knew, again, it was a way of making money and a way to be coming out of the existence of living in a caravan. He was always a battler, and he had to make a noise to be heard, if you like, and one of the ways of doing that was playing incredibly aggressively, like few other drummers at the time, if any.

And he was a loud personality as well. John was a typical, as we call them, Brummie character. He liked his beer, he liked to have a good time, and that transcended into Zeppelin without a doubt. And the later stories where he got a little more notorious, you normally found John Bonham in the middle of it, though I think there was also a lot of insecurity about him being away from his family, which also affected that. But in the early days, his teen years and his early 20s, he was loud and he wanted to be heard, and that was by personality a major tool in the drum kit was never be a lesser player in bands. Because again, in the '60s, the drummer was in the back. When you got to the louder rock and the amplified rock of the late '60s, you'd have Ginger Baker and people like that, who made the drum sound much more a part of the group, and again, that was very evident in Zeppelin.

November 1970. Warhorse issue their debut, on Vertigo. The band's most notable member is Nick Simper, ousted Deep Purple bassist. The album is fairly heavy and Deep Purple-ish, but a wallflower compared to *In Rock*.

November 1970. Grand Funk issue their fourth album, the double *Live Album*, which helps cement the band's somewhat dubious reputation as a hard rock band.

November 12, 1970. Mike Saunders, later known as Metal Mike Saunders, in Rolling Stone, commenting on an album from a year earlier, Humble Pie's *As Safe as Yesterday Is*, says, "*Safe as Yesterday Is*, their first American release, proved that Humble Pie could be boring in a lot of different ways. Here they were a noisy, unmelodic, heavy metal-leaden shit-rock band with the loud and noisy beyond doubt." He further called the band's current album, "more of the same 27-th rate heavy metal crap." This is considered the first instance of the complete two word phrase heavy metal used to describe music.

Budgie drummer Ray Phillips, on the genre labels of the day:
I'm exactly the same as Burke in rejecting this metal tag for Budgie, because you had your underground bands right? Elmer Gantry's Velvet Opera was underground; Cream was an underground band, perhaps the first, actually. In the early days this music generally was referred to as underground. Then you had rock music, and when you got to rock music it was Led Zeppelin, Black Sabbath, Deep Purple, Budgie, all these sorts of bands. But then it moved onto heavy metal. Well, we were always a rock band. Anything after that was a title which we just added on, if you like, to expand the metal market. Budgie, Led Zeppelin, Black Sabbath, Deep Purple... nothing to do with metal music—it was rock music. That's how we'd always seen it.

Interestingly enough, then what you had was rock music, but then you had the pop awards. Two separate things all together. Then they decided to call it the Rock and Pop Awards. I took offense to that because, myself, I worked at it. In rock music, we were all musicians that worked hard and had built up great reputations as musicians. With pop music, not to say that those people never worked hard to build up a reputation, but this attitude of playing in pop music certainly wasn't as high as in rock music. So you got Jimmy Page, Tony Bourge, Tony Iommi, all musicians of a high standard. It was almost like the industry decided, well if we called it the Rock and Pop Awards, it'll lend a bit more importance to pop music. They were two separate things. That's why for us, we were a heavy rock band or a rock band or a classic heavy rock band. Then metal came along.

Budgie bassist and vocalist Burke Shelley on heavy metal:
I think maleness is a big part of it. Because men are just attracted to the aggressiveness of this music. Just as they would subscribe to certain magazines, or watch a war movie, they'll get into heavy metal. There's this sort of macho angle to all this, which tends to be there as you're a younger man. If it's still there when you get older, I tend to think there's something wrong with you (laughs). I don't know; no, I don't really mean it like that. But it's something you should sort of grow out of.

November 20, 1970. Emerson, Lake & Palmer issue their self-titled debut. More of a prog band, nonetheless there was volume, bombast and violence to the way ELP strangled classical music. There was also double bass drum work on a track called "Tank."

ELP guitarist and vocalist Greg Lake on acoustic ballads in ELP:
It was strange! But I think it was one of things that people liked about ELP, really, the dynamic of it. One moment, the band would be very intense and screaming and loud and powerful, and the next minute it would be beautiful and gentle and soulful and emotional. I think if a band is purely instrumental, it cuts itself off from a lot of people, because people really relate to songs, you know, mostly to songs. They enjoy instrumental music, but for some reason it seems to be songs that connect with people more easily.

November 28, 1970. Slade's *Play it Loud* is issued, on Polydor UK, the first under the shortened Slade name. The album is moderately heavy for late 1970, mixing booming riffs with psych, pop, blues, all told, arriving at a prescient hard pub rock, doubly prescient in that the blueprint for the band's UK glam sound is here as well. Triply, if one includes the band's adoption of a vague, mixed skinhead fashion sense.

> Original Judas Priest vocalist Al Atkins:
> Absolutely brilliant, Slade were. What a band. They come from Wolverhampton, which is the next city across, so they were a local band. They sort of broke down the barriers. I know Noddy Holder quite well and we played with Slade three or four times when I was in Judas Priest. We topped the bill over them just once; the rest we had to open up for them. But great band. Really, really loud band, they were, for the time as well. They'd sort of got this wall of sound; it was incredible, the volume they played at. Considering Judas Priest is supposed to be more of a hard rock band, they sort of blew us off.

December 1970. Lucifer's Friend issue their quite heavy self-titled debut album, featuring the very heavy "Ride the Sky," which opens with what can only be described as a Horns of Jericho effect.

> Lucifer's Friend vocalist John Lawton:
> I think a lot of the influences came from Sabbath, Purple... I'm not so sure about Heep? I hadn't heard so much about Uriah Heep, only a couple of tracks from various albums. I was never a Heep fanatic in that respect. So I'd say more of the influences came from Sabbath, Purple, and lots of Gothic stuff that was around the time. We always played how we felt.

December 1970. Sir Lord Baltimore issues their debut album, *Kingdom Come*, which is famously heavy, meaning that this is invariably the first obscure album that enters the discussion of early heavy metal albums. It deserves to be part of the dialogue, even if there's a dated quality to it which frustratingly ghetto-izes the record into the predictable pen with other early American records.

> Sir Lord Baltimore drummer and lead vocalist John Garner on where the band found inspiration to be heavy:
> It's part of the wild nature inside of all of us. We either tap into it or we don't; we suppress it. But we did not suppress it. Of course, back in those days, peace, love and happiness was the persona of the way of things in that era. And you know,

nobody knew how bad drugs were. So we smoked a lot (laughs). So we got a little wild, and we were naturally a little wild, and it came out in our music. I just loved heavy stuff back then. I still do. I feel a sense of power when you hit a bass drum and it feels like somebody punched you in the chest, or if the guitar is like grating and sounding really heavy and cool. Of course, back then the technology was a lot different, and you couldn't sound as heavy as you could today. I used to scream like a maniac. The music was primal, and when I was at the Fillmore, I almost blacked out, I've got to tell you. And I was so thankful to God that I didn't (laughs). I put a scream out that was a little above my body's ability. But we always gave it all we had—I know I did.

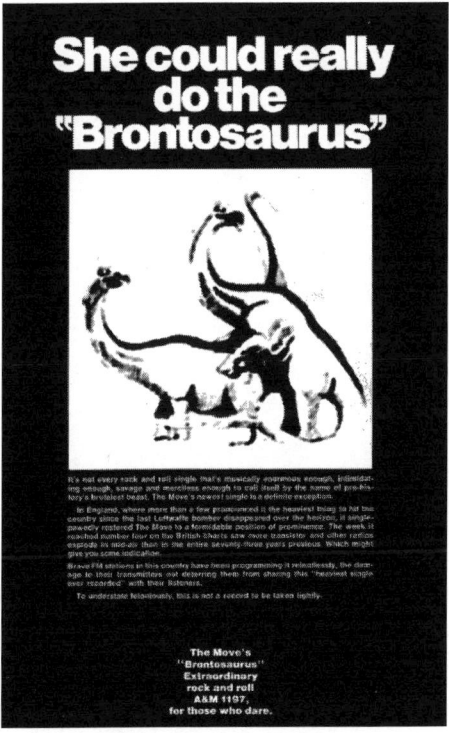

December 1970. The Move issue their third album, *Looking On*, featuring dirgy, crushingly recorded hit single "Brontosaurus" which ad copy calls "the heaviest single ever recorded."

December 1970. Graham Bond, occultist, issues an album of wide-ranging spiritual practise on Vertigo, called *Holy Magick*. A second one, *We Put Our Magick on You* is issued in '71.

December 1970. Free issue their fourth studio album, *Highway*. The band is, on evidence of the songs all over the records, not particularly heavy, yet the popularity of the band's anthems suggests an appetite for simple songs with blocked and boxed power chords, a formula taken forward to Bad Company and then utilized as well by Foreigner, Kiss and AC/DC.

December 1970 – March 1971. Led Zeppelin record tracks for what would be their career-topping fourth album, at Headley Grange, acting somewhat hard rocky with the concept of looking for uncommonly lively room sounds, allowing for bleed and echo.

Led Zeppelin bassist and keyboardist John Paul Jones on recording at Headley Grange:

Headley Grange was a big cold, damp house. You had very large rooms which were very echoey. You had a big stairwell which was even more echoey. The sound on "When the Levee Breaks" happened because Bonzo was so loud in the room we were playing in—because it had these hardwood floors—that we pushed his set out into the hall (laughs), into the stairwell, because the sound was smashing around all over the place. And we just stuck a couple of mics up and got this huge drum sound. So things like that came by accident. And you'd have amplifiers in the cupboards and amplifiers outside in the garden but it was quite good fun.

In general, everybody pitched in. We were four musicians. It was very tight unit on the road. It's very hard to separate things. Robert was more lyrical and

I helped in arranging and Bonzo was also very important. From what I've read recently, or over the years, or from what comes back, I don't know what people think drummers do generally. He would start things that would spark tunes off. But everybody did. You would come in with your own ideas and you'd be jamming. It's an organic process of four people. It's wasn't like a situation where one person does everything. With respect to production, there are times where I would have liked to have had a lot more bass, to be honest. But I don't know, Page did most of the mixing and they came out the way they came out. Some of them were produced strange, but then again some of them were quirky in a way that you love, you know what I mean (laughs)? I mean the sound on "Levee Breaks" is odd. It's just a really odd sound, but I kind of like it.

December 4, 1970. Wishbone Ash issue their debut album, a self-titled. Not a proto-heavy metal act, nonetheless the band is remembered as the first UK act to popularize twin lead guitar soloing, a heavy metal signature as practiced by Thin Lizzy, Judas Priest and Iron Maiden. Of note however, this particular album includes some heavy material for its vintage, as well, demonstrating copious twin lead, as heard on its rockiest tracks, "Blind Eye," "Lady Whiskey" and "Queen of Torture," and periodically through the jammy rest of it.

Wishbone Ash guitarist and vocalist Andy Powell on what kind of band Ash were:
Well, that's the big question, isn't it? Yes, we have many elements but we are what you might call eclectic to some degree. I think it's one of the reasons it's hard to pigeonhole us and probably why we've existed so long as a band. This changing of musical hats is also probably the reason we've not had the really big-time success like some of our contemporaries. Musically speaking though, it's been an interesting ride. The twin guitars have always been a constant.

Wishbone Ash producer Derek Lawrence:
I came about them because Ritchie Blackmore said, "This band has got twin guitar and they're really good." And that's what knocked me out. More, it was early on with Ted Turner and Andy Powell, because Ted was more of a bluesy player and Andy was more of a classical player. And that whole different thing really works nice for me.

Iron Maiden guitarist Dave Murray on the source of Maiden's twin leads:
Personally, when I started out, I was listening to the blues guys, Hendrix and that sort of thing, Santana, Free, and then a band like Wishbone Ash and then Thin Lizzy. I really dug the stuff they were doing. We didn't go out to try and emulate these guys, but it was there subconsciously, when the songs were being put

together. There are those areas where you say, okay, that would be nice, there's a melody, and you put a harmony on top of that. It kind of sweetens things up a little bit when you've got a heavy driving sound. Basically Wishbone Ash got us into that headset.

Recap

With the turn of the decade, the hierarchy of heavy metal gets turned completely on its head, with the axis shifting from the hapless trinity of somewhat accidental, possibly uncommitted metal bands of America—Blue Cheer, MC5 and The Stooges—toward the serious bloody-mindedness of the Brits.

Blue Cheer already in 1969 had dropped out of the game, but in 1970, MC5 would issue the wiry and retrograde *Back in the USA*, which made the statement that *Kick Out the Jams*, was in fact, that fiery perhaps only because it was live. The Stooges, conversely would stay heavy but weirdly get worse at it, or at least more squalid. Flipped to a positive, one might call *Fun House* more punk rock than the first one. Sure, I'll buy that, along with more garagey, stoopider, more Blue Cheer. All of which adds up to the band falling behind, as far as we jean jacket-with-patch metalheads are concerned.

Oh, sure, there would be American bands to replace them, but the American hard rock sound from 1970 to 1973 would underwhelm with refried riffs, hang-ups on Cream and Zeppelin, boogie rocking the handlebar moustaches. So Bloodrock, Grand Funk, Cactus, Mountain and even the wildest of the bunch, Sir Lord Baltimore... oh they make a lot of noise, but nobody's busy putting together *Sad Wings of Destiny* here.

The UK had its own bunch of these mid-tier bands as well giving us records in 1970, heaviest of the bunch coming from the likes of Toe Fat, UFO and Atomic Rooster, with their fine second of the year, *Death Walks Behind You* (mainland Europe contributed as well, through Golden Earring and Lucifer's Friend). Of note, Led Zeppelin would issue *III* this year as well, driving home the point that they are much "more" than a hard rock band—which, remember, is the same thing as less of a hard rock band if you do the math!

Turning the amp up to about seven, the fourth most important album in 1970 (and maybe the eighth overall, if you take in the preceding history), is the debut from Uriah Heep called *Very 'Eavy Very 'Umble*. If not for being preceded by the witchy record discussed below, and if not being matched concurrently in time by the Wagnerian record discussed below, one might have been able to declare, cogently, Uriah Heep as the inventors of heavy metal. Indeed, the band and their sound were nothing like what had come before, were roughly as heavy as anything that had come before, but were just so slightly overshadowed by two other acts from 1970—no other way to put it.

So, finally and most crucially, drum roll please, 1970 knocks us on the head with the answer to our titular question—and then circles back for a few more kicks until we're black and purple. The answer is that Black Sabbath invented heavy metal through the release of the first Black Sabbath album, *Black Sabbath*, on February 13, 1970. But hold on, we're adding a twist, which is why we needed one more chapter to adequately tell the tale.

And the twist goes like this. Quite simply, my plan or desire was to include what Deep Purple was going to do in 1971 before declaring Black Sabbath the inventors of heavy metal. It's a new idea but an intriguing one, and one that looks to fairness in determining both bands' intensity of intention, or put another way, their love of heavy metal.

Now, of course, the only reason we are talking about Deep Purple at all is because of the huge metal boots the band put on for their June, 3, 1970 album *In Rock*. Sitting outside your shaggin' wagon in bellbottoms and floppy hat in the summer of 1970, one might have called it a draw between Black Sabbath and Deep Purple, with Black Sabbath being first by fully three and a half months, but then Deep Purple turning in a record which was more heavy metal in a few departments, better, more polished, more musical, and, yes, somehow a better invention. In blunt terms, it wouldn't be out of line to see *Black Sabbath* as a 1969 album, with all its jazz and blues and jam, and *In Rock* as a 1976 album, given that it's not much different that Rainbow *Rising*.

By the end of the year, however, Black Sabbath has returned with the punishment of power that is *Paranoid*, and one would be inclined to call the contest wickedly won for the Sabs. Deep Purple still might have been framed more musical, a posh experience for the discerning London metrosexual, but the metal mentality so deliciously forged by Black Sabbath on their second record is so intensified, it's kind of time to stop talking about classical keyboard runs and who has faster songs. Plus I can't hear myself think.

But like I say, that wouldn't be fair, would it? Because with *In Rock*, Deep Purple earned themselves the right to prolong the contest until they too had two Jensen Interceptors in the drive (and, no the fact that there was a Mk. 1 of the band is neither here nor there). And so we keep an open mind and see what 1971 will bring.

Chapter Four

Titanium: 1971

1971. Lester Bangs becomes editor of Creem, after being fired by Rolling Stone after a negative review of a Canned Heat album. Lester was a famous and extreme rock critic and was actually quite metal-friendly. It is said both the terms punk and heavy metal were made popular in the pages of Creem. Creem was started in Detroit and later moved to a suburb of Detroit called... Birmingham!

1971. Tear Gas issue their second and last album, a self-titled. Much heavier than *Piggy Go Getter*, *Tear Gas* is in fact heavy enough to compete with most records on that characteristic from either 1970 or 1971, save for the very heaviest. However, the style is still a transitory one, bridging psych, blues and prog to the new power chord rock. However most of the time, the arrangement includes very thick and distorted guitars.

1971. The band formerly known as Soft White Underbelly, Oaxaca and Stalk-Forrest Group becomes the much riffier Blue Öyster Cult, which get signed to Columbia.

Blue Öyster Cult bassist Joe Bouchard:
In the first months that I joined the band, Sandy Pearlman took me to a Black Sabbath show, and it was in Staten Island if I'm not mistaken. And it was the first time I had seen anything like that. They were really loud because it was like a movie theater and we were in the back row, and back there it was still definitely loud. So Sandy was excited about it, and I don't know, I think he mentioned it would be great if you guys could do more music like this. And so later on after that we started working on our demos for Columbia with producer Murray Krugman. Murray definitely wanted heavy. And I think that it made sense. It was the turn of the decade, 1970, going into '71 and I was ready to do anything (laughs). I was right out of college, I had really not ever played a lot of professional shows, so that seemed like a good idea to me—start over fresh. Moved on from Soft White Underbelly, started over fresh with a sort of heavier attitude.
I think one of the reasons Clive Davis signed Blue Öyster Cult was because he had just about signed Led Zeppelin. And so I'm thinking that this must have happened maybe six months before we did our audition. And of course Peter Grant all of a sudden snatched Led Zeppelin away from Clive Davis and took it to Atlantic. And I think that Clive was a little pissed-off. And Atlantic had done a real good job promoting Led Zeppelin, so I think one of the reasons he signed us—because we are not his style at all—was that he was still mad (laughs). He was still mad about losing Zeppelin. Nobody said anything at the time but it is pretty well common knowledge that Peter Grant was flirting with Clive Davis to get a

deal with Columbia. At the same time Sandy had connections at Atlantic and he shopped us around to them and I forget who else. And luckily Clive was still pissed-off enough to sign us (laughs).

Blue Öyster Cult drummer Al Bouchard:
What happened was we were presented to them as being a hard rock band that could be their answer to Black Sabbath, and the person who sold them on that idea was Murray Krugman, who was a project manager and became our producer, and his main job was to make us heavier and more mysterious and darker. And he did that. He worked with us on that first record on every song and tried to make it dark and heavy and mysterious. Grand Funk Railroad and Alice Cooper were big around that time. So there was some heavy-ish kind of groups, but I would say that one of the different things was that we were a little less blues-oriented and more just strange. Especially after we met the Alice Cooper guys; then we really started developing our own sound.

1971. Aerosmith's classic lineup solidifies, as they begin the work of becoming an infinitely more interesting Yardbirds, a much more interesting Rolling Stones and a slightly more interesting Led Zeppelin.

1971. Alamo's self-titled debut on Atlantic represents the rare occurrence of a heavy band from the American south.

1971. Three Man Army's *A Third of a Lifetime* is issued, on Kama Sutra.

1971. South African hard rock band Suck issue their one and only album, *Time to Suck*, which includes "War Pigs," probably the second earliest instance of a Sabbath cover, after Flower Travellin' Band's rendition of "Black Sabbath" in late 1970.

1971. Monument issue *The First Monument*, which is not heavy but totally occult.

1971. Germany's Jeronimo issue their self-titled debut, on Bellaphon. They are one of many bands we could discuss as representative of the slingshot effect from having Deep Purple and especially Black Sabbath make a splash in 1970. In effect, Bang and Sir Lord Baltimore represent the most famed of these bands, but there were many others. Purposely, we will not be name-checking them all for two reasons: a) it's 1971 and we are just past the invention inauguration; and b) there's an uncomfortable level of obscurity that even if some of these very heavy records (especially from countries other than the US and the UK) were issued in 1969, the level of their influence on others, and thus, arguably, importance to the story, diminishes.

Still, credit where credit is due: each of these acts could be dissected as to when they had written and maybe performed some of their very heavy songs. To be sure, we would find many Sabbath-like tracks played sporadically in basements, garages and clubs—even festival dates—before 1970. The author's own *The Collector's Guide to Heavy Metal: Volume 1: The Seventies* contains reviews of dozens of these records, certainly if 1972 is included, amongst the 3700 albums discussed in the book (but I must say, I missed Jeronimo!).

One thorny issue in the construction of that book dredges another debate: there has been a spate of music released from this era throughout the CD age that is derived from rehearsal tapes, demo tapes, live shows, and, yes, unreleased professional studio sessions, that muddies the waters with respect to the concept of invention. To reiterate, with this book we are trying to articulate the idea that the band who invented heavy metal is one and the same with the band that released the best case full-length LP of heavy metal. Well, perhaps we should specify that not only should the album have some commercial significance, but that it actually got injected into the marketplace at all.

January 1971. New York's Dust issue their first of two albums, a self-titled. Fairly heavy for the day, the band would push further into the metal discussion than they normally might have on the strength of music due in part to the macabre cover art of this album, as well as the Viking warrior cover art of the second and last album, *Hard Attack*.

> Dust guitarist and vocalist Richie Wise:
> Dust was probably one of the fastest, loudest rock bands in America, ever produced (laughs). We were real influenced by the early British hard rock bands, starting with, to me, the first hard rock bands like the Yardbirds, leading onto the whole Cream and Jimi Hendrix blues-based rock. Then there's Jim Marshall coming up with the Marshall amps and Bonham with the big drums. We just loved that stuff, and we were sort of glued at the hip with what we were doing. We didn't say much about it, but when the three of us played it was loud and fast. The albums were really more diverse. Given the fact that... I'm really starting to think about what really happened. I didn't think about it much when we were 20 years old doing this stuff, but looking back, Cream used to make albums that were very different from their live shows. They had a lot of those different little Jack Bruce melodic types of songs. And so when I look at the albums, I think we were doing stuff, things that were more reminiscent, sometimes, to a Stones country vibe, when the Rolling Stones used to do some things that tended towards country blues, just like Cream doing some melodic stuff. So the albums were a little different. Of course there were some real heavy fast and loud distorted stuff on the two albums, but that's where we were at.

January 1971. Alice Cooper's third album, *Love It to Death* is issued. The album would be certified gold on November 6, 1972, further proving the popularity of dark rock, even if Alice was more so psychologically and visually heavy than through the evidence of the playing, arrangement and production of the songs on their transformative hit album. Billboard calls the band "the first stars of future-rock." Biggest hit on the record was "I'm Eighteen," which, although essentially a morose ballad, paints the picture of the young metalhead who might be a fan of Alice, Sabbath, Deep Purple or The Doors.

> Alice Cooper on *Love It to Death*:
> *Love It to Death* changed a lot of thinking about what was going on in music. It was a really hard-edged, Detroit, eerie... you know, it had classical things in it, but you could tell that this band was not classically-oriented. But all of a sudden you would hear this classical piano that would come in, over top of all this horror. And that's why it's really unique. You know, at that time, I've got to be honest with you, *Love It to Death* was a really hard record to make. We were going from the point of being a really odd... I

mean, to the point where Frank Zappa loved *Pretties for You* because it was just so bizarre. He said, "I couldn't even teach the Mothers of Invention to play this stuff, it's so weird." *Easy Action* as well... you listen to those albums, and you say, this is a good psychedelic band here, but no direction at all.

When Bob Ezrin got hold of us he said, "Look, everybody wants to love you guys, but there's nothing to hang the handle on. I mean, you guys have no handle, no musical handle." So he took us for eight months. We sat in Detroit in a barn, ten hours a day, and we learned how to play. And I developed a sound, Alice's vocal sound, Dennis developed a bass sound, Glen had a guitar sound, Neal had a drum sound. So when *Love It to Death* came out, it was the first time people heard it and said, "That's Alice Cooper." It had its own sound. You know, when you heard Jim Morrison, you always knew it was Jim Morrison. When you heard Mick Jagger, that's Mick Jagger. This time they heard it and said, "That's Alice." So we had an identification there; people could identify with us now.

MC5 drummer Dennis Thompson on Alice Cooper's move back to Detroit: The powers that be in New York, when they came to Detroit and found us, well then they hired The Stooges and The Frost, and more bands got signed as they came to Detroit and recognized the talent. Alice Cooper got signed. They were an L.A. band who came to Detroit to get muscled up. Because when they first came out here and played, they were god-awful. They were a sideshow, clown carnival band. They came to Detroit and the attitude in Detroit was kick out the jam or get off the stage; I mean, you know, play and play well, play really well. And they really, really improved, really tightened up and got some strength to their music.

Alice Cooper on "I'm Eighteen:"
"Eighteen" was just a riff we used to jam to, to warm up. I remember when we first started to do "Eighteen," it was in Detroit; we used to rehearse in this dump. And everybody had a bottle of Boone's Farm Apple Wine. It was just the worst; I mean, I don't think it's ever seen anything except chemicals. It was just the worst, and we'd all have a bottle of that and that was just the chord progression (sings it), and it was a good riff for everybody to warm up and jam a little bit on, and Bob Ezrin kept hearing that and he kept saying, you know, that's really a good riff. And he would listen to us rehearse and he'd say let's make something out of that. And again, it's one of those things that I would like to say, it was during the war, the end of the war, and there was always that controversy of, "I'm a boy, I'm a man." I can go get killed for my country but I can't buy a beer. So "Eighteen" was that juxtaposition of being both. And then, when it sounded like a complaint, then it turns the corner. It says I'm 18, I've got angst, I don't know what I am, I don't know if I'm a boy or a man, and I like it! And that was the selling point of that. It was the fact that instead of I hate it, it was I'm 18 and I like it. And everybody related to that and said, "Yeah, I dig being screwed-up."

Alice Cooper drummer Neal Smith on the band's "heavy metal" stage show:
We just wanted to be memorable onstage; I think that was the first thing. You know, we were certainly aware of Screaming Jay Hawkins and Arthur Brown, and in those days, in the late '60s. Nobody even had a word for Screamin' Jay Hawkins back in those days, or Arthur Brown, who would come on stage with this big flaming helmet he had on top of his head (laughs) and a big sceptre or whatever he was holding. And lyrically The Doors were doing the same thing. We may have been more influenced by the dark side of The Doors and taking it into a further dimension. After *Love It to Death*, we were starting to find our niche. We were all art students in college and high school, and we were also fans of the old horror movies, all the way from *Frankenstein* to *Wolfman*. Dennis wrote "Black Juju" and we would all brainstorm. We had the idea of putting the sheets over us; this was even after the door for "Nobody Likes Me;" and we still used the feathers. And we had "Dead Babies," even though it's not about killing babies; it's about parental neglect, child neglect. So we thought okay, we'll just do a theatrical thing for "Dead Babies" and "Ballad of Dwight Fry," and we'll execute Alice on stage. We'll put the singer in an electric chair. Without a doubt, we were big fans of the horror movies and that sort of thing. Our influence went beyond musical to theatrical with movies and Broadway.

Alice Cooper producer Bob Ezrin, on hard rock making inroads to radio:
Because I was living in it and was in that world every day, that was my reality. All of us just felt like we were the true American sound and radio was catching up. I was working with those guys and living with them in Detroit, hanging out with them and Nugent and the MC5 and Jimmy Osterberg, you know, Iggy, and all of these people at that time, and I had produced Mitch Ryder right after the first Alice Cooper album—I did Mitch Ryder, also in Detroit. And so I spent a lot of time there, and from that point of view, being my first real experience in an American city, being into an American city's culture, as opposed to just being a visitor, from that point of view, everything was rocking and hard. Everything was larger than life. The people were loud and brash and the bands were heavy, and to me that felt like the seed of the next revolution. So I just thought this was a true expression of where American youth was. I didn't see it as a dangerous thing to do. I thought it was absolutely natural. And maybe that was good. Maybe in our ignorance, we just stormed ahead and did what we did instead of worrying about what was expected of us.

January 1971. Mountain issue *Nantucket Sleighride*. Mountain's heaviness retains many vestiges of the blues boom and psychedelic rock, and thus fails to impress in terms of inventiveness against the British bands.

Mountain guitarist and vocalist Leslie West:
You know, VH1 just had this thing called the 100 Greatest Hard Rock Bands of All Time. Sammy Hagar said that Mountain was the first American heavy metal group. That made me feel great.

Mountain drummer Corky Laing on where Mountain got their heaviness:
    Well, I think Leslie's always had a big sound. When Leslie hooked up with Felix, at the time, Eric and Jack were playing so loud. The first set of amps we ever got, came from Jimi Hendrix. He had his Sunn amps he used to use. See what happened was, he was using the same rehearsal studios, he was buying the new

shit, and then for some reason we had the same agency—not management, but agency—as Jimi Hendrix, so it came from volume. We had the amps. Leslie was a heavy Who freak. So I mean, you're talking about volume.

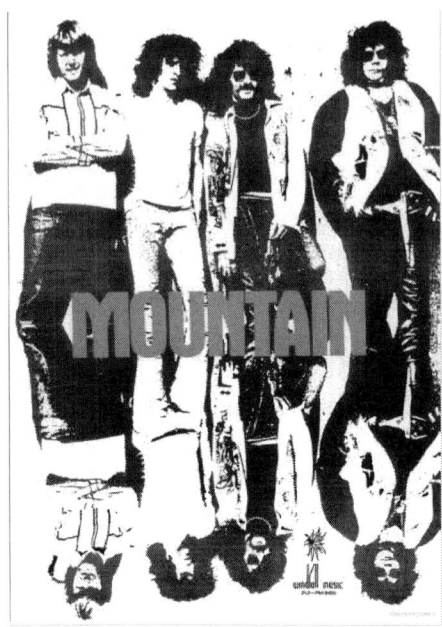

So we started playing as a trio, and even though the organ and the keyboard were in there, those were for special tones and special colour. But basically, the size of the amps. You know, Felix had six huge amps up there when he was playing. And Leslie of course had about six Marshalls, and when you're playing like that on stage, we were a pretty loud band.

I don't think it was called metal at the time. It was just hard rock. And frankly, it was overwhelmingly loud. And of course Felix put on the record, "Play this record loud!" That was the first time it was ever on a record. It was a joke in the band, as Leslie, when he had his band, which made a record Leslie West *Mountain*—the record was called *Mountain*—and he had a drummer named Norman D. Smart on it. And Norman said, "You know, anything you can play loud, you can play soft." And that was the exact opposite of what Leslie thought. It wasn't a very good thing for Norman to say, because he got blown out of the band. He couldn't play loud; he didn't want to play loud. He wanted to play country drums, you know?

In any case, yeah, I had no problem playing loud. I had timbales, which were probably the loudest drums you could buy; that's what I had. I said, when I went in there with Felix, "Do you want me to change the timbales?" And they said, "No, they sound like machine guns." And if you look at the first couple of records, they were timbales—there were no tom-toms. I used timbales for the first year, year-and-a-half. And they were loud. I mean, they cut through anything.

That's as much as I can say about the heavy metal part of that. Let's put it this way, it's a lot of fucking fun to play that shit. You're working out. You're working out like a gladiator. You are a musical gladiator, is what you are. No more is it soft church shit. This isn't that soulful little gospel thing. This is gladiator work. I mean, the places we were playing weren't exactly what I would consider acoustically beautiful. We were playing circus places. That's where we used to play. You would go into a circus and set up the equipment, and playing basically tents and stuff, in those days. And you would play hockey stadiums—that's what you were left with.

UFO drummer Andy Parker:
Those first couple of Mountain albums—I use to play the crap out of them; that was a great band. Leslie West was Michael Schenker's favourite guitar player. I remember him going, "For me he has the best tone." I never saw them live, but I loved their material and I liked the guitars—it was a similar lineup to UFO. I mean, the drummer had double kicks and they had this great guitar player. That kind of music just really appealed to me. So there was some good stuff coming out of the States, including Grand Funk and Blue Cheer. I remember just how big and impressive Grand Funk Railroad were. To British people, that was America in a nutshell—big and bodacious.

January 1, 1971. US release date for Black Sabbath's *Paranoid*, through the band's US deal with Warner Bros., and America quickly learns that Black Sabbath (and *Black Sabbath* and "Black Sabbath") was no fluke. There is so much intention toward this self-made style of music that the band comes off as, in essence, *doubling down* on heavy metal.

Deep Purple guitarist Steve Morse on Black Sabbath's role in the invention of heavy metal vs. that of Deep Purple:
Sabbath is a good point, because there is definitely a slow thing there. At the time we used "heavy" in the early '70s, to describe the way Purple did "Hush," because it was a tune from the south, I believe. And it's their cover version of it, but they did it in a heavy fashion, which meant more emphasis on rhythm and guitar solos and fills, and generally a little slower, like Vanilla Fudge, when they did "You Keep Me Hangin' On." That was a heavy version, and it was slowed down with a more straightforward rhythm. So the term heavy, really, referred to something that was direct and maybe in a narrow tempo range of being slow and heavy. And a lot of the Black Sabbath stuff was written that way, and things like "Smoke on the Water" fit that perfectly as well. But in a way, "Highway Star" had too much energy to be called a slow heavy tune. That was more like the beginning of thrash metal (laughs).

January 16, 1971. ZZ Top issue *ZZ Top's First Album* which proves to be amply heavy blues rock, setting the template for the band's first four albums and for considerable success and for Foghat.

ZZ Top guitarist and vocalist Billy Gibbons on the magic of the blues:
On the surface, it's perceived as a pretty easy to digest, rather simplistic form of art. And that can be a little bit misleading. Even Jimmy Reed records, it was two guitar players and a drummer. But the sophisticated inter-rhythms and the syncopated interweaving musically are very complex. It can be a real challenge to deliver it as it was invented. We're just the interpreters. But to listen to the inventors and what they did to such a beautiful art form is pretty fascinating. And let's face it, the British were the ones who came to the rescue. It was on the verge of becoming invisible. And with that English tendency to take things down to the level of genetics, they really understood how to re-weave it and present it in a really attractive manner.

Early 1971. Foghat forms from the ashes of Savoy Brown, providing a graphic example of a hard blues band becoming more of a mix of a hard rock or heavy metal band with boogie rock, very much what both Status Quo and UFO did between 1969 and the mid-'70s, Yardbirds to Zeppelin, Earth to Sabbath, Moving Sidewalks to ZZ Top.

Foghat drummer Roger Earl:
Lonesome Dave summed it up rather well one time. He said, "Foghat is like a blues band except that we turned it up to ten." You know, instead of using little Fenders and stuff we had big Marshall stacks or Hiwatts. Interestingly enough I remember when Dave was still alive, his son Jason had collected a number of bootleg Foghat tapes from early days and it sounded like a speed metal band. I don't know why but a lot early days with Foghat... it was maybe trying to make up for the fact that we didn't have decent PA systems so you played as hard and as loud and as fast as you could. There's a definite relationship between blues, rock 'n' roll and speed metal; I mean they are all kind of close.

If I had started my career ten, 15 years later, maybe in the mid-'70s or late '70s as opposed to back in the '60s, I might have had a different attitude on music. In fact Dave and I both used to enjoy listening to some of the metal bands. When they came out we would sit there and have a chat about how fast they were playing. But these types of music are very close. They sort of grow out of each other. Dave and I would often sit down and jam, and play stuff with ridiculous tempos. They are very close and using not more than a couple of chords. Three is about the limit I think, isn't it? I remember when we were recording "Fool for the City." We were rehearsing and getting the arrangements down, and I said, "Hey Dave, how many chords are in this song?" And he knew what was coming, and he said, "It's only three, Rog." I said really? He said, "Yeah, no, the other ones that you are hearing, they're just passing chords; they're not real. If you play really, really fast they disappear and you're back to three chords."

Early 1971. Cosmopolitan mainland European band Toad issue an admirably heavy self-titled album on Hallelujah/RCA; *Tomorrow Blue* follows in early '72 and both are engineered by Martin Birch.

Early 1971. Germany's Hairy Chapter issue their third album, *Can't Get Through* which is one of the heaviest albums ever released as of the beginning of 1971. It is the band's third, but first true banquet of metal. On Bacillus Records, the album is produced by Dieter Dierks, famous for his work with Scorpions.

February 1971. Uriah Heep issue their second album *Salisbury*, which necessarily prompts a take-away for the band's heavy metal legacy, through a reduction in intention. Alas, the band now may have become less heavy metal than one of their comparatives Atomic Rooster, and no-where in the league of their usual comparative, Deep Purple.

Uriah Heep guitarist Mick Box on the Hammond and the band's signature sound:
Don't forget, the Hammond organ is like taking a big wardrobe around full of clothes. It's just a very heavy lumpy piece of equipment. But the best thing about the Hammond organ, is that you've got all the dynamics, that we have in our music. It can be romantic, very soft, very quiet and very aggressive. And it has all

of those qualities, pretty much the same as a guitar, really. And when we started out, really, we went into the studio as a four-piece, and when we heard what was coming back we decided we would embellish it with keyboards. And at the time, I was a very, very big Vanilla Fudge fan, and with their Hammond organ and distorted guitars and the volume, we thought, yes, that would be fantastic. So we started putting some keyboards onto the music we already recorded, and that suddenly became the template of what Uriah Heep was going to be about, and it became an exciting part of what we do.

Uriah Heep keyboardist Ken Hensley: *Salisbury* is just me trying to be a classical composer, which is silly, really. But I heard Deep Purple's *Concerto for Group and Orchestra* and I decided I wanted to have a bash at doing something like that. And it was a very exciting time because we were working with the brass and wind orchestra and everything and I'd never done anything like that. The lyrics are not particularly fantastic, but the whole theme of doing a 16-minute track with an orchestra was quite ambitious, I think.

Uriah Heep guitarist Mick Box on forging the Heep sound:
Basically, we've always looked for a home to write good melodic rock songs. And we've always had a positive message, which over the years has become a godsend, because people write to me now and say our music has helped them through hard times in their lives. As well, there's the Hammond organ and the vocal harmonies. That's about it, really. And there was a real creative spirit in the '70s. When you would get your record deal, you would sign for five or six albums and the canvas was wide open. That's why you had so much experimentation. In terms of influence, Deep Purple weren't so much an influence but a contemporary. We used to rehearse in the same space, this big community hall in Acton which was just split into two sections. But our sound was just down to the lineup at the time. We would just jam and get off on the vibe of all of us learning at the same time, to be honest. It was the joy of playing and respecting each other's abilities.

Deep Purple bassist Roger Glover, on comparisons between Deep Purple and Uriah Heep:
In a word, yes (laughs). I remember, the first time I ever saw Uriah Heep was on television, and we'd come back from a gig somewhere and it was a flat we had in Fulham. Jon Lord and I and Ian Paice, I think we had arrived back, it was late at night, and it was one of those late-night rock shows. There was a band on and we sort of looked at it, and Jon went over to the TV, turned it up, and we listened to it for a bit, and Jon went back over, turned it down, and said, "I don't fuckin' believe it. They just ripped us off! They're doing all our tricks, all our trademark bits and pieces, the silly guitar bit, the organ..."

And that's how I first saw Uriah Heep. In fact, their nickname used to be You're All Sheep. However, credit where credit is due—they are a band that has survived. And any band that survives, really, is due a pat on the back. They did carve their own career out of it. I mean, I think they were uncomfortably similar to us at times, but I think that's a serious form of flattery, if you like. And they have carved their own thing out and we became friends and in fact we've worked with them since. I saw Mick Box a couple of months ago at a European festival, and what did we do? Hey, big hug. They're a nice bunch of guys and they're survivors. So I don't hold any grudges. But in answer to your question, that's how we felt at the time.

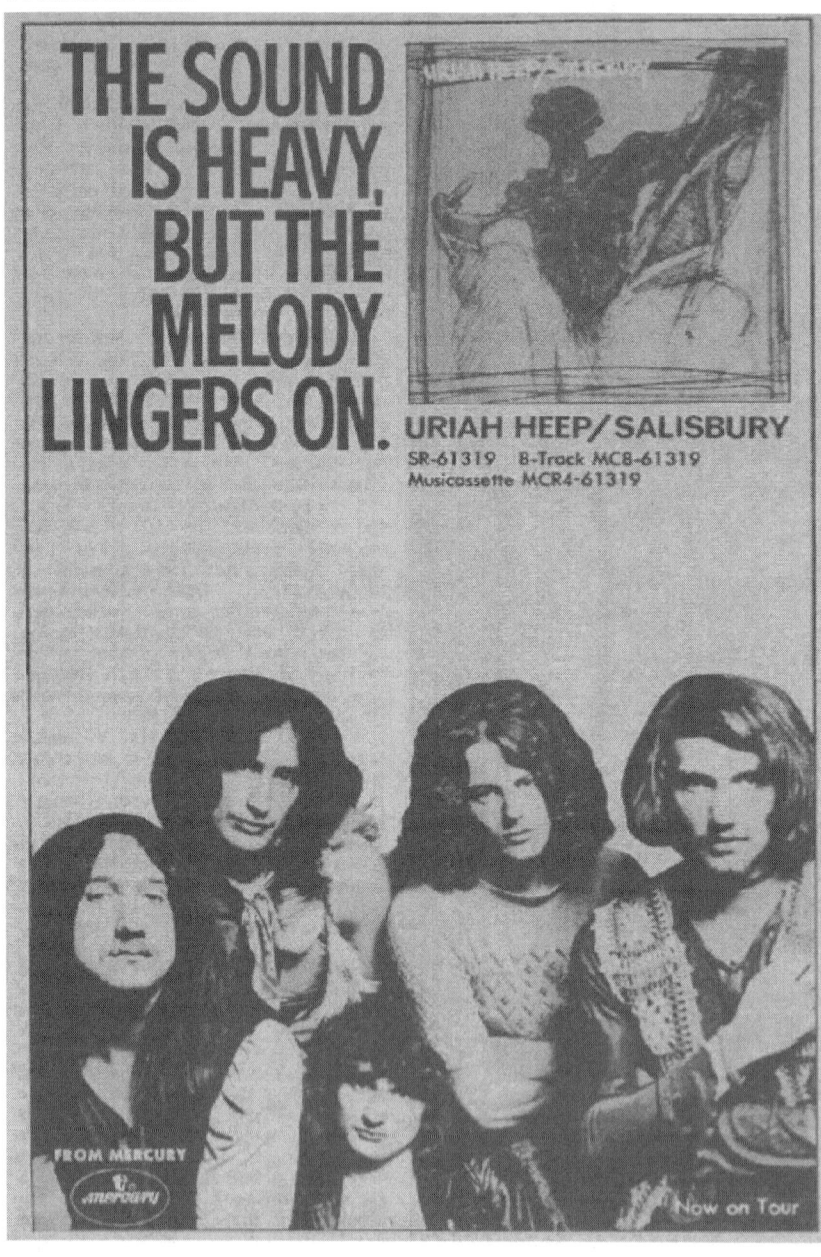

Deep Purple guitarist Ritchie Blackmore on comparisons between Deep Purple and Uriah Heep:
To be quite honest, they were coming up at the same time and they had a good vocalist going, but I think there was a bit of copying going on there. To be quite honest. Because they were like about a year behind us. And I know them quite well; yeah, there was. It was a bit kind of disconcerting, when I'd meet them. David Byron would say, "Hey, we're catching you guys up!" Everything revolved around catching you guys up. And there would be periods when I would hear certain little throwaway things I would do on stage. I used to do a Bach piece, just as a novelty thing, and then suddenly Mick Box would be playing it next time I saw him. So there was some copying going on there. I'm not having a go at them, but you know when somebody is listening to you and copying you. It's not just coincidence. They were a very good band, and I love stuff like "Lady in Black" and "Gypsy;" some of my favourite songs.

Later Uriah Heep bassist Trevor Bolder on those pesky comparisons with Purple:
We've tour quite a few times with Purple. I mean, we're similar because of the Hammond organ. But they don't have any harmonies at all, and of course we use five-part harmonies, with basically every song, and they just have the one front man. I suppose it's heavy rock from the same era, and Purple are a bit like us in a way, in that they've had lots of members in the band (laughs). But I suppose that's about as much as I can compare us, really. I suppose we're more of a Hammond band, and they're much more of a guitar band with one vocalist.

February 1971. Bassist John Deacon joins Queen, completing the lineup.

February 5, 1971. Black Sabbath begins studio work on *Master of Reality*, amidst US tour dates, likely unaware that they will soon be issuing sounds so heavy that they will, by some measures, never be out-heavied, in part through use of down-tuned guitar past previous levels already pioneered by Iommi.

Future Black Sabbath manager and musicologist Sandy Pearlman:
Down-tuning creates a kind of unnatural chordal universe. I don't mean that badly. There's something intensely disturbing about down-tuning. It reads to the auditory cortex as heavier. It creates more positive chordal congestion. Well, you're a guitar player—you know what I'm saying. It's a very important resource. And I believe Hendrix was the first one to exploit it, and then of course, Sabbath exploited it very nicely.

Black Sabbath guitarist Tony Iommi on *Master of Reality* being his most down-tuned album:
    Yes it is. As time went on, I spent more time working on the guitar. The first couple of albums were very, very quick. We didn't have time to work on the guitar sound (laughs). We were in, done it and out. But as time went on, from

Master of Reality onward, we had more time to work on sounds, on everything, really. The down-tuning, I got it more from myself, because when I chopped the end of my fingers off, I found it difficult to bend strings. And on the first couple of albums, of course, in those days you couldn't get gauge strings. They were all sort of heavy strings. So I had to make my own set up. When I had chopped the ends of my fingers off, I had to come up with ideas that would work for me.

So I made my own set of light gauge strings. And how I did that was I got two first banjo strings, and then I got a regular set, and I dropped it down, until I found the right gauge for me. You know, instead of using the sixth string that was in the set, I would throw that away and then use the fifth as the sixth, and do it like that, until I found one that was comfortable for me. And of course, it was a problem tuning it. My old Gibson in those days, you could bend the neck, you could move it easily, as soon as you touched it. So tuning was very awkward at that time. But I had to do it. I realized that I had to change my whole style of playing, play in a way that suits me and not anybody else. So that's what we did. And of course, later on, I tried using every string tuned down, to get the same effect. But it worked also in the sound as well. Again, it's an experiment, just to get a different mood for songs. And of course, when you do it live, you have to do the same live. The last tours we've done with Ozzy, when we play "Into the Void," I had to use a guitar that is tuned down a step.

February 24, 1971. Cactus release their second album, *One Way… Or Another*, which, like the debut, is pretty heavy, but steeped in styles past.

> Cactus guitarist Jim McCarty on being called "America's Led Zeppelin:"
> No idea; it's a mystery to me. I don't know where that came from. It's embarrassing for me. Maybe that came from the label. I would not compare Cactus to Led Zeppelin at all. I don't think you can compare anybody to Led Zeppelin. It's a unique thing unto itself, and they definitely left their recorded legacy. What we heard most back then, was that the band got blasted. The critics hated the band. It just got torn apart for the two years it was together. They didn't think it was anything special. It didn't really mean much to me what they thought. It was what I thought, and musically it just got to a point where it wasn't working, in my estimation.

March 1971. Sweet experience their first international hit single, "Funny, Funny." "Co-Co" follows in June of 1971. Neither pop number points to the lustre and heft of the band's sharply modern metal songs which will arrive with admirable regularity between 1973 and 1977.

March 19, 1971. Jethro Tull issue their fourth album, *Aqualung*. Still clearly not a heavy metal band, Ian Anderson and crew nonetheless became an even greater part of the conversation due to the hit status of the record's title track, plus other high profile heavy-ish tracks like "Cross Eyed Mary" (later covered by Iron Maiden) and "Locomotive Breath." In retrospect, it's easy to understand why lay people would think Tull a hard rock act—the three radio hits from this hit record were the album's heaviest tracks, along with album track "My God" which garnered less radio exposure.

Jethro Tull flutist and vocalist Ian Anderson:
Hard rock fans like us probably because they feel a sense of being deprived of real music, and they need to somehow exercise a little bit of sensitivity and maturity into their musical tastes. I think that's the only possible reason. I mean, I don't mind a bit of loud rock music from time to time. But I find that if it's just repetitive and the same kind of thing all the time, about ten minutes of it and I just want to run for cover. So it is a little odd. I have to say that I've never been a fan of rock music, and particularly incessant loud rock music. It's never appealed to me ever. And one of the reasons I didn't like The Who is that they were so bloody loud! It was just all-out all the time, and I just felt that was pretty boring. Same with a lot of bands that go under the general title of hard rock or heavy metal. It's just all on the same level, and I think music, great music, has dynamic range. It has sensitivity, it has contradictions, it has its ups and it has its downs, and when the guitar or the amplifier is turned up to number 11 from start to finish, frankly, it just becomes a little one-dimensional for me. I like something a little different. As an acoustic musician, that's part of what I'm here to do, is to bring a little sensitivity to the world of rock music, and try to show people different levels at which music can be exciting, without necessarily being ear-splittingly loud.

Spring 1971. Jacksonville, Florida's Blackfoot breaks up for a short period while Rickey Medlocke joins Lynyrd Skynyrd as their drummer. Blackfoot will eventually challenge ZZ Top for the mantle of heaviest southern rock band.

April 1971. Irish power trio Skid Row issue their second and last album, *34 Hours*.

Skid Row guitarist and vocalist Gary Moore:
God, we were listening to stuff like Cream, again being a three-piece band. But I don't have great memories of that band. When I listen to it now I think, oh shit, what was I doing? And I'm sure people who played music for a long time feel that way about stuff they've done earlier on. But particularly that band for me, the rhythm section was so busy. It was just like everyone was showing off. And the bass player, Brush Shiels, I think he saw me as this kind of little prodigy—because I was 16 when I joined the band—someone to show off to people. And he was encouraging me to play faster and faster, just so much emphasis on speed, showing off chops and all the shit that meant nothing, really. But I was so young at the time, I didn't really know what was going on so I went along with it. But I'm not really too keen on all that music. I just think it was very messy and frantic. There's a bit of a King Crimson vibe as well, in all that unison, the fast breaks and stuff. But King Crimson was ten times better at it than anyone else so there wasn't much point getting into that. To be honest, when I joined that band, all I wanted to play was blues, but that's not what they were into. I came out of the blues into that band and I was asked to join and I wanted to get away from home at the time, because I was having a lot of problems at home in Belfast, and it was a great opportunity to get into a band. And Phil Lynott was in the band and it was him really that attracted me to the band and we became friends through that. Music sometimes is very strange.

April 1971. Stray issue their second album, *Suicide*. It is one of the top 15 or so heaviest albums of 1971.

April 1971. Bloodrock issue *Bloodrock 3* and the glory years are already behind them.

April 1971. Free break up, although there would still be a live album issued during the downtime, followed by a fragile union for two more studio records.

> Free bassist Andy Fraser on whether he got the credit that was due to him in the band:
> Yes, I was credited where due, and haven't spent any time second-guessing what others may or may not have assumed. I don't take anything away from Paul Rodgers, I tried to learn all I could from his skills as a singer and songwriter. I am aware that most people see a band first and foremost through the singer. He strongly influenced me. I will let him speak for himself. Only a fool would not take advantage of learning all one could from one's partners. And I felt we were all in a four-way marriage—learnt from everyone, but some marriages end in divorce... Free was a state of spirit. And I think that's why Free broke up: because we lost that spirit. Paul I think was in the beginning phases of wanting to put together a Bad Company-type of thing, which was a slimmed-down, two-dimensional version of Free, sort of stadium-ready and not too sensitive. I miss that side of him, by the way, because he's written some of the greatest mellow songs. But when we started to become a cover band of ourselves, that's when you're not free. Fame and fortune are no substitute for freedom. I want to be free and remain free.
>
> Free drummer Simon Kirke on the break-up of the band:
> Koss was not a leader, he was quite weak and frail at the time and was going through a bad drug period. Paul Rodgers was much more robust and, quite frankly, was more rewarding to work with. I was getting worn with Koss's habit. Andy was a great player but we never really got on, Boz was a lot more fun, and Tetsu was the most precise. Essentially, Free had charm and was innovative, while Bad Company were more professional and commercial.

April 1971. Grand Funk issue their fourth studio album, *Survival*.

April 1971. Blue Cheer issue their sixth and last album (until a reunion for '83's *The Beast is Back*), called *Oh! Pleasant Hope*.

April 1971. The Amboy Dukes is now Ted Nugent and the Amboy Dukes, and onto their first live album, *Survival of the Fittest*. The cover features a picture of Ted and no other band members, suggesting a solo future for Ted, a future that will have him contributing greatly to heavy metal history from 1975 to 1980. The album was recorded at Eastown Theatre, opened in 1931, closed in 1980. Most of the big rock acts of the day played there, along with the Grande Ballroom. Ted is still adding to his reputation as a guitar hero, but with songs that are a combination of psychedelic, proggy, dated and nowhere.

Amboy Dukes drummer K.J. Knight:
We were high energy rock 'n' roll. That seem to be the way all the bands were back then—MC5, Stooges—and we were all inspired by Mitch Ryder and the Detroit Wheels for sure. Mitch was definitely the godfather of Detroit rock 'n' roll. But we were definitely what you would call a high energy rock 'n' roll band, and not psych. Ted was always really conservative. I don't think he ever saw himself as a hippie. He was very much anti-drugs, so I would say that we weren't a hippie-type of band or a head band. And because the music was written by Ted, his influences were the Rolling Stones, and definitely Jim McCarty of the Detroit Wheels.

I'll tell you what, man. Ted was the ultimate showman. I mean, back in the day, he would get on top of two-stacked-high Fender amps and jump off the amps and land standing on his feet. Before his solo, he would go backstage and change into like a loin cloth and come swinging out from a rope tied to the rafters, back on stage. And his brother, Johnny Nugent, who is one of the guys in the road crew, he would take a Styrofoam wig head, and place it on top of the amp, squirt some lighter fluid on it and light it on fire, and Ted would have his bow and arrow onstage and he would shoot the flaming head off. Ted was a fantastic shot, and he would hit it, and the crowd would go crazy! He had terrific energy, fantastic showman, and that rubbed off on the rest of us too. He was definitely a very competitive individual, and probably the most self-confident individual I've ever known. So yeah, he was very competitive. We always went out there every night with the attitude that we were going to blow everybody away.

Ted Nugent on heavy metal:
You know, I never liked the term heavy metal. To me, heavy metal represents some stupid white guy who hasn't learned personal hygiene yet and wears a leather jacket or a Levi jacket because it's the trendy thing to do, which I spit in the face of. I think that's all just cheap and transparent and meaningless. I was influenced by all things black and rhythm and blues. I've never been influenced by heavy bands. Obviously the Yardbirds and the Stones and to some degree the

licks on the Led Zeppelin records. But heavy metal has never done anything for me. I don't consider my favourite bands heavy metal, my favorite bands being Aerosmith and Cheap Trick and Van Halen and ZZ Top. I think those are all rhythm and blues bands. In the case of Van Halen, it's just rhythm and blues-tinged pop with a real rock 'n' roll energy level, mostly delivered by the front men, David Lee Roth and the incredible style of Sammy Hagar. As a functioning band, Eddie and Michael and Alex are the consummate high energy rhythm and blues rhythm section. They are so rhythmical, they can't just be lumped in with that. I certainly wouldn't insult them by calling them heavy metal. I consider heavy metal things like Judas Priest, which I enjoy, and Black Sabbath and Dio but I just think it's too Caucasian for me.

April 25, 1971. Japan's first heavy metal band Flower Travellin' Band issue *Satori*, their third album and first of original material. *Anywhere*, from October '70 included a cover of "Black Sabbath." The album is consistently heavy, with various interesting distortion textures, but is also quite jammy and experimental.

April 26, 1971. End of Black Sabbath's tour in support of *Paranoid*.

April 30, 1971. Thin Lizzy's self-titled debut album, followed by the *New Day* EP on August 20, 1971, provide no inkling that this would one day be one of the world's most cherished hard rock bands. Nor do they give clue to the fact that the band would become the pioneers of twin lead guitar work in a heavy metal context—that would have to wait for Eric Bell to be replaced by Scott Gorham and Brian Robertson.

May 1971. The UK's Pink Fairies (ex-Deviants) issue their hard hippie debut, *Never Never Land*. Drummer Twink would later become, briefly, a member of Motörhead. The free festival freaks have some riffs.

May 1971. The first well-documented usage of the term heavy metal is contained in a May 1971 issue of Creem, embedded in a review of Sir Lord Baltimore's *Kingdom Come*. Mike Saunders (see earlier November '70 reference) notes that, "Sir Lord Baltimore seems to have down pat most all the best heavy metal tricks in the book." Creem critic Lester Bangs subsequently has been credited with popularizing the term in the early 1970s when describing bands such as Led Zeppelin and Black Sabbath. "Heavy metal" may have been used as a derogatory term initially by a number of music critics but was quickly adopted by its adherents. Of note, Bill Ward is credited with the term downer rock, which essentially meant the heavy metal of Black Sabbath, the specific reference being to the fan base's predilection for "downers and wine." Generally speaking, the term entered the lexicon briefly but was replaced by the new descriptor, heavy metal.

May 26, 1971. Work on Black Sabbath's *Master of Reality* is completed with the final work on "Sweet Leaf" and "Solitude." The band have created a symphony of riffery that crushes the claims (pointedly, not theirs, but ours—and after many years, I might add) of Deep Purple with *In Rock*, not to mention the far less metal mix of Deep Purple's salvo for 1971, *Fireball*.

Additionally, *Master of Reality*, through its immense guitar sound and redlined production, would trump the substantial work Black Sabbath themselves had laid down to date through its two records we've pronounced the first bona fide metal albums, along with *In Rock* from Deep Purple and *Very 'Eavy, Very 'Umble* from Uriah Heep. The effect of *Master of Reality*, therefore, on the story and the plot line, is that it reduces the importance of *In Rock* concerning our titular answer, swinging the leaden pendulum back to Black Sabbath as the one band worthy of being called the inventors of heavy metal.

Black Sabbath engineer Tom Allom on *Master of Reality*'s massive guitar sound:
Yes, it's a huge sound. We recorded that in a studio called Morgan. Quite a big room. That was sort of deemed to be the way that the guitar sounds were going. Yes, it is a fatter sound. That album took a hell of a long time. That took four weeks. By then they were a huge band, but they came in the studio with practically nothing written. Totally different from the first album, which was completely written, done, bang, out. Which is very often the case with a band. They get on with it with the first album because they've had several years to get that together.

Black Sabbath manager Jim Simpson:
Well, to be honest with you, I like Black Sabbath best and I like Paranoid second best and I like Master of Reality third best. You've got to remember, we... well, let's get it right. We spent a long time on the material that went into the Black Sabbath album. There's probably two years worth of work there, and then Philips wanted the second album six months later. Also, I think when you establish something new, and you create something new like that, the first step is the greatest, and it's also the song collection of all your thoughts and ideas. Paranoid, itself, the album, was slicker, and I was going to say less honest—I don't mean less honest—but less from the heart. I think the Black Sabbath album was a real emotional creation; they did it because they'd all reached a point where they were thinking exactly along the same lines musically, and this was their first child. I think by the time it came to the second birth, they'd done it all before a little bit, nattily enough, but it didn't have the same sort of innocence of the first. I think any musician, anyway, as he gets better, you become more guileful and find ways of doing things and it's not quite as much from the heart—anyone.

June 1971. Budgie issue their very heavy self-titled debut. *Budgie* was recorded in 1970, lending the band credence in terms of their importance to the story vis-a-vis temporal proximity to Black Sabbath's accomplishments of 1970. Producer of the album is Black Sabbath producer Rodger Bain, who would go on to produce Judas Priest's first album as well.

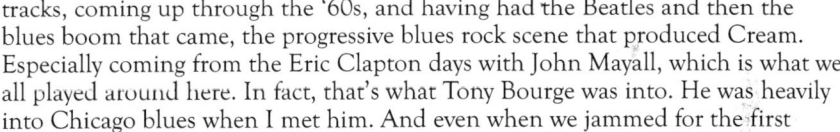

Budgie bassist and vocalist Burke Shelley:
In those days, we were still reverting to older influences, like rock 'n' roll feels or blues tracks, coming up through the '60s, and having had the Beatles and then the blues boom that came, the progressive blues rock scene that produced Cream. Especially coming from the Eric Clapton days with John Mayall, which is what we all played around here. In fact, that's what Tony Bourge was into. He was heavily into Chicago blues when I met him. And even when we jammed for the first time, we jammed on "All Your Love," which is on John Mayall's album. It had to do with guitarists who were in those bands, like Peter Green, Eric Clapton—Jeff Beck, there's another one. Amazing. At the time. Those were our influences: bluesy rock and rock 'n' roll.

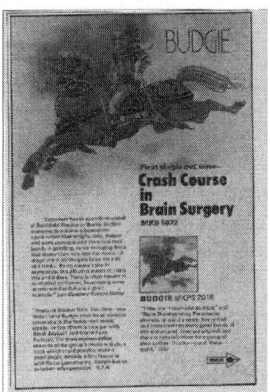

Budgie drummer Ray Phillips:
Rodger had the Black Sabbath experience under his belt. They were an English band, we were a Welsh band and from what I gather, Black Sabbath, especially Ozzy, he was a bit of a tear-away; we were never a tear-away in Budgie. I think Rodger would have a lot more control over the Budgie situation than he would with the Black Sabbath situation. And when Rodger came with us, it was, what can I say, the magic that came from that three-piece band. I remember I was speaking to Dave Howells at MCA Records, and he said what impressed him with Budgie was, we'd go from something really heavy and all of a sudden we'd just switch straight over to really light. So I

think the work with Rodger was a coalition of the four of us. It was almost like a coalition between me and Rodger, between Burke and Tony, between Burke and Rodger, between Tony and Rodger, and the whole band and Rodger.

June 14, 1971. *Black Sabbath* is certified gold, proving that the band's scary music didn't scare everybody away.

Led Zeppelin expert Dave Lewis on Black Sabbath's path to success:
With Black Sabbath, and even earlier as Earth, they certainly paid their dues. They got out there and they got in a van. They went up and down the country, they went to the States, second on the bill to Mountain, and I think the press reacted to that positively because they certainly worked hard to get to where they were. And because their audience had grown through them being visual in concert, a lot of credibility was gained by that as well.

July 1971. Judas Priest, now including Ian Hill and KK Downing, record a demo at Zella Studios, consisting of "Holy is the Man" and "Mind Conception."

Original Judas Priest vocalist Al Atkins on the band's inspirations to be so heavy:
I'd always been in bands which embraces progression. Whatever was happening, we'd go and see something new and say, I like this, let's try it, whether it be Cream or whatever. You'd always watch another band do something on a different level. So yeah, obviously when we formed Judas Priest in '69, Sabbath had already made a name for themselves. Oh, this is great. We need to go

down this route. And we got the name and hit the road, and that was it. It was a fantastic time. We played with Sabbath around that time. Tony Iommi took us under his wing and he managed us for about 12 months. He thought Judas Priest was going to be the next biggest thing. But Sabbath were one of the biggest influences. Led Zeppelin as well. It was the main bands playing around; with Jimmy Page coming out of the Yardbirds, that was a great band as well, great guitarists in there with Jimmy and Jeff Beck. I liked some American bands; we did a couple songs by a band called Quicksilver Messenger Service from America, which we beefed up a bit. So a lot of influence, but more on the heavy side.

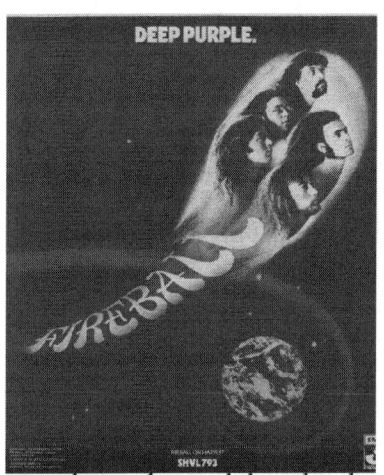

July 1971. Deep Purple release *Fireball* in the US and Canada. The album is issued in Sept. '71 in the UK and Europe. The album's title track is widely considered one of the first speed metal and even thrash metal tracks of all time. There are other heavy songs amidst the wide variety of styles pursued, but the consensus was that the band was taking a shocking and light departure juxtaposed against *In Rock*. In some quarters, *Fireball* is viewed as the band's Led Zeppelin III. It is for this reason that we will close the books on our suspended judgement on whether it was Deep Purple that invented heavy metal instead of Black Sabbath. In other words, had *Fireball* been even heavier and flashier and riffier and more future-forward than the already highly inventive *In Rock*, then Black Sabbath, with their two records, might have been surpassed. It isn't and they aren't. We waited patiently to see what Deep Purple would do in 1971, and what they did is write some non-metal, some average metal, and one pioneering track in "Fireball." Verdict: *Black Sabbath invented heavy metal.*

Guitarist Yngwie Malmsteen on *Fireball*:
I grew up in a country that was barren. I mean, there were a lot of trees, a lot of moose. There was hardly any TV, hardly any radio. I didn't wake up in a barrage of media like kids do today, in between the cable TV and the DVDs and video game and this online stuff. There was nothing. There was really nothing there. So in other words, when I was eight years old, when I first heard Deep Purple *Fireball*, that was my first introduction to rock music. And, what an introduction, eh? Those double drums. It had such an impact on me, it completely decided my destiny. That moment. On my eight birthday, I knew exactly what I was going to do for the rest of my life. There was no doubt, no single-minute spectacle of doubt in my mind, in any fibre of my body, what I was going to do with my life. There was nothing that was going to stop me. Nothing was going to stop me from doing what I wanted to do, from that point on. I knew it.

And actually the year before, I saw Hendrix on TV, and that was in fact huge too, because that was when I wanted to play guitar. I saw him smash and burn the guitar in Monterey. It was only that. It wasn't a musical impact, because it was on the TV news. "Yesterday, Jimi Hendrix died," and boom, there it is. Wow, I like that. So I already had a guitar and I started playing it that day. But when I heard songs like "Demon's Eye" and "Fools," it was like a whole universe had just been opened to me. There was nothing comparable to that, around me. Nothing! I didn't see any other bands. I'd never heard Led Zeppelin or Black Sabbath; I never heard anything like that.

A couple weeks later, I saved up enough money to go buy—which I didn't know at the time; I just wanted another Deep Purple album—and they gave me *In Rock*. That was the left hook, you know (laughs). And that floored me again! And I lived on those albums for many a good year. And it just... as far as I'm concerned, looking back at it, I'm really happy that those were the albums I got. Because if I would've gotten maybe something else, it would've turned out a little different.

Black Sabbath bassist Geezer Butler on Deep Purple:
Well, somebody must like them (laughs). I've never really been a Deep Purple fan. I'm not even really into metal, to be honest, or hard rock. I like mellow stuff and jazz stuff. I liked *Machine Head* when that came out; I thought that was a good album. But then, I'm not a big fan of keyboard-orientated music; I thought there was too much keyboards on it for me. As for comparisons, we didn't see any rivalry. It just sort of divided a lot of people. A lot of people liked Sabbath, a lot of people like Purple, and then when we got together with Gillan later, some people were really pissed-off and some people thought it was brilliant.

Blue Öyster Cult bassist Joe Bouchard:
The first time I saw Deep Purple we were in Chicago, and we had a day off. And we went to a Deep Purple show at some amphitheatre out of town. And it was pure pandemonium. We were just blown away. They started out with "Highway Star." They had the red lights, like the cop lights going, and there was smoke. The place went absolutely nuts. It was really good. That was like a good hard-rocking show, and it was the classic Deep Purple lineup.

Deep Purple keyboardist Don Airey on the Hammond and its place in Purple:
It's the hardest keyboard to play. You spend many years learning how to do it—it's a fine art, and you never get to the end of it. But it's something that can really compete with the guitar, in terms of sound. My Hammond with Purple, I've got two Leslie cabinets, plus I've got a 100-watt guitar amp, and you know, I'm making quite a noise there. I think they stopped making Hammonds in about '76; the company went bankrupt, I think. So they haven't made one since. Suzuki has the rights to it, and they make a digital Hammond, which is pretty good, but I mean, for the old sound, you've got to have an old Hammond. Unfortunately they made about a half-million of the things, and a lot of them are in people's homes. People bought them in the '50s and the '60s for their homes, and now of course, maybe the original player died off, and there's a widow left, and she's in her 90s, so she wants to celebrate her 100th, and you find these things.

Hammonds are the most over-engineered keyboard ever made. They last. I mean, my Hammond will last a lot longer than I will (laughs). I've actually got a few. When I joined Purple, I bought Jon Lord's Hammond. He said he was going in a different direction, and he kind of would leave it with the band. And that Hammond has a long history. It belonged to Christine McVie of Fleetwood Mac.

So it's been on the road, to my knowledge, since 1967, and hasn't had a lot done to it. They just go on and on and on.

The Hammond I use now has been specially built for me. There's a place called The Hammond Store up in Connecticut, and there's a wonderful man named John Haburay who's in charge of it, and he's made it a lot more travel-proof. He's put it in a new case and it's on these legs. I think it's called a chop, is what it's called. And he's modernized two Leslies. I've had this new instrument about a year now, and it gets better every year. Even the band's noticed that there's something going on (laughs). As for Jon's, we're still using it. We have a B rig; we're so busy that we have to leapfrog gear a lot. So the Jon Lord one is in the B rig, but I don't think it likes being the B rig. I can feel the life coming out of it. You know, 42 years in the service of British rock.

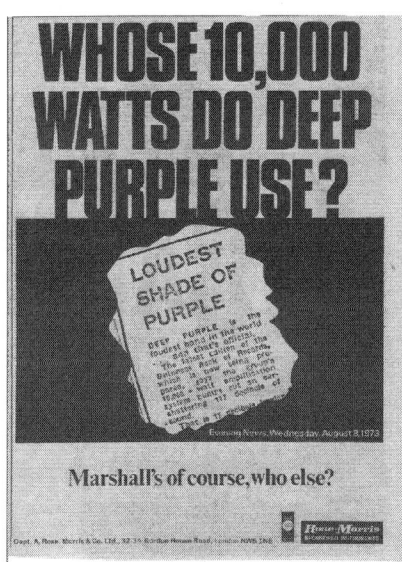

Scorpions guitarist Uli Jon Roth on Ritchie Blackmore:

Ritchie was totally a trend-setter. His approach to playing the guitar was very, very unique when he first came out, and it is still unique. There are very few people in the music business who were able to do like three totally different things and make them all work. You know, like Purple, Rainbow, and then Blackmore's Night. It's a very unique gift that he has, a very musical gift, and a great popular gift also. Like, I couldn't write a riff like "Smoke on the Water." Some people maybe laugh about it because you used to hear it in every music store. But you know, that's an achievement. And it's a gift.

I always felt he was a guitar player who sounded exciting, and he was never afraid to go close to the edge. And there was always danger in his playing. And this is what I like. I like players who don't do the expected thing. They take chances and go for the dangerous moments, and not just be self-complacent. And very often I prefer those kinds of players to the players who are like all smooth and maybe super-refined, and where every note is in the pocket. I guess I'm more fascinated by the aspect of creativity in the making, and with Ritchie you always get that, this element of real excitement. It was always fresh. And even if they played the same songs for the umpteenth time, they weren't afraid to improvise on stage, which most bands are. Purple never played them the same.

Also, another thing that I really liked about Ritchie, whenever I saw him live, he always has a great tone. And he had very much his own tone, and I respond to that. I respect players that have a unique tone, a very good ear for sound. And so he sacrificed the playability of the instrument for a great tone. Because it's not easy to do these sounds with an almost clean guitar, the way he used to play.

July 1, 1971. First date of Black Sabbath's *Master of Reality* tour, St. Paul, MN.

July 2, 1971. MC5 release *High Time*, their third and last album. The band change their sound for the third time over three records, including some degree of heaviness in tracks like "Skunk (Sonically Speaking)," "Sister Anne," "Gotta Keep Movin'" and especially "Poison," but also much jazz.

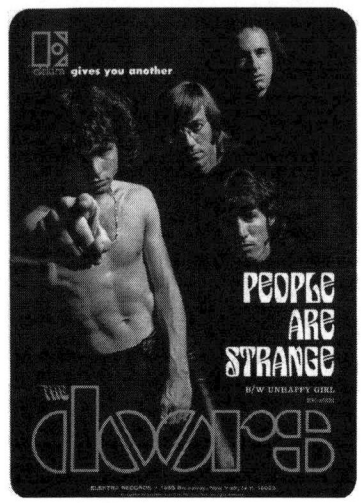

July 3, 1971. Death of Jim Morrison, surprisingly, of little consequence to the heavy metal story, even from a persona or icon point of view.

July 21, 1971. Black Sabbath issue, simultaneously in the UK and the US, *Master of Reality*, a bulldozer and house-wrecker of a record that triple-underscores the intention of the band that invented heavy metal. Other than two tossed-off mellow instrumentals, every track on the album, through production, riffery, even vocals and arguably lyrics, is of a heavier metal than this band had crafted in 1970 or would ever craft in all the years moving forward. In fact, by certain definitions and measures, one could argue that the next nearly 44 years of music has not produced songs "heavier" than "Sweet Leaf," "Into the Void," "Children of the Grave," "After Forever" and "Lord of this World." To their credit, Billboard, after complimenting the band on some "gently evocative songs," also says "a certain amount of doom is provided for diehard fans," citing the song "Into the Void." Is this first use of the term doom as, clearly, a descriptor of a type of music?

> Black Sabbath drummer Bill Ward on *Master of Reality*:
> *Master of Reality*, when you listen to that, you're hearing a band that are already pretty much veterans. I think we probably already had at least one tour of the world under our belt, and at least three or four tours of America, multiple tours of Europe. So the band on *Master of Reality* was a band that had lived together and had been playing together nearly every single day. I mean, we hadn't left each other sides. So with *Master*, I think you're listening to what is a definite upgrade in the musicianship. Ozzy's voice at times... I mean his voice is just incredible. So there are some, what I would call physical differences. We were probably at that point at our peak of working the hardest we had ever worked. And after *Master of Reality* was completed, it was necessary for us to kick back a little bit, because we hadn't stopped. We had been on the road, on and off for three years. We hadn't stop work at all. In terms of the sound of that album, recording procedures change quite a bit very quickly. The equipment that we used with *Paranoid*, in comparison with the equipment we used for *Master of Reality*, there was a major difference. For instance, *Master of Reality* was done on a 24-track board so that brought us up to almost a kind of Beatle-esque level, whereas *Paranoid* was done on an eight-track board.

August 1971. Philadelphia's Bang record a concept album called *Death to a Country*, only to have it shelved for 40 years. The band however landed a record deal with Capitol off of the effort, issuing a self-titled album in February of 1972. Definitely quite heavy and aspiring to doom, *Bang* is invariably paired with Sir Lord Baltimore's *Kingdom Come* when discussion turns to the earliest nascent heavy metal records out of America in the early '70s. 1972's *Mother/Bow to the King* reinforces a degree of heavy metal intention from these underground legends. 1973's *Music*, not so much. The band's *Death to a Country* material unfortunately finds the band only occasionally Sabbatherian, somewhat psych, somewhat folky, typically hung up on the '60s like any number of American bands not doing a good job with heavy metal.

August 1971. Buffalo, Australia's first metal band, forms, in Sydney, Australia, issuing a very heavy debut in 1972. The band is signed to Vertigo, same label as Black Sabbath.

September 1971. Free issue their fifth album, and first live album, *Free Live!*. The band were broken up at this point.

September 10, 11, 1971. Black Sabbath's only shows ever with Led Zeppelin, in Syracuse NY and Rochester NY respectively. It is no secret that Led Zeppelin politely and discreetly looked down their noses at Black Sabbath, tacitly getting the view across that their own band's sense of adventure and subsequent grab-bag variety across their albums pointed to greater intellectual substance. This, of course, ignores the fact—as does the trite dictum, "We have something for everybody on this album"—that 30 minutes is 30 minutes, meaning that as soon as you spend some of those minutes elsewhere, you are exploring less of another genre.

> Led Zeppelin expert Dave Lewis offering the classic defence:
> The prime example of allowing space and the use of loud and soft on the first Zeppelin album would be "Babe I'm Gonna Leave You." You can have this crescendo of composition going over six minutes into a loud and soft scenario. And again, with Zeppelin, there were always acoustic guitars from the beginning. If anyone should have been shocked by Zeppelin III, well, they should have gone back to Zep I and "Babe I'm Gonna Leave You" and "Black Mountain Side." So again, with the metal genre—and I think Zeppelin was unfairly pushed into that, and I'm not trying to be a snob about it—but I they were pushed into that limited genre, which I think in some cases metal has been. Not always. I'm saying there was always much more to Zeppelin than a metal thing. Jimmy had a vast canvas he wanted to cover, and part of it might have been riff-orientated rock, which is what it was, but that was never going to be the end of it. It wasn't just going to be about Marshall amplifiers turned up to 11; Zeppelin was always much more than that.

September 27, 1971. Black Sabbath's *Master of Reality* is certified gold, proving an insatiable appetite amongst Americans for moaning "downer rock" dirges about weed and climate apocalypse.

> Black Sabbath drummer Bill Ward on *Master of Reality*'s bruising "Into the Void:" "Into the Void"... I wasn't aware that there was an influence from any other band. That was Black Sabbath at its absolute height, when it was absolutely coming alive. And at that point Geezer was writing really strongly and the band at that point was unbelievably tight. We were really becoming confident and we had just done a couple of world tours. That was a science fiction one about how we were all fed up at the time and wished we could just get into a rocket ship and blast off.

Late 1971. Belgian band Irish Coffee issue a self-titled album on Brain Trust—fairly heavy but dated.

Late 1971. Sir Lord Baltimore issues their second (and last) album, a self-titled.

> Sir Lord Baltimore drummer and lead vocalist John Garner on the second album:
> Well, the main difference between them, was, quite honestly, I knew that the first Sir Lord Baltimore had an adolescent, imperfect quality about it—it was very raw. And we thought our tempos constantly went too fast, and we needed something to stabilize that, right? So we got Joey Dambra, Louis' brother, who was a much more anchored kind of guitar player. His tempo was more steady. Louis used to just speed up and speed up into the cosmos. And actually it was a mistake, because we didn't realize that people loved that first album the way it was. I know I didn't, because I was listening to groups like Led Zeppelin, and I'm hearing a perfect recording—the tempo is always perfect. And I'm thinking, hey man, that's how we've got to become, more perfect with our tempo and things like that. Not realizing that being crazy was what people loved that about us so much.

October 1971. Scorpions record what will become their debut album, *Lonesome Crow*, issued in February 1972. The band begin their distinguished career at the hard rock end of what is known as Krautrock, but become concise and modernly metallic by the time of their third album.

> Scorpions vocalist Klaus Meine:
> Is there anything German in our music? I don't know... That's a good question! Obviously, we're from Germany but we grew up with English and American music which was such a strong inspiration for the young band. Very early on, in the '70s, we went to England and France, to Japan and America, we toured, and then became an international band. I think our music was never German. It's always had this Anglo-American influence; we never tried to be a German band! We are Germans, yes, but not in our music. When we grew up, there was schlager music, this pop music kind of thing. Krautrock? Yeah! Today it's kind of culty, and people say, "Ah, Krautrock!" But when the Krautrock thing came up back then, in the early '70s, it was like all the international stars in big music magazines: they got big articles and nice features and it was like they were putting us down and making us very small. It was like, push, push, push, when, especially when we were a young band, we needed support to gain the confidence. We felt there was no support and it encouraged us to go to foreign countries. We went to England in 1975 just to figure out, "We are German but we sing in English. Are we good enough? Are we strong enough to survive among the English who invented rock 'n' roll?" This was always like a challenge, and so very soon we became an international band.

October 1971. Uriah Heep issue *Look at Yourself*. The album is recorded in July of '71. Suddenly, Uriah Heep are back in the conversation of bands who were heavy early, given the album's heft embodied in tracks like "Tears in My Eyes,' Shadows of Grief," "Look at Yourself" and "Love Machine." Even with a degree of keyboard-centicity, the band were at this juncture creating a sound that was heavier than doppelgangers Deep Purple. To put a finer point on it, the band's metal mix through three albums was roughly on par  with Purple's, but in terms of production values, "Gypsy," "Tears in My Eyes" and "Shadows of Grief" achieve a muscular Purple pageantry of production purpose Martin Birch and band would never find, coming closest on 1972's

Machine Head. In a sense, the supposed copiers had beaten the originals at their own game, achieving a sonic strength that would be disingenuous of Purple to deny—disingenuous as well if they denied that Gerry Bron's sound represented the perfect hi-fidelity balance of guitar, keyboards, drums, bass and balls.

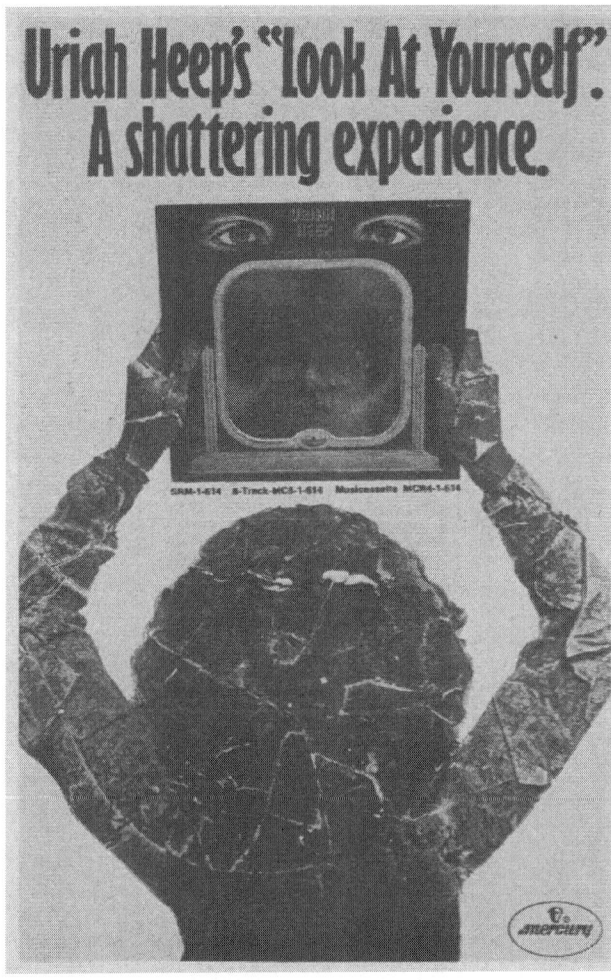

Uriah Heep keyboardist Ken Hensley on *Look at Yourself*:

It's an interesting album from a number of standpoints. First of all, it's the first album we recorded on 16-track. And it's the first record we did at the new control room at Lansdowne, with the new mixing console. So our scope was increased a lot. I remember the sessions very well, because they were done with a lot of enthusiasm. I remember Manfred Mann being involved, Osibisa being involved in the title track and so on. I don't remember all those things particularly fondly, but I do remember them being part of the evolution of the record. We made the record in about six weeks, I think. This was typical for us because we were on the road the rest of the time. We were making a record every nine or ten months at that time. And you can debate the wisdom of that from now until the cows come home, but the fact is, at the end of the day, when we sat down and listened to the final playback, which is always an interesting moment, most of us just said, "Eh, we don't like it." And in fact we said, "I think we have to re-record most of the songs, because they just sound terrible."

We were actually suffering from burnout. So the engineer, in his wisdom said, "Okay guys, I'll tell you what. Go away, take a week off, come back here a week from today, we'll listen to the record again. If you still hate it, we'll re-record it." And we went back a week later and we loved it. We had just gotten totally burnt-out on it and way too close to it. We couldn't be objective. We were just making sort of a blind judgment, and a week later, we all felt better.

I remember the album too, because, it was the album that really launched the band in North America. It was the first time that we were able to get into that market and penetrate that market at all, with the help of a massive tour with Three Dog Night. So yeah, it was a very important album for a lot of different reasons. By the time we got to Look at Yourself, I was feeling much more comfortable writing for the band and specifically writing for David. And I had written a bit on the first album, for which I wasn't given credit because of conflicting publishing deals. I'd written a lot on the second album, Salisbury.

We were really feeling our way around, trying to find a musical direction, a final musical direction. On Look at Yourself, I think we got pretty much close to that. By this time I felt that, from the writing standpoint, I had a lot more leeway. I had kind of established a good rapport with the band and with Gerry Bron as the producer. And I had to establish myself as being the leading provider of material for the band's recording. But it was merely the fact that I was beginning to understand how great of an interpreter David was, that left me more scope to experiment with songs such as "Tears in My Eyes."

Uriah Heep guitarist Mick Box on "July Morning:"
I think that "July Morning" is one of the best examples of the way the band was developing at that point in time. It introduced a lot of light and shade into our sound. It was magic, a very powerful song that encompasses everything that Heep stands for then and now. Beautiful dynamics from the band. Manfred Mann playing over on the end section with his mini moog. No practice—he just played it and we recorded it in one or two takes from memory.

Uriah Heep producer and Bronze Records founder Gerry Bron:
Uriah Heep were not the greatest musicians but they were very good, and as a team—it's like a football team—they succeeded, whereas other groups who had better musicians didn't succeed as they didn't really want to. Uriah Heep were absolutely determined to make it and they made it because they had their passion. My passion was putting them together; their passion was to be successful. I don't think it's just the money—they wanted to be successful because they believed in what they were doing. I don't think you can succeed unless you want to.

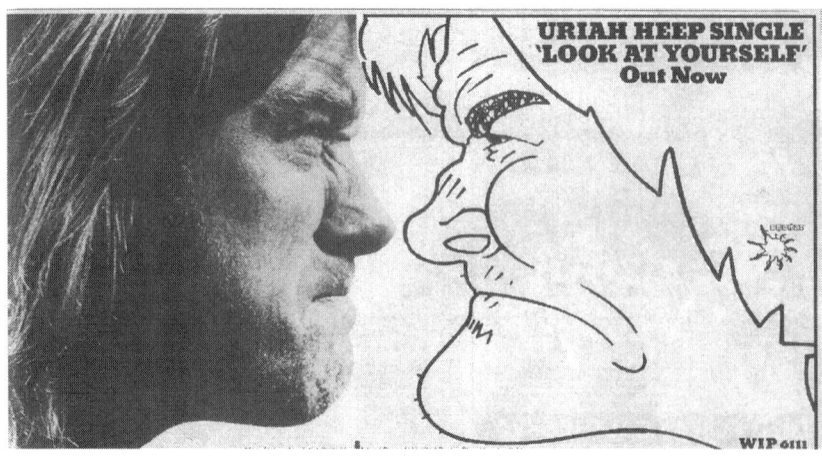

October 1971. UFO issue their second album, *Flying*, which surprisingly, finds the band diminishing their degree of intention in terms of heaviness, a bad career move given the times.

UFO drummer Andy Parker: You know, I don't know where that came from, that whole "One Hour Space Rock" thing. I often wonder, how did we come up with that? What made us decide to do that? I guess it's just where we were at; I guess we were just experimenting, thinking, okay, the first album had a lot of short poppy tunes on there, the record company was cool, let us do what we wanted, and we were just experimenting. There was a lot more jamming back then. And there was a lot more acid going 'round too. People were tripping and taking mescaline and going, "Wow, that's cool" and then doing a solo for 15 minutes.

UFO vocalist Phil Mogg on the band's early influences and joining forces with Schenker: Free, Humble Pie, Led Zeppelin, these were all bands that were playing around at the time. We were weaned on the Yardbirds and The Animals like everybody else. And when Michael joined for *Phenomenon*, he was the lucky link. It made our sound, which I think is very British and a little bit European. With Michael in it, you can hear German or Teutonic notes or notations in his playing. So it's a very European rock band, second or third generation.

October 1971. Bloodrock issue *Bloodrock U.S.A.*, their fourth album, and fourth for Capitol Records.

October 1971. UK's Lucifer issue their "Don't Care/"Hypnosis" single, with more singles and the *Big Gun* album to follow in 1972, which, although completely Satanic, is experimental synthesizer music. Not to be confused with Canadian Moog pioneer Morton Garson and his Lucifer that issued *Black Mass* in the same year, which is also experimental synthesizer music.

October 8, 1971. The Move issue their fourth and last album, *Message from the Country*. The band were transitioning into Electric Light Orchestra at this point.

October 8, 1971. Hawkwind issue their second album, *In Search of Space*, which finds future Motörhead legend Lemmy joining the fold. The band is becoming part of the UK freak festival crowd, along with Edgar Broughton Band and Pink Fairies.

Hawkwind guitarist and lead vocalist Dave Brock on the band's hard rock influences: I actually I used to listen to a lot of blues and jazz and I suppose playing heavy chords comes out of that, I should imagine. Probably a bit of that, and some LSD and off you go. A few chords played loudly through a stack with echo, and there you go (laughs). Prior to me getting Hawkwind together, I toured Holland in the '60s with a band called The Famous Cure, and we would tour around with all the famous Dutch bands of the time, and I suppose really sort of roundabout '65, '66, '67, there was a great influx of blues in Europe. A lot of the old blues musicians were coming over and playing, and lot of electric blues was really heavy sounding. Really, very powerful, some of the old Muddy Waters, Howlin' Wolf, all these old characters, really exciting, quite heavy bands.

October 18, 1971. Cactus releases their third, also pretty heavy album, entitled *Restrictions*.

November 1971. Del Bromham and Stray issues their third album, *Saturday Morning Pictures*, on Transatlantic, a record that is similarly heavy to *Suicide*.

November 1971. Status Quo's fourth album, *Dog of Two Head*, the last of their late-fer-dinner British blues boom phase before seeing the heavy metal light, as evidenced by "Big Fat Mama."

Status Quo guitarist and vocalist Rick Parfitt on Quo adding heavy metal to their bag of tricks: Well, it's just something that I love, that kind of heaviness. In our own music, we were fortunate enough to be in a band that is capable of producing that kind of weight and that kind of chording. And to me, it's a very sexy rhythm; it always has been—it's a real turn-on to play it. When it's really on the money, sometimes, even still these days, it puts the hairs up on the back of your neck. It's just a wonderful style to play, and I'm so pleased we found it. And it's been panned over the years with people saying that we only play three chords. But we play them in a certain way that nobody else plays the. You know, the 12 bar shuffle now... bands go, hang on, I'm not sure we can do that, because we're going to sound like Quo. So I think we've established that by this point—and I'll settle for that.

November 1971. Grand Funk issue *E Pluribus Funk*, but by this point, the band does not figure in the story of heavy metal, nor would they want to.

November 1971. Sweet's first full-length album, *Funny How Sweet Co-Co Can Be*, the first and last full-length of the bubblegum version of the band, before the discovery of riffing as evidenced by the majority of *Sweet Fanny Adams* from April of '74.

November 1971. Alice Cooper's fourth album *Killer* is issued. The album is quickly certified gold, January 28, '72, proving the popularity of ghoulish shock rock, heavy metal for the eyes, if not necessarily for the ears. In fact, incredibly, there's not a single song on *Killer* that could be called heavy metal, a fact that has been deadened (poisoned?) in the pop culture consciousness by the album's very heavy metal cover art (front, back and inside) and by what happens on stage when Alice and his subversives come to your town.

Alice Cooper bassist Dennis Dunaway:
My favourite is *Killer*, in the respect that that was the first album we did where we knew people would be listening. On *Love It to Death*, we went into the studio coming off of two fairly unsuccessful albums. Even though they made the charts, they weren't putting food on the table. And when we went into the studio for *Killer*, we knew people would be buying the album. So our playing abilities were improving just at a time when we met Bob Ezrin, but then by the time we got to *Killer*, we had learned a great deal about proper studio techniques.

Alice Cooper drummer Neal Smith:
We were very anti-hippie all the time, and the only thing is, as things progressed, we were always decadent, but we were decadent even when we were poor. And so, you know, it was Dennis' idea, when you open up the album cover on *Love It to Death*, the most unusual thing was Alice's eyes. And it was the whole inside of the album cover, and when you look inside the pupils, you see a picture of the band. But that idea for the eye makeup came from Dennis. He found a handbill in New York at Carnegie Hall with the eyes on it, and he suggested that Alice try it onstage and we did, and we used it ever since. So that's where that idea... but we were doing that all the time. We just wanted to come up with things that were different. You know, people called us Dada rock in the middle, and in the beginning, and they also called it third generation rock, and they were trying to come up with a name because they just couldn't figure out what the hell we were doing.

November 1971. Humble Pie issue a double live album called *Performance: Rockin' the Fillmore*, which many long-in-the-tooth hard rock practitioners consider one of the greatest live albums of all time.

> Humble Pie drummer Jerry Shirley on the band getting heavier over time:
> We started out a lot quieter and more acoustic, but, if you listen to the early records, there's plenty of heavy stuff on there. We just found that that was something that we could easily conjure up on stage, and impress people with onstage, better than we could the acoustic side. So it made sense. America liked to be kicked in the ass, and that's what we were obviously good at, and we dropped the acoustic stuff kind of early, and just went with the stuff that got people's attention.

November 1971. Mountain issue their live/studio odds 'n' sods album *Flowers of Evil*, as hard rock in America continues to prove less than impressive in the aggregate, lying in wait to return with the likes of Blue Öyster Cult, Montrose, Aerosmith, Kiss, Ted Nugent and Van Halen in that chronological order.

November 1971. English glam merchants Mott the Hoople issue their third album, *Brain Capers*, their heaviest to date. Still, Ian Hunter and crew rarely think like proto-metal makers, more so just including hard rock in their mix at times. The band, however, is often brought into the edges of the discussion due to the heavy look of the band live—five long-haired guys in wild clothes and a lead singer looking menacing in sunglasses. The onstage presentation falls between that of Alice Cooper, New York Dolls and Aerosmith, Mott presenting a whirlwind of post-hippie colour that many associate with hard rock.

November 1971. Nazareth issue their self-titled debut album, which is considerably heavy for 1971.

November 1971. The self-titled from Kossoff Kirke Tetsu Rabbit is issued. The album is an offshoot project of Free members.

Nazareth vocalist Dan McCafferty: That's just what we wanted to play. We were young and full of piss and vinegar, and rock music had to be aggressive, because that's how you felt. You know, you went to join the national "baaaah" party or something, you know what I mean? It was the energy and anger that went on with a lot of things that were going on politically in your home place. It was a difficult youth, really. So I guess that's where that came from. I have no regrets about it, by the way. I have no regrets about it at all. You see, when we started, we were a band. And then we were a rock band, and then we were a hard rock band, and then we were a heavy metal band. So this wasn't us that was making up these titles, it was journalists. Because in the '70s, when I first started, we were signed to the same label as Genesis. Genesis, Jethro Tull, Nazareth, Led Zeppelin, Deep Purple, Uriah Heep—you could like all of them and nobody cared. But then all of a sudden the press became quite large, in a way. And they had to put you into pigeonholes or boxes. So that's what happened there. So I always just thought of us as a rock band, to be quite honest. But then the other thing in my life that I've been is the new guys in the club, the most promising newcomers, and then I was a dinosaur for a while. And then I was legend. A legend was a lot easier than being a dinosaur, with all the scales and all that.

Nazareth guitarist Manny Charlton:
The first two albums that we did, we were all over the place musically, and genre-speaking. But when we played live we went out as a four-piece and basically played hard rock, with Marshall stacks and a lot of drums and stuff. And Dan screaming his head off. And that seemed to go over really well. So we were puzzled at the time as to why our records weren't selling but we were doing well live. And so we decided the best thing we could probably do was get as a producer a musician that understood what we were trying to do. And we'd been playing dates with Purple in the States and Europe, so we knew Roger Glover. And we were into guys that were producing their own bands, and we knew Roger was producing Purple at the time. And Pete Townsend was an influence working with The Who, and Jimmy Page with Zeppelin, so basically we asked the three of them. We asked the three of them if they would be interested in producing the band, and Roger got back to us first and really wanted to do it. So we went yeah, well we know the guy anyway, we're mates, let's have Roger do it, which turned out to be our first really heavy album, which was *Razamanaz*.

Nazareth bassist Pete Agnew:
Being a rhythm 'n' blues-based "hard rock" band, Nazareth have always listened to every other kind of music except hard rock, so our influences are wide-ranging. What we call Scottish rock—and that goes for most of the Scottish rock bands of the '60s and '70s—is heavily influenced by American music rather than the English rock bands who tended to influence one another. The Scottish settlers who went to America tended to move to the south and were largely responsible for what we know today as country music, which with black blues influence became rock 'n' roll, so in a roundabout way you could say our ancestors had a great deal to do with creating Scottish rock. Little did they know what they were starting! In Scotland, in the mid to late '60s, all the bands were heavily into soul music, as were the people who came to dance. The vocalists on the Stax and Tamla labels were—and still are to a great extent—the best in the world. To this day Dan and I would name Otis Redding as the best singer the world has heard. Also the great riffs that peppered soul music were an inspiration in later years to the creators of heavy or "hard" rock: many is the soul riff that has been changed around a wee bit and used as the basis of some of our best known rock songs.

November 8, 1971. Led Zeppelin's untitled, widely called IV, is released. The album has sold 23 million copies in the US (third highest selling album overall) and 37 million worldwide. The album in summation is quite a bit heavier than III, containing tracks like doomy blues "When the Levee Breaks," frenzied, fuzzy, boogie metaller "Rock and Roll," heavy metal rocker with only a passing nod to the blues "Black Dog" and the world's most famous power ballad (a heavy metal trope tagged and identified years later) in "Stairway to Heaven." Considered one of the greatest rock songs ever, it is travesty to call "Stairway to Heaven" a power ballad, but in crass terms it does indeed include one trope that power ballads were built upon, the idea of mellow bits that build to a loud wind-up. Billboard called the album a "powerhouse," going on to identify four "heavy" tracks.

Led Zeppelin bassist and keyboardist John Paul Jones on "Stairway to Heaven:" I remember "Stairway to Heaven" was done kind of around the fire, a big fireplace, sitting around drinking cider. Page had a few things worked out on the guitar. He had these different sections and he was just playing them through and I remember picking up... I had brought all my recorders and my bits and pieces and I picked up the bass recorder and started playing that run-down with the guitar. Then Robert started jotting a few lyrics down. It was a very organic process, as most of our music was. Somebody would start something and somebody would follow, and it would turn into something else and you would sit down and work out what sections you've got and you'd put them together. It was all very easy, very relaxed.

Led Zeppelin engineer Andy Johns on "Stairway to Heaven:"
After we had worked there for a while, I took them to Island Studios, which was a very, very nice place, and I asked Jimmy, "You know, we need to have some kind of song that is a building song, that is dramatic and has a lot of dynamics." "Oh, I think I've got something you might like." And then the next Monday, whatever it was, and he comes in, and that was "Stairway to Heaven." Which was tracked in an unusual fashion, with drums, acoustic guitar, and John Paul Jones was playing this upright Hohner—or maybe it was a Hofner—electric piano, so there was no bass.

So I did a bunch of bottom end, so that the left hand on the electric piano would supply some kind of support for everything. And then he put the bass on, and I could see this was going to be quite something. And then I think Jimmy put the electric rhythm on, and then it was time for the 12 strings. And you know, normally, Jimmy would play his 12 strings through a Vox, and I said, "No, no, no, let's do it direct. Because we'll get more of a pure bell-like quality." "Oh, all right then." So we did that and we doubled it up, and it started to really come alive. There was a little bit of a hassle with the solo, but these days, if somebody takes half an hour for a solo, you're lucky. Back then, it was supposed to be done in two or three takes (laughs).

Nothing was ever hard to get. They would just come in and play, because they were all so good. There was never a struggle to get a decent groove. Like with the Stones, sometimes you would sit there for days and days and days and days, just trying to get a basic track. But they were all so very good, and Pagey had his hands on the reins, and John Paul would come up with some very nice special ideas, and off they would go, bang, and it's pretty much done. And Robert would sing, and it wouldn't be any torture at all. He would get a vocal in a couple, three takes.

In fact, I remember on "Stairway to Heaven," we'd just about finished everything else, and John Paul had done the recorders on the beginning and the end. Robert is sitting at the back of the control room, and I said, "Robert, it's your turn to sing." "Oh really? Well, I'm not finished with the lyrics. Can you play it again?" And he's scribbling away on this pad. "Okay, I'm ready now." And I think it was just two takes with one punch somewhere or another, done.

Led Zeppelin bassist and keyboardist John Paul Jones on "Rock And Roll:"
The lyrics might have been influenced by some old song, I don't know. The first I heard of it... I mean, basically Bonzo just started playing (laughs). He just started playing, and I think his drums were still out in the stairwell and it just kind of turned into an immediate jam. Robert, sometimes, just to get the song going, would use lyrics that he knew, and then he would change them; sometimes not (laughs).

Led Zeppelin engineer Andy Johns on John Bonham's infamously heavy drum sound on the fourth album:
   By the time the fourth record came along, it was my idea to use the Stones mobile, which I'd been working in with the Stones and one or two other acts. And we would go to Mick Jagger's house, Stargroves. I'm fairly sure that's one of the reasons he built it, was because it was called Stargroves (laughs), which was somewhat Spartan, not a lot of furniture, but a great recording space. And Jimmy said, "Well, how much would that cost?" And I said, "Well, the trucks are £1000 a week," which was quite a bit of money back then. "And then Mick's house's £1000 week." And he says, "I'm not paying Mick Jagger £1000 pounds a week, for some bloody place. I'm going to find somewhere else."
   So he did. He found this sort of down-at-the-heels, old farmer's mansion-type place, Headley Grange, and I'm glad that he did, because that's how I got the "When the Levee Breaks" drum sound. Because the lobby was like the lobby, you know? And there were stairs that would go up, and there would be a landing, and then the stairs would go up again and there would be another landing—it was three or four floors. So the ceiling was a very high ceiling. So I thought, I'm going to try this on Bonzo. Because he was always moaning about his sound, bass drum especially.
   And so they were all going to go down the pub. And so I said, "Wait a minute, John. Why don't you stay behind; I want to try something." So we carted his kit out of the room we had been working in, where everyone had been playing, set him up in this lobby with the high ceilings, and I just used two mics, very directional, M160s, and Jimmy had brought along a Binson Echorec, and I put that up the middle and compressed the hell out of the whole thing. And because it's like that halftime vibe, there's plenty of room for the compressors to recover, and, you know, you hear the room come up. And Jimmy convinces himself to this day, that it was his idea. But Jimmy wasn't even there. He was down at the pub.

Aerosmith producer Jack Douglas on Led Zeppelin's production:
I loved it. I absolutely loved the Zeppelin productions. It wasn't particularly fidelic, but that real super-open sound was amazing. I knew Eddie Kramer; he was a friend of mine. It wasn't a terrible mystery to get that stuff because it was recorded on fairly modern stuff. So I mean it wasn't as much of a mystery. You have a wide-open, empty kind of arrangement, and so if you want to emulate that in the production sound, it wasn't all that difficult, but if you wanted to emulate what Richard Perry or George Martin was doing, that was a bit more difficult. There was some mystery in it. I became really good friends with George and I worked with him. But at a Columbia convention in Los Angeles, I met Richard Perry for the first time. He really was a hero of mine. And Richard came up to me and he introduced himself, and of course I knew who he was, and he said, "I just want to ask you, how did you get that sound on *Rocks*?" He says, "I study it and I listen to it and I can't figure out what the hell you're doing!" And I almost fell over, you know? It was really amazing to hear that from my hero.

November 12, 1971. Guitarist Steve Hackett uses a tapping technique on *Nursery Crime*'s "The Return of the Giant Hogweed." Tapping would become a regular manoeuvre in heavy metal guitar soloing in the 1980s, popularized by Eddie Van Halen on 1978's "Eruption," a "song" that very much inspired many future players to enter into this life, along the lines of the Beatles on *Ed Sullivan* and Kiss through *Alive!* and *Destroyer*.

December 2, 1971. Led Zeppelin's "Black Dog"/"Misty Mountain Hop" is issued as a single, pairing the album's riffiest song with another fairly rocking number. A further single from the fourth album (by this band that apparently didn't put out singles) would emerge two months later, pairing another couple of hard hitters, "Rock And Roll" with "Four Sticks."

> Led Zeppelin bassist and keyboardist John Paul Jones on the fourth album's resident heavy metal song:
> "Black Dog" I wrote on the train (laughs). I didn't have an instrument. I write them in my head. Literally, I didn't even have manuscript paper. I have a system my father taught me, where you just use numbers and pluses and minuses and you can write a melody down on anything. As long as you've got a pen and a piece of paper, you can write music.
> And I remember coming back, I think it was from Page's house, after rehearsal. Yes, I remember, I was listening to one of the cuts off of *Electric Mud*, Muddy Waters and there was a riff that they did that kept going around and round. You thought it was going to stop and it didn't. And I thought, it would be great to write a riff that just kind of went around and round (laughs). So I just sat down and as I said, I was in the train thinking about this, and sure enough, it popped into my head as these do. So I got it down quick so I wouldn't forget it.
> I didn't actually do the arrangement, if you know what I mean. The vocal arrangement kind of dictated how that went. It didn't seem that Robert wanted to sing actually over the riff, so it kind of made sense that he sang a bit, then we played the riff, then he sang a bit more. Then Page did the other half (sings it), and then Robert did his stuff over that. Most of the stuff we did worked that way. Somebody would bring in an idea and the whole band would work on the idea and then we would add bits to it. And eventually it would become something through sort of an organic process. Out of all the different elements would come the final song.

December 4, 1971. The Montreux Casino burns down during a Frank Zappa concert, the fire started by a fan shooting a flare gun into the flammable ceiling. And now, from a burnt hotel, we have a song called "Smoke on the Water," a 1972 classic from Deep Purple blessed with a riff that sums up heavy metal music for millions of people, perhaps more than any sequence of stacked chords ever recorded.

Recap

As our journey draws to a close—with a big fire in Switzerland!—let's first dispense with the seeds and also-rans as the hippie generation runs out of steam and headlong into a decade of decay, impeachment, more Viet Nam, oil embargos and shortages, hostage crises, a rotten Big Apple, Nixon, Agnew and Jimmy Carter, Allman Brothers fan.

In the UK, which is so much of the heavy metal story of the '60s, the '70s, and even more so the early '80s and then dead to us by the close of 1983 (that's another book), Judas Priest cut their first demos, Thin Lizzy arrives but folky, and Nazareth and Budgie put forth records of some heaviness, especially Budgie. Indeed, that first Budgie slab would have meant something had it been in the 1970 mix, but here in 1971, as we'll discuss, there's much more to talk about on a whole different exciting and creative level.

Bigger but not of utmost importance is the arrival of Led Zeppelin's fourth album, considered that band's masterpiece (I'd go for *Physical Graffiti*) and one of the greatest selling albums of all time. How it needs to be framed for our world however is that the album is quite a bit heavier than *III*, even if still, there's a datedness to the band even when they are cooking up metal. I think it's safe to say that Led Zeppelin are over-rated. Why? Well, let's start with the fact that they are rated so highly, like, *best band ever*. So it's reasonable to ascribe a little bit of over-rating there. But putting aside "Black Dog," the inventive acoustics, the sounds and arrangement on "Misty Mountain Hop," when Zeppelin made metal, they weren't that hot at it. Sure, we'll get some of that on the magnificent *Physical Graffiti*, and indeed the band were pioneering and prescient in context for their first two records. But on *III*, the fourth or *Houses of the Holy*? Nah.

And what's happening in America in 1971? Alice Cooper puts out two celebrated albums of their Doorsy dark rock, but in the process, fool everybody that they are a heavy metal band. And to be fair, a discussion could be had about how much heavier the band would have come off on stage, even musically, especially in conjunction with the gravely heavying factor of their visuals. Otherwise, there's Cactus and Mountain doing some heavy work, but neither were truly accepted. Ted Nugent makes waves toward going solo, and we see the birth of Blue Öyster Cult, Aerosmith, Foghat and ZZ Top. Do you see a trend there? Because I do. Fold Cactus and Mountain into 'er, and soon the US will be mounting a boogie rock 'n' roll an' riffery revolution—Uriah Heep *Salisbury* this ain't. Handlebar moustaches, Nudie suits, flares and platforms and blue jeans for miles... America will indeed rock hard, beginning in and around 1973, but the vibe will be more *Weekend Warriors* than *Sad Wings of Destiny*.

Which brings us to the conclusion of our tale, and the affirmation that we do indeed have an answer to the question: Who invented heavy metal?. As a reminder, the reason we took our timeline to the end of 1971 was, essentially, to see if we were correct and accurate in saying Black Sabbath invented heavy metal. And what 1971 was going to do for us was tell us who was faking, whose heart wasn't in it, who might have indeed stumbled upon metal, and maybe, just maybe, who didn't like heavy metal.

I'm going a little too far there, to be sure, but some of that applies to the bands we are going to drop away from our discussion, leaving the answer double-underscored that, yes, Black Sabbath deserves to be called the inventors of heavy metal. Those bands that were in fray, or that we left in our fray, a fray of our own conceit and construction, granted, were Uriah Heep and Deep Purple. So what happened with these two bands in 1971? Uriah Heep managed to fire off two albums. *Salisbury* was a ponderous step away, with Ken admitting further copying of Purple on his part, this idea of quite fancying the *Concerto* album. But then Heep bounced back with *Look at Yourself*, an admirable slab of much heaviness, but also one with a dose of prog. But Heep were behind the creative ball a bit with the debut, losing a few marks, and so putting those three records together, it's a good story to tell, but not great—and nor were Heep particularly early.

More serious is the case of Purple. Let's not forget that to some degree, *In Rock* is the best heavy metal—maybe even the heaviest heavy metal—album of the first year of proper metal, 1970. And so it has been because of that that we carried on past the first filed heavy metal patents to 1971. And so what happened in 1971?

Alas, Purple came back with one record, *Fireball*, and the total effect was a bit underwhelming, the album offering much heaviness, but also some funkiness, some psych, a jokey country tune, and only seven tracks in total.

And so in the aggregate, we have three musty, dreary records from Mk. 1 Purple, a classical album, *In Rock* and *Fireball* up against whatever those working class lads from Birmingham are up to, as walls upon the foundation of the formidable paring of *Black Sabbath* and *Paranoid*. Well, as it turns out, what they were up to was *Master of Reality*, and our assertion that Black Sabbath invented heavy metal is affirmed, swathed and mummified in gauzy power chords.

As raved about back at the diary entry for this deafening quake of a record, the five stone-cold killers on *Master of Reality* could be considered, by some measures, as heavy as one can make music. And let's just put it on record, of the three remaining tracks, one is a mellow song and two are short instrumental intros, and all of them could be played at a funeral without double-takes from the extended family. But back to the finger-in-socket music, sure, there's faster, there's more technical, there are heavier vocals, but a purer, more powerful expression of heavy metal intention… Black Sabbath was meant to make this music, and then they got down to work and made this music. Zeppelin, Purple… they came, they saw, they dabbled, they looked down their noses and said, "How can you do just one thing?"

Well, as lovers of metal know, there are myriad interesting things to do with the language without needing a parallel language, and Sabbath embraced that and worked their black and white magic within it. And this is therefore how we arrive at our conclusion, to reiterate, not through the rote and accepted version of events that Black Sabbath invented heavy metal with their first album, but that Sabbath had ascended heroically past the challenge of *In Rock*, and proved to their millions of beloved fans, through *Paranoid* as well, but especially through *Master of Reality*, that in their heart of hearts, they were one with the metal-loving masses of the world, inventing with resolute intention, this triumphant music called heavy metal because they understood the magic within its making.

Anthony Frank Iommi, master of riffs, and most pertinently, if you were forced to pick one person... Tony Iommi invented heavy metal.

Ozzy's voice or persona isn't particularly heavy metal. Putting aside that Bill is a fairly jazzy drummer, it would also be highly illogical to ascribe the invention of heavy metal to a drummer. But Geezer? Well, revisit what Jim Simpson and others have said. One could argue that coming up with the very name Black Sabbath, and then the lyrical direction of the band, that this was the catalyst for Tony to go where he did.

Credits

Interviews With The Author

Included in this book are quotes from interviews the author conducted over the past 20+ years with the following folks, most of them multiple times—which was the lynchpin point that caused me to chuck listing them more formally with dates, as we'd be chewing up pages back here. Thanks to all for making this hobby of a job a joy to wake up to every day. Other than material from my own interviews, a buddy of mine, Dmitry Epstein has allowed me to quote from some of his chats, so those names have been added, late in the process, below as well. Dmitry's smart and historical hard rock scholarship can be seen at dmme.net. Finally there's the odd few words quoted from some old Billboard reviews as well as one-liners from a few journalists around the etymology of the term heavy metal—these are credited in situ, i.e., at the entry.

Pete Agnew, Don Airey, Tom Allom, Ian Anderson, Carmine Appice, Mark Arm, Ron Asheton, Scott Asheton, Al Atkins
Gavin Baddeley, Johnny "Bee" Badanjek, Ritchie Blackmore, Trevor Bolder, Al Bouchard, Joe Bouchard, Mick Box, Don Branker, Don Brewer, Dave Brock, Gerry Bron, Arthur Brown, Jack Bruce, Geezer Butler
Manny Charlton, Neville Chesters, Fast Eddie Clarke, Mick Clarke, Malcolm Cope, Suzanne Cusick
Dave Davies, Michael Davis, Jinx Dawson, Jack Douglas, John Drake, Chris Dreja, Dennis Dunaway
Roger Earl, Jack Endino, Bob Ezrin
Barry Fey, Kim Fowley, Andy Fraser, Ace Frehley, Herb A. Friedman
John Garner, Russ Gibb, Billy Gibbons, Ian Gillan, Roger Glover, Paul Gurvitz, John Gustafson
Peter Hammill, Ken Hensley, Steve Hill, Randy Holden, Norman Hood, Terry Hook, Mick Hopkins
Tony Iommi
Andy Johns, Clive Jones, John Paul Jones, Henry Juszkiewicz
Shirley Kent, Simon Kirke, K.J. Knight, Christopher Knowles, Wayne Kramer
Corky Laing, Greg Lake, Jack Lancaster, Derek Lawrence, John Lawton, Dave Lewis, Steve Lyman
Yngwie Malmsteen, Vinny Martell, John Mayall, Dan McCafferty, Paul McCartney, Jim McCarty (Yardbirds), Jim McCarty (Cactus), Klaus Meine, Phil Mogg, Ronnie Montrose, Gary Moore, Steve Morse, Dave Murray
Ted Nugent
Ozzy Osbourne
Ian Paice, Carl Palmer, Andy Parker, Sandy Pearlman, Dickie Peterson, Ray Phillips, Jonathan Pieslak, Mike Pinera, Andy Powell
Paul Rodgers, Francis Rossi, Uli Jon Roth, Jim Rutledge
Burke Shelley, Brush Shiels, Jerry Shirley, Nick Simper, Jim Simpson, John Sinclair, Neal Smith, Sylvain Sylvain
Phil Taylor, Dennis Thompson
Jaan Uhelski, Mick Underwood
Eric Wagner, Jeff Wagner, Bill Ward, Leslie West, Paul Whaley, Brad Whitford, James Williamson, Doug Wimbish, Richie Wise, Dave Wyndorf
Malcolm Young

Design Credit

The visual splendidness of this book was created by one Eduardo Rodriguez, who can be reached at eduardobwbk@gmail.com.

Photo Credits

The shot of the Mapledurham Watermill (as seen on the cover of the *Black Sabbath* album) used for the front cover was shot by A&R legend Monte Conner, who himself has figured prominently in the discovery and support of so many pioneering metal bands through his work with Roadrunner Records and beyond. The shot of Geezer Butler at the end of the book and the shot of Tony Iommi and Bill Ward on the back cover are from the jaw-dropping archive of Rich Galbraith, who can be reached at rtgenid@suddenlink.net. The shot of Tony Iommi at the end of the book comes from my Spokane buddy Ben Upham, who can be reached through magicalmomentphotos.com.

About The Author

At approximately 7900 (with over 7000 appearing in his books), Martin has unofficially written more record reviews than anybody in the history of music writing across all genres. Additionally, Martin has penned 52 books on hard rock, heavy metal, classic rock and record collecting, and contributed to another half-dozen. He was Editor In Chief of the now web-only Brave Words & Bloody Knuckles, Canada's foremost metal publication for 14 years, and has also contributed to Revolver, Guitar World, Goldmine, Record Collector, bravewords.com, lollipop.com and hardradio.com, with many record label band bios and liner notes to his credit as well. Additionally, Martin worked for two years as researcher on the award-wining documentary *Rush: Beyond The Lighted Stage* and on *Metal Evolution*, an 11-episode documentary series for VH1 Classic, and is the writer of the original metal genre chart used in *Metal: A Headbanger's Journey* and throughout the *Metal Evolution* episodes. Martin was also consultant on Banger's series for VH1, *Rock Icons*. Having lived in Toronto for 26 years, Martin and can be reached through martinp@inforamp.net or www.martinpopoff.com.

Martin Popoff – A Complete Bibliography

Who Invented Heavy Metal? (2015)
Sail Away: Whitesnake's Fantastic Voyage (2015)
Live Magnetic Air: The Unlikely Saga of the Superlative Max Webster (2014)
Steal Away The Night: An Ozzy Osbourne Day-By-Day (2014)
The Big Book Of Hair Metal (2014)
Sweating Bullets: The Deth And Rebirth Of Megadeth (2014)
Smokin' Valves: A Headbanger's Guide to 900 NWOBHM Records (2014)
The Art Of Metal (co-edit with Malcolm Dome; 2013)
2 Minutes To Midnight: An Iron Maiden Day-By-Day (2013)

Metallica: The Complete Illustrated History (2013)
Rush: The Illustrated History (2013)
Ye Olde Metal: 1979 (2013)
Scorpions: Top Of The Bill (2013)
Epic Ted Nugent (2012)
It's Getting Dangerous: Thin Lizzy 81-12 (2012)
We Will Be Strong: Thin Lizzy 76-81 (2012)
Fighting My Way Back: Thin Lizzy 69-76 (2011)
The Deep Purple Royal Family: Chain Of Events '80 – '11 (2011)
The Deep Purple Royal Family: Chain Of Events Through '79 (2011)
Black Sabbath FAQ (2011)
The Collector's Guide To Heavy Metal: Volume 4: The '00s (2011; co-authored with David Perri)
Goldmine Standard Catalog Of American Records 1948 – 1991, 7th Edition (2010)
Goldmine Record Album Price Guide, 6th Edition (2009)
Goldmine 45 RPM Price Guide, 7th Edition (2009)
A Castle Full Of Rascals: Deep Purple '83 – '09 (2009)
Worlds Away: Voivod And The Art Of Michel Langevin (2009)
Ye Olde Metal: 1978 (2009)
Gettin' Tighter: Deep Purple '68 – '76 (2008)
All Access: The Art Of The Backstage Pass (2008)
Ye Olde Metal: 1977 (2008)
Ye Olde Metal: 1976 (2008)
Judas Priest: Heavy Metal Painkillers (2007)
Ye Olde Metal: 1973 To 1975 (2007)
The Collector's Guide To Heavy Metal: Volume 3: The Nineties (2007)
Ye Olde Metal: 1968 To 1972 (2007)
Run For Cover: The Art Of Derek Riggs (2006)
Black Sabbath: Doom Let Loose (2006)
Dio: Light Beyond The Black (2006)
The Collector's Guide To Heavy Metal: Volume 2: The Eighties (2005)
Rainbow: English Castle Magic (2005)
UFO: Shoot Out The Lights (2005)
The New Wave Of British Heavy Metal Singles (2005)
Blue Öyster Cult: Secrets Revealed! (2004; updated 2009)
Contents Under Pressure: 30 Years Of Rush At Home & Away (2004)
The Top 500 Heavy Metal Albums Of All Time (2004)
The Collector's Guide To Heavy Metal: Volume 1: The Seventies (2003)
The Top 500 Heavy Metal Songs Of All Time (2003)
Southern Rock Review (2001)
Heavy Metal: 20th Century Rock And Roll (2000)
The Goldmine Price Guide To Heavy Metal Records (2000)
The Collector's Guide To Heavy Metal (1997)
Riff Kills Man! 25 Years Of Recorded Hard Rock & Heavy Metal (1993)

See martinpopoff.com for complete details and ordering information.